SUFISM, PLURALISM AND DEMOCRACY

SUFISM, PLURALISM AND DEMOCRACY

Edited by
Clinton Bennett and Sarwar Alam

SHEFFIELD UK   BRISTOL CT

Published by Equinox Publishing Ltd.

UK: Office 415, The Workstation, 15 Paternoster Row, Sheffield, South Yorkshire, S1 2BX
USA: ISD, 70 Enterprise Drive, Bristol, CT 06010

www.equinoxpub.com

First published 2017

© Clinton Bennett, Sarwar Alam and contributors 2017

All rights reserved. No part of this publication may be reproduced or transmitted in any form or by any means, electronic or mechanical, including photocopying, recording or any information storage or retrieval system, without prior permission in writing from the publishers.

British Library Cataloguing-in-Publication Data
A catalogue record for this book is available from the British Library.

Library of Congress Cataloging-in-Publication Data
Names: Bennett, Clinton, editor. | Alam, Sarwar, editor.
Title: Sufism, pluralism and democracy / edited by Clinton Bennett and Sarwar Alam.
Description: Bristol, CT : Equinox Publishing Ltd, [2017] | Includes bibliographical references and index.
Identifiers: LCCN 2016032326| ISBN 9781781792209 (hb) | ISBN 9781781792216 (pb)
Subjects: LCSH: Sufism--Political aspects. | Sufism--Political aspects--Case studies. | Islam and state. | Islam and state--Case studies.
Classification: LCC BP188.7 .S84 2017 | DDC 297.409--dc23
LC record available at https://lccn.loc.gov/2016032326

ISBN: 978 1 78179 220 9 (hardback)
       978 1 78179 221 6 (paperback)

Typeset by CA Typesetting Ltd, www.publisherservices.co.uk
Printed and bound in the UK by Lightning Source UK Ltd., Milton Keynes and Lightning Source Inc., La Vergne, TN

Clinton dedicates this book to his father-in-law, Samuel Sarker and his other relatives by marriage in Bangladesh and to his Indonesian friends and former classmates.

Sarwar dedicates this book to all children including Annika and Ghaleeb.

CONTENTS

Tables and Maps ix
Abbreviations x
Acknowledgements xii

INTRODUCTION
Sufism, Pluralism and Democracy:
Contexts, Comparisons and Critiques
  Clinton Bennett 1

SECTION I
Multi-Contextual

1
Sufis, Saints and Politics in Islam: An Historical Survey
  Clinton Bennett 25

SECTION II
European/Euro Asian Contexts (Kosovo/Albania and Turkey)

2
Sufism as a Working Spirit in Globalization and Pluralism: The Case of the Hizmet Movement, a Turkey-oriented Global Islamic Network
  Heon C. Kim 53

3
A Paradox of Political Mysticism: The Bektashi Sufi Order as an Islamic Esoteric Community and Factor in Albanian National History
  Stephen S. Schwartz 71

SECTION III
A Middle Eastern Context (Iran)

4
Sufi Politics in the Contemporary West: The Role and Definition of Sufism in the Works of Javad Nurbakhsh (1926–2008)
  Milad Milani 91

SECTION IV
South Asian Contexts: Bangladesh, Indonesia and Pakistan

5
Anti-Saint or Anti-Shrine?
Tracing Deoband's Disdain for the Sufi in Pakistan
Charles M. Ramsey — 103

6
Sufis as Shapers of Pluralist Political Culture:
The Examples of Bangladesh and Indonesia
Clinton Bennett — 121

7
In Search of God, In Search of Humanity:
Vilayat-e-Mutlaqa of Hazrat Delaor Husayn Maizbhandari
Sarwar Alam — 147

SECTION V
Literary & Theoretical Underpinnings

8
Two Beloved Sufi Poets of the Punjab:
A Case of "Hearing without Listening"
Nikky-Guninder Kaur Singh — 177

9
Looking Inside the Heart: The Universal Appeal of God and Humanity
as Reflected in Ibn al-'Arabī's *Fusus al-Hikam* and Maulana Rūmī's
Mathnawi Manawi
Sayed Hassan Akhlaq Hussaini — 201

CONCLUSION
"Corporate Islam" versus Sufi Islam and the Articulation
of the Present
Sarwar Alam — 223

Bibliography — 230
Index — 244

TABLES AND MAPS

Table 1: Some of the Most Popular Sufi Orders	2
Table 2: Active Political Parties with Sufi Links	35
Table 3: Status of Democracy in Muslim Majority States	44
Map 1: Countries with Muslim populations above 50%	10
Map 2: Comparative Size of Bangladesh and Indonesia	124

ABBREVIATIONS

AKP	*Adalet ve Kalkinma Partisi* (Justice & Freedom Party, Turkey)
AW	Awami League (Peoples League, Bangladesh)
BNP	Bangladesh Nationalist Party
BTF	Bangladesh Tarikat Federation
BTK	*Bashkësia e Tarikateve të Kosovës* (The Kosova Sufi Union)
DPR	*Dewan Perwakilan Rakyat* (Peoples Representative Council, Indonesia)
EIU	Economist Intelligence Unit
FIS	*Front Islamique Salut* (Islamic Salvation Front), Algeria (banned)
GOLKAR	*Partai Golangan Kariya* (party of the functional groups, Indonesia)
HAMAS	*Harakat al-Muqawama al-Islamia* (Islamic Resistance Movement)
MPR	*Majelis Permusyawaratan Rakyat* (Peoples Consultative Assembly, Indonesia
NGO	Non-Governmental Organization (not-for-profit)
OIC	Organization of Islamic Cooperation (f. 1969) (previously Conference) intergovernmental agency with permanent observer status at United Nations
IOJ	*Islami Oikkya Jote*
IS	Islamic State, also ISIL (Islamic State of Iraq and the Levant) & ISIS (Islamic State of Iraq and Syria) are all self-designated names of terrorist organization controlling areas in Iraq and in Syria with various affiliates
ICMA	Association for Indonesian Muslim Intellectuals
JATMN	*Jam'iyyah Ahlith Thoriqah al-Mu`tabaroh al-Nahdliyyah* (Association of Followers of Respected Sufi Orders)
JI	*Jamaat-e-Islami* (Bangladesh, deregistered as a political party)
MB	*Ikhwan-ul-Muslimin* (Muslim Brotherhood, founded in Egypt)
MENA	Middle East and North Africa (geographical region)
NU	*Nahdatul Islam* (Awakening of the Scholars, Indonesia)

9/11	refers to the terrorist attack carried out by *Al-Qaeda* operatives on September 11th 2001. The terrorists hijacked and crashed two planes into the twin towers of New York's World Trade Center, attacked the Pentagon and crashed another hijacked plane in Pennsylvania killing in total over 3,000 people
PDI-P	*Partai Demokrasi Indonesia Perjuangan* (Indonesian Democratic Party – Struggle)
PKB	*Patai Kebangkitan Bangsa* (National Awakening Party, Indonesia)
PKS	*Partai Keadilan Sejahtera* (Prosperous Justice Party, Indonesia)
PNI	*Partai Nasional Indonesia* (Indonesian Nationalist Party)
PPTI	*Partai Politik Tarekat Islam* (Muslim Tarekat Political Party, various name changes but retaining the PPTI abbreviation)
PPP	*Partai Persatuan Pebangunan* (United Development Party)
7/7	refers to a series of coordinated terrorist suicide bombing attacks on London's transportation system on July 7th 2005 killing 52 people in total. The attacks were carried out by four radicalized British Muslims (three born in the UK) inspired by Al-Qaeda
ZIDRA/BRDIA	Serbian and Albanian initials for the Community of Aliite Islamic Dervish Networks in Yugoslavia, predecessor of BTK

ACKNOWLEDGMENTS

We are indebted first of all to all those who contributed to the special issue of the journal *Comparative Islamic Studies* and to this volume. Contributors represent a variety of disciplines, backgrounds and nationalities. At least seven languages were used in researching the material presented in this book: Albanian, Arabic, Bangla, Farsi, Punjabi, Turkish and Urdu as well as English. All contributors more than demonstrated deep commitment to this project despite the fact that it took much longer than planned. Partly, this was due to attempts to recruit additional contributors but also because Clinton Bennett was hospitalized right in the middle of the project. Then, after he had taken up his pen again, a number of contributors asked for extensions to enable the completion of field work research, which hopefully benefits the volume but which also contributed to the slippage of deadlines. We are therefore grateful that everyone involved remained patient to the end, not least of all Janet Joyce, our long-suffering publisher. It was her idea to tie this volume and an issue of the journal together, which Equinox also publishes. It was a privilege to co-edit that issue which hopefully whetted some readers' appetites for this book even if they have had to wait longer for it than they may have expected. Valerie Hall at Equinox and all the team that helped produce, design, typeset, copy edit and proofread the book also deserve our thanks. Errors, though, are to be attributed to Bennett and Alam since like it or not the proverbial buck stops at their editorial desks!

As it happens, given that, sadly, there is more Islamophobia in the media today and in the discourse of some Western politicians than there was when we began, our book may be more relevant and timely due to its delay. Islam and Muslims are routinely presented as somehow always problematic so perhaps this effort at exploring an alternative perspective is even more critical. We also want to acknowledge the advice of others who offered suggestions, criticism and encouragement including the original, anonymous reviewer. Our academic colleagues merit recognition, too, especially our librarians for helping us access material in-house and through the Inter Library Loan system. We very much appreciate their assistance. Finally, our wives and families more than deserve mention in these acknowledgments for their moral and often also practical support. Clinton Bennett's dedication refers to his father-in-law, Samuel Sarker and to his other relatives by marriage in Bangladesh from whom he has learned much that he draws on in his writing. His dedication also expresses gratitude to Indonesian friends and former classmates who deepened and extended his interest in their homeland, and added considerably to what he claims to know about it, which is much less than he pretends! Sarwar Alam's dedication is to all children including Annika and Ghaleeb.

Clinton Bennett (SUNY New Paltz)
Sarwar Alam (University of Arkansas)

INTRODUCTION

SUFISM, PLURALISM AND DEMOCRACY: CONTEXTS, COMPARISONS AND CRITIQUES

Clinton Bennett

DEFINING THE SUBJECT MATTER: WHO QUALIFIES AS SUFI?

Sufism (*taṣawwuf*) is usually described as Islam's mystical tradition. Unfortunately, mystical is a somewhat arcane word that does not readily convey what Sufism is or what the term means. It is also often called Islam's esoteric tradition. This makes it sound covert. Certainly, Sufism focuses on the inner experience of faith rather than on its external and legalistic aspects. Perhaps it is best understood as a set of devotional and contemplative practices, spiritual techniques and theological beliefs that are customarily linked with membership of fraternities (*ṭarīqahs;* paths), each with their particular rituals and teachings. These fraternities are headed by teachers who trace a spiritual lineage through their own mentors back to Muhammad (known as a *silsilah*). The burial site of the fraternity's founder is often where the current head's lodge is located. Professed members of the fraternity and also non-members may visit the shrine, sometimes performing set rituals. Some orders have distinctive dress, although many do not.

All who practice Sufism want a deeper, more intimate relationship with God. This involves traveling along a spiritual path away from a self-centered, egotistical and often material oriented life to one that centers on God, which also prioritizes others' needs. Thus, Sufi lodges are places of hospitality, of learning and also of healing, with hospitals and other social welfare institutions attached. Known as travelers (*sālikūn*), initiates pass through a series of stages or steps (*maqaamat*) toward annihilation of their ego (*nafs*) and may receive, in turn, "states" (*aḥwāl*) that reward their progress. Typically, the former are repentance, watchfulness, renunciation, poverty, patience, trust, and acceptance. The latter include ecstasy, intoxication and intimacy. The large initiatory fraternities are transnational although they may be more numerous in certain regions. The following are some of the most popular.

Table 1: Some of the Most Popular Sufi Orders

Name	Origin	Region/Regions
Naqhsbandiyya	Named for Baha-ud-Din Naqshband Bukhari (d. 1398) but founded in the twelfth century	Widespread across Asia and the Middle East
Chīshtiyya	Began in Chist, Afghanistan about 930 CE founded by Abu Ishaq Shami (d. 940).	Especially strong in South Asia
Qādiriyya	Founded by Abdul Qadir-Gilani, (d. 1166).	Arab world
Tijāniyyah	Founded early 1770s by Sīdī 'Aḥmad al-Tijānī	Dominant in West Africa
Suhrawardiyya	Founded by Diya al-din Abu 'n-Najib as-Suhrawardi (d. 1168).	Arab world and Indian Sub-continent
Mewlewī	Founded by Jalāl ad-Dīn Muhammad Rūmī (d. 1273).	Arab World, former Ottoman provinces and Central Asia

The great Sufi masters, some of whom are discussed in this volume, often used poetry to express their theology. Many spoke of "unity-of-being" (*waḥdat al-wujūd*) referring to the belief that ultimately all that exists is of God and from God and will return to God. Annihilation (*fanā*, "to pass away") of the *nafs* leads to "unity" (*baqā'*) with the divine, or deification, which some Muslims took to be blasphemy, for which al-Ḥallāj was executed in 922 CE after crying out *Ana 'l-Ḥaqq* (I am truth). However, another way of understanding Sufism's spiritual goal is to achieve such intimacy with God that experientially, as when two lovers embrace, the "us"-"other" distinction seems to vanish. The renowned legal scholar al- Ghazālī (d. 1111), who turned to Sufism after experiencing a dark night of the soul, interpreted al-Hallāj's language as metaphor. His mistake was to speak about the unspeakable, to describe what defies description, what is to be experienced not spoken about. Intoxicated with spiritual ecstasy, al-Ḥallāj confused the wine with the wine glass when what he meant was "*'tis as though it were the wine glass*" and so misspoke (see al-Ghazālī & Gairdner 2010: 61). Sufis were accused of preferring their own rituals over Islam's mandatory duties, such as the five daily prayers. They were criticized for elevating the esoteric over the exoteric, abandoning legalistic Islam. Al-Ghazālī stressed that Muslims should keep esotericism and exotericism in balance. Sufis, he said, should observe all the pillars of the faith and imbue their observation with inner meaning. On the *hajj* (pilgrimage at Mecca), they travel within their hearts toward the divine within as well as physically along the pilgrims' route. Al-Ghazālīan-type Sufism for many represents an orthodox version. Hussaini's chapter in this volume skillfully surveys what two of the most influential Sufi masters taught on the divine-human relationship and the soul's journey toward God.

Attempts to describe the origin of the word Sufi as derived from the Arabic for wool (*Ṣūf*) because early Sufis wore woolen habits can suggest, as does the word mystical, something obscure about Sufism. The explanations often neglect to mention that wool was symbolic of poverty, which for Sufis is a desired spiritual state and practice. The term may also derive from the Arabic words for purity (*Ṣafā*), and bench (*suffa*). The latter refers to the bench outside Muhammad's home in Medina on which the pious or pure in heart liked to sit. The very earliest Sufis were not highly organized; those interested in exploring spirituality gathered informally around a teacher or studied at his lodge often called a convent in the literature. Exactly when this began is unclear but figures such as Hasan of Basra (d. 728) and even earlier Salman the Farsi (d. 656), a companion of Muhammad, feature prominently in the lists of lineages, so can be identified as pioneer Sufis. Some restrict the term "Sufi" to teachers (*murshids*), known variously as shaykhs (also sheikhs), *pīrs* and *marabouts* depending on location (Arab world, the Iranian/Farsi or Persianate cultural zone and Africa) and to their licensed deputies (*khalīfahs*). Women as well as men feature in the ranks of renowned Sufi teachers beginning with Rābiʻa (d. 810), who shifted emphasis from divine wrath to divine love. Others may call professed disciples (*murīds*) Sufis, that is, initiated members of the fraternities, or *ṭarīqahs (turuq)*. Others may use the term for those who occasionally attend a Sufi ritual, or visit a Sufi shrine or to anyone whose practice of Islam is Sufi-influenced. Ramsey's chapter in this volume discusses how "Sufi" is understood and used today in Pakistan, where "'Sufi'… does not refer to glorified mystics but rather to mendicant deviants," for whom there is widespread disdain. In Indonesia, there are Sufi associations whose founders' are unable to trace their spiritual lineage to Muhammad that some Sufis call non-Sufi or "pseudo-Sufi" (Zamhari 2010: 1). Some of these fraternities blend Sufi beliefs and practices with aspects of Indonesia's endogenous religion. Critics see this as syncretistic. The *Jam'iyyah Ahl al-Thariqah al-Mu'tabarah* in Indonesia, set up in 1957 by Sufi members of the *Nahdlatul Ulama* (NU), did not extend *mu'tabarah* (respectable) status to these movements which sidelined them from taking part in the political arena as Muslims (Zamhari 2010: 1).

There are also movements that have Sufi roots but criticize traditional Sufism, condemning saint veneration, prayer to saints (*Tawassul*), celebrating saints' birthdays (*'urs*), pilgrimage or visits (*Ziyārah*) to shrines for example but retain some Sufi practices especially *dhikr* (repetition of the divine names, or remembrance). In Chapter 5, Ramsey describes this critique in the context of Pakistan. Called "neo-Sufi" by scholars, members may also be considered Sufi although not everyone will accept this. The contributors to this volume may use "Sufi" to describe a teacher but they may also use the term more inclusively to refer to people whose Islam is flavored by Sufi thought or practice. Geoffroy does not equate Sufism with what he calls "brotherhoodism" pointing out that there were Sufis before *ṭarīqas* and so "there may be a Sufism after them as well." In his view, the brotherhoods "are not in good health." Where leadership has become hereditary, heads are more concerned with administering property than spiritual direction. There is, he says, a rediscovery of "spirituality within Islam, but in an environment that is broader than that of the brotherhoods" (Geoffroy 2010: 199). How many people today identify as Sufis? Geoffroy cites Saāīd Hawwā's claim (made in 1980) "that ninety percent of all Muslims had, in one way or another, a link with Sufism over the course of the centuries" (2010: 198). In Senegal, where according to Pew Research, 92% of the population admit a Sufi affiliation, this percentage still applies. Elsewhere, when neo-Sufis and non-*ṭarīqah* Sufis and those whose faith and practice is Sufi-flavored are included, the number may be much higher than the Pew statistic indicates. Hizmet (see Chapter 2) is an example of a non- *ṭarīqah* form of Sufism with "millions of the members" and "thousands of educational institutes and dialogue platforms over the world." Nonetheless the Pew Research Centre's, *The World's Muslims: Unity and Diversity* (2012a) is an important source of data and analysis. After Senegal, Pew lists Chad with 55% then eight other African states with the ninth, Uganda equal with Bangladesh at 26% but with a much smaller Muslim population (2012a: 3).

We find criticism of Sufi belief and practices in classical, more modern and contemporary sources. Some reject the doctrine of unity-of-being, some reject the role played by teachers and the teacher-student relationship involved in this; others condemn visiting shrines as un-Islamic. Some denounce Sufi teachers as charlatans, who take advantage of their disciples. Some, indeed, are very wealthy. Claims that Sufi masters can heal the sick, read minds, fly through the air or perform any number of supernatural acts, also attracts criticism. The charge of syncretism is common, not only against localized versions in Indonesia and elsewhere but against the whole phenomenon of Sufism. Alleged sources include Buddhism and Christianity. European scholars, who warmed to Sufism because they recognized affinity with Christian mysticism, wrote positively about Sufism while at the same time removing it from its Islamic roots. Sufis were good Muslims who were really to be seen as Christians in disguise. Sufism, thus, was deconstructed. In Chapter 4, Milani warns of the danger of Christianizing Islam, interpreting it through a Judeo-Christian lens. In Chapter 9, Hussaini refers to how Rūmī's commitment to universality meant that he explained "his mystical ideas independently from religion." Sufism almost certainly does draw on thinking from outside Islam but sees truth as universal, thus the distinction between an Islamic and a Buddhist source is artificial and false. God has spoken through all religions, although God speaks most fully in Islam. Hussaini's chapter on Ibn al-'Arabī and Rūmī (whose poetry is popular in the West) describes their great reverence for Jesus, whom al-Hallāj had regarded as the sublime example of submission to God. Others criticize Sufis for lack of interest in the health of the wider Muslim community, in helping translate Islam's social ideals into practice. Despite Sufism's humanitarian tradition, Sufis are regularly criticized for being too other worldly. They ascribe too much authority to their teachers, which challenges that of scholars of Islam's legal tradition and even that of Muslim rulers. They should engage more with political systems, some say.

Sufis past and present may be seen to be indifferent about who sits in the palace as long as they are able to contemplate the divine. Yet some movements that criticize Sufis for their alleged other worldliness owe Sufism a debt in terms of their organizational structures and social welfare programs, including the Muslim Brotherhood (founded 1929 in Egypt) which combines a political with a social mission. *Hezbollah*, regarded in the West as a terrorist organization, may have adopted its considerable involvement in social welfare from Sufi examples which helps attract support and local legitimacy. It has won seats in Lebanon's parliament. Lebanon saw a Sufi organization, *Ahbash*, active in politics in the 1990s (see Chapter 1) and currently ranks second highest on the Economist Intelligence Unit's *Democracy Index* among Arab states. The essays in Ridgeon's *Sufis and Salafis in the Contemporary Age* (2015b) help shed light on the ambiguous, complex and shifting relationship between Salafists and Sufis.

Criticism of Sufism may originate from the left as well as from the right, from fundamentalists or Salafists on the one side such as those influenced by the thought of Muhammad ibn 'Abd Al-Wahhab (1703–92) and from liberal or modernist Muslims from the other side. Salafists look to the era of the first three generations of Muslims as the ideal that should be replicated. In Indonesia, the large *Muhammadiyah* association of modernist Muslims was critical of Sufism, although recently members have begun to find it attractive. An example of a progressive, modernist thinker who criticized Sufis is Muhammad Iqbal (1877–1938), the influential Indian Muslim philosopher and poet. Yet Iqbal's own thought was indebted to and in some respects imbued with Sufi metaphors, idioms and language. Iqbal wanted humanity to fully embrace the task of partnering with God in stewarding creation, thus allowing God to realize potentialities that are presently dormant. Iqbal's "superman" may be God-like but remains human. Sufis' "otherworldliness," he wrote, obscures the vision of "Islam as a social policy" (Iqbal & Sheikh 2012: 119).

THE VOLUME'S AIMS AND OBJECTIVES

Iqbal's critique helps to set the stage for introducing the purpose of this volume. Sufism today remains a popular form of Islam. Traditional orders, neo-Sufi organizations, people whose beliefs and practices are Sufi-influenced who have no formal association with Sufism, are found in every Muslim-majority state and non-Muslim majority states as well. Some orders have declined. Some *ṭarīqahs*, run by descendants of the founders with no real spiritual insight, do operate more or less as money-making enterprises. Many, though, continue to offer spiritual advice, training and discipline. A number of factors, traditionally linked with Sufism, have attracted attention recently in relation to the phenomenon of militant or as some insist on naming it, radical Islam, that is, acts of terror carried out by self-described Muslims including 9/11, 7/7 and the Paris bombings and armed conflict in Syria, Yemen, Iraq and elsewhere. Coupled with this, there are Islamists and Salafists who want to transform Muslim-majority countries into Islamic states, which raises fears that non-Muslims would become second class citizens, that women's rights would be limited, that seventh century penal codes would be imposed, that popular participation in political systems would be curtailed, and many freedoms and rights would be restricted. Such regimes would be authoritarian, not democratic. Pluralism, freedom of thought and speech, would be endangered. Pointing to the democratic deficit that does exist in Muslim-majority states (see Chapter 1), some argue that when Islam is linked with governance, or privileged within the legal system, autocracy follows. This view correlates lack of democracy in 26 out of 47 Muslim-majority states with Islam as a causal factor. Those for whom democracy is the pinnacle of social and political organization may regard living in a democracy as a human right.

This raises questions about whether Islam actually is incompatible with democracy, which some Muslims claim or are certain interpretations, not Islam per se, incompatible? There are in fact many different types of governments across Muslim-majority space, and currently 17 qualify as in some measure democratic. This includes several that are secular. As IS recruits young Muslims from Europe and North America as well as from Muslim-majority states to fight its wars and commit acts of terror, or of so-called *jihad*, in Islam's name, some in the West speak of Islam as their enemy. Some think that it needs to be rooted out of Western societies. On one hand, in this volume Milani states that:

> it cannot be generally said that Islam is necessarily democratic or pluralistic in practice. This would be to impose a 'Eurocentric' view based on a sense for existing modern social democratic notions that do not have an historical basis in Islamic literature.

On the other hand, it can be argued that Muslims have litigated the *are Islam and democracy compatible issue* and adjudicated in the affirmative. According to Khan (2009) it is a non-issue. He writes, "The challenge is not to argue that Islam and democracy are compatible – that debate is settled" but "to go a step further and show how an Islamic democracy may be conceived and what its constitutive principles and architecture will be (2009:16). Yet the majority of Muslim-majority states are not democratic and none are currently classified as fully democratic, so there is still a debate to be had about how more might become democratized, and how might those that are improve their democracies. What resources exist within Islam, if any, that can aid this process? What exists that can offer disenchanted youth an alternative to hate, violence and extremism? Sufis, traditionally, are open and tolerant toward diversity, respecting other faiths and even emphasize commonalties. Some accept non-Muslim initiates. Does this predispose Sufis toward accepting pluralism, which is necessary for the development of liberal democracies in which all enjoy equality regardless of gender, faith, sexual orientation or race? Sufis regard peace, inner peace and social peace, as essential for spiritual health, and have a reputation for pacifism and non-violence. Although there are exceptions (see Chapter One) Sufis do seem unlikely recruits for jihadist missions.

A number of recent texts explore the possibility that Sufism could help to counter extremism, or combat Salafism including Lombardi *et al.* (2012), Muedini (2015) and Ridgeon (2015b. In addition, the 2007 RAND Corporation report, *Building Moderate Muslim Networks,* encouraged the US and its partners to cultivate Sufis as allies in the task of countering extremism (Rabasa, *et al,* see especially 73–74, 102–103). Among those consulted, the report acknowledges one of our contributors, Stephen S. Schwartz "for his valuable insights on Sufism" (.p. xxv). This volume is offered as another contribution to this topic. It began as a type of sequel to the earlier collection of essays, edited by Bennett and Ramsey, *South Asian Sufis* (2012), that explored Sufism's health in that region where, historically, it has had a significant presence. The volume was interested in how traditional orders have adapted to change, how they deal with the accusation of heterodoxy from reformists and from other Muslim critics. It was also interested in the development of neo-Sufi movements. Several chapters, too, explored political involvement by Sufis although that was not a major focus of the volume as a whole. A number of those involved in the earlier volume, including Bennett and Alam, who are co-editing this book, however, wanted to give further consideration to this aspect in the context of current suggestions that Sufism has a role to play in combatting radicalization of Muslim youth to aid counter-terrorism strategies. What do the leading Sufi masters say about respect for the religious other, and does this encourage Sufis to embrace or affirm pluralism? Are there examples of Sufis embracing pluralism in the public sphere?

Are Sufis offering alternatives to Islamist agendas and ideas about governance? Are there resources in Sufism that might challenge the assumption that Muslims will automatically end up with autocratic systems that restrict non-Muslim rights, and impose a top-down, unquestionable version of Islam denying internal diversity? Are there actually any impulses toward democracy in Sufism, which prima facie does not appear to be obvious? One of Alam's chapters in *South Asian Sufis*, in fact, examined three Sufi-related political parties in Bangladesh, thus demonstrating that despite the accusation of political quietism, some Sufis are active in the political arena. This opened up enquiry into where else Sufis are engaged or have been engaged in this way, what success have they had and what might Muslims in other contexts learn from their experience.

EXPLORING CONTEXTS AND INVITING COMPARISONS

This writer's first chapter resulted from reading and research stimulated by the questions posed above about identifying contexts where Sufis are politically engaged. It is mainly a review of available literature and digital media, although he has visited a total of seven Muslim majority states including several that feature in this chapter. It offers an overview, partly historical but substantially contemporary, of Sufis and political engagement, a multi-contextual enquiry intended to invite comparison. In addition to earlier political engagement by Sufis in Lebanon, the chapter examines post-2011 Egypt, where three Sufi-related parties now exist and also Bangladesh, more fully covered in other chapters. The chapter also mentions the Sufi-roots of Turkey's current governing party, and refers to earlier Turkish leaders' membership of the Naqshbandi order. It briefly describes how, in the state that has the highest democracy ranking for the Arab world, Tunisia, more people are turning to Sufism to assist in the process of national healing. Resources are recommended below to help more detailed exploration of contexts, including Senegal and Morocco that are touched on but not exhaustively.

This book makes no assumption that Muslim-majority societies should develop any particular form of democracy, or imitate any Western state. Khan (2009) thinks, for example, that Iran, which most Western commentators "dismiss as a totalitarian regime run by clerics" does not receive enough credit for being "more democratic than most regimes in the region, and certainly more than the pro-West, pro-United States Iran under the Shah" (2009: 15). At the February 2016 election, more women (17, an increase of 8) won seats than clerics (16, a decrease of 11). Democracy varies greatly across the world, with different ways of electing legislators and chief executives (first past the post, proportional representation, presidential or prime-ministerial systems, federal or unitary, not to mention constitutional monarchies).

Some systems allow a candidate to win the popular vote yet they can lose the election. Democracy cannot function without choice thus pluralism is a necessary foundation. This is why pluralism is one of this book's main foci, and a major consideration for measuring the status of democracy globally. However, while it is assumed that affirming pluralism is a condition for democratic governance, affirming equal rights across race and religion, for example and allowing a choice of political options, there is no assumption that a democracy in a Muslim-majority state must adopt Western style secularism. Khan (2009) comments that belief in the "*separability of church and state*" (not, he says, in their separation) "is ... one of the enduring myths of modernity," because neither "pure religion" nor "pure politics exist in real life" (2009: 16–17).

Muslims want Islamic values to inform legislation, though they do not necessarily wish to implement classical legal interpretations, which would restrict rights and freedoms of women and minorities among others. Just as the United Kingdom has an established church and qualifies as a full democracy (ranked 16th), so Muslim-majority states can have an established religion and still evolve democratic systems as long as adherents of all religions are free to practice their own, or none, and do not suffer discrimination. Islam as a state religion while rigorously safeguarding the rights of non-Muslims may be preferable to Indonesia's insistence on "monotheism" as a national principle. This leaves atheists and agnostics open to the charge that they undermine the state's philosophical foundations. There may be issues about how a state religion is financed compared to others that raises questions about fairness, though. When formulating a critique of democracy as it develops in Muslim-majority space it is important to be equally critical of defects in democracies in Europe and North America, which are not perfect. Perhaps by exposing an alternative Islamic face, that of the peace-affirming, other-faith respecting Sufi from that of jihadist terrorists, more people will see contradictions between what it means to be Muslim, and the actions of so-called Islamic terrorists. Despite the insistence of some that these jihadists are "Islamic," they contravene Qur'ānic prohibitions, the actual meaning of *jihad* and classical Islamic rules of engagement to such a degree that, arguably, they are something other than Muslim. Some will want to find ways of assisting Sufis, if indeed they have a role to play, in the task of promoting, strengthening and running democracies. This could be a more valuable long-term contribution to world peace and stability than existing aid, or the sale of arms to several authoritarian Muslim-majority states. Although there are large Muslim populations in such non-Muslim majority states as India, where they constitute 20%, the Russian Federation, where Islam is the second largest religion and in France (10%) our focus is on states where Muslims are in a majority. Map 1 indicates where Muslims are the majority (47 states).

10   *Sufism, Pluralism and Democracy*

Map 1: Countries with Muslim populations above 50%. All belong to the OIC (Syria is suspended).

Separation of powers is probably a prerequisite for democracy, which means that an established or state religion should not have the power to approve, revise or veto legislation. Salafists have proposed systems that do elect representatives to Assemblies but they usually restrict who would be allowed to stand (pious Muslims approved by an oversight body) and vest an agency, such as Iran's Guardian Council, to sanction or veto regulatory measures (called legislation elsewhere). This is the Islamist option. Islamists see Islam as a political-social-religious unity (*din-wa-dawla*, a term often used by the *Ikhwan-ul-Muslimin*/Muslim Brotherhood [MB]), and insist that Muslims must live under the authority of Islamic Law. This limits the scope for human initiative. Islamist parties aim to create Islamic States, with the eventual goal of a restored caliphate or equivalent global entity with legal and political jurisdiction over all Muslims. Islamists may pragmatically accept the notion of a "sovereign state" as an interim measure on the way to achieving the goal of a unified Muslim polity but essentially see this as non-Islamic; "Islam does not stop at any border," stated the Sudanese Islamist leader Hassan al-Turabi (1983: 242). Many Islamist parties, though, mainly operate constitutionally and legally within existing systems participating in elections. This includes the *Ikhwan-ul-Muslimin* (MB) which won the 2012 election in Egypt (see Chapter 1) before being ousted from power and *Jamaat-e-Islami* (JI) in Bangladesh. JI has not had as much success at the ballot box but in alliance with a more moderate Muslim party has had cabinet seats. MB and JI have attracted accusations of inciting or involvement in violence but cannot be characterized as terrorist organizations, unlike Hezbollah, *Harakat al-Muqawama al-Islamia* (HAMAS), Al-Qaeda, Islamic State (IS) and their affiliates whose goals are similar but who justify violence as their modus operandi. Hezbollah and HAMAS combine constitutional and extra-constitutional tactics. Muslim critics of Islamism, however, see it as a political ideology that compromises Islam as a spiritual, religious faith in the hearts of women and men. Many think that Muslims can separate religion from the structures of the state, that union of these was circumstantial under Muhammad, not prescriptive or normative. The *Qur'ān*'s ethical and religious teachings are universally binding, not its penal prescriptions which were time limited although they may signal when a severe punishment is appropriate.

This book also uses the terms Islamic party, Muslim party and Islam-oriented party to describe, for example, *Adalet ve Kalkınma Partisi* (AKP) in Turkey, Bangladesh Nationalist Party (BNP) in Bangladesh and *Patai Kebangkitan Bangsa* (PKB) in Indonesia. These want to see Islamic values imbue and inform legislation and the law of the land but do not usually advocate that classic interpretations of Islamic Law must replace existing systems. On the other hand, while calls by Muslims for Islamic Law alarm non-Muslims in the West, there is a need to distinguish negative *sharī'ah* such as amputation for theft, stoning for adultery from its positive emphases on forgiveness, mercy and reconciliation that Muslims may prefer over retributive justice. BNP has used more Islamist rhetoric at times but while in office did not introduce any radical, Islam-based legislation. It operated within the existing system, which after the beginning of Bangladesh's democratic restoration it has helped shape. Nor has AKP in Turkey, as yet, introduced Islam-based legislation or changed the state's secular identity, which is enshrined in the Constitution. It has made Islamic content more explicit in the educational curriculum. PKB (with many Sufi members), whose Sufi founder became head of state, is wholly committed to the national philosophy, *Pancasila*, which includes the principles of national unity, democracy and belief in One God but which does not privilege Islam over other religions. In Indonesia, as Chapter 6 shows, the more Islamist PKS and other Islamist parties have drawn closer to what the PKB represents. Only one out of a total of nine parties currently operating, that either have roots in Sufism, close ties with Sufism or a formal link, represent the Islam-oriented option. The Islamic Constitutional Movement is Islamist, although it detests *Jamaat-e-Islami* (JI) as non-Islamic. Yet the relation between Sufis and Salafists is complex. Bangladesh's military ruler from 1982 to 1990, whose rhetoric was Islamist, regularly consulted his *pīr*, of whom he was a devout disciple while in pre-2011 Egypt, Sufis accepted state sponsorship, as they have elsewhere.

MORE CONTEXTS AND CHAPTER SUMMARIES

When this volume was originally planned, there was an over emphasis on South Asia, due to both of the editors' backgrounds. A reviewer whom the publisher commissioned to comment and critique our proposal pointed this out and suggested that other contexts should be added. Accepting this as valid, the editors sent out additional invitations in an attempt to extend coverage to more contexts. That effort was only partly successful. Some gaps were covered, some were not. In the end, as many editors have experienced, not every promised chapter materialized, which did help relieve some anxiety involved in possibly needing to disinvite several people to ensure that the book would not become too lengthy. Chapter 1's inclusion of many contexts is meant both to introduce this book's focus in more depth and to compensate lack of specific contributions on several of the contexts it discusses. We were also given the privilege of editing a special issue of the journal, *Comparative Islamic Studies* 9.1 (2013), which aimed to whet potential readers' appetites for this volume and to help keep its size manageable. Three articles were published in the Journal, one on Bangladesh, one on Egypt and one on Malaysia, thus three contexts, two Asian (where 60–62% of Muslims live) and one from the Middle East and North Africa (MENA) (where 20% of Muslims live), were covered. This actually correlates fairly well with the relevant demographics. In the pages that follow, most chapters focus on one specific context, several, however, deal with movements or a thinker that impact multiple contexts. In the end, the geographical coverage in this book has three chapters whose main or sole focus is on South Asia/ South East Asia. Thus, three out of the seven chapters on specific contexts deal with Asia. These are those on Pakistan, Bangladesh and Indonesia (one chapter is a comparative analysis of Bangladesh and Indonesia). Of the four on or rooted in other contexts, one is Middle Eastern, Iran and two fall into Europe and Euro Asia, namely Kosovo/Albania and Turkey. Thus, the Muslim-majority states in Europe are almost fully covered. The final two contributions are categorized as literary theoretical, and do not really have geographical foci. Not counting the theoretical essays, the distribution of three on South Asia and three on other contexts is reasonably well balanced in terms of demography, although despite the multi-contextual chapter there are gaps.

Filling the Gaps

The obvious gaps are sub-Saharan Africa and Central Asia. Some might want to see more on the Arab world within the Middle East. Sadly, there is not that much to report on democratization in the Arab world apart from setbacks. It is too early to assess post-2011 developments in Egypt and even Tunisia until another peaceful transition of power takes place, while Libya, Syria, Yemen and arguably Iraq are currently failed states. Credit should be given to Morocco (culturally Arab) and Jordan for shifting toward becoming fully democratic constitutional monarchies and to Lebanon and Palestine for achieving relatively high scores despite problems not all of their own making. Jordan's advocacy of pluralism within Islam through *The Amman Message* (2004) and of interfaith relations through *The Amman Interfaith Message* (2005) and *A Common Word* (2007), both initiated by the Royal Hashemite Court, challenge the Islamist agenda. Nonetheless, while a volume such as this could not hope to cover every context, it is to be regretted that attempts to recruit contributions on Africa and on other MENA states were unsuccessful. There are, though, some studies that help to fill these lacunae such as Muedini, which has chapters on Algeria, Morocco, Pakistan, one on the Central Asian states of Chechnya and Uzbekistan and one on efforts to recruit Sufis to aid counter-terrorism and to counter radicalization of young people in Britain and North America. Looking at the former Soviet states introduces a different dynamic; these states were previously under socialist regimes. Kosovo, of course, which is discussed was also under socialist rule. A very recent text, by Hamid (2016) looks at Salafists and Sufis in Britain, at their organization, relations with British society, and rivalries. Both gain and lose support and, in his estimate, fail to offer young British Muslims much help in constructing a viable British Muslim identity. There is also much that is relevant to the concerns of this book in Ridgeon (2015). While the current situation in Egypt is outlined in Chapter 1, this writer highly recommends Ladjal and Bensaid's important and timely article (2011). Mention should also be made of Rozehnal (2007) on Pakistan, while Werenfel's 2013 article on the reentry into the political arena of Sufis across the Maghreb covers several MENA states. On Morocco, Bouasria (2014) examines the interplay between Sufis and the political sphere from the colonial period until today, categorizing relations as acquiescent or dissident. There are also references to Indonesia. The linkage between Indonesia and Morocco as fertile for comparison dates from Geertz *Islam Observed* (1968), the first text by a leading anthropologist with "Islam" in its title. Interestingly, though there is indeed a strong rationale for this comparison, it began accidentally. Geertz was looking for another research field after his work in Indonesia and was thinking about East Pakistan. However, he thought that it might be "too unhealthy for" him "and his family." Then at a conference someone suggested Morocco, and he continued his pioneer interpretive anthropology there thus influencing many of us who work in comparative Islamic Studies (Geertz & Ross 1992: 151). Two texts discussing African contexts are recommended to fill that gap in this volume; Diouf (2013) on Senegal and, although less recent, Nimtz (1980) on the coastal city of Bagamoyo in Tanzania. Describing "societal divisions" based on ethnicity (1980: vii), Nimtz found that during the colonial period the *ṭarīqahs* helped mobilize African's against German rule while post-independence they are socially and politically engaged in promoting the interests of Tanzania's Africans. Touched on in Chapter 1 and the contextual backdrop for Chapter 3, as the first Muslim-majority state to enshrine secularism in its constitution, Turkey presents some very particular circumstances that merit more detailed treatment. Here, Axiarli (2014) provides in-depth analysis of the political and Islam-related background of the current regime (which has Sufi roots).

Chapter 2

Kim's chapter on "the Hizmet movement, a Turkey-oriented global Islamic network" presents "a case study to look at how Sufism is actually lived in and interacts with today's secular and pluralistic contexts." It has much to say about Turkey but situates the movement in its global context. Kim's doctoral work was on Fetullah Gülen, the movement's founder but he undertook additional fieldwork to bring this chapter up-to-date. He described Hizmet (which means "service;" following his use, this is not italicized) as "keeping its distance from traditional Sufi orders" while also depicting "how the tolerant, adaptive and inclusive feature of Sufism was reactivated both theologically and practically for interfaith dialogue and peaceful coexistence in today's pluralistic and global world." Gülen was blamed by the Turkish government for fomenting the attempted coup in July 2016 but no evidence for this has been presented. Bennett also includes a segment on Gülen in Chapter 1 as an example of a prominent Sufi-influenced teacher who draws on Sufis principles to argue in favor of democracy and interfaith dialogue. The other thinker discussed in that brief segment is the late and much missed Fatima Mernissi, partly to ensure that at least one female voice is present in this text.

Chapter 3

Schwartz's chapter takes us to Kosovo. He also refers to other former Yugoslav republics and to Albania, thus covering the region in Europe where Muslims are a majority apart from those who live in the European part of Turkey. This was, of course, socialist space. Not yet fully recognized as a sovereign state (Serbia recognizes its autonomy not its independence), Kosovo is still healing from the wounds of war in the former Yugoslavia (1991–2001) that resulted in this Serbian but culturally and linguistically Albanian territory seceding in 2008. Albania, for its part, has a history of cordial interfaith relations. It was the only German-occupied country during World War II where the size of the Jewish population increased. Our memories are short. It is easy to forget the role that self-declared Christians played in demonizing Balkan's Muslims and attempting to eradicate their presence and cultural heritage through the crime of genocide. Kosovo, historically sacred for Serbian Christians, was a target of ethno-religious cleansing. During this conflict, Muslims were victims not victimizers despite the tendency to always cast them in that role (see Bennett, 2014: 90–125 on the

Bosnian and related conflicts). Post-2008, Kosovo's government is perhaps uniquely committed to reconciliation and interfaith dialogue and has sponsored a series of international conferences, in which Kosovo Sufi Union participated. Schwartz was a panelist at the first two. With 20 out of 120 seats in Kosovo's Assembly reserved for different ethnic communities, inclusivity is a state policy. Yet there is a question about how inclusive Kosovo's Sufis are vis-à-vis the Bektashi (*Bektāshī*) order (founded 1501), which played a major role in spreading Islam in the region. The order presents "'the other Islam' to the world ... an Islam that despises miss-rulers, promotes mutual respect between believers in all religions, and cultivates the faith of the heart rather than falling into the trap of obsession with *shāri'a*h." With Sunni, Shia, pre-Islamic and some say Christian elements, it has been labelled syncretistic or as *ghulāt* (extreme). Schwatz describes it as "liberal Shia." The Ottomans outlawed the order in 1826. Sometimes, Sufis seem to find it easier to embrace pluralism when their partners are non-Muslim than when they are seen as deviant Sufis (as in Indonesia where the *Nahdatul Islam* (NU) related Sufi association regards local orders as heterodox). Schwartz's personally engaged chapter recounts how the Bektashi are tackling the issue of their own inclusion within Kosovo's Sufi Union, providing a somewhat different perspective from most other chapters in this volume.

Chapters 4 and 5

In Chapter 4, Milani explores the contribution of the Iranian thinker, Javad Nurbakhsh who died in 2008. Nurbakhsh's thinking developed within the particularities of Iran's "cultural heritage" but he also attracted non-Iranian followers, and interest across the globe. Nurbakhsh led the "newly defined Persian Sufi tradition, the Nimatullahi Khaniqahi," an offshoot of Iran's second largest *ṭarīqah* that also has a substantial following in Azerbaijan. Milani makes it clear that Sufis range from conservative through moderate to more radical religiously and politically. However, Nurbakhsh "managed to shift the direction of a largely conservative Nimatullahi attitude toward a secular project that stood in the face of dogmatic religious elements in Iran, and later abroad." This included disassociating Sufism from "formal religion." He left Iran after the 1979 revolution. Applying Garry Tromps' "payback" and "retribution" concept and Pierre Bourdieu's "Theory of Practice" to his analysis, Milani offers an important cautionary note: "the experience of the Khaniqahi Nimatullahi in Iran offers an inversion to the view that Sufism is somewhat a pluralistic and democratic force *ipso facto.*" Thus, "such revered attributes need to be examined within their proper socio-political context, and not viewed as the *sine quo non* of Sufism." While placed in the contextual category, this chapter is an important theoretical contribution to the volume, warning that "Sufi ideas about altruism and universalism did not emerge in a vacuum." In fact, the way that

NU affiliated Sufis in Indonesia regard some Sufi-related movements and the *Bektāshī*'s struggle for inclusion in Kosovo should caution us against assuming that Sufis always embrace pluralism.

Ramsey's chapter on the Deoband movement follows. This is rooted in a South Asian context, Pakistan. However, the Deoband movement (began 1866) is also well represented among British Muslims, so analysis is relevant for that context too. Ramsey lives and works in Pakistan. His doctoral work (to be published by Brill) was on the important Indian reformist thinker, Sir Sayyid Ahmad Khan (1817–1898) for whom Islam's religious ideals and aspects, not legal/political formulations, are universally binding for Muslims; "I acknowledge," he said in an 1884 speech, "the original religion of Islam, which God and the Messenger have disclosed, not that religion which the '*ulama*' and blessed *maulavis* and preachers have fashioned" (Ramsey 2015: 295). Analyzing Sayyid Ahmad's untranslated Urdu work on the Bible in his PhD, Ramsey concludes that his view of scripture was that "prophetic texts share a greater consonance than dissonance if universal principles are applied to regulate interpretation" (Ramsey 2015: Abstract). Sayyid Ahmad drew heavily on Sufi exegesis in his approach. This has an echo in how cultural mediators in Bengal dealt with Hindu narratives (see Chapter 6 below). Sayyid Ahmad's response to British power in India can be seen as an accommodation. He rejected the call to regard India as a place of war, arguing that under British rule it qualified as a place of safety where Muslims were free to practice their faith's religious aspects. He wanted, though, his College (founded 1875, now Aligarh Muslim University) to combine Islamic and Western learning. Cooperation with the British would help redress the balance that Hindus were outstripping Muslims by taking advantage of what the West offered educationally, scientifically and socially.

The Deoband movement's response was midway between the most radical, who declared *jihad* against British rule, and Khan's. The background to all three was the revolt of 1857. The Deoband minimized contact with the British, retreating to their rural seminary (now one of the largest in the world) where they set out to purify Islam, ridding it of Hindu and other influences. Once Islam was renewed, more Arab-flavored, Muslims would again become God's chosen. Yet the founders had strong Sufi ties and never totally condemned Sufi practices. Thus, the actual Deoband-Sufism relationship is complex. Ramsey asks how "does this contribute to an understanding of the complex interrelation of Sufism, pluralism, and democracy." Pointing out that Deoband itself embraces diversity (which may surprise some who assume that it is monolithic) which he explores in some detail, Ramsey's analysis of texts, preaching and digital media concludes that "the vast majority" of Deobandis in "Pakistan are neither anti-saint nor anti-shrine, though they share clear expectations of what devotion to these must not entail." Deoband may in fact be categorized as a post-*ṭarīqah* form of Islam. Deoband, he says, "does not have an innate or predetermined political agenda." However, most of Pakistan's extremists are not graduates of Deoband seminaries but of Westernized universities. There is support for a Taliban-style state but little enthusiasm for armed struggle to achieve this. The Deoband, considered as a post-*ṭarīqah* form of Sufism, may not represent an impulse toward democracy but nor are members likely to join violent, regime changing uprisings.

Chapter 6

Next, this writer's second chapter straddles two South Asian contexts, Bangladesh and Indonesia (technically South East Asia). Indonesia ranked, at 49th, in first position for a Muslim-majority state on the EIU's *Democracy Index* 2015 (48th in 2016).[1] Turkey, at 97th (2015 and 2016), although routinely described as the only Muslim democracy, is relatively high on the scale but less democratic. Yet Indonesia has not attracted as much attention as Turkey and so invites closer investigation. Although there is a strong argument for a separate chapter on Indonesia in this book, this writer decided to offer a comparative study of Indonesia and Bangladesh, which at 86th on the 2015 *Democracy Index* also ranks highly (promoted to 84 on the report for 2016). He thought a long time ago that a comparative study of these would be worthwhile when he read about how Geertz almost tackled this in the 1960s although much of what this chapter covers took place more recently. Given their current ranking, these two South Asian states (where a combined 22% of all Muslims live, more than in Arab space) qualify for in-depth analysis. What role have Sufis played in shaping their national and political cultures that currently represent multi-party, broadly secular, developing but not yet full liberal democracies? If it is the case that Sufism is a contributing factor in the democratization of two *and not just one* Muslim-majority state, this strengthens the chances that resources exist in Sufism that promote pluralist democracy. This does not challenge Milani's proposition that Sufi openness and support for democracy "need to be examined within their proper socio-political context, and not viewed as the *sine quo non* of Sufism" because the thesis here is that these two South Asian contexts represent cultural milieus that, mingled with Sufism, allowed these "revered attributes to blossom."

Chapter 7

Alam's chapter supplements Bennett's second contribution by exploring the legacy of Sayyid Delaor Husayn Maizbhandari (1892–1982) grandson of Maulana Sayyid Ahmadullah Maizbhandari (d. 1906), the founder of the Maizbhandariyya *ṭarīqah*, Bangladesh's only indigenous order by analyzing his text, *Vilayat-e-Mutlaqa* (8th edition, 2001). Today, the Maizbhandariyya is affiliated with one of the Sufi-related parties that embrace religious pluralism, democracy and a secular system of governance. It won two seats in 2014. Alam's chapter explores how Husayn's teaching of *jatidharmanirbisese* (regardless of caste or creed), preference for ethics over ritual religious practice and "of religious pluralism and accommodation over conflict ... might be a model for national integration, which in turn may resolve the tension between the secular and the religious in modern Bangladesh." Again, tolerance, openness and commitment to democracy are seen to be grounded in a specific context. No automatic relationship may exist between being Sufi and supporting democracy but the presence of certain cultural currents might release some dormant potentiality toward this.

Chapters 8 and 9

The final two chapters are categorized as theoretical-literary in this volume. Singh's chapter presents the work of two Punjabi poets who attract admirers from across faith divides, and extol gender equality, humanism and universality. This is an opportunity for readers to become acquainted with her subjects, Bullhe Shah (1680–1758) and Waris Shah (1722–1798) who are likely to be less familiar than the subjects of the final chapter. To help us here, she uses her own published translation of their Punjabi verse, *Of Sacred and Secular Desire: An Anthology of Punjabi Lyrical Writings from the Punjab* (Singh 2012). Like Sufis in Bangladesh and Indonesia, religious identity blurs as these poets "sumptuously utilize Hindu imagery." Instead of appreciating the "multivalency of their poetics" scholars frequently end up placing them either in a Muslim category or in a Hindu category, missing the "dazzling diversity of the human spirit" that shines through their work. Singh's analysis draws on Hans-Georg Gadamer's theory of literary hermeneutics. Her chapter also tackles the controversial issue of veiling, which Waris Shah saw as "suffocating and oppressive" thus offering a feminist perspective.

Hussaini's chapter on universality in the work of two of the most celebrated Sufi masters, Ibn al-'Arabī and Rūmī, is again less contextual than theoretical and literary, looking at how this provides theological ground for a pluralist worldview. Hussaini's work is an insightful investigation of the subject material, which also provides readers with copious citations from primary sources. He argues that the notion of tolerance so powerfully and beautifully expressed in their work "is substantial, rather than accidental." It goes beyond a pragmatic acceptance of diversity for the sake of social harmony because it roots plurality in the divine reality. He writes, "This is the positive pluralism that encourages people to observe more faces of God's manifestations through religions."

THE CONCLUDING CHAPTER

In the Conclusion, co-editor Alam re-iterates that this book is offered as part of a conversation which he characterizes as one between Islam past and Islam today. Distinguishing Sufi Islam from what he describes as "monolithic mainstream Sunni Islam" or following Vincent J. Cornell (2014) "corporate Islam" (although this book includes Shia perspectives) he describes the first as creative and dynamic, thus adaptive to change and the latter as "frozen in the past." Drawing on Qur'ānic reference and the content of this book, Alam articulates the case that Sufism, which is prone to inter-religious openness, affirmative of gender equality and pacifist, offers Muslims today an alternative to Salafist/Islamist Islam, perhaps one that is also pro-democratic. Alam links Sufis' acceptance of diversity and democracy, suggesting that the former might provide a foundation on which democratic institutions could be built. He equates the present with modernity, arguing that Sufism is better equipped than "corporate Islam" to recognize signs of God's self-disclosure in the present.

Call for Comparisons and Critiques

This composite text is intended to enable comparison between contexts, those discussed and those covered in some of the texts recommended above. It is also intended to invite critical discussion of Sufism's role or lack of one in the political arena, to challenge too positive an assessment of this. Although all contributors write as scholars who aim at objectivity, a degree of passion does color these pages. Clearly, some contributors do lean toward supporting, in theory, the contention that Sufis typically embrace religious openness, respect for other faiths, and see human values as the best basis around which societies should be organized. This writer has often taken the critical paradigm of exposing prejudice, false and biased representation of Muslims, into his academic work. He is convinced that misrepresentation can be dangerous in an already divided world. Accounts of Islam that demonize Muslims, and analysis that always sees Islam as problematic, may have serious consequences for world peace and international relations. The current xenophobic rhetoric of some Western politicians alongside the revival of right-wing nationalisms that demonize racial, religious and cultural others bodes ill for preserving pluralist political cultures in the West. Several Western states' democracy rankings have been downgraded including those of France and the USA. Some want to demonize all Muslims, wherever they live. The development of democracy in Muslim-majority space may help combat this very negative view of Muslim societies. The possibility that Sufis might take valuable insights and impulses with them into the democratization process, at the very least, is worth even more critical attention than this single volume can offer.

Contributors, though, did not intentionally allow *a priori* assumptions to skew their findings. Nonetheless, the contributions published here tend to suggest that Sufis may be allies in the global task of strengthening and extending democracy. What mitigates against this possibility is the fact that Sufis have cooperated with dictatorial regimes and reached accommodations with a range of political realities. They appear to have done so, however, to guarantee their own ability to continue their activities in the social welfare and spiritual-devotional spheres. Survival even under regimes they dislike arguably overrode becoming the cause of more conflict through revolt or political dissent. Contributors are aware that the complexities involved in discussing the role that Sufis have played and play politically make it problematic to argue for an automatic relationship between being Sufi and support for democracy and for that matter embracing pluralism. Without ignoring this, however, taken as a whole the contributions in this book are sympathetic toward the view that, depending on other contextual factors, Sufism can help democracies develop. As a hypothesis, this should be subject to critical scrutiny. In the light of Milani's cautionary proposition, which this book takes seriously, this hypothesis is presented as *plausible, tentative but unproven*. Everything on offer in this book, based on contributors' research, represents scholarly investigating and theorizing that invites critique. Hopefully, this book will become part of and promote a wider conversation.

A NOTE ON CITATION AND STYLE

Finally, one technical matter is that authors were allowed to choose whether to use endnotes or not. Endnotes, when used, are for additional information; most citations are referenced in the text although some appear in the notes when appropriate. This might compromise the book's stylistic cohesion but reflects the editors' desire for contributors to enjoy a degree of literary freedom within their customary and familiar writing habits. The requirement to follow an unfamiliar template can hamper scholarly production. However, the editors have tried to standardize spelling and use of diacritics. This book leaves un-italicized words that are commonly used in English, such as shaykh (also spelled sheikh in English) Muhammad, caliph, Qur'ān, Shia (for *Shī'ah*) (although Quran is now widely used too) as well as Sufi (Ṣūfī) and uses traditional spelling for Mecca, Medina, for example that have become English words. It uses diacritical marks for technical words, and has tried to be consistent with this but may not have always succeeded. It sometimes anglicizes words such as *ṭarīqahs* (rather than *turuq*) for the plural (though contributors may use a localized version, such as the Turkish *tarikak*). We usually use *ḥadīth* (which is plural) for plural and for singular (*aḥādīth*). Errors and inconsistencies, in the end, are the editors' fault, not individual authors'.

Notes

1. The EIU report for 2016 was published in January 2017 while this book was being copyedited. References to the Democracy Index are mainly to the 2015 report but some data has been inserted from the 2016 report, when appropriate, to up-date the text.

SECTION I

Multi-Contextual

1

SUFIS, SAINTS AND POLITICS IN ISLAM: AN HISTORICAL SURVEY

Clinton Bennett

THE ENIGMA OF SUFI POLITICAL ENGAGEMENT

On the one hand, Sufis are widely perceived as politically quietest, largely disengaged from politics. Sufis may be content with any government, authoritarian or democratic, religious or secular under which they are left free to pursue their spiritual goals. On the other hand, a current trend looks to Sufism as an antidote to Salafist and Islamist agendas. The latter's ideal Muslim political system may include elections. However, they would also restrict who can stand, the rights of some citizens based on religion, sexual orientation and gender and the role of modern notions of what is humane with reference, for example, to legal penalties. A Sunni Salafist state might look a lot like the Shia majority Islamic Republic of Iran. Some claim that a natural affinity exists between Sufis and democracy, that they accept pluralism more readily than some other Muslims. Thus, Sufis may be recruited to help counter radical Islamists and to combat radicalization of Muslim youth to aid counter terrorism strategies.

This chapter, though, takes seriously from the beginning the problem of arguing in favor of some automatic cause and effect relationship between Sufism and support for democracy, which should not be taken for granted. It cites ambiguities and contradictions in actual practice that makes any simplistic association of Sufism with democracy rather naive. In reality, the relationship between Sufism and political engagement is at best enigmatic. Yet Sufi leaders and their communities may, historically, have challenged dominant political systems, offering value-based alternatives which arguably represent more support for a Sufism-democracy association. Drawing on Charles Lindholm's historical anthropology, this chapter suggests that thriving Sufi orders effectively functioned as micro-states, providing viable alternatives to the larger Islamic polity, whose values Sufis rejected. Arguably, Sufis did opt out of public life in the wider Islamic polity yet the fact that they did so was itself a political act. Conversely, there is also a long tradition of Sufi masters legitimizing and opposing political leaders, offering a spiritual alternative to how political authority was validated.

Having identified several contexts where Sufis are currently engaged in the political sphere, usually supporting pluralist democracy, as well as no few where Sufis have acquiesced with authoritarian regimes, this chapter turns to some recent theoretical underpinning for a Sufism-democracy linkage. The chapters on earlier Sufi thinkers, including two of the most eminent, suggest an historic openness to pluralism but democracy did not feature in their discourse. Summarizing the contributions of *Fethullah Gülen* (which Chapter 2 analyses in more detail) and of Fatema Mernissi, it proposes that Sufism's affirmation of pluralism, dialogue and respect for others may predispose Sufis to prefer democratic, open systems. over authoritarian ones that seek to impose religious and social conformity on all citizens and discriminate against some on the basis of creed, gender and other identities. As Milani proposes in chapter 4, though, this never occurs in a vacuum thus circumstances and specific cultural factors all play a role. However, analysis of the Economist Intelligence Unit's *Democracy Index* indicates some possible correlation between Sufi political activism and how Muslim majority states score, which strengthens the case in favor of a possible Sufi-democracy link given the right confluence of factors. This correlation, on the one hand, might be conjecture, on the other, it can be proposed as a plausible hypothesis for investigation and scrutiny and possible refutation.

SUFISM'S AMBIGUOUS POLITICAL RECORD

Brief Historical Survey

In support of the view that Sufis are predominantly apolitical, many examples of Sufi disengagement from politics can be cited, both from history and from contemporary contexts. Werenfels (2014) suggests that, "Combining Sufism and politics, at least in theory, would appear to be something of a paradox, as the essence of Sufi philosophy is spirituality and retreat from worldly affairs" (2014: 282). She points out that Sufi teachers did not write any political treatises (2014: 283). Yet an argument can be made that Sufis have, in fact, quite often taken part in political life. Muedini comments that "while some Sufis are apolitical, many are not" but argues that it would be a mistake to assume that politically engaged Sufis automatically fall into one category "in terms of attitudes toward the state... use of violence, and ... support for the protection of human rights" (Muedini 2015:14). As Milani writes in this volume, "Sufis and Sufi groups, today, can be among those least receptive to change as well as sometimes seen to embrace (even instigate) social and ideological transformation." Yet challenging the claim of political disengagement, at least two states, the Emirate of Asir in the nineteenth century and the Kingdom of Libya in the mid-twentieth century "had Sufi origins" and as Sedgwick (2015) comments, "states are political entities" (2015: 118). Examples can be given of rulers in the pre-modern period sponsoring Sufism for a variety of reasons. For instance, in Egypt the early Ayyubid sultans funded Sufi teachers, encouraging the formation of *Khanaqahs* (teaching centers) to help revive learning following the intellectual decline that had taken place in the latter days of the Fatimid dynasty (Ladjhal & Bensaid 2011: 3). At a time when effective political and military power was in the hands of regional rulers, advised by his Sufi teacher, Abbasid Caliph al-Nasir (d. 1225) turned to the institute of the *futuwwa* (occupational, trade and charitable guilds) to increase his base of support. He made himself head of a warrior *futuwwa*, then set about initiating "other rulers into his brotherhood, including the Prince of Syria and the King of Ghazna." The aim was to re-unite the fragmented caliphate as a single community, drawing on Sufi ideals of chivalry and charity to maintain "social solidarity" and the caliph's role as society's symbolic center (Lindholm 2002: 129). Although not formally affiliated with Sufism, these guilds applied Sufi ethics to their work. Many members also belonged to Sufi orders. In this way, the Ayyubids in Egypt and al-Nasir both contributed to how Sufi organization developed. Abdelaziz (2013) describes how in the early Mamluk period, Mohamed Ibn 'Aṭā'Allāh al-Sakandarī (d. 1309) forged an alliance with the Sultan that helped create political stability after years of turmoil, as well as establishing a place for Sufi studies at one of Islam's premier seats of learning.

Trimingham refers to overlap between the *futuwwa* and the emerging initiatory fraternities of the time, "the organization of the orders...owes much to that of the guilds...as the latter had a grandmaster...and a hierarchy of apprentices...companions and master-craftsmen, so the religious orders acquired a hierarchy of novices, initiates and masters" (Trimingham, Spencer, and Voll 1998: 25). On the one hand, "the organization of the religious orders owes much to that of the guilds," while on the other hand "the tariqas sanctify such secular associations" (1998: 25). Over time, some occupational guilds came to be "linked with particular orders" (1998: 176). The Sufi teacher, al-Suhrawardī (d. 1234) dedicated his classic *'Awarif al-ma'arif* ("The Givens of Knowledge") to al-Nasir (Ernst 1992: 15). Subsequently, shaykhs of the Suhrawardī order were very loyal to the sitting ruler, disavowing "revolt against any king, no matter how unjust" (Ernst 1992: 15). During the colonial period, Sufis led freedom struggles, for example, in North Africa against French rule, in Libya against Italian rule, against Egyptian-British rule in Sudan, against the Dutch in Indonesia while in Chechnya Sufis have a long history of fighting Russian imperialism which continues today. Elsewhere, though, Sufis chose to ally themselves with colonial powers, resisting attempts "to overthrow [these] whether from a nationalist or Islamic direction" (Lieven 1998: 361), which complicates analyses. In Senegal, Sufis accepted French patronage in return for freedom from interference in running their "internal affairs." Sufis gained economically from cooperation with the state, which for its part benefitted from a strategy that minimized risk of political opposition (Muedini 2015: 9). As many as 92% of Senegalese claim membership of a Sufi order. Senegal is now classed as a flawed democracy by the EIU's *Democracy Index* because of the governing party's centralization of power since 2009 but the country's relative stability is credited to the role Sufi leaders still play in mediating between their members and the government (Diouf, 2013: 2). In India, the British followed the example of earlier rulers by recruiting Sufi shaykhs into their system of patronage. Under Mughal rule, many shaykhs enjoyed the benefit of land grants and revenue collecting rights. In Sind, the British allowed shaykhs certain privileges, including exception from appearing in civil courts and seats at *darbars* (gatherings of nobility) with the most honored sitting closer to the front, realizing that shaykhs' help in maintaining law and order especially in frontier zones was vital (Ansari 1992: 49–50).

More Recent Sufi Political Engagement

It is easier to challenge the claim that Sufis have been typically apolitical than it is to establish any particular link between being Sufi and support for specific systems of government, or political ideologies. More recently, in the pre-Arab Spring era, Sufis both opposed and supported authoritarian regimes. In Mubarak's Egypt, they allowed themselves to be sponsored by the government via patronage of the state-sponsored Supreme Council of Sufi Orders and various prestigious appointments including at Al-Azhar, over and against the anti-Sufi Muslim Brotherhood, which opposed Mubarak (Brinton 2016: 136). Former Grand Mufti, Ali Gumah, a Sufi, did his best to discourage the pro-democratic movement that ousted Mubarak (Elmasry 2015). This patronage helped provide the regime with religious legitimacy; the regime, though did not especially want Sufis to have much of a political role perhaps realizing that Sufis might actually oppose its authoritarian rule. Muedini suggests that authoritarian governments choose to "work with Sufis because they…view such groups as nonpolitical, and thus a minimal threat to their political existence" (Muedini 2015: 15). Earlier, Pakistan's military leader, Ayub Khan, in power 1958–1969, had also tried to recruit Sufis to legitimize his admittedly modernist policies, taking control of shrines in order to "link his secular government to the religious authority of the Sufi establishment" (Cesari 2014: 51). About 17% of Pakistanis claim membership of a Sufi order, although actual numbers of those who practice a Sufi-flavored form of Islam may be much larger.

According to Ladja and Bensaid, "no serious clash of any kind has ever been recorded between the Sufi orders and political authorities" in Egypt, "whether under the monarchy or British occupation, or under the revolutionary regime of 1952" (2011: 10). However, when some members of the Supreme Council found themselves opposed to Mubarak's choice for the new grand shaykh, Abdul Had al-Qassabi, following the 2008 vacancy, they formed the Sufi Reform Front and "filed legal suits... challenging" al-Qassabi's appointment, and submitted "complaints to relevant authorities" (Ladjal and Bensaid 2011: 10). They saw al-Qassabi's appointment as an overreach of political authority into the religious sphere. In Syria, some Sufis joined the MB in the anti-Assad coalition, the Islamic Front (founded 1981). Such willingness to accept patronage from authoritarian regimes may indicate that Sufis fear that democracy would benefit their Salafist critics who, once in power, would legislate against their interests and dismantle democratic institutions. Muedini (2015) explores the patronage of Sufis by mainly authoritarian governments in a range of different contexts arguing that they offer sponsorship primarily to combat extremism but that Sufis who accept this also calculate whether cooperation with or resistance to the state is in their best interests. Cooperation often increases their ability to extend the services they provide and their own influence within society (2015: 12–13). Muedini also discusses sponsorship of Sufism in Britain and in the USA as part of anti-terrorist strategies. Similarly, Corbett (2017) describes US and British official interest in cultivating relations with Sufi leaders and organizations pointing out that from the 1990s, "US policymakers began to regard Sufism as the moderate Islam they sought". The US State Department, she writes, increasingly saw Sufis as "peaceful, apolitical, and moderate" and "all other Muslims as extremists" (Corbett 2017: 71; 88; see also 99–100). Her study is especiallly valuable because it draws on a decade of research based in a particular community of Sufis in New York city. In the UK, the government encouraged the formation of the Sufi Muslim Council shortly after the 7/7 terrorist attacks (Muedini 2015: 158–59). Pew Research (2010) reports that some see this "as a blatant attempt by the government to co-opt traditional Sufism for political purposes" (2010: 8). In her 2014 article on the political re-emergence of Sufi orders in the Maghreb, Werenfels also stresses how Sufis who accept sponsorship from authoritarian rulers do so for their own reasons. She emphasizes that while for their part authoritarian regimes sponsor or court the favor of Sufis to gain religious legitimacy, Sufis respond as "actors with their own social, political and economic interests that may or may not overlap with those of the regime and that might twist system reforms in ways to better serve themselves" (2014: 276). What follows, she suggests, "can best be described as a *do-ut-des* (I give that you may give) process, in which bottom-up and top-down interests coalesce" (2014: 284). Sufis in the Maghreb have chosen to cooperate with Islamists as well as with authoritarian rulers but also propagate "messages that are not necessarily in line with values or practices important for upholding the current (authoritarian) rules of the game" (2014: 291). In Tunisia, the only Arab country ranked as a "flawed democracy" on the EIU's 2015 *Democracy Index*, which has the 3rd highest score for a Muslim majority state, despite attacks on Sufi shrines during 2012 Sufism is experiencing a revival. More people are "eyeing Sufism as a means of individual and collective healing as the country faces a multifaceted crisis with complex and overlapping economic, political and spiritual problems" (Ghanmi 2016). According to one poll, 43.1% of Tunisians visit a Sufi shrine at least once annually (Ghanmi) although Pew reports that only 1% claim a Sufi affiliation. Having launched the Arab Spring, Tunisia remains (so far) its only success story. This is less an example of Sufi political activism than of Sufis becoming part of a national dialogue, thus contributing to debate on important issues. This healing process was made possible when, having won a plurality in the 2011 election, the Islamist Ennahda party, which was widely perceived to restrict civil rights if it gained power, voluntarily stepped aside so that a new Constitution could be negotiated with the goal of national reconciliation. Adopted in 2014, it has strong guarantees on religious freedom and human rights. Islam is the state religion. In the 2014 election, 68 women won seats (out of 217), the highest percentage for an Arab state.

Sufi Affiliated Senior Politicians

Similarly challenging the apolitical view, politicians with Sufi affiliations have held senior offices in Muslim-majority states. Among these, Hussain Muhammad Ershad, Salafist in his views, was President or rather dictator of Bangladesh from 1982 to 1990 when he regularly consulted his Naqshbandi *pir* on matters of state. Even after Ershad was jailed for corruption, he won seats in parliament; since 1996 he has supported the secular Awami League, in whose government his party has had a cabinet post. President Abdurrahman Wahid (1999–2001) of Indonesia, who for many was a living saint, was liberal and pro-democratic but was impeached for incompetency and cronyism. In addition to heading the *Patai Kebangkitan Bangsa* (PKB/National Awakening Party), which won 12.6% of the vote in the 1999 election, 51 out of 462 seats, Wahid led the world's largest Muslim organization, *Nahdlatul Ulama* (founded 1926). On Wahid, see Chapter 6 of this book. His thinking also represents a recent example of theoretical underpinning for a Sufi-democracy link. The *Nahdatul Islam* (NU) runs a large network of *pesantren* (Islamic boarding schools, whose curriculum includes Sufi teachings), 44 universities, many hospitals and other charities. A significant number of NU members identify as Sufi practitioners. Turkey's current president, Recep Tayyip Erdoğan, a Sufi, has attracted negative comment for public references to Sufi ideas about deification, suggesting that this reveals ambition to govern as a God-like figure (Shoebat 2015). Earlier, Turkey's prime minister 1983–1989 and president 1989–1993, Turgut Özal, a member of the Naqshbandi order, benefited from Sufis' support, as did Neçmettin Erbakan (deputy prime minister 1974: 75–77, 77–78 and prime minister 1996–97) who regularly consulted his shaykh on social, economic and political issues. Özal was very open about his Muslim identity. Several Turkish leaders, including Tansu Çiller, Turkey's first and so far only woman prime minister (1993–96, deputy prime minister 1996–97) have carefully juggled their Turkish, Muslim and secular identities.

Sufi Affiliated Political Parties

Sufis have established a number of political parties that aim to offer secular, democratic alternatives to Salafist agendas. One of the earliest forays into modern politics by Sufis took place in Lebanon (where 9% claim membership of a Sufi order, Pew 2012a: 3, Q32), when the Pan-Sufi *Ahbash* (Society of Islamic Philanthropic Projects, or *Jam'iyyat al- Mashari' al-Khayriyya al-Islamiyya*) organization (founded 1930) "ran two candidates in Lebanon's parliamentary elections, one of whom, Dr Trabulsi, won a seat in Beirut" in 1992 (Hamzeh and Dekmejjian 1996: 225; an important early contribution on Sufis and politics). Pro-democracy, the *Ahbash* "call for religious moderation, political civility, and peace" and "an enlightened Islamic spiritualism within a modern secularist framework" (Hamzeh and Dekmejian 1996: 224). However, in 2005 two members were jailed for alleged involvement in the assassination of Rafiq Hariri, after which, although these men were later exonerated, "the organization began a steady retreat from politics" (Choufi 2013) perhaps disillusioned with its experiment at political activism, a pattern which may currently be repeating itself in Egypt.

Indonesia's *Patai Kebangkitan Bangsa* (National Awakening Party) (PKB) formed in 1998 is discussed in more detail in Chapter 6. This party's Sufi leader, Abdurrahman Wahid was president from 1999 to 2001. Although PKB's share of seats remains modest the current leader, Muhaimin Iskandar, the Wahid's nephew, was vice-chair of the People's Representative Council from 1999–2004 and 2004–2009 and since then has served as minister of manpower and transmigration. Three other PKB members sit in the current Cabinet. While not explicitly Sufi-affiliated, PKB counts as a Sufi-related party that has had a degree of electoral success and a role in governance. Similarly, Turkey's *Adalet ve Kalkınma Partisi* (AKP) qualifies as Sufi-related but is not officially Sufi affiliated. AKP's origin lies in the National Order Party (founded 1970, banned 1972) which reformed as the National Salvation Party in 1971 until that was banned in 1980, then as the Welfare Party (1983) which became the Virtue Party in 1983 and finally AKP in 2001. The Khalidi branch of the Naqshbandi order has had a high level of involvement in each iteration of Turkey's religious party (parties have had to reform after military interventions). The National Salvation Party was part of a coalition government from 1974 to 1978 when its leader served as deputy prime minister. The Welfare Party led a coalition government between June 1996 and June 1997. It was forced to resign when the military threatened to intervene to protect Turkey's secular constitution. It self-defines as "conservative democratic." However, a "fundamental premise … is that one may be a Muslim culturally and a democrat politically" (Axiarlis 2014: 115). AKP has governed Turkey since the 2002 election. It briefly lost the majority in June 2015 (with 258 out of 550 seats) but regained this in November's snap election (with 317 out of 550 seats). Although Turkey's president has to sever links with a political party, Recep Tayyip Erdoğan the current president (since 2014, prime minister from 2003–2014) and his predecessor Abdullah Gül (2003–2014; prime minister from 2002–2003) co-founded and led AKP. The AKP remains committed to joining the European Union, which is "the most significant indicator of the" AKP "government's espousal of a modern democratic agenda (Axiarlis 2014: 115). Constitutional amendments in 2010 removed immunity for taking part in the 1980 coup from military personnel and limited military courts' jurisdiction over civilians. Cornell and Kaya (2015) describe AKP as "with only slight exaggeration…a coalition of religious orders." It is the most successful, so far, of any Sufi-related party. Gül, Erdoğan, interior ministers Abdülkadir Aksu and Beşir Atalay and close to a dozen other ministers during Erdoğan's tenure belong to the same Sufi lodge, the *İskenderpaşa* as had Erbakan and former presidents Süleyman Demirel (1993–2000; seven times prime minister between 1965 and 1993) and Turgut Özal (Cornell and Kaya 2015).

In Egypt, *Al-Tahrir Al-Masri* (Liberation Party) (founded by members of the 'Azmeya order), the *Ḥizb Ṣawt al-Ḥurriyyah* (Voice of Freedom Party) (founded by members of the Rifa'iya order) and *al-Nasr al-Sufi Party* (Victory Party) (founded by various Sufi leaders), all established post-2011, aim to mobilize support for social democracy against Salafist alternatives. They have also said that they welcome Christian members. The Victory party has called for an investigation into the funding of the Salafist Al-Nour Party and its "views on Egypt's Coptic Christians" in January 2015 (Ahram online 2015). Abu Azayim, the 'Azmeya shaykh, told one reporter that the aim of the World Federation of Sufi Orders (*Al-Ittihad al-'Alami lil-Turuq al-Sufiyya*, founded 2013), which he also heads, is to "promote peace in the world, fight against Salafism and convince all Muslims to take the path of modern Islam," (Borsatti 2010). The Mubarak appointed Grand Shaykh al-Qassabi denounced these parties' formation as divisive, possibly "leading to greater social rifts" (Harvard Divinity School Religious Literacy Project). He stated that Sufis should "promote religious thought, not politics" (Cesari 2014: 148). There are an estimated 10 to 15 million Sufis in Egypt where 9% of the population claim membership of a Sufi order (Pew 2012: Q3). Hassan (2011) suggests that Egypt's Sufis prefer a party similar to Turkey's AKP. Abu Azayim "travelled to Turkey to examine" AKP's "political experience...armed with the hope of creating" a "body that could reflect the... voting power of Sufis" (2011: 5). A number of prominent Sufis also gave public support to Abdel Fattah El-Sisi's successful 2014 presidential bid when they met with him in May, saying that Egypt needed a strong military man to deal with its current crises (Jones 2014). This support for the military strong-man could indicate that, having dabbled with electoral politics, Egypt's Sufi shaykhs have reverted to their earlier position of passivity and compliance "with general government policy," although lack of success may also lie in "political immaturity" and "weak political organization" (Ladjal & Bensaid 2011: 15). The Liberation Party and Voice of Freedom, too, "strictly represented" the membership of their founding orders "and failed to unite other Sufi orders" (Ladjal & Bensaid 2011: 14). The large number (over 40) of new parties would have contributed to the difficulties of becoming politically viable at the ballot. In their study of the recent "political journey" of Egypt's Sufis, however, Ladjal & Bensaid call it a "failure" (2011: 1).

Three Sufi-related parties have campaigned in Bangladesh, the Zaker Party (founded 1989 by Ershad's *pīr*, Hasmat Ullah of Atroshi, d. 2001, who was said to have 10 million devotees), the Islamic Constitutional Movement (founded 2002, linked with the Sabiri branch of the Chīshtī order) and the Tariqat Federation (founded 2005, linked with the Maizbhandari, see Chapter 8 on this indigenous Bangladeshi order). Zaker and Tariqat mobilized against militancy and Salafist parties in alliance with the secular Awami League, which has governed since 2008, although Zaker withdrew from the alliance in 2008 to contest a number of seats by itself. ICM opposes Awami, although with the other two Sufi parties it vehemently denounces the *Jamaat-e-Islami* (electorally the most successful Islamist party in Bangladesh). Alam (2012), who discusses these parties' formation, argued that although they did not achieve electoral success, they represent a "creative initiative" by Sufis designed to "expand their space in... political culture" (2012: 176). The Tariqat Federation won two seats in the 2014 election. The large *Tablighi Jamaat*, which may have over 100 million adherents worldwide (although it has no official membership mechanism) "is and always has been unwilling to participate in political debates" but "typically, Tablighis support the Awami League" (Uddin 2006: 162). About

26% of Bangladeshis claim affiliation with a Sufi order. However, close to 50% may identify with Sufism to some degree. Tablighi, which is usually categorized as "neo-Sufi;" rejects saint and tomb veneration and some Sufi teachings but uses such Sufi practices as *dhikr* (remembrance, a devotional act) and emphasizes inner renewal.

In Pakistan, the *Awami Tehreek*, founded in 1999 by the Sufi teacher, Muhammad Tahir-ul-Qadri, promotes democracy, human rights and justice. Tahir ul-Qadri won a National Assembly seat in 2002 but resigned in 2004. In 2010, Tahir ul-Qadri issued his *Fatwa on Terrorism and Suicide Bombings*, in which he wrote:

> Terrorism in its very essence symbolizes disbelief and is a rejection of what Islam stands for. When the forbidden element of suicide is added to it, its severity and gravity becomes even greater (2010: 35).

Tahrir ul-Qadri's neo-Sufi *Minhaj-ul-Quran* (founded 1987) organization has branches in over 80 countries. Several of these parties have had little or no electoral success. One held the presidency. One is currently in power. However, their existence challenges the claim that all Sufis are politically inactive. Islamist parties have seen relatively little electoral success either with a few exceptions such as the Freedom and Justice Party, founded by MB members, in the 2011–2012 Egyptian election, which can be explained in terms of its long organizational history of opposition to the ousted regime compared with most other parties, which were new. MB members had won seats in pre-2011 parliaments (which exercised little power) becoming the largest oppositional group in 2005 with 88 out of 444 seats. However, this result was more or less rigged by the government to create the impression of free political expression. The Freedom and Justice Party gained the largest number of seats (42.7%; 213 out of 498 seats; allies won an additional 22 seats) and the presidency (with 51%) in 2012. Both President Mohamed Morsi and the government were overthrown in a military coup on July 3rd 2013. Although elected democratically, the suspicion was that they would institutionalize their policies and perpetuate their power. Their draft Constitution did reduce judicial independence, lacked protection for free expression and allowed civilians to be tried in military courts. MB and the Freedom and Justice Party were subsequently banned. Bangladesh *Jamaat-e-Islami* (JI) is also currently excluded from electoral politics in Bangladesh. Morsi's ousting repeated the military intervention that occurred in Algeria in 1991 after the Islamist *Front Islamique Salut* (FIS) (Islamic Salvation Front) won 48% of the vote in the first round of parliamentary elections. Fear that FIS would radically alter the state's secular constitution saw its opponents shut down the election process. FIS, though committed to *din-wa-dawla* (unity of religion and state) advocated an electoral system and said that it would safeguard minority rights (see Bennett 2005: 245–47). Thus, Islamists have had some electoral success. This is because they offer an alternative agenda to that of post-colonial regimes under which the majority of people have not prospered, which are also often corrupt. After winning local elections in Algeria, FIS had gained a reputation for honesty. HAMAS won 74 out of 132 seats in the 2006 Palestinian National Authority elections which also qualifies as success. This can be explained as popular frustration with lack of real progress toward viable statehood. Due to arrests of HAMAS legislators by Israel and an international aid embargo, HAMAS limited its control to the Gaza strip. *Hezbollah* has won seats in successive Lebanese elections, too with cabinet seats since 2005 and runs one fifth of local municipalities. *Hezbollah* has stated that "constitutional democracy" is "the best political system for Lebanon" (Wiegand 2016: 111). By providing social services and healthcare, *Hezbollah* meets needs that the government does not which earns support at the ballot box.

In Bangladesh and Indonesia, electoral support for religiously affiliated parties has recently declined in favor of secular or *de-facto* secular ones. What can also be said is that the Sufi-related parties, in contrast to Islamists, appear to support the forming of liberal democracies within a broadly secular framework, although one that allows Islamic values to inform legislation and policies. However, no religious body would have a veto or sanctioning authority.

Table 2: Active Political Parties with Sufi Links

Country	Party	Sufi Link or Affiliation	Electoral Record
Pakistan	Awami Tehrik (f. 1989)	Linked with neo-Sufi Minhaj-al-Quran and the Qadiriyya.	One seat 2002–2004 held by founder.
Indonesia	PKB (f. 1998)	Close ties with *Nahdatul Islam* (NU) and its affiliated association of Sufi orders.	Held presidency 1999–2001 and 51 seats out of 462; 2004, 52 out of 678; 2009, 28 out of 692; 2014, 47 out of 692. Four MPs currently serve in the Cabinet.
Turkey	AKP (f. 2001)	Strong ties with Naqbshbandi-Khalidi order	Governing party since 2002. Currently Presidency and 315 out of 560 seats.
Bangladesh	Zaker Party (f. 1989)	Founded by a Naqshbandi shaykh currently led by his son.	0
Bangladesh	Islamic Constitutional Movement (f. 2002)	linked with the Sabiri branch of the Chīshtī order	0
Bangladesh	Tariqat Federation (.2005)	linked with the Maizbhandari	Won two seats in 2014.
Egypt	Victory Party (f. 2012)	Various Sufi leaders	0

| Egypt | Voice of Freedom Party (f. 2012) | Rifa'iya order | 0 |
| Egypt | Liberation Party (f. 2012) | 'Azmeya | 0 |

Sufi-Salafi Relations: a Complex Phenomenon

Sufism attracts the opposition of Salafists yet it would be wrong to assume that these two are mutually incompatible. Their actual relationship is complex and it can be argued that Salafist movements represent a particular transformation of Sufi ideals into practice, thus "in their continuities as well as in their contradictions, Islamic fundamentalism and Sufism have helped construct each other as modern subjects," while both strive "to conceal this mutual dependence" (Weismann 2007: 30). Ridgeon (2015b) usefully explores the complex relationship between Salafists and Sufis. Geoffroy (2010) points out how almost all Salafist reformers "come from the school of Sufism, which they criticized on this or that point, but to which most never ceased to belong" (2010: 136). In addition to the Sufi background of such prominent Salafists as Muslim Brotherhood's founder, Hasaan al-Banna (1906–1949) (although he was excommunicated for founding the organization) and the founders of the Deobandi movement, (1867) (see Ramsey in this volume), the prominent preacher and academic Yusuf al-Qaradawi calls for "an elision between the scholarly discipline of the Salafists and the ethical virtue of the Sufis" (Gauvain 2013: 305 n. 103). Although widely known for an anti-Sufi stance, the Muslim Brotherhood's original 1928 charter "stipulates that the new *salafi* movement would have as its base 'a Sufi reality'" (Geoffroy 2010: 137). Sufism's legacy can be seen reflected in the Brotherhood's social welfare work and in its emphasis on the need for personal renewal. Sayyid Qutb (d. 1966), regarded as a founding father of Islamic fundamentalism, director of MB's propaganda department for many years, believed that inner renewal of faith is a prerequisite for social transformation. Islam, he wrote, must "first be transplanted in the hearts of men" as "living reality" (2006: 50). The Indonesian thinker, Hamka (1908–1981) a prominent member of *Muhammadiyah* (founded 1912, Indonesia's second largest Muslim organization) championed a type of Salafist Sufism in his book, *Tasawuf Modern* (1939) arguing that Muslims should develop spiritually while adhering to Islam's external forms, thus combining Sufi and Salafi foci although unlike al-Ghazālī (d. 1111), who had also advocated this he rejected the *ṭarīqah* system. When some Indonesians, spurred on by anti-Sufi rhetoric, stripped their practices of what was "suspected of not being in conformity with Qur'ān and Hadiths, they found themselves left with a faith that lacked "deeper spiritual meaning." Thus, Hamka encouraged them to cultivate an inner spirituality "guided by the outward forms of conventional Muslim religiosity" but "accompanied by a deeper emotional richness" (Howell 2001: 711). Ibn Taymiyyah (d. 1328) one of the preferred classical thinkers among contemporary Salafists had a complicated relationship with Sufism, of which he was critical. However, he is included in a medieval manuscript recording *silsilah*, and was buried "in a Sufi graveyard" (Ridgeon 2015a: 145). The Muslim Brotherhood's position on democracy is also complex. It denounces democracy as un-Islamic yet members, officially as independents pre–2011, regularly stood for and won parliamentary seats, as noted above. As well as enjoying strong Sufi links, "leading representatives of the various branches of the Brotherhood [MB], including Hamas, have been honored guests at AKP conventions" (Cornell and Kaya 2015).

SUFIS AS LEGITIMIZERS OF POLITICAL AUTHORITY

Internal Organization of Sufi Orders

The great initiatory Sufi fraternities so well-known today, such as the Chīshtī, Naqshbandi, Qadiriyya and the Rifa'iyya developed during the eleventh and twelfth centuries, creating an enduring organizational structure for Sufism that had not previously existed. Early Sufism saw less formal circles of students gathered around a teacher resembling the pattern found elsewhere in the Muslim world around non-Sufi scholars and their followers. These circles consisted of individuals attracted to the teacher, pursuing their own goals with a "bare minimal of institutional rules" and a largely transient, rather than permanent, population (Trimingham, Spencer, and Voll 1998: 5). Believing that the way of the Sufis was for an elect, these early masters only taught those whom they considered qualified to learn (see Ernst 1985: 44). Manṣūr al-Ḥallāj, executed for heresy in 922, annoyed his mentors when he began to preach indiscriminately to anyone who would listen, abandoning "the tunic of the Ṣūfīs" for the "'lay' habit (probably the *kabā*, a cloak worn by soldiers), in order to be able to speak and preach more freely" (Massignon and Gardet 1986: 99–100). With the rise of the orders, most who chose the Sufi path now followed one teacher, while previously some would move from master to master. Initially, the orders had a "minimal of rules to regulate their life in common" (Trimingham and Voll 1998: 166) and the master's role was limited to "spiritual matters" (1998: 167). However, more elaborate rules and organizational structures evolved over time, with the shaykh at the head, several *khalīfahs* under him in charge of "district or town sections," some with their own sub-leaders beneath them. The master-student relationship also became permanent and central. A city "might have many sectional sub-groups" (1998:174) (titles vary and sometimes denote different functions).

Within the orders, distinctions were drawn between novices, fully professed initiates and associates who received "little Sufi training" but were "trained to take part in the ritual" (1998:176). There may be several grades of affiliation (1998:188) as there are of spiritual attainment with accumulating responsibility, such as teaching others at a designated level. Over time, the masters' exercise of authority, too, extended beyond spiritual matters into other areas of life so that they came to function like "medieval European feudal lords" (Quraeshi 2010: 110). Shaykhs often situated their *khaniqas* at intersections of rival tribal territories, "where they could function as centers for trade and mediation" helping to maintain peaceful relations (Lindholm 2002: 191). Their temporal as well as spiritual authority enabled orders to function as "their own small sacred empires within the larger ... state, complete with a centralized administrative organization ... tax collection through voluntary donations and access to the military force of tribal chiefs." Under regimes in which Islamic principles were marginalized and a corrupt elite exercised power, Sufi shaykhs could exercise authority more locally that substituted for that of the caliph, emir of sultan. Life at the state-level might be "de-sanctified and fragmented" but at a micro-level, Sufism offered a sacred alternative, a more integrated, unified life often crossing class and clan divisions (Lindholm 2002: 193). Werbner's recent investigation of Zindipir's brotherhood suggests that maintaining peace in a turbulent prone region is a central concern of *pīrs*, who "have a stake in peaceful coexistence and tranquility, which enables them to expand their cult networks across a region and to reach different ethnic and religious population." Their "pragmatic accommodation to different regimes," she says, "militates against violence" (Werbner 2012: 26). Although Sufis have taken part in violent uprisings, these appear to have responded to extreme provocation often during colonial or foreign rule. Lay members, too, rather than leaders of Sufi orders, probably engaged in these armed struggles although some were supported by shaykhs. Sufi teachers may not specifically disapprove of "the soldier's profession on principle," says Ernst but do regard this as an occupation that "limits ... the possibilities of spiritual advancement" (Ernst 1992: 101). About half of Zindipir's disciples serve in the Pakistani military. However, Werbner observed "it is as civilians that they join his cult" (Werbner 2003: 133). It can be argued that Sufis are unlikely to find joining a radical fighting force such as al-Qaeda or ISIS very attractive. On the other hand, Schwartz (below) refers to the Army of Men of the Naqshbandi Order in post-2003 Iraq which might or might not be seen as a response to extreme provocation.

Sufis and Worldly Power (Mulk)

There may be no detailed political treatises written by Sufi teachers but there is a large body of lore, "written and oral ... on the spiritual and worldly authority of Sufis, or Muslim holy men" (Eaton 1993: 30). According to the eleventh century Iranian Sufi, 'Ali Hujwiri (died c. 1072), the Sufi saints "govern the universe" causing rain to fall, plants to grow and Muslims to gain victory over non-Muslims (Hujwírí and Nicholson 1976: 213). He enumerated various ranks of a hierarchy headed by the *Qutb* (axis), who together constitute a divine court with power to loose and to bind (Hujwírí and Nicholson 1976: 214). The *Qutb* is the most honored living saint, tasked with convening the council. Mirroring the number of prophets according to Islamic tradition, it is said that at any given time there are 124,000 *'awliyā'*, or living saints. Despite the council's hierarchical nature, "mutual consent" of its members is necessary for any decision or act, which could be seen as an impulse toward democracy. Eaton points out that this vision of authority as "dependent on a hierarchy of saints" clashes with that of the "independent sultan and his dependent 'herd', the people" (1993: 31) and arguably with that of a single caliph who legitimizes the authority of regional rulers. Eaton also points out, though, overlap between these two views of how authority is exercised. For example, "the Arabic term *walī*, meaning 'one who establishes a *wilāyat*' meant in one tradition as a 'governor' or 'ruler' and in the other 'saint' or 'friend of God'." Also, "the crown (*tāj*) used in the coronation ceremonies of kings closely paralleled the Sufi's turban (*dastār*), used in rituals of succession to Sufi leadership" (1993: 31).

Sultans certainly did possess and exercise power but some Muslims could not but question whether they or the Sufi saints "had the better claim" to represent "God on earth," given the luxurious lifestyle of the former compared with the comparatively simple lives of the latter and their teachings on the nobility of poverty. Neither the caliphate nor the sultanates were ever officially secular but ways were found to minimize the role that Islamic values played, including those related to economic justice. Sufi concern for physical as well as spiritual welfare represented a truer Islamic alternative. Over time, Sultans found it prudent to look to "spiritually powerful Sufis" rather than to a perhaps remote, distant and even discredited caliph to legitimize their rule. These Sufis could also withdraw support for rulers whom they considered no longer fit to exercise authority. Thus, they acted as looseners and binders, fulfilling the classical role of the *ahl al-hall wa'l-'aqd*, who selected or elected the caliph (Black 2011: 106). Eaton's seminal study of Islam's rise in Bengal chronicles how a succession of Muslim rulers patronized "Chishti shaykhs" who in turn legitimized their rule (1993: 56). As Lindholm comments, the "hierarchy of saints" could be seen as superseding "the corrupted" and even "crumbled hierarchy of secular power" (2002: 190). Even today, the kings of Morocco use a synthesis of their status as Sufi saints and descendants of Muhammad to re-inforce royal authority (Geertz 1968: 55). More recent Salafist opposition to Sufism, too, as well as being in part theologically motivated, has a political dimension. The fact that Sufi shaykhs do exert political influence and that this is not subject to the control of the formally trained legal scholars who would run a Salafist state means that they can represent a challenge to that state's authority system.

SO IS THERE ANY LINK BETWEEN BEING SUFI AND DEMOCRACY?

The fact is that Sufis have supported authoritarian, anti-democratic as well as democratic rule, which makes it *prima facie* difficult to argue that they are naturally more sympathetic toward democracy than Islamists are. Sufi orders are not democratic. Members pledge total spiritual obedience to the Shaykh. Shaykhs succeed their predecessors by nomination or through birth, not by election. Senior officers are appointed by the Shaykh. On the other hand, in contrast to the powerful legal class whose members usually represent elites, those who exercise authority among Sufis frequently "arose among the people" and were not "the children of scholarly elite, but instead were often of lower and working class background" (Lindholm 2002: 189). The Pakistani Sufi master, Zindapir of Ghamkol Sharif (d. 1999), refused to attend a meeting of Sufi shaykhs convened by dictator Zia-al-Haq saying that if a *faqir* even tried to influence politics, he ceased to be one (Werbner 2003: 91). According to Werbner, Zindapir stated, "God is not elected, and to become a Sufi you do not need to be elected" (Werbner 2003: 119). Of course, few religious institutions are internally democratic, although they may support democracy in the public sphere, to a lesser or greater extent.

In fact, the master-craftsmen of the *futuwwa* did elect their heads (Lewis 1937: 30). There are, of course, Muslims who argue that Islam and democracy are incompatible, which others refute. The latter often view the Islamic traditions of *shūrā* (consultation) as a form of democracy although they may argue that the combination of religion and politics under Muhammad is non-binding, made necessary by historical circumstances while in different contexts Muslims may separate religion and state in favor of a secular democratic system. Thus, they may regard Islam as primarily *din*, a spiritual path rather than a political-social-legal and religious system. Supporters of the "Islam is a religion not a state" view include Ali Abd al-Raziq (1888–1966), Sir Sayyid Ahmad Khan (1817–1898) and Abdurrahman Wahid, who was taught by al-Raziq (see Chapter 6). Among Sufis, as the above survey shows, some have accepted sponsorship by non-democratic, authoritarian regimes and others have aligned themselves with Salafists which challenges any claim that a cause and effect relationship exists between being Sufi and advocating democracy. On the other hand, some Sufis have supported democratic reforms. It could be the case that their support for democracy is quite unconnected with the fact that they happen to be Sufis. Or, might there be some elements within Sufism that lend themselves toward affirming democracy and the freedoms that democracy requires? A number of Sufi-influenced Muslims have suggested such a link, including Fethullah Gülen (born 1941) and Fatemah Mernissi (1940–2015) who offer some theoretical underpinning for a Sufism-democracy link, even if this link is not as Milani states "the *sine quo non* of Sufism".

Fethllah Gülen

Gülen's movement (a service-oriented, non-*ṭarīqah* expression of neo-Sufism) has a following of some ten million (although, like Tablighi, it has no formal membership) argues strongly that Islam and democracy are compatible and that "tolerance," "freedom" and "democracy" are essential pillars for any healthy society. People should be able to "choose different beliefs, religions and pursuits" (Carroll 2007: 26). According to Koc, Gülen draws on "the Qur'ān, the Sunnah, and the intellectual tradition of Sufism in order to establish a clear precedent within Islam for cultural co-existence" 2012: 10–11). He has consistently supported a multi-party political system since Turkey adopted this in 1946. Gülen advocates a "dialogic Sufism" that invites people to relate to others as members of the same species. Sufi openness to dialogue follows from its emphasis on love for *all*. Early rules of companionship (Ṣuḥba) to order the common life of Sufis required respect for individual spiritual freedom (Trimingham, Spencer, and Voll 1998: 167). Among his 11 principles of Sufism, Gülen lists "overflowing with Divine Love and getting along with all other beings in the realization (originating from *Divine Love)* that the universe is a cradle of brotherhood," and "giving preference or precedence to the well-being and happiness of others" (Gülen 2006: xiii). True human transformation "relies on one's love for" God and "consequently for all humanity" (Kim 2008: 230). Arguably, democracy provides the best framework within which these principles can be practiced. Gülen, whose movement is involved in de-radicalization initiatives in Britain and elsewhere, has repeatedly condemned acts of terror (see Al Banna). "A true Muslim," he says, "cannot be a terrorist" (Keles and Sezkin 2015: 18).

Fatema Mernissi

Mernissi combined human rights and pro-democracy advocacy in her native Morocco with her distinguished academic career as a pioneer Muslim feminist scholar. In *Islam and Democracy* (1992) she argued strongly in support of Muslims choosing secular political systems in which they would be able to practice their faith free from compulsion, suggesting that "once disassociated from coercive power," Islam would "witness a renewal of spirituality" rather than, as many Muslims fear, die out (1992: 65). Muslim rulers stifle dissent, insisting on conformity. Imaginative, speculative thought, said

Mernissi, threatened the palace's grip on power because more often than not it stresses individuals' rights to question and to think for themselves, which challenges the notion that anyone can exercise absolute authority. Rather, "any authority that does not come from the people" that is, from "thinking, responsible" individuals free to decide their own acts "does not bind their will" (1992: 34–35). She praises how Sufis "found in religious texts everything they needed to bolster the idea of the thinking, responsible individual" (1992: 34) which, against the rulers' insistence on absolute power, gave people back their rights (1992: 92). Violence represented the only way that opposition to rulers could be expressed, which traditionally resulted in repressive counter measures. The health of Muslim societies depends on re-establishing intellectual, artistic and religious freedom that best flourishes in democracies. Mernissi ended her book by summarizing *Farīd al-Dīn 'Aṭṭār's Manṭeq al-ṭayr* (*The Conference of the Birds*). The world's birds fly off to find the mythic *Simorgh*, a "fabulous being." Finally, 30 birds arrive at his "legendary fortress" only to learn after all their effort and trials along the way that there is no distinction between the *Simorgh* and themselves, for he was the "mirror set before" their "eyes" in which they saw "their own unique reality." All were one. "The community, indeed the whole world, can be a mirror of individualities." Embracing pluralism makes us stronger (1992: 173). Thus, Muslims should accept diversity of opinion within Islam and engage in "unlimited dialogue" with others "to create that global mirror in which all cultures can shine in their uniqueness" (1992: 174).

Affirming Sufism's Pro-Democratic Impulse

Sufism's traditional view that "truth" is singular (*wujud al-haqq*) and that truth may find diverse expression has tended to affirm religious pluralism as God-given. Ibn al-'Arabī (d. 1240) pioneered the view that since faith is God's gift and not a human work, it is also independent of the particular religious identity people profess (see Chapter 10). All are children of One God. God lives in every heart, thus all religions may be seen as containing truth and as deserving of respect (Hameed 1993: xxxiv). Ibn al-'Arabī regarded Islam as "the religion of God," in contrast to other religions which are humanly conceived but saw all religion as "for God" and also as "acknowledged" by God (Ibn al-Arabī and Austin 1992: 113–14). In the Indian subcontinent, there is a long history of Sufi teachers attracting Hindu disciples. Non-Muslims continue to visit many famous Sufi shrines, which this writer has observed (see Singh in this volume). In this volume, Sarwar discusses the contribution of Sayyid Delaor Husayn Maizbhandari (1892–1982) who, in the context of East Pakistan (and later Bangladesh) promoted human unity, arguing that "the state should observe tolerance toward diversity and maintain neutrality toward various traditions and practices or *acardharma*." Pemberton (2012) explores how, following a terrorist attack at the Chīshtī shrine in Ajmer, Rajastan in 2007 by right-wing Hindus, Sufis responded by launching a program to combat communitarianism, promote inter-faith harmony and peaceful relations. She notes that "Chīshtī orders in India have long welcomed foreign visitors, and many do not require those seeking to become disciples to convert to Islam, which has also attracted many disciples from the West" (2012: 280). *In the West*, Hazrat Inayat Khan (d. 1927), also from the Chīshtī *tradition*, whose spiritual legacy is preserved by the Sufi Order Ināyati, "did not require his followers to formally accept Islam" (Hermansen 2012: 249). The order continues to offer spiritual teaching to people of any faith. Assuming that affirming religious freedom and allowing different political parties to function is an essential feature of a democratic system, even if it cannot be convincingly argued that an automatic relation exists between Sufism and support for democracy, it is logical that Sufis might find a state that limits religious freedom and freedom of thought unacceptable.

As Muedini points out, Sufis can be "quite restrictive of equal rights when it comes to issues such as gender equality" (2015: 14). However, it is also the case that there are no few women of note in Sufi history while today "a growing number of women play major roles in Sufism, giving spiritual direction to men and women, whether the place is Tunis, Beirut, Istanbul, or Delhi" (Geoffroy 2010: 29). For Ibn 'Arabī, for example, "God, as the point of conjunction between opposite, contains the principles of both male and female, principles which take part equally in that cosmic union which is realized in any coupling, whether of plants, animals, humans, or other" (Geoffroy 2010: 28). He did, though, interpret Qur'ān 2: 228 to mean that women are ontologically subordinate to men (al-'Arabī & Austin 1992: 276) but also pointed to Muhammad's saying that he loved women, perfume and prayer, which he says gives "precedence to the feminine over the masculine intending to convey thereby a special concern with ... women" 1992: 277). Gender equality, with freedom of thought and religion, are foundational democratic rights. That four Muslim majority states where Sufism remains popular, namely Bangladesh, Indonesia, Pakistan and Turkey have had women leaders may not be accidental.

CONCLUSION: ANALYZING THE DEMOCRATIC DEFICIT IN MUSLIM-MAJORITY STATES

Finally, the possibility that the presence of politically engaged Sufis actually does promote the development of democratic systems could find support in an analysis of where Muslim-majority states rank on the EIU *Democracy Index* for 2015 (see Table 3.[1] This uses 60 indicators covering the electoral process and pluralism, the functioning of government, political participation, political culture and civil liberties to measure the status of democracy

44 Sufism, Pluralism and Democracy

Table 3: Status of Democracy in Muslim Majority States

Category	Country (all are members of the OIC)	Rank	Region	Colonial Legacy including League of Nations' Mandates and Zones of Hegemonic Influence
Flawed Democracies				
Category begins at 21.	Indonesia	49 (48 in 2016)	South East Asia	Dutch
	Tunisia	57	MENA	French
	Malaysia	68	South Asia	British
	Senegal	75	West Africa	French
	8.51% of Muslim Majority states (47)			
Hybrid				
Category begins at 80	Albania	81 (unchanged 2016)	Europe	Former Ottoman province, socialist 1944–1991
	Bangladesh	86 (84, 2016)	South Asia	British
	Mali	= 88 with Ukraine	West Africa	French
	Kyrgyzstan	= 93 with Kenya	Central Asia	Russian/Soviet
	Turkey	97 (unchanged 2016)	Euro-Asia	Not officially colonized but finances subject to European oversight 1878–1914.
	Lebanon	102	MENA	French mandate 1920–1946/
	Burkina Fas0	106	West Africa	French
	Morocco	107	MENA	French/Spanish
	Nigeria	108	West Africa	British
	Palestine	110	MENA	British mandate 1920–1948; under Israeli occupation.
	Sierra Leone	111	West Africa	British
	Pakistan	112	South Asia	British
	Iraq	115 (114, 2016)	MENA	British mandate 1920–1932
	27.66% of Muslim Majority states			
Authoritarian				

1 *Sufis, Saints and Politics in Islam*   45

Category begins at 117.	Mauritania	117	North Africa	French
	Algeria	118	MENA	French
	Jordan	120	MENA	British mandate 1922–1946
	Kuwait	=121	MENA	British protectorate 1899–1961
	Niger	=121	West Africa	French
	Egypt	= 134	MENA	British (effectively from 1882 to 1922)
	Qatar	= 134	MENA	British protectorate 1916–1971
	Guinea	= 136 (with China)	West Africa	French
	Kazakhstan	140	Central Asia	Russian/Soviet
	Oman	142	MENA	British protectorate 1820–1970
	Gambia	143	West Africa	British
	Djibouti	145	North East Africa	French
	Bahrain	146	MENA	British protectorate 1880–1971
	Afghanistan	147	Central Asia	
	United Arab Emirates	148	MENA	1820–1971 protection treaty with Britain.
	Azerbaijan	149	Central Asia	Russia/Soviets
	Sudan	= 151	North East Africa	Anglo-Egyptian 1899–1956
	Libya	153	MENA	Italian
	Yemen	154	MENA	Partly British
	Iran	156	MENA	British/Russian sphere 1907 to 1919; British to WWII
	Uzbekistan	=158	Central Asia	Russian/Soviet
	Tajikistan	=158	Central Asia	Russian/Soviet
	Saudi Arabia	=160	MENA	British sphere of influence end WWI to 1932.
	Turkmenistan	162	Central Asia	Russian/Soviet
	Chad	165	Central Africa	French
	Syria	166	MENA	French mandate 1923–1946
	Least democratic: North Korea	167	East Asia	Japanese 1905–1945
	55.3 % of Muslim states (four are unranked)/50.9% of all states.			
Based on EIU *Democracy Index 2015: Democracy in An Age of Anxiety*, Table 2: 24–28.				

(Economist Intelligence Unit 2016: 48–58). Section 53 under "civil liberties" measures: "The degree of religious tolerance and freedom of religious expression," asking:

> Are all religions permitted to operate freely, or are some restricted? Is the right to worship permitted both publicly and privately? Do some religious groups feel intimidated by others, even if the law requires equality and protection? (2016: 57).

Although currently no Muslim-majority state is categorized as fully democratic, of the four within the "flawed" category (numbered 21 to 79), Indonesia (ranked 49), Tunisia (ranked 57; 69 on the 2016 index), Senegal (ranked 75) are all places where Sufis play significant roles either politically or as shapers of cultural values. Sufis' traditional openness toward pluralism would contribute to scoring higher in the first area that the Index measures, at the very least. Indonesia was ranked 53rd in 2012, so has risen by four places. Bangladesh was 84, so dropped two places (it is again at 84 in 2016). Tunisia was "hybrid" in 2012, equal with Albania at 99. According to some political scientists, Tunisia would need to undergo two or more peaceful transitions of government, though, to qualify as more fully democratic. Albania, where Sufis originally spread Islam and remain significant shapers of culture (see Chapter 3), is now at the top of the hybrid category for Muslim-majority states (at 81). Flawed and hybrid are counted as democratic; authoritarian as dictatorial. Flawed are deficient in one or more area, such as political participation, election irregularities, underdeveloped political culture or restrictions on the media (2016: 45). On this scale, Norway ranks as number one (the USA was number 20 but slipped to joint 21 with Italy in the "flawed democracy" category in the 2016 Report which lists only 19 states as full democracies). It may or may not be significant that 10 of the fully democratic states are constitutional monarchies, with seven in the top ten. Moving down into the "hybrid" category (where restrictions on freedom, lack of transparency and other factors compromises democracy, from 80 to 116 on the scale) four of the "hybrid" Muslim majority states out of thirteen, Bangladesh (86), Turkey (97), Lebanon (102, second highest ranked Arab state) and Pakistan (112), all have substantial Sufi populations and some degree of documented Sufi engagement in the political arena (for the rankings, see *Democracy Index 2015,* EIU 2016: 4–8, Table 2). Given the problems that Lebanon has had to deal with, not all of its own making with influxes of refugees, foreign intervention and Iran's support for Hezbollah, which aims to create an Iran-type Islamic state in Lebanon and to destroy Israel, Lebanon should be given credit for achieving the score it has. At 110, Palestine scores above Pakistan, despite lacking full sovereignty, continued Israeli occupation and the split in control between Gaza and the West Bank. Authoritarian states may hold elections but "these have little substance" (EIU 2016: 46) and they restrict many freedoms.

Statistics are provided for 167 states. Some, including four members of the Organization of Islamic Cooperation (Brunei, Comoros, Maldives and Somalia), lack the necessary data to be ranked. Ten out of the 57 OIC members have Muslim populations below 50%. Their statistics are not used in this analysis. Nigeria, which according to Pew (2012), has a Muslim population of 48.8% is included; other sources cite 50% (such *The World FactBook*). This is also the fifth largest Muslim population, above Egypt at sixth. The EIU report refers to progress represented by Nigeria's first democratic transfer of power (2015: 3). Of the 43 Muslim-majority states for which the data is available, 16 are Arab (17 if Morocco, technically Berber but culturally Arab, is counted) and 27 non-Arab. Three Arab states are classed as in some measure democratic (Iraq, Lebanon and Palestine; four if Morocco, is included). The other 13 are non-Arab. The total number of Muslim-majority states that count as democratic is 17 (39.53% of the 43 that are ranked, or 36% out of the total Muslim-majority states of 47; it is unlikely that any of those for which data is unavailable would qualify). The last decade has witnessed a decline in the global health of democracy. Several Muslim-majority states have moved down the ranks, including four that have "descended further into chaos and war (2016: 35) namely Iraq (which, at 115, still ranks as hybrid and therefore democratic), Libya (153), Syria at 166, one above North Korea, is the least democratic and Yemen at 154. With Somalia all four can be considered as failed states. Only Syria, though, ranks lower than Saudi Arabia (160); where Sufism is more or less officially proscribed, though it would be conjecture to draw any direct link between this and the state's authoritarianism. Out of 51 states categorized as authoritarian, 26 (50.98%) are Muslim majorities. Therefore, there is a democratic deficit in Muslim-majority space. However, 25 other non-democratic states *are not Muslim*. Since only 8.9% of the world's population live in full democracies, the state of democracy in Muslim space needs to be discussed in relation with those non-Muslim states where democracy is also weak or compromised. Analysis should identify what factors hinder democracy in non-Muslim space that might also hinder democracy developing in Muslim-majority space. Questions include: who has access to education; how healthy is civil society; who, historically, exercised power; are the same group in power today; who have been and still are excluded from power and whether there are specifically Islamic factors that hinder democracy's development or is this attributable to non-Islamic factors. How states were created by departing colonial power or by the victors of World War I also requires attention. Did their borders take note of ethnic, religious and linguistic differences or commonalities? How does the colonial legacy of centralized, non-democratic authority influence post-colonial developments? Given the downgrading of several European states as well as a lower score for North America, which has seen a "significant decline in democracy" (2016: 9) analysts should not jump to conclude that the problem is always related to Islam. The EIU describes 2015 as a year of anxiety, as "perceived risks and threats – economic, political, social and security – is undermining democracy" 2016: 1) across several regions. Response to the Syrian refugee crises and the rhetoric of xenophobic, anti-immigrant politicians, has nothing to do with Islam except that some concerned encourage Islamophobia and want to pit the West against the Muslim-majority world. While the Middle East and North Africa had the biggest decline regionally in 2015, "more countries (10) registered an improvement in their scores than recorded a decline (9)" (2016: 23). In MENA, 13 countries are classed as "authoritarian" (including Egypt, previously a "hybrid" democracy) representing 50% of the total for Muslim-majority states (six are in Central Asia, 7 in Africa). In the 2012 index, Egypt, Libya, Morocco, Mauritania and Niger had moved up from authoritarian to "hybrid;" Egypt (where Sufis are politically active) and Libya are again "authoritarian" (134, 153 respectively); Morocco (with an historic relationship between the monarch and Sufism) remains hybrid (107). Chapter 6 in this book is a case study of two South Asian states, Indonesia and Bangladesh (respectively measured first and seventh among Muslim majority states) where Sufism has helped create political cultures that affirms the rights of non-Muslims alongside Muslims within secular frameworks (de facto or constitutionally defined).

About the Author

Clinton Sarker Bennett holds degrees from Manchester, Birmingham and Oxford Universities. His Birmingham PhD thesis was published as *Victorian Images of Islam* (Grey Seal, 1992; Gorgias, 2009). A Fellow of the Royal Asiatic Society (FRAS) and of the Royal Anthropological Institute (FRAI), Bennett has combined an academic career with church-related jobs and practical involvement in improving interfaith relations. He is an ordained Baptist minister. In the UK, he helped mosques acquire charitable status and Muslim neighborhood associations funding for community programs. A former missionary in Bangladesh (1979–82), he later served on the staff of the British Council of Churches (1987–92) and took part in several World Council of Churches' interfaith consultations. He currently sits on the Inter-religious Convening Table of the National Council of Churches USA. Academic posts include Subject Leader for Religious Studies at Westminster College, Oxford (1992–98) where he was also an Assistant Chaplain and Associate Professor of Religion at Baylor, TX (1998–2001). Between 1985 and 1992, Bennett was Honorary Associate Minister of a multi-racial, inner-city congregation in Birmingham, UK. He has authored a dozen monographs as well as chapters in edited volumes, book reviews, encyclopedia entries and journal articles. He is Section Editor for North Europe and Team Leader for Western Europe with the Brill series, *Christian-Muslim Relations: a Bibliographical History* (covering 1500 to 1914, directed by David Thomas). His recent work focuses on contemporary Muslim spiritual and political movements, and issues related to citizenship, identity and belonging in multi-cultural contexts. A naturalized US citizen, Bennett teaches Religious Studies at State University of New York at New Paltz. He is also a founder member of the Center for Middle Eastern Dialogue (2008).

Notes

1. The EIU's Democracy Indexes are published early in the year following the year under review.

SECTION II

European/Euro Asian Contexts (Kosovo/Albania and Turkey)

2

SUFISM AS A WORKING SPIRIT IN GLOBALIZATION AND PLURALISM: THE CASE OF THE HIZMET MOVEMENT, A TURKEY-ORIENTED GLOBAL ISLAMIC NETWORK

Heon C. Kim

Contrary to the modernist and secularist prediction of the decline of Sufism in the modern world, Sufism continues its vitality in many parts of the Muslim world today. It has shown remarkable strategies for survival in the face of changing and challenging contexts of modernization, secularization and globalization. Innovational forms and movements along with traditional Sufi orders have emerged to show diverse manifestations of Sufism in its dynamic interaction with secular and pluralist contexts.

Responding to this trend, this chapter examines the Hizmet movement, a Turkey-oriented global Islamic movement, as a case study to look at how Sufism is actually lived in and interacts with today's secular and pluralistic contexts.

The Hizmet movement is known as one of the most visible Islamic civic movements in the world today. A worldwide survey on the most influential Muslims remarks the movement is "one of the best connected and therefore one of the most powerful networks competing to influence Muslims around the globe, making it likely to have an enduring impact on the modernization of Islam and its engagement with Western ideas."[1] *Time* magazine also counts Fethullah Gülen (b. 1941), the founder and spiritual guide of the movement, as one of "the world's most intriguing religious leaders."[2] Indeed, the movement showed a rapid and successful expansion over the globe in just last two decades to have millions of the members with thousands of educational institutes and dialogue platforms over the world.[3]

Like many studies, this chapter notes the success of the movement. Yet, unlike them, this chapter looks at the movement from the angle of Sufism to figure out intrinsic factors of its success, which are little examined. For this, it traces back the historical evolvement of the movement, and draws out Sufi elements of the movement in each period. In so doing, this chapter makes salient the role of Sufism in the development of the movement in a way illustrating how Sufism provides a working spirit to the movement to succeed in secular, global and pluralistic contexts.

CONTEXTUAL BACKGROUND

A much debated issue in relevant studies is whether or not the Hizmet movement is a *tarikat* (Sufi order in Turkish). This question is still pivotal to clarify the nature, identity and purpose of the movement. Outsiders, especially opponents of the movement, do not hesitate to consider the movement as a *tarikat*. Yet, for insiders, their movement has never been a *tarikat*, and thus cannot be considered as such. For a proper placement of this issue, it is necessary to look at the movement in a broader context of Sufism in modernity and a specific context of the Kemalist secular politics in modern Turkey.

The decline of Sufism in the face of modernity was once predominant in academic discourse; for a brief account of the discourse, see Bruinessen and Howell (2007: 5–9). Many scholars predicted the incompatibility of Sufism and modernity, the inevitable decline of Sufism and its eventual death. As predicted, most parts of Muslim societies observed the decline of Sufism in the process of modernization and secularization. Secular modernist thought, which basically saw religion as the opposite side of the rationalism in modernity, swept over the world to direct people to this-worldly matters eschewing from irrational mystical religious experience. In this broad context, other-worldly and mystical dimensions of Sufism in general and fatalism, superstition and ecstatic intoxication of Sufi orders in particular, were constantly fading out (Trimingham 1998: 249–50). In addition, a traditional Islamist claim, which pictured Sufism as a non-Islamic innovation (*bid'a*), revived to blow out popular Sufism. This anti-Sufi trend widely spread by modern Islamists like Sayyid Jamāl al-Dīn al-Afghānī (d. 1897) and Muhammad Abduh (d. 1905), who stressed the incompatibility of *taqlīd* (blind obedience of disciples to their Sufi masters) and *ijtihad* (Islamic scientific reasoning) (Sirriyeh 1999: 65–167). Sufism was eventually blamed as a cause of the decline of the Muslim world in the face of modernity and the western advancement. In a different sense, the secularist states in the Muslim world claimed Sufism was as a major reason for state stagnation and implemented anti-Sufism policies into domestic politics. Over the twentieth century, political anti-Sufism was well grounded to shake the social roots of Sufism in many Muslim countries.

However, against the backdrop of modernist, secularist and Islamist anti-Sufi politics and as opposed to the modernist prediction of the decline of Sufism, the end of the twentieth century observed that Sufism and Sufi orders were not only still alive but also continued to provide a basis of popular religion in many Muslim societies. For instance, Valerie Hoffman observed the continuing vitality of the Egyptian Sufi orders, which showed characteristics of sobriety and non-violence while eschewing from politics (See Hoffman 1995). Itzchak Weismann's study demonstrated how the Naqshbandi tradition in India and Syria in the face of modernity reformulated itself toward renunciation of specific Sufi terminology, even the term Sufism (Weismann 2007: 115–28). Indonesia also showed the resurgence of Sufism. In contrast to Clifford Geertz's prediction of the decline of Indonesian Sufism, Julia Day Howell's work depicted the emergence of new institutional forms of Sufism. She particularly observed a turning towards Sufism without engaging in the practices of Sufi orders, and illustrated how this turning created a mood of "disengagement of tasawuf from tarekat" in the Indonesian Islamic revival (see Howell 2000, 2001). Bennett also describes these developments in Chapter 6 of this volume.

Sufism in modern Turkey was not immune to this broad context of the decline yet vitality of Sufism. In the late nineteenth and the early twentieth centuries when modernization quickened the last breath of the Ottoman Empire, Sufism and its related movements, be traditional *tarikats* or non-orthodox movements, were in decline (See Lewis 1968: 408–409). This decline continued to hit a new low with the establishment of the Kemalist Republic in 1923. Having witnessed the fall of the Ottoman Empire, the new Republic of laicism blamed Sufism and its related organizations as a reason of Turkish backwardness and as a cause of the state's divisions. As a result, the Republic legislated a ban on *tarikats* and their activities by *Tevhid-i Tedrisat Kanunu* (Law of the Unity of Education) issued in 1924. This ban and related policies initiated the political anti-Sufism at a state level. Since then, as Spencer Trimingham noted, "the [Sufi] orders became a direct object of attack by the secularizing movement, being regarded as something not merely decadent, but politically reactionary and dangerous" (Trimingham 1998: 253). The political anti-Sufism was lethal for Sufism and *tarikats*, producing an image problem in society against *tarikats*, and labeling them with negative connotations. This gave rise to, as Hakan Yavuz underlined, "a tendency in the usage of secularist Turks promiscuously to designate virtually any organized Islamic groups as a tariqa" (Hakan 2003: 181). It was this context that Gülen's thought of Sufism was grounded in to form the Hizmet movement.

The Birth of the Hizmet Movement

When Gülen was 25 years old in 1966, he began to serve as an official imam of the Kestanepazari Qur'ān School at Izmir, south western part of Turkey. During this service that continued until 1971, he taught young people Sunni and Sufi interpretations of Islamic doctrine (see Erdoğan 1995: 98–99). For an effective teaching, Gülen elaborated summer camps, which were innovatively operated by his own educational system. He combined *madrasa*

(Islamic school), *tekke* (Sufi lodge) and *mektep* (military academy) to raise integrated youths who would be well-disciplined and religiously motivated with scientific knowledge.[4] The summer camps with this new educational system were highly successful, as Gülen later recalled that "taken as such, discipline of military, morality of *tekke* and knowledge of *madrasa* became an integrated whole in the camps, which formulated our first step into the world that we imagined" (Erdoğan 1995: 122). From the youths in the first summer camps, the first and core devotees to Gülen's thought emerged.

The success of the summer camps soon led to the establishment of dormitories and rented houses as the daily residences of high school and college students. These residences also used the same educational system of the camps. Following the Qur'ānic verse of *Nūr* (The Light), Gülen called these residences *Işık Evler* or Light Houses, and considered the places of the Prophet Muhammad and great Sufis like Abu Hamid al-Ghazali (d. 1111) and Ahmad al-Faruqi as-Sirhindi (d. 1624) as an example of *Işık Evler*. In Gülen's preparation, *Işık Evler* were ideal places in which the residents could best realize *ihya* (revival) of their Islamic orientation and pursue spiritually meaningful life while living in and interacting upon the secular world (Gülen 1997a: 13). In *Işık Evler*, students followed instructions of their *ağabey* or seniors, fulfilled daily Islamic obligations, and contemplated by reciting litanies and Gülen's teachings, while doing their school work to succeed in a secular society.

With this initiation, *Işık Evler* became the nucleus of Gülen's educational network and foundation of the Hizmet movement.

Early Challenges and Continuing Success

The educational activities of the summer camps and *Işık Evler* show the deep involvement of Sufism in forming the movement. For this reason, however, the early community of the movement faced challenges.

Having suspected Gülen's educational activities as a part of religious activities of *Nurcular*, the followers of Bediüzzaman Said Nursi (d. 1960), the military coup in 1971 arrested Gülen on charges of being involved in and associated with the *Nurcu* movements against the secular law, and violating the Article 163 that defined religious propaganda as a crime.[5] Gülen was imprisoned for seven months, and then released but his public lectures were prohibited. Instead of reacting against this oppression, Gülen guided his followers to be more careful and accepting of given contexts and challenges, while eschewing from politics. At the start of its existence this guidance secured the movement and gave it distance from political activism that some of the *Nurcu* movements had shown (see Yavuz 2003: 183). Gülen was leading his movement neither to be a solely other-worldly focused *tarikat* nor to be a political movement. Instead he guided the movement to be a civic movement that bridges religiosity and secularity in line with his educational system. For this, however, he felt it necessary to make use of political means and to establish positive relationships with politicians. Consequently, Gülen would later make links with leading politicians such as Necmeddin Erbakan and Suleyman Demirel, former Prime Ministers of Turkey.

In 1974 when the post-coup civilian government passed an amnesty law, the ban of Gülen's public lectures was finally lifted. He began to speak in diverse places, not only in mosques, but also in coffee houses and lecture halls. Moreover, Gülen also visited different parts of Turkey to deliver a series of lectures, which put an emphasis on the compatibility between Islam and science. These public lectures gathered attention from the public, who, as Muslim Turks, inherited Islam as a lifestyle with its millennium history but still lived in a secular society. Accordingly, his movement also grew enough to establish educational institutions, including the Foundation for Turkish Teachers and the Foundation of Middle and Higher Education. The movement also published a periodical magazine titled *Sızıntı* in 1979. Focusing on the compatibility between science and Islam, the magazine aimed to provide a Muslim identity to a new generation in a secular society and to aid them to cope with the modernization and secularization processes (Yavuz 2003: 183). Since then, *Sızıntı* served as a main platform to spread Gülen's thought and the movement's activities to a wider audience.

Significantly to note, in this period, Gülen solidified his dream of *Altın Nesil* or Golden Generation.[6] *Altın Nesil*, in Gülen's definition, is a generation with minds enlightened by positive science, with hearts purified by faith, who would be an example of virtue and who would burn with the desire to serve their nation and humanity, and who would live, not for themselves, but for others (Gülen 1998b).

To Gülen, this generation is not new, but modeled by the Prophet and the Four Caliphs.[7] Gülen inspired his movement to follow this model to train youths who could harmonize "hearts purified by faith" and secular science to live for others. The "hearts purified by faith" is prerequisite for the movement to train youths to be *Altın Nesil*. Such hearts can be acquired via specific qualities including, as Gülen characterized, *muhabbet*, a generous attitude toward friends and enemies, *hamle*, an action to conquer one's egoistic self to help others, and *murakabe*, a consistent self-control and self-censorship (Gülen 1977). Each of these qualities refers to a particular practice and spiritual stage of Sufi path, and thus clearly indicates the influence of Sufism in Gülen's idea of *Altın Nesil*. In another passage, Gülen identified *Altın Nesil* as the people who begin with faith and love (*ashq*), use faith and love for self-evaluation (*muhasaba*), and then make available themselves for other people with action (*hamle*) of self-reflection (*muraqaba*) and close relationship (*muhabba*) (Gülen 1997b: 218). Having embodied these Sufi qualities, one would become among *Altın Nesil* and among whom "would live, not for themselves, but for others." As Marcia Hermansen noted, this spirit infused into the youths in dormitories and camps "to foster a Golden Generation that would restore, heal, and carry forward the best potentials of humanity in harmony with a modern and pluralistic world" (Hermansen 2015: 26).

For Gülen, to raise up *Altın Nesil* of these Sufi qualities is an ultimate goal of the Hizmet movement, and to do so, it is necessary for the movement's members to have these Sufi qualities first. In other words, senior members of the movement need to be role models. This aspect is well reserved in the preface of *Kalbin Zümrüt Tepeleri*, a series of Gülen's writings on Sufism:

> Gülen dreamed of a generation that would combine intellectual 'enlightenment' with pure spirituality, wisdom, and continuous activism. Being notably knowledgeable in religious and social sciences and familiar with the principles of 'material' sciences, he instructed his students in most of these areas. The first students who attended his courses in Izmir became the vanguard of a revived generation willing to serve his ideals (Gülen 2004c: Preface).

The task of producing *Altın Nesil* whose hearts were purified by Sufi spiritual qualities was imperative to the movement moreso than any other work including politically engaged activities. Following Gülen's teaching of Sufi spirituality to live for others, the movement focused on civic educational activities instead of engaging in politics. This teaching also led Gülen to invite people to practice tolerance and forgiveness in political turmoil between left and right-wings throughout the 1970s (Balci 2012: 82).

Gülen's vision of moderate Islam and the movement's educational activities spread quickly throughout the 1980s, and the movement emerged to be a major civic and Islamic movement in Turkey. A socio-political shift toward "a more stable and religion-friendly political environment in the early 1980s" effectively helped for diffusion of Gülen's thought that stressed tolerance (*hoşgörü*) for harmonious co-existence with other cultures (Yavuz 2003: 183–88). In particular, the slogan of the Turkish-Islamic Synthesis of then Turgut Özal's government, the first post-military civilian government, worked well with Gülen's moderate Islam and Turkish Muslimness (*Türk Müslümanlığı*) (Balci 2012: 82–83). Simultaneously, this secular yet religious-friendly domestic politics aided the movement to perform its educational activities in earnest. Owing to the continuing success of its educational activities of camps and *Isik Eviler* that combined secular knowledge and Sufi spirituality, the movement opened its first official schools in 1982. Especially, when the Özal's government "passed a series of legislations in 1985 and 1988 that eased the opening of private schools" (Balci 2012: 84) those who were inspired by Gülen's educational philosophy "formed their own independent boards to start dormitories and schools in their own cities."⁸ These private schools opened them up to market competition, and met successfully with the public need for a better educational system (Yavuz 2003: 183). In competing with the public and other private schools, the movement gained its reputation in public in the late 1980s, and enabled the proliferation of schools, dormitories and college preparatory schools in almost every Turkish city and town by the early 1990s (Balci 2012: 84). In 1987, the movement also began to publish its daily newspaper *Zaman*, which since then has served as a primary means of publicizing and popularizing Gülen's thought and vision of Islam in a secular society.

This remarkable success of the Hizmet movement led some scholars to attribute the success to extrinsic factors. For instance, Hakan Yavuz put forward the "religion-friendly" political climate of the 1980s as a main reason of the success (Yavuz 2003: 183). Yet, this could be true only partially and extrinsically. Otherwise, many of the religious movements including the *Nurcu* movements might have succeeded just as the Hizmet movement did. Moreover, as Tamer Balci noted, Gülen and his activities were still under state monitoring so he could not preach until 1986 (Balci 2012: 83). In my analysis, surely, both Gülen and the movement benefited from the political climate, yet it is far fetched to consider the political environment as the main reason for the movement's success. Instead, as this chapter has examined so far and will look at further, it was intrinsic factors such as Gülen's vision of moderate Islam that appealed to people, and his teaching of Sufism that provided spirituality to the members to work hard to succeed in a secular society. It seems clearly that these intrinsic factors played a major role for the movement's success. Indeed, because of the intrinsic religious factors, Gülen and the movement eventually faced a serious challenge from secularists and military elites, which I now turn to.

Fethullahçılar Tarikat

The fast growing reputation of Gülen invoked a reactionary suspicion raised by secularist media and military elites throughout the 1990s, which continues today. In common with his nation-wide fame, the reaction created a nation-wide sensation via media.

Having noted its religious orientation, a number of secularist media began to call the Hizmet movement with *tarikat* nuanced and associated names. Foremost was *fethullahçılar*, "partisans of Fethullah," which underlined the movement as a divisionary/sectarian organization and a potential danger to the secular identity of the Republic.⁹ Notably, the negative naming of *fethullahçılar* was often associated with a label of *tarikat*. Gülen was portrayed as "the shaykh of *fethullahçılar tarikat*" and "a leader of Naqshbandi order," while the movement's educational institutions were called "tarikat schools." This *tarikat*-associated name of *fethullahçılar* served effectively and widely to remind people of "ruinous tarikat" that was once banned with the establishment of the Republic, and thus to post an image to the movement as a harmful institution in society. Once imbued in this way, the *tarikat*-associated name and image of the movement continued in the 1990s and the 2000s as it was continually used by secularist media.[10]

Confronted by the image problem that *fethullahçılar tarikat* brought out against the movement, Gülen repeatedly rejected any involvement in *tarikat*. He said:

> I have stated innumerable times that I'm not a member of a religious order [*tarikat*]. As a religion, Islam naturally emphasizes the spiritual realm. It takes the training of the ego as a basic principle. Asceticism, piety, kindness and sincerity are essential to it. In the history of Islam the discipline that dwelt most on these matters was Sufism. Opposing this would be opposing the essence of Islam. The religious orders are institutions that appeared in the name of representing Sufism six centuries after our Prophet, upon him be peace and blessings. They have their own rules and structures. Just as I never joined a Sufi order, I have never had any relationship with one.[11]

It is clear that Gülen denied any *tarikat* association given his conviction that Sufism was independent of *tarikat*. While Sufism is the essence of Islam, *tarikat* is just one of its diverse historical, social and cultural manifestations. Gülen further pointed out the bidirectional problems of master-disciple relationships typically shown in *tarikats*. The role of the master as a spiritual mediator between God and their disciples is untenable, as it is in discord with *tawhid* (Oneness of God). This may also lead a disciple to follow a master blindly, which would hinder his/her spiritual journey as shown in the claim of being the Mahdi or the Messiah (Gülen 2004c: 146–47). This kind of master-disciple relation may go too far "to prefer sainthood to Prophethood and, favoring the principles and manners established by the founder of their orders over those of the Prophetic way" (Gülen 2004c: 242–43). In this regard, to Gülen, *tarikats* remain vulnerable to deviating from Islam.

Having regarded *tarikats* in this way, Gülen accepted neither himself nor his movement being associated with a *tarikat*. In fact, many of the studies on the Hizmet movement have found no evidence in the movement to support the alleged association of the movement to a *tarikat*. What they found instead is the lack of essential qualities of a *tarikat*, like initiation rites for disciples, and a shaykh or master (see Sarıtoprak 2003: 168–9). Rather than these qualities of a *tarikat*, the movement had secular schools, and the members did not isolate themselves from the society but tried to succeed in a secular society (Sarıtoprak 2003: 168–9).

Then, what is the movement, if not a *tarikat*? To find a proper answer, it is necessary to understand Gülen's appreciation of Sufism independently from *tarikats*, which inspired the movement to be the "Hizmet" movement.

HIZMET AND SUFISM

Despite the various names that outsiders have used – whether negatively *fethullahçılar* or simply the Gülen movement – insiders of the movement within their circle used to name their individual and collective activities as hizmet.

As a generic term in Turkish daily language, hizmet means "service." To the members of the Hizmet movement, it denotes technically "service for humanity," which Gülen has put a great emphasis on as the identity and goal of the movement.[12] Gülen empathetically taught that:

> [T]he worldly life should be used in order to earn the afterlife and to please the One who has bestowed it. The way to do so is to seek to please Allah and, as an inseparable dimension of it, to serve immediate family members, society, country, and all of humanity accordingly. This service [hizmet] is our right, and sharing it with others is our duty (Unal & Williams 2000: 267).

To perform this service, Gülen further stated that "for this movement, religious dimension is important. This religiosity directs not inwardly, [but] more than that, outwardly. [Thus] the concept of *hizmet* is significant."[13] This statement defines hizmet as an outward reflection of inner personal religiosity to conduct "service for humanity." Actually, this concept of hizmet corresponds well with Gülen's ideal of a golden generation, as noted earlier, "who would burn with the desire to serve their nation and humanity, and who would live, not for themselves, but for others." In the same way that Sufism played a founding role in Gülen's concept of *Altın Nesil*, it served to be a working spirit for hizmet. In particular, Sufism for hizmet spins by two wheels, personal spiritual training and active engagement in society, both of which provide a spirituality to do hizmet, service for humanity. This aspect will be clear in the following two points.

First, Gülen presented Sufism as the spiritual essence of Islam to deepen one's inner religiosity. He emphasized:

> Sufism is a name, which was later given to the life and the science of religious and spiritual essence of Islam. It is not necessary to use this name. What is important is to live with the actions of the heart like asceticism (*zuhd*), piety (*taqwa*), perfect goodness (*ihsan*) and knowledge of God (*marifah*), as it is an inseparable part of Islam... no Muslim can be indifferent and impassive to Sufism, Islamic spiritual aspect, which constitutes the essence of religion, fosters its belief and leads one to being a perfect human being (Pope 1998).

Unlike typical Islamist critique against Sufism as a non-Islamic innovation (*bid'a*) and superstition (*khurafa*), Gülen appreciated Sufism as Islamic spirituality, which is essentially an ahistorical and an invisible animating force of Islamic life. As the spiritual essence of Islam, Sufism originates in the Qur'ān and the Sunna to shed light on a spiritual path for "reaching true belief in God's Divine Oneness [*tawhid*] and living in accordance with its demands (Gülen 1989: xv). In his reading, this spiritual path was set forth by the life of Prophet Muhammad, "the truest ascetic in all respects," "the perfect guide of humanity" and "a Sufi master of spiritual profundity," who exemplified an inner purification via asceticism (*zuhd*), piety (*taqwa*), and knowledge of God (*marifah*), and showed perfect goodness (*ihsan*). Gülen further asserted that as represented by the Prophet's life, "the spirit of the Shari'a, which is made up of austerity, self-control and criticism, and the continuous struggle to resist the temptations of Satan and the carnal, evil-commanding self," (Gülen 1989: xviii) and "this spiritual life was practiced at the most sublime level during the Age of Happiness, the Time of the Prophet and the Four Caliphs" (Gülen 2004b: 166). Since then, this has become a model of Islamic spiritual life.

To Gülen, this Islamic spirituality was later named as Sufism. In his conviction, Sufism was by no means synonymous with *tarikats* which, as stated earlier, are only one of many outward manifestations of Sufism. Nor did Gülen approve of intoxication (*sakr*) and theopathic locutions (*shathiyyat*), which became well-known by Sufis like Bayazid al-Bistami and al-Hallaj al-Mansur. To Gülen, although al-Bistami's words of "Glory be to me, how exalted my being is" and al-Mansur's utterance of "I am the Truth" are understandable from the inevitable spiritual states that they were, these utterances are "nothing but a deviation from the true path" (Gülen 2004c: 146–47).

More importantly in Gülen's thought, the ways of *tarikats* put too much emphasis on inner spiritual training or experience to ignore the social dimensions of Sufism that lead one to perfect goodness (*ihsan*). In his conviction, Sufism as Islamic spirituality cannot be just inward seeking (*içe dönük*), but should be outward reflection (*dışa dönük*) of inward religiosity. This is the second aspect of Gülen's Sufism that drove the Hizmet movement to do hizmet – service for humanity.

For Gülen, Sufism cannot be remote from and indifferent to society. It is in a society that the spiritual travelers realize and deepen their "God-consciousness" through daily life. In this sense, Gülen considered "genuine Sufis" as those who, following the footsteps of the Prophet, were not aloof from society, but actively participated in this-worldly matters by disciplining their lives with self-supervision (*muraqaba*) and self-criticism (*muhasaba*). On this basis, Gülen taught that,

> everyone who has planned his or her life to reach the horizon of a perfect, universal human being is conscious of this life and spends every moment of it struggling with himself or herself (Gülen 1998a: 9).

Put simply, Gülen assured "Sufism within society." In his teaching, as exemplified by the Prophet and his companions, any spiritual journey needs to be vitalized by action, and action needs to be vitalized by the constant "God-consciousness" in society. This aspect of Gülen's Sufism was well analyzed by a number of studies. For instance, having compared Gülen's Sufism to Max Weber's theory of "worldly asceticism," Elisabeth Özdalga (2000) coined it as "activist pietism." "Sufism within society" was closely linked to Gülen's teaching of "man of action and thought" (*aksiyon ve düşünce insanı*), which requires an outward reflection of one's inner spirituality in society. As Özdalga noted, this was why the members of the Hizmet movement worked hard in society for their spiritual growth, and in this regard, the Hizmet movement became different from typical *tarkats*.

"Sufism within society" further led Gülen to teach "Sufism for society." To him, one's spiritual journey "toward, in and with God" is to realize a journey "from God." For this, Gülen elaborated each step of spiritual journey, as "journeying and initiation" (*sayr u suluk*), "journeying to God" (*sayr ilallah*), "journeying in God" (*sayr fillah*), "journeying with God" (*sayr maallah*), and "journeying from God" (*sayr anillah*). In the final stage of "journeying from God," ascetics "devote their lives to saving others from worldly and other-worldly dungeons" (Gülen 2004c: 244–62).

This concept of "activist Sufism for others" is what hizmet, service for humanity, meant when the members of the Hizmet movement said "hizmetimiz" (our service). And, this is "the way" that Gülen empathetically taught, as cited earlier, "to seek to please Allah and, as an inseparable dimension of it, to serve immediate family members, society, country, and all of humanity accordingly."

Sufism, Dialogue and Democracy

Being consistent with his teaching of hizmet based upon activist Sufism, Gülen inspired the supporters of the Hizmet movement to go to the world for hizmet, service for humanity, since the 1980s. Although the secular state continually monitored, the schools and the institutes associated with the Hizmet movement continued to succeed in the competitive market of education in Turkey. Based upon this success, the movement began to extend their educational activities to central Asian countries in the early 1990s, and thereby trod the path toward globalization. In the process of its globalization, the movement focused its activities exclusively on interfaith and intercultural dialogue. As Hermansen noted, "the 1990s marked the opening of two major new horizons for Gülen and the Hizmet movement: expansion beyond the borders of Turkey, and dialogue beyond the frontiers of Islam" (Hermansen 2015: 31).

Gülen's representative examples shed light on this path of the movement toward dialogue and globalization. In the 1990s, Gülen started to deliver lectures in other countries, like Germany, Denmark, Netherland, France, Italy and the United States. At the same time, he met with several religious leaders in Turkey, including Patriarch Vartholemeos of the Greek Orthodox Church in Turkey, and David Aseo, the Chief Rabbi of Turkey's Jewish community (Hermansen 2015: 31–33). Gülen's interreligious dialogue activities reached a high point with his meeting with Pope John Paul II at the Vatican in 1998.[14] The Hizmet movement followed in Gülen's footsteps. While establishing the first international Turkish schools in Central Asian countries, the movement began to establish platforms for its inter-religious dialogue activities in the 1990s, which "was to become more prominent within the context of the Hizmet movement's global activities" (Hermansen 2015: 32).

Yet, despite the remarkable success of the movement within the legal boundaries of the secular Republic, the negative image of *fethullahçılar tarikat* was still vivid in Turkey where the military intervention into the domestic politics was effective. In this climate occurred the 1997 military-based soft coup, in which the Kemalist military secularists overthrew the democratically elected coalition government of Necmettin Erbakan and his Refah Party. This coup revived the suspicion around Gülen and his movement as a religious sectarian organization that could dismantle the secular state. Gülen was accused using evidence from cassette recordings of his sermons on an Islamic state. These recordings were fully and sensationally covered in the media in 1999 to indict Gülen and stiffen a *fethullahçılar* image of his movement among the public.[15] The indictment lasted six years but Gülen was finally acquitted by a court in Ankara in 2006.

In 1999, Gülen traveled to the United States for heart surgery and since then has lived there. His residence in the States led the Hizmet movement to accelerate its globalization and develop full-scale dialogue activities. Above all, Gülen's thought of moderate Islam and his open approach to other religions corresponded well with the pluralistic nature of the States. Especially in the context of September 11, Gülen put forward his pluralistic view of interreligious dialogue as a solution of common human concerns and problems. For him, interreligious dialogue "is neither a melting pot nor a mosaic of religions, but rather it is a toolbox for building bridges between humanity's continents and isles" (Yavuz 2003: 181–82).

From his conviction of dialogue, Gülen guided the Hizmet movement to engage in intercultural. Inter-religious and interfaith dialogue on a global level. For this, the movement established a good number of institutions and platforms in the world as advance bases for interfaith dialogue activities. These activities along with its global educational activities led the movement to become a global civic movement, claimed to have over six million members worldwide in 2007. The movement was "known for its efforts to promote tolerance and interfaith dialogue everywhere" (Findley 2015: 14).

2 Sufism as a Working Spirit in Globalization 65

A close look at Gülen's thought makes salient that just as the concept of *hizmet* was built upon Sufism as noted earlier, Sufism provided a working spirit to the movement to engage dialogue with other religious and cultural people for hizmet, service for humanity. In other words, the dialogue activities of the Hizmet movement occurred as a natural sequence of Gülen's appreciation of Sufism.

Sufism for *hizmet* in Gülen's thought is a sprit to promote dialogue and tolerance. In the process of the globalization of the Hizmet movement Gülen taught, directly addressing members,

> If we can spread globally the Islamic understanding of such heroes of love as Niyazi Misri, Yunus Emre, and Mawlana Rumi, and if we can extend their messages of love, dialogue, and tolerance to people who are thirsty for this message, everyone will run toward the embrace of love, peace, and tolerance that we represent (Gülen 2004b: 60–61).

As this teaching indicates, Gülen's conviction about dialogue has an inseparable link with the concepts of love, peace and tolerance through which such renowned Sufis as Misri, Emre and Rūmī showed inclusivism. Gülen tried to revitalize this Sufi inclusivism in today's world where "clashes" among civilizations and religions are anticipated along the line of globalization.[16] To prevent clashes that may endanger humans, Gülen stressed the need for intercultural and interreligious dialogue (Unal & Williams 2000: 193–304; Carroll 2007).

To Gülen, dialogue is an activity that has human beings as its axis to form a bond among them. For such humanitarian dialogue, tolerance and tolerance-based virtues like love, compassion, forgiveness and humility are essential. For this reason, Gülen regarded tolerance and dialogue as "the two roses of the emerald hills of humanity" (Gülen 2004b: 50–53).

This concept of dialogue is intrinsically linked to Gülen's view of pluralism and democracy. As noted earlier, opponents of the Hizmet movement tended to consider it as a potential danger of the secular nature of the Turkish Republic. As opposed to this claim, Gülen advocated the compatibility of Islam and democracy with many passages in his writings and sermons.

To begin with, Gülen lamented that,

> in the Islamic world and particularly in my country, Turkey, it is painful to see how those who speak on Islam and democracy and claim to pronounce in the name of religion have come to the understanding that Islam and democracy cannot be reconciled (Saritoprak & Ünal 2005: 452–53).

To him, this understanding originates in the distinction between the rule of God in Islam and the view of humans in democracy. In Gülen's theological thinking, this distinction is misled, as the rule of God means that "sovereignty is entrusted to humans by God," and this entrusted human rule was practiced in the era of the Caliphate. Thus, Islam is compatible with democracy (Saritoprak & Ünal 2005: 453).

Gülen further pointed out a tendency to consider democracy "in its unaffiliated form." In his words,

> democracy itself is not a unified system of government; it is rarely presented without an affiliation. In many cases, another term, such as social, liberal, Christian, or radical, is added as a prefix. In some cases, even one of these forms of democracy may not consider the other as democracy (Saritoprak & Ünal 2005: 452).

From this, Gülen underlined the pluralistic nature of democracy.

Following this, Gülen acknowledged many versions of democracy, and thereby advocated an Islamic form of democracy. His idea of Islamic democracy is distinctive in its emphasis on spiritual dimensions that Islam and democracy share with democracy. To Gülen, "Democracy is never opposed to the spirit of Islam." And, "the spirit of Islam," as noted earlier, directly refers to Sufism in Gülen's thought. In criticizing the view of Islam as a totalizing ideology, he further argued:

> [T]he spirit of Islam, which promotes the rule of law and openly rejects oppression against any segment of society. This spirit also promotes actions for the betterment of society in accordance with the view of the majority. Those who follow a more moderate pattern also believe that it would be much better to introduce Islam as a complement to democracy instead of presenting it as an ideology. Such an introduction of Islam may play an important role in the Muslim world through enriching local forms of democracy and extending it in such a way that helps humans develop an understanding of the relationship between the spiritual and material worlds (Saritoprak & Ünal 2005).

To Gülen, democracy is a system that satisfies both material and spiritual needs of an individual human being. In this sense, he was confident about the future of democracy, as he said:

> Democracy has developed over time. Just as it has gone through many different stages, it will continue to evolve and improve in the future. Along the way, it will be shaped into a more humane and just system, one based on righteousness and reality. If human beings are considered as a whole, without disregarding the spiritual dimension of their existence and their spiritual needs, and without forgetting that human life is not limited to this mortal life and that all people have a great craving for eternity, democracy could reach the peak of perfection and bring even more happiness to humanity. Islamic principles of equality, tolerance, and justice can help it do just this (Gülen 2004b: 352).

This indicates Gülen's perception of democracy from three components–equality, tolerance and justice, each of which deserves attention.

In Gülen's theology, every human being is equal in terms of "the most valuable being in the universe" and "the greatest mirror of the Names, Attributes, and Deeds of God" (Gülen 2006b). Each of them is given capacity to mirror divinity, and owing to this capacity, s/he is God's most valuable creature who can be "greater than the universe" (Gülen 2004c: 292). Thus, every human being is equal beyond religion, race, wealth and social status. Simultaneously, each human being is unique and different from each other in terms of free-will that God bestowed upon each of them equally (Gülen 2007: 15). By free-will, a human "chooses," and by the ability to choose, each human being is unique. From this angle, Gülen considered freedom. Just as democracy, true freedom directs itself toward both material and spiritual progress, as he said that "true freedom is the freedom of the human mind from all shackles that hinder it from making material and spiritual progress, as long as we do not fall into indifference and heedlessness" (Gülen 2007: 65).

Because every human being is equal and unique, human beings exist in diversity. Therefore, we are dialogic beings in essence. In Gülen's view, it is dialogue that secures human equality, uniqueness and diversity, and thus, dialogue is essential in democracy. From this perspective, he assigned tolerance to be prerequisite not only for dialogue as noted earlier but also for democracy. Gülen asserted:

> Democracy is a system which gives people the possibility of living through their own feelings and thoughts. The tolerance is an important part of its depth. It could even be said where there is no tolerance, democracy cannot be talked about... Without the existence of tolerance it is impossible for democracy to take root. In actual fact, it is imperative for those who defend democracy to tolerate those who do not share their views and open their hearts to everyone.[17]

As such, a basis of democracy is tolerance that enables one to acknowledge others. As noted earlier, tolerance in Gülen's thought is linked to the inclusive feature of Sufism. As a representative example of Sufism-based tolerance, Gülen further presented "Turkish Muslimness" (Türk Müslümanlığı):

> The teaching of tasavvuf [Sufism] remains to certain extent in every corner of our society. Everyone took a benefit from it. The influence of tasavvuf on Turkish society is stronger and deeper than any other Islamic country. A custom such as to see oneself as lower than others; to see others higher than oneself and to give priority to others over oneself was impregnated to this nation from its very beginning by Sufi authorities such as Ahmet Yesevi, Yunus Emre, Mevlana Celaleddin-i Rumi and Haci Bektash Veli (Pope 1998).

Although this teaching of the soft, humble and inclusive Turkish Sufism was directly addressed to the members of the Hizmet movement to provide them spirituality to be tolerant to others, it showed Gülen's conviction of Turksh Islam as an important contribution to a betterment of the democracy system.

From this view of the equality in humanity and tolerance toward others, Gülen evaluated today's world. In his view, people of today face many problems, including the danger of war and clashes, ecological crisis, hunger, and loss of moral values, all of which make them concerned about peace, contentment, ecology, justice, tolerance, and dialogue. At the bottom of all of these problems and concerns, Gülen saw "the prevailing materialistic worldview," which "disturbs the balance between humanity and nature and within individuals."[18] The materialistic worldview causes injustice between materiality and spirituality, both of which are necessary for an individual life as noted throughout this chapter. The existing injustice around materiality and imbalance between materiality and spirituality in turn belittles the need of tolerance and dialogue, which may close the door on democracy.

Against this backdrop, Gülen continued to raise his voice on tolerance, dialogue, justice, democracy, and spirituality for a humane and just world. For this world, according to his writings and sermons, Gülen guided the Hizmet movement to focus its activities on education and dialogue, while inspiring millions of people to be supporters of the movement.

CONCLUSION

This chapter has examined the Hizmet movement by focusing on its Sufi orientations. By tracing the history of the movement, the chapter showed how Sufism was actually lived in the movement to interact with secular, pluralistic, democratic and global contexts of today. As demonstrated, Sufism served as a working spirit to form the movement in the 1970s, to endure various challenges from local politics of anti-Sufism throughout its history, to focus its activities on education and interfaith dialogue, and to become a most visible Islamic global network today.

The findings of this chapter illustrate a form of 'lived Sufism,' which, as opposed to the once popularized academic theory of the decline of Sufism, provides considerable evidence of the continuing vitality of Sufism in a secular context. It also adds another example of Sufism-related movements that keep their distance from traditional Sufi orders. Last but not least, it depicts how the tolerant, adaptive and inclusive feature of Sufism was reactivated both theologically and practically for interfaith dialogue and peaceful coexistence in today's pluralistic and global world.

About the Author

Heon Kim is Associate Professor of Philosophy and Religious Studies at East Stroudsburg University of Pennsylvania. He has also taught Humanities Seminar courses in the Intellectual Heritage Program at Temple University, Philadelphia. As a teacher-scholar, Kim specializes in Comparative Religions, Interreligious Dialogue, and Religion and Spirituality. He has pursued a strong cross-cultural academic career in South Korea, Egypt, Turkey and the USA. Kim received his doctorate from the Department of Religion, Temple University, with a distinction award by his dissertation committee's unanimous vote. He received his BA in Arabic Language from Hankuk University of Foreign Studies, Seoul, South Korea. He subsequently studied Arabic and Islamic theology for several years at Al-Azhar University, Cairo, Egypt. His academic career continued at Marmara University in Istanbul, Turkey, where he obtained an MA degree in Islamic Philosophy. Kim authored *Din Değiştirmenin Entellectual Arka Planı* [Intellectual Background of Religious Conversion] in Turkish (Işık Yayınları, Turkey, 2004), and edited two volumes, *A Just World: Multidisciplinary Perspectives on Social Justice* (Cambridge Scholars Publishing, Newcastle UK, 2013), and *Making Peace In and With the World: The Role of the Gülen Movement in the Task of Eco Justice* (Cambridge Scholars Publishing, Newcastle UK, 2012). Often invited to speak at national conferences, since 2010, Kim has served as a manuscript reviewer of *Journal of Ecumenical Studies*. Kim is the Founder and Chair of the section "Interreligious and Interfaith Studies," and a Co-chair of the section "Religion, Conflict and Peace," for the American Academy of Religion Mid-Atlantic Annual Conference. He currently serves as the President of Interdisciplinary Association for Philosophy and Religious Studies of the Pennsylvania State System of Higher Education.

Notes

1. Cited from www.themuslim500.com (accessed 5 March 2016). The survey has been conducted annually for seven years so far since its first version in 2009, entitled *The 500 Most Influential Muslims 2009*.
2. Cited from http://time100.time.com/2013/04/18/time-100/slide/fethullah-Gülen/ (accessed 5 March 2016).
3. The exact number of the members is not provided by the movement and because of this, the movement is often criticized as a secret organization. Yet, this critique overlooks the nature of the movement, which is a loosely connected civic "movement" inspired by Gülen's teaching rather than a tangible organization or institution. For this reason, many studies on the Hizmet movement roughly estimate the number.
4. Gülen criticized the then existing educational system, which separately run *madrasa*, *mektep* and *tekke*; see Can (1997: 72–87).
5. Gülen was one of 1971 persons who were imprisoned from 1949 to 1971 for vio-

lating article 163. For this number of 1971, see Cemal (1974), cited from Toprak (2005: 291).

6. For the audio clips of Gülen's speech on *Altın Nesil* in 1976 and 1977, see, http://fgülen.com/tr/ses-ve-video/fethullah-Gülen-hitabet/fethullah-Gülenin-siirleri-konferanslari (accessed 9 March 2016).

7. See Gülen's speech on "Altın Nesil Konferansı" at Çorum in 1977, available online at http://fgülen.com/tr/ses-ve-video/fethullah-gülen-hitabet/fethullah-Gülenin-siirleri-konferanslari/36326-altin-nesil-konferansi-corum (accessed 9 March 2016).

8. Cited from http://www.gülenmovement.us/gülen-movement/brief-history-of-gülen-movement (accessed 12 March 2016).

9. See, for instance, Ertugrul Ozkok (1995). "Fethullahçılık ve Tarikat," *Hurriyet*, January 23–30.

10. For instance, *Hürriyet*, a Turkish daily, reported in 2006 that "the influence of Fethullah Gülen, the most famous name of *tarikat*, covers all cities of Turkey, and further extends from Africa to Far East via *tarikat* schools (of the Hizmet movement)" – cited and translated from *Hürriyet* online at www.hurriyet.com.tr/pazar/5097892.asp (accessed 5 March 2016).

11. Gülen (1998b) https://fgulen.com/en/press/interviews-claims-and-answers/25016-claims-and-answers (accessed 7 June 2016).

12. For a most recent discussion on the concept of hizmet in the Hizmet movement, see Marty (2015).

13. Gülen's interview with Nuriye Akman, *Zaman*, 9 June 2003, cited in Kim 2008: 267.

14. For Gülen's meeting with Pope John Paul II, see "Fethullah Gülen and his Meeting with the Pope," *The Fountain* 23 (1998): 14–34.

15. For this indictment, see Baskan (2004: 236).

16. See Huntington (1993: 199). For Gülen's responses to Huntington's theory of Clash of Civilizations, see *Today's Zaman* (English edition) on October 29–30, 2007, which included articles; Ali Ihsan Aydin, "Gülen Sees Peace Wherever Huntington Sees Clash" and Richard Penaskovic, "Fethullah Gülen's Response to the 'Clash of Civilizations' Thesis."

17. Gülen, "Hoşgörü-demokrasi birliği," available online at http://arsiv.zaman.com.tr/1998/10/07/yazarlar/6.html (accessed 15 March 2016).

18. Gülen, "The Necessity of Interfaith Dialogue: A Muslim Perspective," *The Fountain* 3:31 (2000): 4; available online at http://www.fountainmagazine.com/Issue/detail/The-Necessity-Of-Interfaith-Dialogue (accessed 15 March 2016).

3

A PARADOX OF POLITICAL MYSTICISM: THE BEKTASHI SUFI ORDER AS AN ISLAMIC ESOTERIC COMMUNITY AND FACTOR IN ALBANIAN NATIONAL HISTORY[1]

Stephen S. Schwartz

INTRODUCTION

The phenomenon of "political mysticism" in Islam, aside from the history of mahdist eruptions, has been little studied by non-Muslim historians. Yet "political Sufism," to narrow the concept to its most prolifically-visible exemplar, is a leading factor in the Islamic affairs of many countries. However one views the Iranian clerical regime, including its treatment of dissenting Sufis, the Tehran theocracy is pledged to an interpretation of Shia Islam, identified with Ayatollah Ruhollah Khomeini and his revolutionary cohort, that claims to draw significantly on the Sufi classics, Persianate, Turkic, and Arabic. At the other end of the global Muslim social and political spectrum, the Nahdatul Ulama (NU) movement in Indonesia, which has claimed a membership exceeding 40 million and status as the largest Muslim organization in the world, operates networks for education, health, and social welfare while upholding a conventional, Sunni-Sufi doctrine grounded in the Islamic theological classics.

Between the authoritarianism of the Iranian Islamic regime and the moderation and pluralism of NU, there are currently several variations in "political Sufism" largely undetected by non-Muslim observers. The Barelvi sect of Sunni Islam – which is headquartered in South Asia and influences the Muslim diaspora in the United Kingdom and South Africa – accounts for several hundred million adherents, and is an active force in Pakistan, India, and Bangladesh opposing the influence of Wahhabi and Deobandi doctrines. The Barelvis, who have adopted the custom of referring to themselves alone as "the Sunnis" (*Ahl-e Sunnah Wal Jammah*), include an internal spiritual apparatus drawn from the Qadri (*Qadiriyya*) Sufi order. The Qadris are known for their jihadism, as in the Caucasus, and Barelvi elements in Pakistan have wavered in the direction of radicalism. In Iraq, a jihadist body, the "Army of Men of the Naqshbandi Order," was formed in the aftermath of the US intervention of 2003. It has pursued a two-pronged offensive against the so-called "Islamic State" and the latter's predecessor, Al-Qaida in Mesopotamia (AQIM), as well as against the Shia-dominated post-2003 government. Naqshbandi Sufis, more than the Qadris, possess a jihadist legacy.

Assessing these four variants of "political Sufism" one might conclude that such trends are exclusively radical, or at least jihadist. But a more interesting and important example of "political Sufism" is that of the Bektashi community in the Albanian lands (*Komuniteti Beḳtashian* in Albanian).

THE BEKTASHIS

The Bektashis comprise a heterodox component of world Islam. They are liberal Shias – indeed, they are the only indigenous Shia Muslims in Europe, with the exception of a few of their spiritual cousins among ethnic Turks in Macedonia and Thrace (Trakya). In addition, the Albanian lands are alone in Europe in supporting a large and diverse range of Islamic Sufi *ṭarīqahs*. The Bektashis are, like all Shias, extremely devoted to the personalities of Imam Ali, Imam Hasan, and Imam Huseyin, the leading figures in the early development of Shia Islam. For this reason the Bektashis have been labelled a "*ghulā*" sect – excessive in love of Imam Ali – by scholars including Matti Moosa, the standard historian in Western academia of the "*ghulat*" phenomenon (Moosa 1988).

Bektashism is traced to its eponymous apostle, Hunkar Haci Bektaş Veli, who is believed to have lived from 1209 to 1271 of the Common Era and is viewed as the leading herald of Islam among the Turkic peoples. Haci Bektaş Veli is thought to have been born at Nishapur in Khorasan, a region of northeastern Iran productive of ecstatic religiosity as well as of Islamic refugees to Turkey, pressed by Mongol expansionism. Haci Bektaş Veli was a near-exact contemporary of Jalalad'din Rūmī (1207–73) and the two are said to have known each other well. Haci Bektaş Veli is buried, according to tradition, at a complex in a village of the same name in central Anatolia.

Unlike Rūmī, who wrote first in Persian and whose works were then translated into Turkish and were inducted into the Turkish Sunni literary and official theological traditions, Haci Bektaş Veli was a vernacular lyricist composing verse in the idiom of the poor Turkic peasants of Central Asia and eastern Anatolia. The destiny of the Bektashis would turn out very differently from that of the super-contemplative Mevlevi order named for Rūmī. Under the Ottomans, the Bektashi Sufis became the Islamic chaplains of the *yeniçeri* or "new men" [often called "janissaries" in Western commentaries]. The *yeniçeri* served as elite infantry, palace troops, and personal guards to the Ottoman rulers. The link between the *yeniçeri* and the Bektashis originated presumably in the late fourteenth century CE as the Ottoman state consolidated.

These somewhat pale assertions of "Sufi history," which is often distorted in memory, are paralleled by a more inspirational narrative, focused on a legendary Bektashi progenitor, Sari Salltëk Dede. The leading Albanologist, Robert Elsie, has noted that references to Sari Salltëk as a preacher of Islam in Europe first appear in the historical writings of Ibn Battuta (1304–77), where the Islamic saint is said to have been sent by the second Ottoman ruler, Orhan Beg (1326–62) to proselytize for the faith of Muhammad in the Balkan and Eastern Black Sea territories from Rumeli (today's Bulgaria) to Crimea (Elsie 2000). Sari Salltëk is said to be buried in several Bektashi Sufi shrines, including the fifteenth century CE *tekija* [Bos., Sufi lodge complex] at Blagaj in Hercegovina, one of the most significant and impressive Sufi monuments in the Balkans, and a tomb at Babadağ in the Romanian Dobrudja region. Elsie further mentions tombs believed to house the remains of Sari Salltëk on the island of Corfu, at the Orthodox Christian Monastery of Saint Naum on Lake Ohrid in Macedonia, in Kruja, Albania, and on Mount Pashtrik, a peak on the Albanian-Kosova border. Sites ascribed to Sari Salltëk's interment total seven, and pilgrimages to them are common, especially by Bektashis.

Moosa, for his part, cites the Ottoman traveler Evliya Çelebi (1611–c. 1682), recounting that Haci Bektaş Veli went to Rum – the former Greco-Roman Christian lands of Anatolia, Greece, and the Balkans – in the company of Sari Salltëk, Shams al-Din Tabrizi (1185–1248), the spiritual teacher of Rumi, and Muhyid'din Ibn Arabi (1165–1240). This powerful Sufi constellation, whether it existed in history or not, left a deep impression on Balkan Islam, where more conventional Turkish and conservative Slavic Sufis joined with heterodox Albanian Sufis in their affection for Ibn Arabi.

But Haci Bektaş Veli and his legacy became identified exclusively with Turkish and Albanian Islam, and through the centuries, was repudiated and repressed by Balkan Slav Muslim authorities. Whether Bektashism was originally introduced to the Balkans by early *du'at* like Sari Salltëk, it had established a marked presence in Albania by the mid-seventeenth century CE. Shia habits (such as outspoken praise for Khalifa Ali and his fellow martyr Imam Huseyin, and condemnation of the Sunni *khulafa* who opposed them and gave rise to Sunnism) were widespread in Albania, according to Evliya Çelebi (Dankoff & Elsie 2000). It is not impossible that the efflorescence of Shiism and especially Bektashism among Albanians reflected the charisma of Sari Salltëk during the thirteenth century and amid Ottoman conquests, but it could equally have embodied the influence of Alevi-Bektaşi Turkish and Kurdish Shias who, 200 years later, sided with the aggressive Persian ruler Shah Ismail (1487–1524), founder of the Safavid dynasty, unifier of Persia, patron of Shia Islam as the state religion of Persia, poet, and enemy of the Ottomans.

Some of these Alevi-Bektaşis may have been banished by the Ottomans to Albania, considered a wild and vulnerable province on the Christian borderland. John Kingsley Birge, the first English author to write authoritatively on Bektashism, argues that during the Ottoman-Safavid war Shia (i.e. Bektaşi) sympathies were so pronounced among the *yeniçeri* that their military capacity against the Safavids was significantly undermined (Birge 1937). Yet the Turkish Sultans could not move against them until further centuries had passed, and then, as we shall see, a purge of the Bektashis from the Ottoman state was mandated. Additionally, because of their advantageous position in the *yeniçeri*, the Bektashis were able to protect and shelter thousands of disaffected, pro-Safavid Turks and Kurds in eastern Anatolia. It has long been argued that the chief value of the Bektashis to the Sultans consisted in their ability to assimilate fractious elements – from Christian youths Islamized and incorporated into the *yeniçeri* under the system of *devşirme* or "blood levy" to pro-Safavi Shia rebels.

Between the missionary work of Sari Salltĕk (fourteenth century) and the encroachment of the Safavids (sixteenth century), the Bektashi order of Sufis underwent an important restructuring, at the instance of Ballëm Sulltan (fifteenth century CE), the "second pir" of the order after Haci Bektaş Veli himself. According to the authoritative modern Bektashi author Baba Rexheb Beqiri (1901–95), Ballëm Sulltan brought organization to the Bektashis, with administration of all the *tekkeler* [Turkish; Albanian pl. *teqet*, from the sing. *teqe*; Bos. pl. *tekije*, sing. *tekija*, or lodges], and initiated Sultan Bayazet II into the *ṭarīqah* (Rexheb 1970).

Until the onset of consequential demands for the modernization of the Ottoman Empire by the Western European powers, the Bektashis maintained their position as a pillar of the state. With suppression of the *yeniçeri* and their religious partners, the Bektashi Sufis, in the bloody "reform" of 1826, the Bektashis were forced underground and their *tekkeler* and other properties were handed over to the Sunni-exclusivist and *shāri'ah*-centric Naqshbandi order. Imperial loyalists in the Balkans rebelled against the reforms and many Bektashi *babas* (*shaykhs*) were killed at the order of the state.

But the Bektashis were a resilient band of mystics. To escape persecution, Bektashis in the Ottoman empire practiced *taqiyya* or dissimulation, declaring themselves to be Sunnis. The Bektashi spirit could not be extirpated from the Turkish, Kurdish, and Albanian soul. Having adopted *taqiyya* as Sunnis to protect themselves, they had no compunction about becoming Naqshbandi *shaykhs*, with the intention of reviving their *ṭarīqah* and regaining their properties. The ability of the heterodox Bektashis to survive persecution is one enigma of their history, and seems to indicate that unlike the more traditional Sunni Sufis in the Ottoman domains, they drew on vestiges of Central Asian Turkic shamanism and Kurdish mysticism to reinforce their authenticity.

More important, especially for the discussion of "political Sufism," is a paradoxical fact. While they were suppressed and driven to *taqiyya* in Anatolia, and condemned there by the Western powers and Ottoman modernizers as "backward-looking," in nineteenth century Albania, where they had gathered for generations, they suddenly emerged as a leading force in the assertion of national enlightenment and, eventually, independence. Albanians had long declared that they were Muslims and would serve the empire, but that they would not abandon their ethnic loyalty and would never assume Turkish identity. This attitude prevailed notwithstanding that considerable Albanian-Turkish intermarriage existed, and that even in remote Kosova, one of the rough frontier provinces of the empire, the elite spoke Turkish in such places as Prizren. The latter city, known for its beautiful mosques, is the seat of the Sunni Sufi body, the Kosova Sufi Union, or BTK (*Bashkësia e Tarikateve të Kosovës*), of the main Serbian ecclesiastical institution in the Albanian lands, the Eparchy of Raška and Prizren, and of the Catholic Apostolic Administration of Prizren. Nonetheless, Prizren remains known for the important Turkish-speaking element in its population today.

Nicola Guy, a British historian and government official, published a recent study, *The Birth of Albania*. Therein, she follows the analysis of the Albanian-American historian Stavro Skendi (1905–89), who identified three currents in the Albanian National Renaissance or *Rilindja Kombëtare*. The first were the Hamidists, centered in Kosova and mainly Muslim, seeking a restoration of the constitutional reforms enacted in 1878 by Sultan Abdul Hamid II (1842–1918, reigned 1876–1909) and suspended until the Young Turk revolution of 1908. A second tendency, the supporters of the Ottoman "Party of Freedom and Accord," comprised Muslims and Albanian Orthodox Christians, and were prominent in Kosova and in central and southern Albania. They called for Albanian autonomy within the empire. The third and most significant element in the leadership of the *Rilindja*, the "enlightened intellectuals," were drawn mainly from southern Albania and the Albanian diaspora. They, according to Guy, "included Orthodox Christians and Muslims, especially a number of prominent Bektashis and many involved in the earlier cultural and literary endeavors. They were influenced by the enlightenment… and were similar in many ways to the intelligentsia in other European states" (Guy 2012).

THE LEAGUE OF PRIZREN

The foundation of the League of Prizren in Kosova in 1878 is considered by all Albanian patriots and Albanologists to mark the commencement of the *Rilindja*. For most commentators, the formation of the League was mainly a defensive and even a military development, brought about by Russian and Balkan Slavophone aggression during the so-called "Eastern Crisis" beginning in 1875. Russian imperialism, then as now, incited the Orthodox Christians of Hercegovina, Bulgaria, Serbia, and Montenegro to rebellion and war against Turkish rulers, non-Slavic-speaking, and non-Orthodox inhabitants of the region. In this conflict, Albanians were caught between their national desire for greater autonomy in the Ottoman system, and the voracious onslaught of the Russian-backed powers. Russian troops invaded the Balkans and attacked northern Albania, but were defeated by Turkish forces in 1876.

Russia then chose to impose its ambitions in the region through diplomacy. In negotiations with Austria-Hungary, Moscow twice accepted the definition of Albania as a separate component of the Ottoman Empire along with an independent Serbia, Montenegro, and Romania and an autonomous Bulgaria. But Russia secured Habsburg neutrality in a prospective tsarist war with the Sultan, in exchange for Austro-Hungarian occupation of Bosnia-Hercegovina. Beginning a fresh offensive against Turkey, Russia entered Bessarabia (today's Moldova) in 1877. In this phase of its overall plan for expansion and consolidation of its dominions, Russia was more successful in assisting its Serbian and Montenegrin accomplices. Both of the South Slav states annexed significant areas that had been Albanian-speaking historically and expelled thousands of their indigenous inhabitants southward, killing many of the *muhaxhirs* or "refugees for the sake of Islam."

Serbia drove some 200,000 Albanians out of the cities of Nish, Vranje, Prokuple, Leskovac, and Kurshumlia, while Montenegro committed similar atrocities in Tivar, Ulqin, and Podgorica. Journalists at the time commented on the considerable number of deaths and generalized suffering that accompanied the Slav advance. The Turkish military panicked and fled, and as the Russians appeared close to complete victory in the region, the well-known treaty of San Stefano was signed by the Russians and Turks on 3 March 1878, handing the greater part of the spoils of war to a new "Greater Bulgaria." The latter state, although remaining tributary to the Sultan, was intended to include most of Slavic Macedonia, and the treaty turned over a major portion of the Albanian lands (known today in their totality as "ethnic Albania") to Bulgarian, Serbian, and Montenegrin control.

"Greater Bulgaria" encountered opposition from Serbia, backed by Britain. Serbia was irked by the expansion of Bulgaria, and Britain by the extension of Russian influence. Austria-Hungary, which sought confirmation of its occupation of Bosnia-Hercegovina, joined Serbia and Britain in opposing the San Stefano Treaty; Romania, which had opposed the Ottomans but received no substantial rewards, also feared a "Greater Bulgaria," and Greece, which had ambitions in Albania, Macedonia, Thrace, and some border areas, additionally dissented from the San Stefano proposals. Calls for revision of the San Stefano Treaty led to convocation of a Congress in Berlin. Hope among the Albanians that a review of the San Stefano Treaty would free them from the sudden spectre of Slav-speaking domination stimulated the formation of the League of Prizren on 10 June 1878, just prior to the meeting of the Congress of Berlin. Since the fate of Bosnia-Hercegovina, awarded to the Habsburgs by Russian diplomacy, was also to be determined by the Berlin negotiations, a small number of Bosnian delegates joined in the first meeting of the League.

Most of the participants in the League of Prizren represented the areas directly threatened by the San Stefano arrangement: northern Albania, Kosova, the *sancak* [Ottoman district] of Yenipazar/Pazar i Ri/Novi Pazar, and Western Macedonia. The organization of the League had been preceded by defensive efforts including formation of Local Councils for National Salvation and foundation of the Central Committee for the Defense of Albanian National Rights, also known as the Albanian Society of Constantinople, in 1877, in the latter case with the participation of Muslims alongside Catholics and Christian Orthodox believers. The Ottoman metropolis was the original location for activities by three outstanding figures associated with the *Rilindja*, the Frashëri brothers: Abdyl (1839–1902), Naim (1846–1900), and Sami (1850–1904). Born in the southern Albanian town of Frashër, the brothers were Bektashi in their religious culture. Sami Frashëri is also known among Turks as one of the *munevverler* or "intellectuals," pursuing journalism as well as education, under the name Şemseddin Sami Bey (Gawrych 2006).

Although the Bektashis were victimized by the imperial reform measures taken at the insistence of the Western powers, they became acolytes of popular education and outstanding proponents of Albanian-language schooling, which was still prohibited under Turkish rule. When the *Rilindja* began, according to Robert Elsie, possession of Albanian written materials, no matter how trivial, was considered by the Ottoman authorities a more serious crime than murder or banditry (Elsie 2005). Sami Frashëri utilized the network of Bektashi *teqet* in southern Albania to support demands for five basic changes: a single, unitary Albania, with administration by Albanian-speaking officials, Albanian-language schools, a legislative assembly, and development of a budget for education and public works. Sami Frashëri also became prominent as author of a wide range of literary and scientific works, while Naim is honored as one of Albania's greatest national poets, with the Catholic Gjergj Fishta (1871–1940).

Abdyl Frashëri emerged as the main political and intellectual figure in the League of Prizren, but its chief military personality was Ali Pasha Gucia, who had raised an army to resist Montenegrin annexation of his native territory, and who continued fighting for several years. Fishta's national epic, *The Highland Lute (Lahuta e Malcis)* celebrates Ali Pasha Gucia. By these examples – Bektashi leadership in the form of Abdyl Frashëri and his brothers, literary praise as penned by the Franciscan Fishta – the universal significance of the League of Prizren for the Albanians becomes visible. The League anticipated the call to national unity of Pashko Vasa (1825–1892), also a Catholic and a supporter of the League of Prizren, who wrote in his poem "O moj Shqypni" ("O Albania mine") composed in the aftermath of the League's efforts, *"feja e shqiptari asht shqiptaria"* – "The religion of the Albanian is Albanian nationality!" This remains the Albanian national credo today.

The League of Prizren fostered branches in all Albanian cities and towns, and was administered by a General Council and a National Committee. It was conceived as a "lobby" – to employ a contemporary term – that would convince the diplomats meeting in Berlin to prevent the partition of the Albanians by their Slavic-speaking neighbors. The Bektashi Abdyl Frashëri projected a *besa*, or alliance of all Albanians, regardless of religious affiliation, but his strategic objectives were limited to recognition of the Albanian nation, integrity of the historic Albanian lands and their unification in a single territory, along with an end to taxation and conscription. A single Albania would reproduce the nationalist pattern sought by the Bulgarians, Romanians, and Greeks. In contrast with the Southern Albanian, Bektashi-influenced adherents of Sami Frashëri's progressive program, Sunni Muslim Kosovar participants in the League concentrated on loyalty to the Ottoman state, although with considerable autonomy for Albanians, and the defense of Islamic law (*shāri'ah*). And at first, the Turkish regime supported the Kosovar approach.

The Congress of Berlin, however, provided for occupation of Gucia by Montenegro, and the Ottoman authorities chose to accept this unjust decision. When an Ottoman delegation arrived in the city of Gjakova intent on convincing the Albanians to accept the Berlin outcome, it was attacked by gunfire over several days, leaving hundreds dead and wounded. After that, the Turkish court turned its face against the League of Prizren, but Albanian resistance was strengthened.

In the succeeding years, the League of Prizren changed, in two directions. It assumed governance in Kosova; and it gravitated further away from the Ottoman-loyalist and *shāri'ah*-centric sentiments of its Sunni pioneers to accept the progressive program of Sami Frashëri and his Bektashi milieu. The General Council became its legislature, and the National Committee served as its executive. Three ministries were created, with responsibility for foreign affairs, internal order, and the financing of military defense.

The League conducted a successful campaign to repel Montenegrin and Russian soldiers. In 1880 the League met in Shkodra, northern Albania, with equal backing from Catholics, the majority in the north, and Muslims, to call for the autonomy of all Albanians. The next year the League assembled in Prizren and proclaimed a provisional government headed by Haxhi Ymer Prizreni (1821–87), with Abdyl Frashëri handling foreign affairs. The Ottoman court treated the regime created by the League as seditious, and through an extensive military campaign suppressed it, with the conquest of

Prizren itself in 1881. Still, Albanian resistance continued for several years. Abdyl Frashëri was sentenced to prison, and Ymeri Prizreni was assassinated. But the examples of resistance in Gucia and the brief rule of the League of Prizren in Kosova provided evidence that Albanians could fight and, at least temporarily, prevail.

To emphasize, with the goal of freedom for the Albanian nation, the League of Prizren brought together representatives of differing religious communities – Sunni Muslims and Catholics in the north, Bektashis in the south. In addition, the special role of the Frashëri brothers exemplified the dedication of the Bektashis to national enlightenment. Above all, the influence of the Frashëris led the League of Prizren to promote education in the Albanian language as the foundation of national development.

Prizren is of special importance for the Sufi heritage in the Balkans. In the past, the city had a Bektashi *teqe*, founded in 1850 by Adem Baba, who was active with his successor, Haxhi Adem Baba Kovaçi from Gjakova (1841–1927), in the League of Prizren, having cooperated with Abdyl Frashëri and established a branch of the League. But the Bektashi *teqe* in Prizren has been closed since the first world war. At present Prizren is the headquarters of the Kosova Sufi Union (BTK), successor to the former Sufi coordinating body (excluding Bektashis) in ex-Yugoslavia. It is headed by Sheh Adrihysen Shehu, a Rifa'i Sufi, and is located in a Rifa'i *teqe* built in 1893. Along with Bektashis and Rifa'is, Sufis in Prizren have included two now-inactive Sinani *teqet* with *tyrbet* (shrines to Sufi saints), the Tabakhane (built in 1576) and Terzimahallë (seventeenth to eighteenth centuries) The Sinani Begzade *teqe* was opened in 1994. Prizren also shelters a Sa'adi *teqe* and *tyrbe* founded at the beginning of the sixteenth century, two Qadri *teqe-tyrbet*, the Qadri-zinxheri (1646) and Qadri-rezaki (1880), and a Halveti *teqe-tyrbe* (1691). Another esoteric strain of Sufism, the Melamis, came from Gjakova and built a *teqe*, which included a *tyrbe*, in 1892. As a legacy of the most important indigenous expression of Sufism in Europe, these are precious resources that must be protected from political abuse.

The League of Prizren, and its Albanian members, were victims of a phenomenon I have come to call "peace crime." In the name of peace between the Ottomans and the Orthodox powers, the rights of Albanians were ignored; Albanian independence was delayed for more than 30 years, to 1912; and the freedom of Kosova still, even now, remains open to renewed attack. Everybody knows about war crimes, even if many of them have gone unpunished or been minimized by derisory punishments. Peace crimes and peace criminals represent the other side of the present-day international order. In the name of peace, Kosova remains a dependency, with real decision-making in the hands of the European Union and the rest of the "international community." In the name of peace, Serbia presses its claims to deny Kosova its rightful status in Europe. But like Abdyl Frashëri and

Ali Pasha Gucia, Albanians have repeatedly demonstrated their loyalty to the principles that will inevitably assure their complete liberation: cultural enlightenment, refusal of religious-sectarian conflict, and single-minded resistance.

Albania attained independence more than a century ago. The Ottoman system in Turkey was replaced in 1923 by a secular republic. Sufi orders were officially suppressed in Turkey two years later, and the Bektashis moved their world headquarters to Tirana.

The Bektashi Baba, Musa Qazim Bakalli, who died in 1981 aged 101, was one of the greatest personalities in the spiritual history of Kosova. Today his Bektashi *teqe* in Gjakova, an edifice devastated by Serbs during the 1998–99 Kosova war, has been renovated magnificently, and the street on which it stands is named after him. When I first visited the then-ruined *teqe*, in 1999, I was told by its current Baba, Mumin Lama, that the loss of the library at the facility, burned in the destructive Serb attack, was especially hard to bear. Its irreplaceable holdings included a 1,000 page manuscript in which Baba Qazim described his visit, on foot, to India, whence he was drawn by curiosity about Buddhism.

ZIDRA/BRDIA

The passing of Baba Qazim in 1982 had been marked by a memorial issued by the Community of Aliite Islamic Dervish Networks in the former-Yugoslavia, then known by its Serbian initials as ZIDRA and in Albanian as BRDIA. Today that body has become the Kosova Sufi Union (BTK).

In honoring Baba Qazim, "*HU*," the Bulletin of ZIDRA/BRDIA – its title reproduces the Sufi salutation to God – recalled that the Bektashi leader declared when the Sufi group was established,

> I admire your ambition and your youthful *ṭarīqahs* [Sufi orders]... I am sure you will be able to establish in our country a body uniting the *ṭarīqahs* such as has long been awaited. The program you have elaborated and the Statute you have adopted reflects the works of great *shejhs* [sheikhs] and is completely original for the *ṭarīqahs*. I am with you; I want to be an ordinary member of the community of *ṭarīqahs*, and it is a great honor for me.

HU noted that prior to his affiliation with the Bektashi *teqe* in Gjakova, Baba Qazim served at the Harabati Baba *teqe* in Tetova, Macedonia. The Harabati Baba *teqe*, the largest Sufi complex in the Balkans, has been almost completely usurped and vandalized by Wahhabi radicals, incited by the official Islamic Religious Community of the Republic of Macedonia (IVZRM) in a tragic example of fundamentalist pillage beginning in 2002. When ZIDRA/BRDIA was founded, Baba Qazim pointed out,

> there has never been such an organized effort by the *ṭarīqahs* [in the former Yugoslavia]... because we are independent of the *ilmija* [Islamic clerics], we have suffered a lot from them... they even closed *teqet* and prohibited the activity of the *t ṭarīqahs*. As if that were Islamic (Schwartz 2015).

Shejh Lulzim Shehu, based in Prizren and now the public spokesperson for the BTK, met with me during the fourth International Interfaith Conference sponsored by InterfaithKosovo, a state-supported effort with global influence. The event was held in Prishtina, the Kosova capital, 28–30 May 2015. Shejh Lulzim provided instructive documentation on the struggle faced by the metaphysical Islamic Sufis of ex-Yugoslavia after the Communist takeover of the country.

The Yugoslav Communist regime was fully established in 1945. In 1951, financing of *teqet* by *awqaf* (*vakuf*) or Islamic pious endowments typically paying for their maintenance, was downgraded from the central budget of the official Supreme Council of the Islamic Religious Community of Yugoslavia, meeting in Sarajevo.

In 1952, the work of all *tekije* were banned in Bosnia-Hercegovina.

In 1955, the Directorate of the Islamic Religious Community of Serbia noted that 40 *teqet* were active in Kosova, then under Serbian control. But the Sufi institutions did not come under the responsibility of the official religious directorate. The strict repression imposed on Bosnian Sufism could not be attempted in Kosova.

In 1971, after protests and repression in some Yugoslav regions, an Initiative Committee was set up in Prizren to create the ZIDRA/BRDIA. In 1972, however, the Supreme Council of the Islamic Religious Community of Yugoslavia, from Belgrade, ordered the closure of all *tekije*, since, allegedly, "their existence and creation is not in harmony with the interest of the Islamic Community."

This order remained, nevertheless, impossible to enforce in Kosova and other Albanian-speaking areas. In 1973, ZIDRA/BRDIA informed the Commission on Religious Relations of Serbia that they intended to proceed with the formation of ZIDRA/BRDIA. The statement was copied to the *reis-ul ulema* [chief Islamic cleric] of Yugoslavia and to the political authorities in Serb-occupied Kosova. The new group proposed to act within the structures of the official Islamic Community but with "a certain internal independence."

In August 1973, the creation of ZIDRA/BRDIA was obstructed both by the Supreme Council of the Islamic Religious Community, meeting in Sarajevo, and the Islamic Religious Community of Serbia. The former, in Sarajevo, proclaimed that they could not work with *tekije*, or allow the recognition or adoption of statutes by dervish associations. The latter, from Belgrade, specified that it was impossible to agree to or approve of any such activity.

Socialist Yugoslavia adopted a new and liberalized constitution in 1974. One of its stipulations granted Kosova and Vojvodina, as provinces of Serbia, greater political power. The 1974 constitution further removed the barrier to the open functioning of ZIDRA/BRDIA. The Sufis defined themselves as "an independent religious community… with its own administration… which cooperates on a basis of equality with the [official] Islamic Community." *HU* began to appear in 1980, and before his death, Baba Qazim, the Bektashi from Gjakova, contributed to its pages, writing in 1981 on the vocabulary of Bektashi moral teachings. According to *HU*, Baba Qazim was "learned and well-read" in addition to his fidelity to Bektashi principles. His intellectual gifts are illustrated, obviously, by his journey to India and back.

THE KOSOVA SUFI UNION (BTK)

The Kosova Sufi Union (BTK) has reserved positions for 12 Sufi orders in its *majlis* or general assembly. These are the Qadri, Rufa'i, Naqshbandi, Halveti, Sinani, Sa'adi, Shadhili, Bektashi, Mevlevi, Badawi, Bajrami, and Desouki Sufis. The last four orders currently maintain no *teqet* in Kosova, but that is not the case of the Bektashis. To emphasize, Baba Mumin Lama of the Baba Qazim *Teqe* in Gjakova has carried on the noble commitment of his predecessor and is a leading figure in Kosova religious life today. Yet the Bektashis are absent from the BTK.

Shejh Lulzim has advocated for their inclusion in the Union. He says the BTK operates on the principle of a single vote for each Sufi order, although a *ṭarīqah* may have more than one member in the *majlis*. He wrote to me,

> the sovereignty of *tariqats* and *teqet* is respected fully by the Union. The Union does not impose obligations on its members regarding specific dogmas, eschatology, epistemology, cosmology, or doctrine of any kind… but it expects correct *adab* [Islamic manners], *akhlak* [morals], and peaceful relations between all people and all communities.

Bektashi Sufis are an important element in Albanian cultural and social history. They shared the burden of Sufis in pre-1974 Yugoslavia. Their situation in the Republic of Macedonia involves their essential survival in that country. In Albania proper, where the Bektashis once counted at least 30 percent of the population, the 2011 census released by the Institute of Statistics credited the Bektashis with no more than 2.09 percent in a population of three million (Njoftim 2011). This unfortunate datum reflects the suffering inflicted on all religious believers under the brutal, anti-religious dictatorship of Enver Hoxha (1908–85) in Albania.

In 1976, emulating the terrorist "cultural revolution" in Albania's then-patron, China, Hoxha ordered the suppression of all religious activities and the designation of Albania as the "first atheist state in the world." During this dark period, Bektashism was kept alive as an institution by the Gjakova *teqe* of Baba Qazim and a *teqe* founded in 1954 in Taylor, Michigan, USA, by Baba Rexheb. Within Albania proper, the force of the Hoxha regime was applied, according to the academic scholar of Bektashism Frances Trix, such that Baba Bayram Mahmutaj was subjected to 32 years' imprisonment and hard labor. Trix quotes Baba Bayram Mahmutaj regarding the deaths of several Albanian Bektashi leaders: Baba Murteza of Kruja was "tortured and thrown from a prison window." He died in 1946. Baba Kamil Glava of Tepelena was executed by court order in the same year. Baba Ali Tomori, a major Bektashi poet, was liquidated in 1947, as was Baba Shefket Koshtani of Tepelena.

Other Bektashi figures died tragically under Hoxha's rule. Two famous Bektashi clerics, Baba Faja Martaneshi (1910–47) and Baba Fejzo Mallakastra, had joined the political leadership of Hoxha's Partisan movement. They were killed in 1947 when they attempted to convince the then-*Kryegjysh* or Supreme Grandfather of the Bektashis, Abaz Hilmi Dede, to cooperate with Hoxha's dictatorship. Hilmi Dede then committed suicide. According to Trix "Baba Rexheb of Gjirokastër and Baba Bajram of Plashnik estimate[d] that in the mid-1940s there were two-hundred and eighty Bektashi Babas and dervishes [in Albania]. In 1993 there were five Babas and one dervish alive in Albania." Trix declares, I think correctly, that Albanian Catholics and Bektashis were the main targets of Hoxha's war on religion – the first because of their public service in education and the second because of their patriotism and positive reputation among the people (Trix 1994).

Bektashism is a libertarian and progressive religious phenomenon that emphasizes and reinforces values of freedom and social justice. These values are dramatized by the epic of Ashura, when Imam Huseyin was martyred at Karbala, in struggle against the terroristic usurpers of religious authority during his time. For Bektashis, as for other devotees of Imam Huseyin, Ashura is a permanent reality: seekers of truth and defenders of justice are continuously martyred at the hands of the evil "Yezids" who use violence to manipulate and control religious believers. We see this tragic condition reflected in the offensive of so-called "Islamic State" murderers, against Muslims no less than non-Muslims, across the globe. As has been said by others, Sufis, including Bektashis, are peaceful but not pacifist, and must now organize their self-defense in numerous countries.

Bektashis, because of their heterodox Sufi practices as well as their dedication to contemporary principles, including the equality of women and men, secular government, and modern, universal education, are naturally in the front line defending a freedom-loving Islam against radicalism and terrorism. The Bektashis in the Albanian lands are, in my view, those most properly denoted as heirs to the legacy of Haci Bektaş Veli. Still, the Alevi-Bektaşi movement in Turkey is also known for its dedication to secular government, modern culture and education, although it has a more political and leftist character than the Bektashi Community in the Albanian lands. A closer relationship between Turkish and Kurdish Alevi-Bektaşis and Albanian Bektashis would be a positive development for the latter, if it could reinforce their defense against Wahhabi and other Sunni fundamentalist aggression, and as long as the historical development of the Bektashi Community, resulting in its effective "Albanization," is respected. Misguided attempts to return the center of Bektashi attention and activity to Turkey, in my opinion, will not and should not succeed. The same is, I believe, true of failed ventures to establish a link between the Albanian Bektashis and the Iranian Islamic regime. *Bektashism as we know it today is Albanian in heart, tongue, and writing, entirely European and Western in its outlook.*

As an element in this transnational movement toward spiritual liberation, the Albanian Bektashis share in the great responsibility of presenting what I have called "the other Islam" to the world. That is an Islam that despises misrulers, promotes mutual respect between believers in all religions, and cultivates the faith of the heart rather than falling into the trap of obsession with *shāri'ah* or *sheriat*. Bektashis recognize in *sheriat* no more than external ritual, comprising the first and least important step on the path from the ordinary observance of the believer through the higher stages of *ṭarīqahs* – collective spiritual discipline; *marifet* – esoteric wisdom, and *haqiqat* – understanding and fulfillment of unity with God in *vahdeti vuxhudi* – the unity of God's creation.

By contrast, fundamentalist Sunnis and Shias alike have made an idol – and I know how serious this charge must be – of the external religious rules of *shāri'ah*. This disastrous situation of "official" Islam today reminds one of the comment by the greatest Islamic theologian, Al-Ghazālī (c. 1058–1111 CE), the vindicator of Sufism. In his *Revival of Religious Sciences* or *Ihya Ulum Al-Din*, he derisively asked, "What makes you think that the science of the laws... is a science that prepares for the hereafter? He who studies these things to get closer to Allah is downright mad." In considering this, one should be aware that high praise was afforded to Al-Ghazali by Baba Rexheb.

As for the moral and spiritual challenge Bektashism offers to the world, it is best summarized by the declarations of the beloved Albanian poet Naim Frashëri, who wrote in 1896 in his "Bektashi Pages" (*Fletore e Bektashinjve*) as follows:

> Truth and justice, intelligence and wisdom, are supreme.
>
> The faith of the Bektashi is a broad Path lighted by wisdom, brotherhood, friendship, love, humanity, and all the virtues.

On one side are the flowers of knowledge, and on the other the flowers of truth…

Who does good, finds good; who does evil, encounters evil.

Who sins against humanity has joined the beasts…

Humanity is not bound, but free in all ways, and accountable for all actions…

But the human person has a mind which reasons, knowledge by which to make choices, a soul filled with recognition, a heart of discernment, and a conscience that weighs all deeds. This is all one needs – no other help is required. God has granted humanity everything…

The Bektashi Sufis take as the book of their religion the Universe, and especially humanity, because as Imam Ali said, 'The human being is a speaking book, faith is speech, but the ignorant add to it. Faith is in hearts, not in books'…

They who enter the Path leave all vices behind and retain only virtue. With an unclean heart, an evil soul, or a bad conscience, nobody can enter the company of the saints who achieve intimacy with God.

Here one must know the self, for whoever knows the self, knows God…

Brotherhood, peace, love, closeness to God, friendship, good conscience, and other virtues light the Path.

Above all things, love is the beginning and guidance of the Path (Frashëri n.d.).[2]

This essential message was reaffirmed in America in the 1950s when Baba Rexheb wrote, in a briefly-published periodical titled *Zëri Bektashizmës* (*Voice of Bektashism*), about the significance of Ashura and the martyrdom of Imam Huseyin. Baba Rexheb declared that the grandson of Muhammad was persecuted and slain because he defended a constitutional attitude toward religious rule, liberty, and the welfare of the people. Imam Huseyin, according to Baba Rexheb, "kept alive the flag of liberty, the prestige of religious democracy." The people rebelled against the injustices of their rulers and Imam Huseyin joined them in their protest, but the evil usurpers of authority replied with "terroristic actions." This anticipation by an Albanian Bektashi exile in America of the key questions in the relations between Islam and the West a half-century afterward is more than remarkable. The principle of "religious democracy" – meaning democracy *within* religion, not a democracy ruled by religion – is a great challenge to *shāri'ah*-driven conformity in Islam, and the description of Muslim tyrants maintaining their position by terror could be taken from the pages of any newspaper in the world today.

CONCLUSION

Eight centuries after the birth of Haci Bektaş Veli, Bektashism has arrived at a crucial moment for its spiritual inspiration and the humanity it honors. The literary works of Bektashis down to the present, epitomized by Baba Rexheb's volume *The Mysticism of Islam and Bektashism* no less than by Frashëri's *Bektashi Pages*, are impressive in their quantity, quality, eloquence, and lyricism. An authoritative inventory of Bektashi works in Albanian alone would be a major contribution to studies of Sufism.

According to the late Haxhi Dede Reshat Bardhi (1935–2011), supreme leader of the order, the Bektashis were commanded during World War II, after Hitler's armies took control of Albania from Italy in 1943, to save the small community of Albanian Jews, along with several thousand Jews who had fled there from elsewhere in Europe. Jews were hidden successfully, and Albania was the sole German-occupied state with more Jewish residents at the end of the war than at its beginning. Most of the Jews who had escaped to Albania then emigrated to Israel and other places. Albanian "Righteous Gentiles" have been recognized at Yad Vashem, the Holocaust memorial in Israel.

Today the Bektashis are free to teach their beliefs in Albania and Kosova, although they are repressed in Macedonia. Baba Rexheb's indispensable book has been republished in Albania and is widely read. In America, Baba Rexheb made a unique contribution to religious life, deserving of greater attention and study.

About the Author

Stephen Suleyman Schwartz is the Executive Director of the Center for Islamic Pluralism in Washington, DC (www.islamicpluralism.org) and author of the book *The Other Islam: Sufism and the Road to Global Harmony* (Doubleday, 2008). In 2002, he published the bestselling *The Two Faces of Islam: Saudi Fundamentalism and Its Role In Terrorism* (Doubleday, 2002). He is an Adjunct Scholar of the US-based Middle East Forum. During the 1990s he pursued an intensive study of Balkan comparative religion while working as a reporter for the *San Francisco Chronicle* and an editor for the Albanian Catholic Institute in San Francisco. He also completed missions in Bosnia-Hercegovina, Kosovo, Croatia, and Slovenia for the International Federation of Journalists, the Council of Europe, the US Agency for International Development (USAID), the International Crisis Group, the Soros Fund for an Open Society, the Friedrich Ebert Stiftung, the Konrad Adenauer Stiftung, the US Department of State, and the Tony Blair Faith Foundation.

Notes

1. Sources consulted but not cited are included in the References where some are annotated. This article draws extensively on my observations, conversations and time spent in Kosovo and elsewhere in the former Yugoslav republics and in Albania.
2. *Fletore e Bektashinje*, Kryegjyshit Botëror Haxhi Dede Reshat Bardhi. The English excerpt cited herein has been adapted by Stephen Schwartz. It was first published in F.W. Hasluck, *Christianity and Islam Under the Sultans* (Oxford: Clarendon Press, 1929).

SECTION III

A Middle Eastern Context (Iran)

4

SUFI POLITICS IN THE CONTEMPORARY WEST: THE ROLE AND DEFINITION OF SUFISM IN THE WORKS OF JAVAD NURBAKHSH (1926–2008)

Milad Milani

INTRODUCTION

Sufi ideas about altruism and universalism did not emerge in a vacuum. They were the result of specific local reactions to social and political pressures. Traditional Sufi groups are, in effect, extensions of regional movements centered around a charismatic mystic. However Sufi values are defined, Sufi psychological and spiritual morality evolved from a Qur'ānic base and adapted to the regions where the Sufi orders took root. Sufi organizational networks flourished within an increasingly politically fractured realm of Islam. They operated independently of each other, competed with one another for patronage, and regulated their own brand of Islamic morality. Much like the religio-political structure of the wider Muslim world in the era of the post-Rashidun, Sufism was similarly devoid of centralized agency. Beyond a handful of universal principles that broadly defined a Muslim way of life, everyday religiosity was subject to local peculiarities. All in all, there was nothing akin to an operational pluralistic or democratic ideal within the medieval Muslim world. Islam was the rule of the land, and the only religion worth considering, as far as Muslims and Sufis were concerned. In a contemporary setting, however, the reinterpretation of the principles of Sufism in the context of religious pluralism and political democracy gives rise to interesting alternatives to political Islam.

The Sufi publications of Javad Nurbakhsh during the 1990s are an excellent point of reference in this regard. Using this example, it will be argued that Sufism is not only defused, but that it is also, in the case of Nurbakhsh, active in the task of producing an alternative narrative in Islam. Trompf's study on "payback" and "retributive logic" among the cultures of Papua New Guinea (1994) provides valuable insight for a study of regional Sufism. The Sufism of Nurbakhsh works simiarly in an atmosphere of religious retribution. It is an egalitarian and liberal worldview wedded with his own morals of mysticism, which are a result of a charged socio-political atmosphere. Nurbakhsh serves a response or "payback", if you will, to the dominant narrative of Islamization. According to Bourdieu's Theory of Practice, Nurbakh's social action can be analyzed as being motivated by the affects of two forces that provide social agents with the impetus to act. Nurbakhsh is the product of the Iranian ethos, which is a densely layered historical landscape now saturated with Islamic sentiment. Through a reading of Bourdieu, the agency of Nurbakhsh's Sufism is driven by the quiet power of past experiences and unchecked beliefs that are continually reinvested into present actions. Also, that these same qualities of "habitus" give meaning to the social and political climate in which social agents – the adherents of Nurbakhshian Sufism – are located. Bourdieu's theory of "field structuring habitus" and "the contribution of habitus to field" is useful in a study of Sufism that seeks to define and locate Sufi values in the reciprocal relation of the individual to the social environment (Matton 2008: 51).

Contemporary Sufism expresses a healthy variety of attitudes within its own tradition that ranges from the traditional and conservative to the moderate and liberal e.g., from the traditional Qardiriya to the Universal ("new-age") Sufism of Inayat Khan. Sufis and Sufi groups, today, can be among those least receptive to change as well as sometimes seen to embrace (even instigate) social and ideological transformation. This chapter focuses on some elements of the writings of Javad Nurbakhsh (1926–2008), the late master of a newly defined Persian Sufi tradition, the Nimatullahi Khaniqahi Sufi order. In particular, this chapter will examine Nurbakhsh's adaptation of Sufi material for a more democratic Sufi outlook. Most importantly, the modern history of the Nimatullahiya, under Nurbakhsh's leadership (1953–2008) (self-exiled after the 1979 Revolution), demonstrates the strains of domestic politics upon liberal interpretation of Islam, and the need for Iranian Sufis to seek sanctuary within Western democratic societies.

THE IDEAL OF TOLERANCE

This work is specifically focused on the question of tolerance of the "other," in particular with reference to Sufism and the politics of power between the oppressed and oppressors. Sufism generally enjoys a positive representation in the West, popularized by Rūmī and "love" poetry. While Sufism is promoted as the "heart" of Islam, advocates of Muslim orthodoxy quite often see the nature of Sufi practice and its belief system as a contentious issue. For instance some of these concerns can pertain to the Sufis' devotion to the master of the path (*pir-e tariqat*), the idea of spiritual transformation (*fana va baqa*) or the incorporation of music or visual art.

Tolerance is a universal notion that has become almost synonymous with Western values and seen as a "virtue" of the good citizen harking back to the Socratic dialogues of Plato. The point of contention, however, concerns its practice within the societies that adopted its ideal. The Islamic civilization is not itself without this notion of universal tolerance, nor are its citizens free from its uses and abuses. Historically, Jews, Christians, and Zoroastrians were able to live in relative peace under Muslim rule during the Middle Ages, for example, across the Iberian Peninsula and many parts of the Near East and North Africa under Ayyubid rule, but also later in the early modern period during the reign of the Mughal. Still, the toleration of Muslim rulers had its limitations. Muslim attitude to foreign religions, for instance, varied across regions and reigns, and the Muslim propaganda of 'peace' cannot be idealized as a generally applicable policy. Yet it is fair to say that in either the case of Medieval Islamic civilization or Modern Western liberal democracy, the practice of tolerance, in those regions that implemented it, has always had its limits, and its conditions. In the case of Islam in the West, Muslims are welcome to become citizens and contribute to Western democratic societies, yet on some occasions, and to varying degrees, social and legal conditions restrict or prohibit their ability to express aspects of their cultural and religious identity in public life (for instance the banning of the burqa in France). In the case of Sufism in Iran, Sufis are welcome to practice Sufism so long as their practices and ideology, for example, does not contravene the regulations adhered to by the Islamist state theocracy. Rather than place this blame of the misuse of tolerance squarely on religion or even the societies that espoused it, it may be fair to say that tolerance is rather – in a Machiavellian sense – an inclination put into practice when it best suits those who apply it. It may also be said that as a political tool, the application of tolerance almost always serves the dominant party. This is to underline the politics of tolerance, and to approach it à la the master of suspicion, Bourdieu. The assertion can be made that such a perceived libertine notion may be seen as a strategic construction, invented by those that aim to incorporate it to fit a desired outcome. Pierre Bourdieu explained the critical role of 'capital' for social positioning. In *La Distinction* (1984) Bourdieu incorporates his example of "taste" to demonstrate cultural hegemony in the way that the meaning and value of what is considered *tasteful* determines "social distinctions." By extension, social policies can in a similar way be seen to enforce specific standards that are then strictly regulated.

This *tolerance of the other* is therefore seen in two ways: first, as a matter of perspective, in that some societies or communities can in fact afford to be tolerant, or at least appear to be so, more than others simply because it best serves their interests socially, politically, even economically. Secondly, that tolerance of the other is only of relevance from the point of view of those socially or politically marginalized, and completely disregarded by those in a position of absolute power. Trompf's "theory of retribution" (Trompf 1994), underlines the fact that judgment of the other and its associated reciprocations are an inescapable human behavior, albeit, as he explains in both its positive and negative forms throughout *Payback*. Indeed, reciprocity is fundamental to our social conditioning, visible from the remnants of the earliest codes of law and social conduct across archaic civilizations. Societies, and indeed religions, have been based on, and operate on the basis of, a systematic principal of a "price" that has to be paid either through revenge or recompense. It is therefore to be reminded that this fundamental principal of reciprocity "is endemic to humanity" (Trompf 1994: 2), to such extent that individuals are even unconsciously conditioned from childhood as to what is "right" and "wrong" based on the "gifts and withdrawals of parental affection."

SUFISM IN THE WESTERN CONTEXT: THE QUESTION OF PLURALISM AND DEMOCRACY

It is true, however, that the Media more often places the spotlight on hardliner and conservative Islam, while there are a greater majority of Muslims whose moderate-to-liberal worldview is ignored. Principal Islamic doctrine demonstrates an aptitude for far-reaching tolerance, whereby the act of reading the Qur'ān, becomes for Sufis, the contemplative exercise *par excellence*. Even so, it cannot be generally said that Islam is necessarily democratic or pluralistic in practice. This would be to impose a 'Eurocentric' view based on a sense for existing modern social democratic notions that do not have an historical basis in Islamic literature. Having said this, what can be attributed to the Muslim world is a long-standing oral tradition and implicit textual verification of egalitarian and communalist ideals. These in turn are linked to the "West" so to speak vis-à-vis the view that Islam is an ideological extension of the Abrahamic faiths that came before it.

Like the Muslim world, within which Sufism is nourished, the Sufi tradition inherits a rich diversity of views and positions from ultra-conservative to hyper-liberal manifestations. The history of Islamic societies reveals a plethora of religious interpretation across cultures and nations where Islam is either practiced or held as the official religion (see for example, Lapidus 2014). Muslim attitudes traditionally range from literalists to moderate to more liberal outlooks that compete for the representation of Islam. Sufism is one of the voices from within the global Muslim community that (quite often) represents the peaceful and tolerant face of Islam. Where political Islam is currently the version most familiar to contemporary Western imagination, Sufism is then typically seen as the tolerant alternative. This is a forced polarity, and one that is false. As problematic as it may be to draw such arbitrary distinctions, Sufism is the practice of an internal Islam, and as such it can be said that Sufis have traditionally preserved the core spiritual message of Islam, and that charismatic Sufi sheikhs have at times balanced the equation in the face of literalist Islamist views and currents of radicalization and fundamentalism within Islam.

The career of Javad Nurbakhsh is a good example of one such charismatic Sufi sheikh. Using his influence, Nurbakhsh managed to shift the direction of a largely conservative Nimatullahi attitude toward a secular project that stood in the face of dogmatic religious elements in Iran, and later abroad (Milani & Possamai 2016: 7). The Nimatullahi Sufi order is one of the oldest and largest Sufi orders in Iran. It is divided into three primary branches: Monawwar Ali Shahi, Safi Ali Shahi, and the Sultan Ali Shahi or Gonabadi.[1] Monawwar Ali Shahi branch of the Nimatullahi has a greater presence outside of Iran, though the Gonabadi branch is by far the largest and best known of the three within Iran. This is important since Javad Nurbakhsh is linked to Monawwar Ali Shahi "chain," and it is largely due to his efforts that the order has prospered and expanded in the West.

The Nimatullahi Sufi order, which takes its name from its founder, Shah Nimatullah Wali (1330–1431), is one of the major traditional Sufi orders that have successfully adapted to a Western context. The order is embedded in its cultural heritage, exemplifying the Persianate elements within it. During the turn of the millennium, the order had undergone internal upheaval as a result of a decision to rethink its connection with Islamic orthodoxy. Scholars have comfortably demonstrated that Sufism is a strictly Islamic phenomenon, born out of distinct Muslim ethos of the mid ninth-century, in an effort to accommodate external religious and cultural components absorbed through conversion to Islam. Having said this, however, the Nurbakhian interpretation picks up on contrived Orientalist narratives that favor a more exotic origin for Sufism, particularly that of Persia. It is well known that the first step for the aspiring Sufi is to enter Islam, but subsequent to the Islamic Revolution of Iran, and in anticipation of commotions connected to terrorist activities, Nurbakhsh moved to indiscriminately distinguish Sufism from Islam. Thus to his mind, the old ties with formal religion are to be broken, since it is implied that external religion leads to fundamentalism and narrowmindedness. He began to explore the lofty ideals of Sufism beyond the limitations of Islamic orthodoxy couched in a psychological understanding. There is a touch of the *new age* to this reinvention of Sufism by Nurbakhsh, but at its core, it is politically motivated, and aimed at ascertaining "capital" to balance the odds in favor of the oppressed. The "oppressed" are dissidents of the old regime that lost the socio-political battle to an overwhelming desire of the people to overthrow the Shah and his modernist project and install Khomeini as the leader of a legitimate Islamic state. In the West, therefore, the faction in favor of modernist and progressive ideals reformulated its identity under the banner of "Khaniqahi Nimatullahi" order. Nurbakhsh led it. This faction reached a wide global audience, ranging from UK, Europe, Russia, West (and South) Africa, to the United States and Australia. Nurbakhsh was successful in attracting both Iranian and non-Iranian adherents (Lewisohn 2006; Graham 1999; Quinn 1999).

THE SUFISM OF NURBAKHSH

Upon closer observation, Nurbakhsh presents a new form of Sufism, which is to be distinguished from New Age Religious Movements (NRMs) and neo-Sufi categrorizations. This is because Nurbakhsh retained the fundamental components of the Sufi tradition and maintained the core principles of Sufi teaching, and so he never modified the visible form of Sufi ritual by superimposing non-Sufic ideas or integrating religious synchretisms. His rendition was consistent with classical forms of Sufism, yet with one major exception. The production of this new form of Sufism was his adaptation of a Sufism without Islam, or, of mysticism without religion. There are two historical forces that merge in Nurbakhsh's reformulation of Sufism: the anitnomian tradition and the method of the "blame seekers" (*malamatiyya*). In this, Nurbakhsh's Sufism is a deviation from classical Sufism, which was religiously based. It should be noted that the presumption of Nurbakhsh is not without precedent, for it is based on a sentiment that is commonly found within the community of the faithful. It is that many rationalize an act of devotion, such as, kissing the hand of a sheikh or priest, an Icon, the floor of a mosque, and so on, in the following manner: it is not the items that are subject to the kiss but rather, what they represent. So it is that the faithful typically identify their act of devotion not for the sake of the religious item, but for the sake of God. It is in this simple example that the basis for Nurbakhsh's logic is found. This notion of a Sufism without religion will be expanded on below, but it should be said that regardless of Nurbakhsh's own inclinations about Sufi theology, or absence thereof, his ideas were never overtly or necessarily enforced as a *fait accompli*. Any trickle down effect of Nurbakhsh's ideas was generally adopted by members in a nuanced manner; they were mostly free to interpret Sufism in their own way, and to selectively practice traditional elements of formal Islam of their own choosing.

Nurbakhsh's Sufism needs to be understood in the light of the trajectory of thought that unfolds in the duration of his time as head of the Nimatullahi order. To appreciate this unveiling of his attitude toward religion, God and ultimately the Sufi path itself, it is important to take into account the variety of resources that are presently available. This work will draw on a selection of his books, a face-to-face exclusive interview recorded and published online and time spent among the Nimatullahis.[2] The research reveals the order to be represented by a moral spiritual "non-theism," a tendency to not disavow God, but rather preclusion to invoke for the sake of reaching its *truth* (Pourjavady 1978: 224–25). To qualify this "non-theism," in a number of instances Nurbakhsh has expressed that Sufism has nothing to do with religion (see Smith 2008a), and by extension the *God* of the Sufi similarly has nothing to do with the "God" of the biblical tradition (Nurbakhsh

1996: 32–34). I would therefore suggest the preferred definitional phrase for Nurbakhsh's Sufism might be "non-theism" as a qualifier to the more provocative "atheism;" also because of the fact that Nurbakhsh's writings are never without reference to God or a sense of God's presence behind the symbolic language he employs. The real legacy of Nurbakhsh seems to be his demarcation of Sufism from Islam. Sufism is portrayed as having parted ways with the Islamic religion long ago, a fact that Nurbakhsh is only now making explicit (see Forum 2007; Smith 2008a and b).

The works of Nurbakhsh, in particular, a number of his prominent discourses (1996), are heavily centered on the notion of chivalry or *javan-mardi*. Chivalry is a consistent theme through his writings through which the virtues of altruism are heavily promoted, often at the expense of religious praxis and conformism. At times, the faith-based element of his style of Sufism seems to be an unremitting faith in the "master" – recalling such lines from Hafez such as: *be mey sajjadeh rangin kon garat pir-e moghan gooyad* (stain the prayer rug with the wine should the master command you). Selections from his poems (see *Divan-e Nurbakhsh* in particular Feigning Negligence, Love's Bazaar, Love's Treasure etc.) reinforce the view that religion is a mere barrier to God, and that God is not that which is conventionally divulged by representatives of religion. In his *The Psychology of Sufism*, in particular, Nurbakhsh offers a highly technical psychological explanation of the process of spiritual transformation from a state of ego-centredness to spirit-consciousness without recourse to religion. Nurbakhsh's "theology," therefore, does not advocate the conventional view of the divine, but rather the divine as manifest in humane virtues. This is a central point in his Sufism, and it is powerfully demonstrated in his works through heavy dependence on the classic theme of self-realization that is arrived at through the complete destruction of the ego. Yet, this is to be understood, in the context of Nurbakhsh's Sufism, as a modification from classical Sufi ideas about the same process. For Nurbakhsh, the desctruction of the ego, in a post-classical setting, is layered with a special understanding about the ego being enmeshed in religious psychology, needing to be emancipated. In no uncertain terms, Nurbakhsh proclaims a Sufic humanism. The aim of Sufism, as Nurbakhsh proclaims it, is purely epitomized in civil etiquette (*adab*) and moral duty (*khedmat*) (Nurbakhsh 1996: 51), and this is consistently visible across his works.

The motivation behind Nurbakhsh's Sufism is the politics of the age, whereby his post-revolution work is a bid to maintain the sense of freedom of religion that was enjoyed prior to the Islamist regime. Nurbakhsh's circumstances were not the first of their kind in the history of Sufism. The founder of the Nimatullahi order, Shah Nimatullah Wali, to which Nurbakhsh is a claimant, was also forced into exile due to political pressures and the arousal of suspicions of heresy spurred by a rival Sufi faction (Graham 1999). The

Discourses (1996) therefore take pains to illustrate the frustration with religious authorities, and the means to offer individuals a degree of flexibility and accountability of conscience. For example, Nurbakhsh says: "The Sufi's love of God involves no expectation of reward or fear of punishment, for the Sufi does not have any wishes and demands" (Nurbakhsh 1996: 21). Again, "Righteous action refers to acting with no thought of merit of reward" (Nurbakhsh 1996: 16). The general tone of Nurbakhsh's progressive Sufism is for good reasons muffled in the publications, and need to be analyzed carefully in the light of other factors. However, his own position is gradually disclosed in diaspora as can be seen from the interview in 2008 and prior to this already visible in the Internet discussion threads about his decision to relinquish ties between Sufism and religion (Forum 2007).

At this level, then, Nurbakhsh breaks with the conventions of traditional Sufism in order to advocate modernism and progressive thought by demonstrating that Sufism is not only compatible with the "Western" project of modernity, but that it can disseminate its ideals. The Sufism of Nurbakhsh was no longer identified with decadent and intellectually languid forms of Sufism criticized by the likes of Ahmad Kasravi (Ridgeon 2006). It is true, as it is pointed out by scholars that Nurbakhsh's Sufism was catered to the members of the Tehran high society during a time when a certain type of liberal Sufism was becoming fashionable. He further capitalized on the foreign market of interest in the US and UK by setting up Khaniqahs abroad for those who had become interested in the order whilst living in Iran (Spellman 2004: 110). Indeed, he was broadly feeding into the emerging interest in Eastern spirituality in America and Western Europe specifically (Spellman 2004: 110). It is worth remembering that Nurbakhsh's *progressivism* is not original, but rather symptomatic of an emerging current of spiritualisms across the West. This brand of Sufism is, in effect, a reconstruction by Nurbakhsh for the contemporary age and facilitated the national agenda for education and social reform under the Shah's administration. The 1979 Revolution, and subsequent regime change, re-issued a conservative agenda, and interest fell to traditional and conservative Sharia-based Sufism, if at all, leaving Nurbakhsh in a vulnerable position. Of note is the fact that Nurbakhsh's Sufi project did not end with the Shah's modernization project. The local impetus was brought to the global stage, at least as far as the future of Sufism was concerned, by Nurbakhsh, as a follow through, and with a view to compose religion and society in the light of contemporary sensibilities.

CONCLUSION

The Sufism of Javad Nurbakhsh presents a counter intuitive view about Sufism at large. The experience of the Khaniqahi Nimatullahi in Iran offers an inversion to the view that Sufism is somewhat a pluralistic and democratic force *ipso facto*. The argument in this chapter has been that such revered attributes need to be examined within their proper socio-political context, and not viewed as the *sine quo non* of Sufism. The Sufism of Nurbakhsh clearly demonstrates the political underpinnings of liberal and democratic Sufi attitudes, and with it the importance of patronage and intentional alignment of ideals with broader social attitudes and political trends. Two important factors to consider here are first that the Sufism of Nurbakhsh represents the larger picture of Sufi groups that compete for political power within society. Nurbakhsh has many rivals among Sufi orders in Iran, some of whom contest his leadership as *qutb* (or spiritual head) of the entirety of the Nimatullahi tradition. Secondly, the subversive nature of Nurbakhsh's Sufism is informed by his contestation of oppressive state politics that has marginalized his faction. His style of Sufism forms part of the "retributive logic" that is reactionary, but that it enacts the crucial function of "payback" in outlining a politics of the oppressed. Returning to the question of tolerance, it is interesting to recall the Trompfian "theory of retribution," urging the question as to who is the truly tolerant. There is no doubt that the Sufism of Nurbakhsh stands for an ideal rejected by the Iranian theocracy; yet his view is equally prejudiced and constrained by its own paradigmatic flaws. The preoccupation with difference becomes a luxury that the world can perhaps no longer afford. This was an observation made by Trompf in *Payback* some 20 years ago now, and it echoes the core concerns shared in this work: "the world is bleeding to death through misunderstanding over such cultural basic as revenge and concession" (Trompf 1994: 13).

About the Author

Milad Milani is a researcher and Lecturer of Religion at Western Sydney University, Australia. He is also a Member of the Religion and Society Research Cluster, and convenes units of study in the History, International Studies and Politics (HISP) and Islamic Studies majors in the University's School of Humanities and Communication Arts. Formally trained in the multi-disciplinary field of religious studies, Milani is interested in the study of religious beliefs, behaviors, and institutions. He specializes in the area of Sufi historiography and hermeneutics. Milani is the author of *Sufism in the Secret History of Persia* (London: Routledge 2014) and also has a forthcoming manuscript with Routledge, *Sufi Political Thought* (forthcoming 2017).

Notes

1. The second largest order in Iran is the Kawthariyyah order, which has millions of followers in Azarbaijan. See, Nasrollah Pourjavadi and Peter Lambert Wilson, *The Kings of Love: The Poetry and History of the Ni'matullahi Sufi Order* (Tehran: Imperial Iranian Academy of Philosophy, 1978).

2. See also Milad Milani and Adam Possamai, "Sufism, Spirituality and Consumerism: the Case Study of the Nimatullahiya and Naqshbandiya Sufi Orders in Australia," *Contemporary Islam: Dynamics of Muslim Life*, Online (2016) available at http://dx.doi.org/10.1007/s11562-015-0335-1

SECTION IV

South Asian Contexts: Bangladesh, Indonesia and Pakistan

5

ANTI-SAINT OR ANTI-SHRINE? TRACING DEOBAND'S DISDAIN FOR THE SUFI IN PAKISTAN

Charles M. Ramsey

INTRODUCTION

Today it is broadly accepted as axiomatic that the Deobandi in Pakistan are unequivocally antagonistic towards sufism. But how can this be when the founders of the eponymous *Dar ul-'ulum* were themselves prominent leaders in Sufi orders (*tariqa*)?

Established as a grassroots movement for religious education in the wake of the 1857 Sepoy Rebellion in India, the Deoband *'ulama* continue to flourish and to carry the mantle of "custodians of change" with increasingly activist vigour (see Zaman 2004). What are the repercussions of this growth, and how does this contribute to an understanding of the complex interrelation of sufism, pluralism, and democracy?

Much of the present literature on the Deobandi, or those with an expressed affinity with this sect (*firqa*), proceeds from sociological and historical methodologies and has not given sufficient attention to the theologically nuanced beliefs that unite this cohort. One result of this is that the movement is characterized as oppositional both to their mystical heritage and to shrine based devotionalism. An examination of the complex subdivisions within the group draws attention to the present theological fault lines and allows for a more textured understanding of their perceived disdain for the "Sufi."

It is necessary to reiterate from the start that the Deobandi are not a homogenous group. Earlier studies, like those by Muhammad Qasim Zaman, Arshad Alam, and Yoginder Sikand, have noted this but stopped short of qualifying this observation. Contextual differences in the sect, as expressed in Pakistan and India for example, are frequently mentioned as a caveat, but I know of no efforts to examine the internal differentiations. Thus, I proceed with the premise that the identification of such markers is necessary to make sense of the seemingly paradoxical experience of persons self-described as Deobandi but who participate in the devotional practices of Sufi shrines. In these pages we will draw from the vernacular literature, preaching, and digital media to map the taxonomy currently applied to different types of Deobandis in Pakistan.

In contemporary discourse those affiliated (formally or not) with Deoband are divided into two broad categories: Hayati (alive) and Mamati (dead). The nomenclature indicates the divisive issue as pertaining to the physical condition and abilities of holy persons after death. More directly stated: do prophets remain alive in the grave? Is there an enduring connection between their soul and the entombed corpse? The question raises a series of theological questions, but these revolve around a central issue: the efficacy of intercession (*shafa'a* and *tawassul*). Although this terminology has crystalized over the past 20 years, it is reflective of preceding theological differences and so we will begin our study by identifying these. We then proceed to clarify some of the diversity encompassed within the Deobandi grouping in order to note that the vast majority of these in Pakistan are neither anti-saint nor anti-shrine, though they share clear expectations of what devotion to these must not entail. We then conclude with some observations concerning the political implications of this group's increased popularity and social influence.

WITHIN THE CONTEXT OF RELIGIOUS REVIVALISM

The Deoband movement is now one of the most significant strands of Sunni Islam in the world. The loosely affiliated grassroots network of schools has become synonymous with traditionalist resurgence and resistance to Western cultural dominance and its accompanying knowledge economy (see Metcalf 1984). Metcalf's study of the school's 1866 inception has stimulated continuous academic interest and this has been strengthened by more recent work like those of Zaman and Ingran. Of particular interest is their respective studies of the schools' founders, like the writings of Rashid Ahmad Gangohi (d. 1905), Muhammad Qasim Nanautawi (d. 1880), and subsequent luminaries such as Khalil Ahmad Saharanpuri (d. 1927) and Ashraf 'Ali Thanwi (d. 1943) (see Ingram 2009, Sikand 2002: 2–12, Zaman 2007). Our central interest here is to elucidate the opinion of the Deoband *'ulama* concerning the practices and beliefs demonstrated at the shrines of revered Sufi masters (*'awliya*) who embody the mystical facets of Islam (*tasawwuf*).

It is important to note that there are those who dismiss the mystical heritage known broadly as Sufism as not authentically Muslim. But as Carl Ernst has aptly summarized, this is "little more than a political exercise based on contemporary culture clash" (Ernst 1996: 3). My aim is not to deny a historical conflict between juridical (*shari'ah*) and spiritual (*tariqa*) tendencies in Islam, but rather to emphasize that the border between these is porous. Care must be given that historiography not over-simplify the opposition between the Sufi and the Shari' for these have traditionally functioned as two sides of the same coin. As Shahzad Bashir succinctly observed, "Sufism forms an integral and crucial part of the complex intellectual and social landscape [of pre-modern India]" (Bashir 2011: 10, 13). Islam in South Asian is inextricably colored by Sufism. This is incontestably the case with the founders of the madrasa in Deoband, and this remains clearly stated in their formal creed *'Aqaid 'ulema-i Deoband*:

> It should be known that we, as was the case of our teachers (*mashaykh*), adhere to the branches (*farohat*) of tradition schools of jurisprudence (*muqallid*) through Abu Hanifa, the principles and beliefs of Abul Hasan Ashari and Abu Mansur Maturidi, and to the lineage (*tariqa*) and methods of the Naqshabndiyya, Chistiyya, Qadriyya, Suhrawardiyya (Saharanpuri 1907).

Simply put, it is impossible to disambiguate the influence of *tasawwuf* from the study of Islam in South Asia in general, or from the study of the Deobandi movement in particular.

How is it then that the Deoband *'ulama* have come to represent juridical opposition to Sufism, and particularly to the devotional practices in shrines? To understand such developments we must first place the movement against the backdrop of religious revivalism in pre-partition India. We will see that although formal allegiance to Sufi *tariqa-s* has decreased among the *Ahle Sunnah wal jamat*, both the Deobandi and Barelvi schools carry forward the central elements of *tasawwuf* and the underlying theological assumptions. In this light, the Deobandi continue to thrive as post-*tariqa* expressions of Sufi Islam: they are Sufis reforming Sufism.

The origins of the movement must be seen against the backdrop of developments underway in the social and intellectual environment. "In the late Indian medieval period," as Anna Suvorova has convincingly argued, "the idea that the only role of a saint is intercession before Allah and, consequently, that of only a link in the chain of healing, was forgotten" (Suvorova 1999: 12). There were many issues, but the heightened glorification of the saint was of central concern because for many this reeked of polytheism. In the absence of an institutionalized *'ulamā'*, like that of the Ottomans for example, religious leaders such as Shaykh Ahmad Sirhindī (d. 1624), the "juridic Sufi master" sought ways to redirect the community away from a universalist trajectory and towards a more reified practice of Islam.[1] Sirhindī's Naqshbandiyya followers emphasized dogma (*'aqā'id*) and defined principles (*asūl-i sharī 'a*) derived from *sunnah* as the required remedy. Although there are many heirs to this spiritual and intellectual lineage such as Shāh Walī Allāh (d. 1762), the ubiquitous father of Indian revivalism, for our purposes here we underscore the importance of Shah Isma'il, Sayyid Ahmad Barelvi, and the Indian Mujahidin because of their efforts to put these ideas into action as an idealized political system.

This has immediate implications for our study here because the reform of shrine based spirituality was of central concern to the Mujahidin. As most clearly seen in *Taqwiyyat al-iman*, Shah Isma'il (d. 1831) was extremely critical of the excessive veneration of anyone other than Allah as sin of association (*shirk*), be he saint (*'awliya*) or even Prophet. Yet, although the Mujahidin came down heavily on shrine-based worship, it is vital to note that their leaders were actively Sufi. Barelvi's principle means for legitimizing leadership was to recount his spiritual authority derived through the *muraqaba* attained through initiation in the four leading Sufi *tariqa-s*: Naqhsbandiyya, Chīshtiyya, Qādriyya, and Suhrawardiyya. As Mahmud Hussein has convincingly argued, the movement drew from powerful and recognized Sufi idioms in order to redirect devotion away from the cult of the local saint and toward the direct veneration of God through the emulation and intercession of the Prophet. This was reform of Sufism by Sufis.

Challenges to local beliefs and practices, however, were met with stiff opposition from the entrenched nobility who were themselves relatives and beneficiaries (*mutawalli*) of the shrine system (see Haroon 2007: 43; Sanyal, 1996: 204–14). It is essential to comprehend that the entombed saints are regarded as mediators of divine blessing and knowledge (Liebeskind 1998: 226). The Sufi master is "hyper corporeal," and he "spreads himself through time and space in order to protect multitudes of disciples (*murids*)" (Bashir 2011: 187). Such exalted authority became a natural means for social influence, and it was not long before the substance of religious authority became a primary means for temporal power (Haroon 2007: 38). State patronage reinforced this social authority and enlarged its wealth. The *mutawalli* functioned (and continue to do so) as an intermediary elite with the power to legitimate both temporal and spiritual leadership, and to connect political leaders with large swathes of people (Gilmartin 1984: 39–42; Eaton 2003: 267). This dynamic continues to play out today in Pakistan, even as the balance gradually shifts towards an activist *'ulama'* who can leverage power in favor of their own social clientele (Alam 2006: 175–77).

The war of 1857 sets the stage for the formal beginning of the Deoband movement. In the wake of the "revolt," punitive measures were taken against the Muslim community in general, but against the *'ulama'* in particular Jaffer (1981).[2] Some like Sayyid Ahmad Khan integrated into the government systems of the British Raj, but others like Naunatwi and Gangohi, the founders of Deoband, resisted and were intent on promoting a parallel society that would preserve and sustain a communal leadership structure. As Metcalf observed, in the absence of wealthy patrons – the established nobility and estate owners – Deoband would have to create "a new clientele composed of ordinary lay Muslims who would fund this *madrasa* as well as be its social base" (Metcalf 1984: 97). Although space does not permit a larger description of their vision and works, it is important to reiterate that these were Sufis, and that they have overtly carried forward the mantle of juristic Sufism from the preceding generations.

But is this the case today? The answer to this question depends on the definition of Sufism. Although there has been an obvious distancing between the Deobandi *'ulama'* and both formal initiation in Sufi orders (*tariqa*/silsillah) and certain practices of shrine based spirituality, Deobandis continue to draw from the same sources of authority as its founders. To address this question we now turn to some of the differences prevalent in the movement today. Here we reaffirm that the group is not monolithic: there is considerable diversity of response towards the various facets of spiritual belief and praxis. First we will explain that there is a spectrum, and then indicate how this serves to clarify the main camps within the Deobandi movement in Pakistan. Then, from within these we will draw particular attention to those that most virulently oppose "Sufism" and seek to understand what this entails. In this way we can question how a theological movement whose founding leaders were Sufi could mutate into its antithesis, at least in some popular understandings.

DIVERSITY WITHIN THE CAMP: WHAT DOES IT MEAN TO BE DEOBANDI?

To place our study in proper perspective, it is worth noting that nearly one third (over 484 million) of the world's 1.57 billion Muslims live in South Asia. Of the four historical schools of jurisprudence (*madhab*), the largest grouping in Pakistan is the Hanafi, which draws from the authority of Abū Ḥanīfah, or Nuʿmān ibn Thābit ibn Zūṭā ibn Marzubān (d. 772 in Baghdad). Although a thorough contrast cannot be made here due to space constraints, the other major Hanafi group is known as the Barelvi, named after the home of its founder Ahmed Raza Khan (d. 1921). This school is unapologetically Sufi and has continued some of the devotional practices that the Deobandis oppose. There is also a significant group called the Ahl-e Hadith, which does not conform to one particular school (*ghair muqalid*). Each of these traces its roots back to the legacy of Shah Wali Allah and his influential sons and students, and as such they provide a spectrum of positions that are differentiated by the manner in which divine grace is presently accessible.

Sunni mosques in South Asian population centers tend to self differentiate among these three schools of interpretation (*firqa*). Though accurate statistics are lacking, it appears that the Barelvi remain numerically larger, though Deoband has produced a greater number of leaders (*imams*) and the balance is shifting. According to Tariq Rahman's study charting the growth between 1988 and 2002 in Pakistan, enrolment in Deoband *dini madaris* has completely outpaced all other Sunni competitors. There was exponential growth across the board, but Deoband saw the most dramatic exponential growth from 1779 to over 7000 and there are no signs of abatement. This trend can be seen in all provinces, but growth in the Punjab outstripped all others. To place this into perspective, according to a 2002 report by Pakistan Human Rights Commission, over 250,000 of a total of 600,000 students in the Punjab are enrolled in *dini madaris* rather than private or public education (Jaffrelot 2015: 544–46). This statistic is important because it indicates that our subject concerns far more than the 'mercenary *madaris*' of the Afghan frontier, but rather represents what is increasingly the garden variety Muslim in Pakistan. In other words, the group discussed here, the Deobandi, is one of the largest and most dynamic groupings within Sunni Islam.

THE CURRENT TAXONOMY

As noted above, in contemporary discourse the Deobandi are divided into two broad categories: Hayati (alive) and Mamati (dead). The nomenclature indicates that the division is primarily derived from beliefs pertaining to the physical condition of the Prophet Muhammad after death. The central question, as Sheikh Muhammad Yasir explains, is whether persons remain alive in the grave, or not? "Is there an enduring connection between the soul and the entombed corpse"?[3] And, if one is alive, then can the person interact with those in the present physical world? The answer for the Hayati is: yes. The Prophet actively intercedes for persons. As he received the *durud* from angels traveling to his grave in Makkah, he mobilizes divine grace on their behalf. This raises the subsidiary question of whether this status of hyper-corporeality is divinely ordained to Muhammad alone, or has it been granted to all prophets, or also to holy persons such as the caliphs and saints (*'awliya*). The Hayati view is representative of the traditional Hanafi (*Ahle Sunnah wal Jamaat*) belief. These believe that persons remain alive and conscience in the grave, even while enjoying different degrees of access to the intermediary realm (*barzakh*). The Mamati, however, vehemently disagree and claim that death creates a division between these realms that cannot be crossed. The normative Deobandi view, as recorded in the creed (*aqidah*) is that of the Hayati. However, the steady increase of support for the Mamati position over the past decades indicates that disagreement on the issue of intercession has become a major faultline within the movement.

As is the case of most theological debates, there is textual support for both positions within the Qur'ān and Hadith. In the Qur'ān, references to intercession occur mainly in negative terms. The Day of Judgment, for example, is described as a day on which no intercession will be accepted (2:48, 23; 74:48–9; 82:19). We read there, "Guard yourselves against a Day when no soul will stand in place of another, no intercession will be accepted for it, nor any ransom; nor will they be helped (2:48)." And again, "You who believe, give from what We have provided for you, before the Day comes when there is no bargaining, no friendship, and no intercession (2:54)." However, it is also stated that intercession is exclusively the domain of Allah. It is recited in Al-Zumar (39:44), "Say, 'All intercession belongs to God alone; He holds control of the heavens and the earth; in the end you will all return to Him'." There are also passages indicating that intercession is possible by divine permission (20:108–9; 2:254–5). Thus while intercession belongs solely to Allah, it is apparent that this may be extended through certain exalted persons (10:3; 20:109; 21:28; 19:87; 34:23; 4:64 12:97–8). Indeed Surah al-Ma'idah (Q5:35) seems to encourage one to seek such intercession: "O you who believe! be careful of (your duty to) Allah and seek means (*wasilla*) of nearness to Him and strive hard in His way that you may be successful." Historically, the majority Sunni view is that the Prophet's intercession (*shafa'ah*) on Judgement Day is the key to eternal bliss.

The Mamati, like the Salafis, hold that it is sinful to seek intercession from those who are no longer alive. They regard such belief as tantamount to polytheism (*shirk*). As Sarfraz Khan Safdar wrote in *Taskin us-sadur*, "The grave is empty, there is no one there... if the grave of any prophet is opened then the onlookers will see the prophet without any sense of feeling and without any movement" (Khan 2010: 37). This is a view shared by a significant cadre of contemporary Deobandi *'ulama* spread across the provinces of Pakistan. Some of the most notable include Maulana Ghulam Allah Khan, Mufti Muhammad Tahir, Nur Muhammad, Qazi Shamsuddin, Pir-i Tariqat Sayyid Inayatullah Shah Bukhari, and Muhammad Ameer Bandealwi. As to the issue of intercession these regard the tomb not as a nexus of spiritual power, but rather as a memorial for the departed. The deteriorated corpse is all that remains because the "soul" has departed to another realm. This is a rejection of the corporeality of the deceased, and of their ability to intervene in the affairs of this present age. To invoke the dead is to speak to an idol; it is harmful addition (*bi'da*) to Islam, and the practice should be avoided lest it cause confusion and erroneous belief (*fitna*).

Nida-i haqq by Muhammad Hussain Neelvi is a key source for ascertaining the Mamati contentions. Neelvi takes to task eminent Deobandi luminaries like Rafi 'Uthmani (brother of Taqi 'Uthmani) and Amin Safdar Okarwi for being "too close to Barelvi: you became Sufis, you worship graves" (Neelvi n.d.: 18–19.)[4] He emphasizes four particular points of contention: the location and condition of the spirit after death (*hayat ar-ruh*); the permissibility of listening to the dead (*sama' muat);* the intercession of others (*tawassul*); and, the relation of the soul and the body after death (*azab-i qabr*). He is adamant that the dead depart to another realm and cannot intercede.

> To attempt to listen or invoke them is to place faith upon that which is other than Allah. To seek this intercession is to deviate from the clear teachings of the founders of Deoband, who directly opposed this Barelvi view and practice (Neelvi nd: 2010).

The "Sufi," by this definition, is one who believes in the viability of the deceased and the intervention of the departed in the affairs of the living. The belief in intercession, and the practices with seeking mediation are singled out as the central difference, the focus of their disdain.

However, as already noted above, the majority Deoband position is that of the Hayati. This is not unexpected in light of the strong ties of the founders to Sufi *tariqas* and particular shrines as was normative in South Asian Islam. With regard to the belief in intercession, the Hayati claim that the Deoband founders were unambiguously clear that holy persons remain alive in the grave and are able to intercede for the living. The foundational source most often cited is *Al-muhannad ala al-mufannad* by Khalil Ahmad Saharanpuri, which has been translated in Urdu as *'Aqaid 'ulema-i Deoband* (the creed of the scholars of Deoband) or simply as *'Aqaid ahle sunnah* (the Sunni creed):

> It should be known that we, and our teachers (*mashaykh*), conform (*muqallid*) to the branches (*farohat*) [of traditional authority] of Abu Hanifa, the principles (*asulon itiqadat*) of Abul Hassan Ashari and Abu Mansur Maturidi, and to the linked paths (*tariqa intessab*) of the Naqshabandiyya, Chistiyya, Qadriyya, Suhrawardiyya. We do not accept anything without reference to Qur'ān, sunnah, *ijma*, or statement (*qol*) of an Imam (Saharanpuri 1907: 8).

Furthermore, as Saharanpuri proceeds to explain, this is in accordance with the chain of authorized guidance:

> For us, and our *mashaykh*, it is permissible in prayer to seek intercession from prophets, saints (*'awlya*), martyrs (*shahid*), and the righteous (*siddiqain*) during their life or after death… [In this], by the mediation (*wasilla*) of an esteemed person (*fulan buzurgh*), the acceptance and efficacy of your prayers to Allah may increase (Saharanpuri 1907: 31).

The authority of the 1907 text is attested by no less than 18 *'ulama'* of the Masjid Haramain (Makkah); and more recent editions include signatories from the highest echelons including Muhammad Yusuf Banauri, Abdul Haq Haqqani of Akhor Khattak (JUI-S), Muhammad Sadiq of Bahawalpur, Zafar Ahmad 'Uthmani of Sindh, Shamsul Haq (President, Vafaq ul-madaris al-Arabiyya Pakistan, Muhammad Idris (Jamia Ashrafiyya Lahore), and Mufti Muhammad Shafi (father of Taqi 'Uthmani of Dar ul-'ulum Karachi). These are the most senior *dini madaris* leaders in the nation. This is incontestably the standard and mainstream Deoband position.

5 Anti-saint or anti-shrine? 111

The attestations are important because the Mamati argue that the founders' position has been misrepresented. One reason for this is that the founders are assumed to carry the mantle of Shah Isma'il and to be on a mission to establish the domain of true faith by expunging harmful innovation (*bi'da*) (for a summary of these points see Isma'il·(Isma'il 1924: 14–17). The rationale is that Gangohi linked *bid'a* with *shirk*, the sin of association. This can occur in three ways: a practice that opposes *sunnah*; a practice done with the similar purpose or consistency as *sunnah*, though it is not included within the remit; or by conflating the permissible with the obligatory. The application of this definition has been applied to forbid a number of activities, festivals, and traditions, which though not mentioned in Hadith, are regarded as harmful. As Ingram explained, Gangohi was averse to a range of practices, including the adorning of certain clothing, not because these are forbidden in Islam, but because they reflect a confusing affinity with other traditions, whether Hindu, Jewish, or Christian. These practices are deemed as *fitna*, and are "*haram*" and "acts of unbelief (*kufr*)" (Ingram 2009: 483).

This position with regards to intercession, however, is difficult to sustain against clear statements made by other founders that present a far more dynamic relationship between the deceased and those who remain. Qasim Nanautvi, for example, explicitly addresses this issue in stating:

> Concerning the issue of the present life of the Prophet, the elders of Deoband are unanimous in this pronouncement. Concerning the Holy Prophet (pbuh) and all revered prophets, the elders of Deoband believe that these remain alive in their graves; and their holy bodies (*abdani muqadsa*) remain safe; and their elements (*ansar*) are in the realm of *barzakh* in a state similar to that of this world, the only difference is that they are no longer bound to the principles of shar'iah, but they pray (*namaz*), and the *darud* prayed during the holy fasts are heard without the necessity of mediation. This is the consensus of the hadith scholars (*muhadisn*) and theologian (*mutakalamim*) of the Ahle sunna wa jamat Khan 2010: 37–39).

This founder again sustains the view that holy persons remain alive and responsive from within the grave. In his depiction the grave functions as a portal to the intermediary realm of *barzakh*; the soul remains connected with the body and responsive to the living. It is for this reason that Deobandi stalwarts like Ibn al-Hassan 'Abbasi have concluded that,

> it is right (*jaiz*) to seek intercession (*wasilla*) from the Holy Prophet and the righteous elders (*buzurghon*); it is meritorious (*sawab*) to go on pilgrimage to the grave of the Holy Prophet; and it is meritorious and right to request intercession (*shafa'at*) and to petition (*istagasa*) the Prophet for justice, or to cry out to someone other than Allah (for greater detail see Nanautivi 1992).

In summary, although the body remains confined to the vicinity of the tomb in the present world, the soul of the righteous remains active and mobile within another realm. This is not limited to the exalted, but includes even the less righteous who can avoid the stifling darkness of the grave and have a window opened to the other realm through the prayers of others. The prevalent view is that all believers who have committed sins must undergo temporary punishment after death, but that all Muslims are destined to eventually enter paradise. The question then is how best can this punishment can be remitted or shortened. As we will consider below, reflection on this subject is helpful both for understanding theological trends but also for establishing a more nuanced understanding of the spectrum of ideas currently under discussion, but also in defining the broad category of Sufism.

SUB-CATEGORIES

Within the majority Hayati group, there are also sub-categories. One major distinction therein is that between the Farohi (lit. branches) and the Asuli (lit. root, or principle). The term Farohi does not pertain to an organized faction, but rather is a descriptor applied to those that do not ascribe to a defined set of principles for reifying Sunnah. These adhere to a variety of opinions – like the branches of a tree – for determining what specifically is required in the multifarious activities of daily life such as what to wear, how to groom, where to pray, and what to do at a shrine. The Asuli, on the other hand, derive a set of principles from the commentaries and teachings on Sunnah of the leading Deoband scholars to establish prescribed norms. Authorized traditions (*khabar*) of the Prophet and of the *rashidun*, the first four caliphs, once deemed as conclusively authentic (*hujjat*), are accepted as Sunnah and accepted as revealed guidance (*wahy ghayr matlu*).

The determinant power of these principles becomes more clear in light of a further distinction between the Asuli, that of the Tanzihi and Takfiri. The vast majority of those associated with the Deoband movement can be categorized as Tanzihi, including each of the Hayati representatives listed above. The descriptor is self-styled by *'ulama*, and it refers to their emphasis upon correct behavior. These take a hard line against *fitna*, that is disorder, error and sinful activity.[5] The Takfiri (from *kufr*) share the concern, but carry this name because of the willingness to declare someone as no longer Muslim because of a particular issue. Maulana Fazulllah of the Taliban and Shah Abdul Azziz of Lal Masjid in Islamabad, to name two of many possible examples, claim that to depart from Sunnah, the conclusive guidance ascertained from the established principles, is to commit *kufr buwa* and to depart from Islam (Sial 2012: 10–15). This is a highly sensitive issue in traditional jurisprudence that is never taken lightly particularly because the verdict can carry the penalty of death. Once someone is declared to be openly opposed to Islam (*kufr buwah*), then the burden of explanation shifts to why they should not be killed rather than spared. Hence, Tanzihi and Takfiri opinion on intercession may be identical, but these differ in response to the implications of disagreement. According to my respondents, the Hayati Takfiri regard the Mamati not as misinformed, but rather as *kufr* because they reject the guidance of Sunnah on the issue of intercession.

This leads to a final difference observable among the mainstream Hayati Tanzihi. This is the difference between the Mutashadat and Mutadil. The former will seek to implement the required behavior with force if necessary, whereas the latter seek to "lovingly" convince others of the necessity of compliance to a particular belief or practice as necessary for Muslim fidelity. Highly recognized public figures like Tariq Jameel of the Tablighi Jamaat and Siraj al-Haq of Jamaat-e Islami, for example are Mutadil, and this also includes the vast majority of *'ulama* serving in a government capacity, whether in the *awqaf* or in government mosques.

In order to further clarify these descriptive terms, it is helpful to consider the issues pertaining to a visit, for example, to the Datta Sahib shrine in Lahore. This is one of the most frequented in the region, and one is certain to encounter a large number of Hayatis on a visit there. Of course, these will not approve of visitors who partake in hallucinogens or hashish, or who dance and play drums (*dhol*) in order to invoke some form of ecstacy. The entombed saint, though revered, is not to be worshiped, so songs and prostrations should clearly be directed to Allah alone. They will not approve of those that kiss the shrines, nor will they like those who bow or prostrate towards the marble tomb. They will certainly abstain from such activity. However, one will lay flower wreaths on the grave, and perhaps purchase an ornate sheet (*chador*) that was laid over the tomb or request an amulet (*tawiz*) from one of the initiates. He will be happy that the shrine is divided into male and female sections so that modesty (*purdah*) can be protected, and will likely have explained all of this to those accompanying on the visit. He also may seek opportunities at the shrine to preach and instruct others in these matters. Some will even dedicate multiple days to this task as a form of religious service so that others can benefit from correction. The Takfiri, on the other hand, will regard those who break these rules as incomplete Muslims, and like the Tanzihi Mutashadat will most likely not seek confrontation in such an established venue. In smaller shrines though, or in areas where they have greater control, these may indeed intimidate or attack the shrine or its leadership in order to communicate the severity of illicit behavior. All of these, however, while firmly believing that the correct procedures should be followed, will seek the intercession of the saints and the Prophet to support their petitions to Allah for success and eternal bliss for themselves and their loved ones, both living and departed.

THE PARADIGM APPLIED

A presentation of the descriptors applied among the Hayati is indicative of diversity within the tradition. It also draws attention to the varying degrees of severity by which different persons go about implementing the demands of faith. However, belief in the corporeality of the prophets and saints, and the blessing of their propinquity, remains a commonality amongst the majority of Deobandis. Further, this is a commonality shared with the Barelvi. This observation generates an important question: if there is agreement on such a central issue, why then is there such animosity between these two camps?

The differences are subtle but important. The Hayati concern is that the clear guidance of Qur'ān and Sunnah not be diluted by an effused spirituality that might come close to worship of the person, whether saint or prophet. As Maulana Rafi Uthmani, Grand Mufti of Pakistan and Director of Darul 'ulum Karachi, explained in his open letter to the Barelvi in 2009, "Deobandi and Barelvi schools agree upon the fundamental principles and sources of Islamic law...the nature of the Deobandi's conflict with the Barelvis concerns the ways of implementing of rules and laws" (Hayat 2012: 18–19). In this estimation, the problem is not belief but boundaries. Behavior and belief, even that passed down through revered *mashaykh*, must be sieved through the Sunnah and Qur'ān. The Hayati guard against the exaggerated exaltation of a saint's power – and of the heirs who carry this grace – to a greater degree than their Barelvi counterparts.

Underlying these differences is an enduring philosophical difference on the "Unity of Being" (*wahdat al wujud*) and the pre-existent "light of Muhammad" (*nur-i Muhammadiyya*). Though some western literature projects these as peripheral and outdated, this is not the case for much of South Asia. As Tahir Tanoli, Director of the Iqbal Academy in Lahore, has explained: "Belief in the 'unity of being' (*wahdat al-wujud*) was seen as obligatory for all Muslims" (Tanoli 2013: 202–204).[6] The Persianate world accepted Ibn al-'Arabi's doctrine of *tawhid* as axiomatic. This paradigm provided the forum to consider and experience the interrelation of the Creator and the created. However, there are diverse perspectives on what *tawhid* actually entails. This was the case for Shah Wali Allah and his Nashbandiyya Sufis, and it is the case amongst the *'ulama* today. What these share in common is the realization that the utter differentiation between the Creator and creation, or 'master' and "servant," is a logical impossibility. Belief in the efficacy of intercession in the present world, by persons dead or alive, infers that the divine attributes remain active in the cosmos and can – in some way – be wielded as embodied grace.

The central conflict, however, is not between the Hayati and Barelvi, but rather between these and the Mamati. There is a growing effort, whether from the Ahl-i Hadith or Wahhabi, to invalidate this view of intercession.

One way that the Hayati and Barelvi have pushed back is through the rhetoric pertaining to the honour of the Prophet. On the 40th day (*chalea*) after Mumtaz Qadri's execution, for example, there were mass movements to demand that he be beatified as a national hero for assassinating Governor Salman Taseer. As Syed Hamad Ali has explained, though it may seem counterintuitive, this was not a move to overthrow the government but rather to establish the severity of tampering in any way with matters pertaining to the exalted status of the Prophet. "The Barelvis have for years been touted in certain western and liberal Pakistani circles as the more moderate answer to Saudi-exported Wahhabi or Salafi versions of Islam," he writes, "[but] in fact, the Barelvis came out more fiercely than others in condemning the death sentence to Qadri. This is due to their supposedly stronger attachment to the Prophet Muhammad."[7] Although a blasphemy case has not been brought as of yet against the Mamati, this is not altogether beyond the realm of possibility. In essence, the contestations between the Barelvi and Deobandi, and with their opponents, revolve around the degree of devotion to be given to the Prophet of Islam.

IMPLICATIONS FOR POLITICAL SOCIETY

What does this mean for society and governance? First it is imperative to note that the term "Sufi" in Pakistan today does not refer to glorified mystics but rather to mendicant deviants. Many Deobandis indeed disdain this latter connotation, even while maintaining a high estimation of the former. It was to elucidate this complex historical heritage that I have sought to introduce distinct terms of reference that are reflective of the internal heterogeneity. As a component portion of the Ahle Sunna wal Jammat, the Deoband '*ulama* are part of a long tradition of Sufis who are reforming Sufism. I am not saying that the political hopes of this modern nation state rest upon the wandering mendicants, the *malang* and *qalandars*, but rather that perhaps there is something in the broader spiritual heritage that has stimulated a resilient social cohesiveness and aspiration to pluralism. If Sufi is not the current term to describe the advocates of such values, then Deobandi is also not the term to describe those who oppose such aspirations.

Again there is a range of political views represented among the Deobandi '*ulama*. The Takfiri – whether theologically Hayati or Mamati – regard their coreligionists as being in the process of becoming fully Deobandi. Dissonant leaders are those who have not actualized the ideals inherent in the teachings of the elders. As the name implies, this is the inherent belief that those who do not embrace the breadth and depth of changes required for fidelity to the divine plan demonstrated in the reification of Sunnah are in fact inimical to the actualization of Islam. The political outworking of this is *khoruj* (lit. departure, or exodus): resistance to the system of governance and its leadership. This can be violent or non-violent, but it entails direct opposition because the government is regarded as un-Islamic. Some adhere to this view, but most do not.

There are also those from among the Tanzihi that seek to impose a change of system from within the current constitutional framework. This is the effort of many involved in the Jamiet-e-Ulema-Islam (JUI). Even here there are two branches. The JUI-S, named for Sami ul-Haq is active along the Afghan frontier and has consistently supported the Taliban. Their *dini madaris* have provided recruits to many factions intent on bringing about regime change and further institutionalizing this version of *shar'ia*. The JUI-F, led by Fazlur Rahman, is more integrated into the current system and often serves as an intermediary to mediate dialogue and greater national cohesion in the most restive areas. The move towards greater participation is recent, but very important. Islamist supporters have worked to undermine the government systems so as to create instability. This has led to the creation of parallel systems and economies in these regions.

Both factions idealize the political ideology implemented by the Taliban in Afghanistan prior to the NATO invasion, but disagree on how this is to be brought about in Pakistan. According to Hassan Madni, Director of Islamic Studies Department at Jamia al-Islamia in Lahore,

> The Taliban achieved power in Afghanistan through their individual struggle and enforced an ideal Islamic system there. Our religious scholars fully supported it. In contemporary Islamic history, if we see Islam enforced anywhere and peace achieved it was in Afghanistan under the Taliban regime (Sial 2012: 88).

He would like to a similar system in Pakistan so that the country no longer functions as a Muslim majority democracy founded upon western ideas, but rather as an Islamic state established according to traditional jurisprudence. The difference, as again Madni explains, is that, "I have a clear opinion about this democratic system but I do not believe in armed or violent struggle to change it." However, as the ballots reveal, this idea has not found popular support. The Takfiris, however, regards the current means of legislation as analogous with *taghut* (idol/despot), and apply the commands ordained in the Qur'ān and Sunnah for condemning false deities (Sial 2012: 63). There is no shortage of evidence for this party's disdain for its competitors, and the vitriol has resulted in an inventory of attacks against shrines across the country. But as argued throughout this chapter, this is a particular sub-group within the larger movement. If this were the majority view then the landscape in Pakistan would look radically different.

This is not to deny, however, the obvious distancing between most Deobandi *'ulama'* and traditional Sufi orders (*tariqa/silsillah*), or the differences in emphasis and practice that exist between the Deobandi and Barelvi. Differences in style, emphasis, and practice continue to divide communities and it often plays out in heated contestation over the appointment of mosque leadership. However, the belief of the Hayati Deonandi with regard to belief in the efficacy of intercession by the prophets and saints, both living and dead, in the present life and in the hereafter, is practically identical to that of the Barelvi. It would be of benefit for future studies to explore the theological differences in a more systematic and extended manner than what could be attempted here. The effort is to provide some texture to the broad category of Deobandi that appears so frequently in the literature. A taxonomy points towards the need to differentiate between the mercenary *madaris* of the Afghan frontier bent on establishing the Taliban government, and the quietist views of some of their Indian counterparts like Syed Arshad Madani, President of Jamiat Ulema-i Hind (India), who claim they are ready to give "even to the last drop of blood for the secular constitution."[8]

Deobandi refers to a large and dynamic group that does not have an innate or predetermined political agenda. Though they would never use the term secular, it is important to recall that constitutional democracy endures in Pakistan because of Deobandi support. Were the entire movement to shift positions and see the officials and the system from a Takfiri position and call for *khoruj*, then the government could not persist apart from civil war. But this is not the case. The senior elected officials in the present as and previous governments hail from prominent shrine families (*mutawalli*) and continue to draw from an extensive and interconnected relational network. The bounds between these and the political center remain strong despite the growing rejection of the feudal landlord system that has crippled institutional development. Perhaps if a greater number of the *'ulama* sense a clarity in position, similar to that of the JUI-F, then these custodians of change could leverage their pulpits for greater advocacy and accountability in local governance.

The roll of the *'ulama* and the *dini madaris* in Pakistani's electorate will continue to increase. As already noted, the ratio of students enrolled in *dini madaris* compared with private and public schools is indicative of the importance of this form of education in determining the agenda and priority of national development. From all indications this percentage continues to increase. For some this is a matter of belief, but for many it is a basic practicality. Children need food and basic schooling, and religious learning opens the possibility for employment and status. This form of education directly affects childhood development and has unalterable consequences upon the nation's workforce. According to Tariq Rahman's study, there has been exponential growth in enrolment over the past two decades across the board, but Deoband has outpaced the other Sunni schools. This trend can be seen in all provinces, but the highest rate of growth was seen in the Punjab. Although affiliated political parties have not done well in the polls, this young crop of voters and activists may yet change the game.

An increase in political participation from the Deobandi social base is not something to be feared but rather encouraged. The group is composed primarily of the rural and urban poor, and this demographic remains greatly underrepresented in a political arena that continues to be dominated by a feudal elite. It is important to recognize that an increase in participation does not correlate with votes for militant extremism. Recent research indicates that the most radical extremists are not the product of Deoband madrasas, but rather of modern and westernized universities.[9] As Tahir Mehmood Ashrafi, former Chairman of Pakistan's Ulema Council, explains:

> [youth] are absorbing new religio-political ideologies which are distinct from those held by Deobandi, Barelvi, and Ahl-e-Hadith schools of thought. Takfiri ideology is gaining ground among students of mainstream educational institutions. This is, however, not the case in madrasa where religious scholars at least guide their students on critical religious issues (Sial 2012: 88).

If Ashrafi is correct, then a shift in perspective needs to come about to where the traditional religious leaders, the *mullah* and the *'ulama*, are not regarded as the problem but rather as a vital part of the solution to Pakistan's quest for peace and sustainable development.

CONCLUSION

In contemporary discourse those affiliated (formally or not) with Deoband are divided into two broad categories: Hayati (alive) and Mamati (dead). The terminology indicates that one of the most significant faultlines in the movement concerns the efficacy of intercession (*shafa'a* and *tawassul*). Although this terminology has recently crystalized over the past 20 years, it is reflective of established differences within South Asian revivalist literature concerning the physical condition and abilities of holy persons after death. Our observations, preliminary as these may be, indicate that the vast majority of the Deobandi in Pakistan are neither anti-saint nor anti-shrine, though they share clear expectations that behavior and beliefs associated with types of Sufi behavior and shrine based activity not lead to *fitna*. The term Sufi remains ambiguous but it is increasingly understood to promote syncretistic practices and involvement with the occult. Nevertheless, present leaders understand fidelity to tradition to incorporate elements of *tasawwuf*. This adds further agreement to the classification of the Deobandi as an example of post-*tariqa* Sufism. It also identifies the continued centrality of hyper-corporeality as a core element of faith.

About the Author

Charles M. Ramsey is dually appointed as Assistant Professor of Religion and Public Policy at Forman Christian College (A Chartered University), Lahore, Pakistan. He has lived and worked in the Indian Sub-Continent since 2000. He holds a PhD in Islamic Studies (University of Birmingham, UK, supervised by David Thomas), an MA in the History of Religion (Baylor University, TX, USA where Clinton Bennett was his first reader), and PGC in Poverty Reduction (Centre for Development, Environment, and Policy at University of London, SOAS). Ramsey is a Research Fellow at the Centre for Dialogue and Action at Forman, a member of the Common Word Movement, and has served as Advisor to the National Peace Committee for Interfaith Harmony in Pakistan. Current research interests include Islam and Modernity, South Asia, Peace Building, Spiritual Theology, and Scriptural Hermeneutics. He has been awarded grants from the British Library and from the US Institute for Peace, and the Institute for International Education. Some of his works include: *God's Word, Spoken and Otherwise: Sayyid Ahmad Khan (1817–1898), Revelation, and Coherence* in the History of Christian-Muslim Relations series edited by David Thomas (Leiden: Brill, forthcoming); *South Asian Sufis: Devotion, Deviation, and Destiny*, eds. Clinton Bennett and Charles Ramsey (London: Continuum, 2012); and "Orientalist: Friend or Foe?" *Responses Towards 9/11: South Asia and Beyond*, ed. Nukhbah Langah (New Delhi: Routledge, 2016).

Notes

1. See Arthur F. Buehler, *Sufi Heirs of the Prophet: The Indian Naqshbandiyya and the Rise of the Mediating Sufi Shaykh* (Columbia: University of South Carolina Press, 1998. Born in rural Punjab, Sirhindi's insight and acumen led many to accept him as the *mujaddid-i alf-i thani*, the anticipated millennial restorer of the *umma*. His influence was such that within two generations Naqshbandi-Mujaddidi practice supplanted practically all prior expressions of the vast Naqshbandiyya order.
2. This is a descriptive account of life in the prison camps set up for religious clerics on the Andaman Islands following the 1857 war.
3. Sheikh Muhammad Yasir, "Are the Mamatis part of Ahlus Sunnah?," available at https://www.youtube.com/watch?v=UMX2s_nl2vE, *Hanafi Fiqh Channel* (accessed 22 April 2016).
4. Neelvi is a student of Hussain Ali from his home city of Mianwali in Pakistan, who began his education in 1884 in Deoband with Rashid Ahmad Gangohi and Mahmood Mazhar Nanautvi, a student of Shah Abdul Aziz son of Shah Wali Allah.
5. *Tanzihi* also has a theological meaning but that is not the case here. In that usage the term refers to the absolute difference between God and human, as opposed to *tashbi* that signifies closeness or similarity. These are the theological terms applied in discussion of the *wahdat al-wujud* (Unity of Being) with reference to

the interrelation of the creator and creation. I was assured by respondents in this research that this is not the meaning here.
6. This position was not seriously challenged, according to Tanoli, until 1897 when Sayyid Mehr 'Ali Shah (d. 1937) composed *Tahqiq ul-haqq fi kalimat al-haqq*.
7. http://www.theguardian.com/commentisfree/belief/2011/oct/12/pakistan-moderate-salman-taseer-mumtaz-qadri
8. http://sadaewatanjadeed.com/national-integration-conference/, New Delhi, 12 March 2016 (accessed 23 April 2016).
9. Raheem ul-Haque, "Youth Radicalizaion in Pakistan," *Peacebriefs*, no. 167, United States Institute of Peace, 26 February 2014, available at http://www.usip.org/publications/youth-radicalization-in-pakistan

6

SUFIS AS SHAPERS OF PLURALIST POLITICAL CULTURE: THE EXAMPLES OF BANGLADESH AND INDONESIA

Clinton Bennett

A BRIEF COMPARISON OF BANGLADESH AND INDONESIA

Without denying distinctive features, Bangladesh and Indonesia, as majority Muslim states, share many common features. The way that Sufis carried out peaceful proselytization in both contexts, planting Islam within the indigenous cultural and religious milieus, is remarkably similar. In both states, reformist expressions of Islam have found much in these localized versions of Islam to criticize or condemn as deviant. Islamist parties and movements have challenged the dominant ethos of religious pluralism and political inclusivity. In both, this has tended to juxtapose a supposedly purer, Arab-informed version of Islam and localized Islam. Both states have had periods of military rule but since democratic restorations they qualify as democracies, although Bangladesh's democracy is more fragile. Currently, according to the 2016 Economist Intelligence Unit *Democracy Index* Bangladesh ranks as the 84th most democratic country (out of 167) (which is above Turkey, numbered 97) in the "hybrid" category in which Albania at 81 has the highest score for a Muslim-majority state. Indonesia, ranked at 48, has the highest overall score for a Muslim-majority state (and qualifies as a "flawed democracy"), as does Malaysia (65) in the South Asian region (the other two Muslim-majority states in this category are Tunisia and Senegal). In some respects, Bangladesh, the younger state, has looked to Indonesia as a model. In both, a woman or women have held or hold high political office. In both, political parties range from secular (by name or pragmatically), through Islamic to Islamist. At least one party in each has Sufi links. In Indonesia, a Sufi leader served as President, even though he proved unequal to the task. In both, over the past decade, Islamists have performed poorly at the polls, suggesting that Sufi inclined Muslims have succeeded in challenging their ideology and agenda, while in Indonesia Islamist parties appear to be shifting to the center, affirming pluralism, abandoning demands for Islamic systems in favor of policies and legislation informed by Islamic values, the Islamic-oriented option. This chapter critiques the view that Bangladeshi and Indonesian flavored Islam are any less authentic than any other expression of Islam, and suggests that these tap into Islamic principles and potentialities toward democratic and religious pluralism from which Muslims elsewhere can benefit. This chapter, as well as using relevant literature and research, draws on time spent in these two countries. This writer has briefly visited Indonesia on three occasions, beginning in 1973. He has also had Indonesian colleagues. He first went to Bangladesh in 1979, leaving during 1982. During that period, he learned Bangla. He has spent substantially more time in Bangladesh, where he has close professional and personal ties with three visits since 1982, twice undertaking fieldwork researching views on Islam. He lived through some of the events described below, while his wife and members of her family have recounted to him their experience of many other important events.

Indonesia, with a total population of about 254 million, has the largest number of Muslims in the world representing about 13%. Bangladesh, with about 169 million people, has the world's fourth largest Muslim population representing about 9%. The tendency to equate Islam with how the religion is practiced in the Middle East often overlooks the fact that more Muslims live in Asia, indeed in these two states, than in the whole of the Middle East. The Muslim population for Asia is about 62% of all Muslims, or just over three-fifths. Of the 13 Muslim-majority states that the Economist Intelligence Unit's *Democracy Index* (2017*)* ranks as "hybrid" (below "flawed" but still classed as "democratic"), four are in the Middle East and North Africa region (MENA), two in Europe, four in Africa and three are in Asia where, as noted above two are in the higher category, so five out of six are democratic. Counting Brunei, which is not ranked, as undemocratic and including Afghanistan in Central Asia, South Asia, as a region, has the largest number of Muslim-majority democracies. Of the 26 Muslim-majority states ranked as "authoritarian," the highest number (13) are in the Middle East and North Africa, seven are African and six, all with one exception former Soviet republics, are Central Asian. Together, Bangladesh and Indonesia, two Asian states, have over one-fifth of the world's Muslims. Bangladesh, which straddles the Tropic of Cancer, is much more densely populated than Indonesia, which is about 13 times larger. The population of Java is about the same as Bangladesh's, although the island is 7,500 square miles smaller. Straddling Capricorn, Indonesia consists of over 17,000 islands. Bangladesh, which sits astride the Ganges delta, has more or less the same sultry climate as Indonesia. Rivers and canals crisscross Bangladesh, resulting in numerous island-like villages and towns often only accessible by boat during the rainy season. Both states were colonized by European powers. Post-independence, both have had periods of military rule. Both qualify as democratic, although of the two Indonesia's democracy is the more stable and, as noted, scores higher on the status of democracy index. Bangladesh's roots as a nation-state may probably be traced back further than Indonesia's, although both territories have long histories as culturally distinct zones. Bangladesh can look to the Pala Empire (eighth century to twelfth century) for political antecedents, since that Empire covered the entire modern state's territory. Indonesia may look to the comparatively more recent Majapahit empire (thirteenth century to sixteenth century) for an historical predecessor, although it was not until the colonial period that most of the territory of modern Indonesia was unified politically (West Iryan was a German colony until the end of World War I, and several areas were under Portuguese control). The Bangla language has long served as a cultural unifier in Bangladesh, which, spoken by the majority of citizens as their first language, has produced revered literary figures across different religious communities. Indonesian did not emerge as the majority language until the modern period; many citizens speak another dialect as their mother tongue. However, tolerance of religious diversity has an equally long history in both states where there is a similar number of non-Muslims. Non-Muslims in Bangladesh are approximately 11% and are mainly Hindu; Indonesia has roughly 13% non-Muslims who are mainly Christian, although Hindus are the majority on Bali and represent the world's fourth largest community. Bangladesh's largest non-Muslim community, though, pre-dates Islam's arrival, while Indonesia's results from the outreach of Western missionaries. Christians in Bangladesh are about 0.3%.

Both cultures, too, have interesting legacies vis-à-vis the status of women. In Bengal, goddess worship is an ancient tradition; seven *peethas*, sacred sites related to Shaktism, are located in Bangladesh, where veneration of *Sakti* remains popular. Some of the many Sufi teachers who spread Islam in what is now Bangladesh were women, some mythical, some historical with at least one shrine of a woman saint, Garam Bibi in Chittagong (Harder 2011: 322). Some Muslims in Bangladesh still pray to various female deities, such as *Bonbibi* (protector of the forest), *Sitaladebi* (goddess of smallpox) and the snake goddess, *Manasa* (Banu 1992: 102). Bengali women joined in both the anti-colonial and the language movements. The latter morphed into the liberation struggle, during which a number of women helped organize the *Mukti Bahini* (soldiers of liberation). The form of Hinduism that really took root in East Bengal was not strict Brahmanism, with rigid class/caste and gender roles but *Bhakti* that sat much more loosely to class and gender distinctions, and to restrictions on their role. Women marched with men protesting Pakistan's ban on broadcasting the songs of Rabindranath Tagore, who used *Kali* as a metaphor for the land in his much loved poetry. In Indonesia, some areas have matrilineal systems of descent and inheritance, while Atjeh had a series of Muslim women rulers between 1641 and 1699 (Mernissi 1993: 109). Veneration of female saints and ancestors features in Indonesia; some tombs of female Muslim saints

124 *Sufism, Pluralism and Democracy*

Map 2: Comparative Size of Bangladesh and Indonesia: Bangladesh (in black) is superimposed onto the island of Borneo.

which are still visited are located in places considered sacred in pre-Islamic times. Quinn (2016) lists 12 of these with their tomb's location. The mythical deity, *Nyi Roro Kidul*, which is female, is widely regarded as the nation's guardian spirit, without whose help no one can successfully govern. Even

Muslim sultans have claimed her protection, using various techniques to summon her aid. Somewhat to his embarrassment, the founder of Indonesia's first modern mass membership Islamic association, *Sarekat Islam* (SI) (founded 1912) was hailed as *Nyi Roro Kidul*. His meetings attracted large crowds. Rumors circulated that a revolution was imminent (Van Bruinessen 2007: 96). Many SI branches were headed by Sufi shaykhs. These legacies almost certainly impacted both countries' willingness to elect women to high political office, and to how women's social roles are developing. There is an increasingly influential women's movement in Indonesia, where the two largest Islamic organizations, *Persyarikatan* Muhammadiyah (Followers of Muhammad, usually referred to as *Muhammadiyah*) and *Nahdlatul Islam* (NU) each have women's wings which have, for example, championed women's reproductive health rights in recent years (Blackburn 2004:160). In Bangladesh, the 1997 election saw 13,000 women gain seats on municipal councils out of 45,000 female candidates, indicating a high level of political involvement although women remain underrepresented in government posts. While Bangladesh was conquered militarily by Muslims and Indonesia was never invaded by a foreign Muslim power, the way that Islam spread peacefully in these two states, becoming embedded in the cultures of each, is very similar. Perhaps how the majority of Muslims in each state continue to respect religious pluralism, and women's status in each, owes a debt to the proselytization process.

ISLAM'S SPREAD IN BANGLADESH AND INDONESIA

Bangladesh

There is some evidence that Muslim traders had reached East Bengal before Muhammad Bakhtiyar's conquering troops arrived in 1203 (Eaton 1993: 130). However, the presence of larger numbers of Muslims dates from much later. According to Eaton, only a small number of Muslims were present in Bengal until after the Moghul conquest (1576). Until then, comparatively few elite Muslims lived in the capital and in other administrative centers governing a mainly Hindu/animist population (1993: 133). There are many accounts of Sufi preachers, some sword-wielding, temple-destroying conquerors in Bengal from soon after the beginning of Muslim rule. However, these hagiographies, which date from several centuries after their subjects' deaths, reflect later ideas "about how the past ought to have happened" featuring "a decisive break between Bengal's Hindu past and its Muslim future" (Eaton 1993: 73). Rather, the adoption of Islam by the masses in Bengal, indeed in East Bengal, took place over a long period of time but especially during the sixteenth and seventeenth centuries. There is no evidence to link Islam's spread in Bengal with violence or conquest. Muslims had ruled for centuries before mass conversion began. This was due to the preaching of self-appointed cultural mediators who set out to present Islam in ways that attracted adherents of endogenous religious traditions to the exogenous religion. These cultural mediators, almost all of whom were Sufis, adopted and adapted Hindu language and mythology to accommodate and spread Islam's message, thus Allah might be identified with *Niranjan* (the Absolute as beyond objectification or form, a popular name for God in Bengal), Muhammad as an *avatar*, his daughter Fatimah as *Jagat-jananī*, the mother-of-the world (Eaton 1993: 276, 288).

Ways were found to indigenize Islam, associating it with the much loved soil, fauna, flora and waters of the *desh* (land); a Sufi teacher might sit under a tree already revered as holy, or identify himself with sacred fish, crocodiles, tigers or snakes. Over time, these were *pirified*, a process explored by Roy in his groundbreaking work on Bengal's cultural mediators (1983). Many *pīrs* became renowned for their healing abilities. Shah Jalal (d. 1346) arrived from Yemen with a lump of soil which he found was an exact match with that of the place in Sylhet where he settled, as his teacher had instructed him (Eaton 1993: 212–13). Hindu heroes and deities could be seen as among the 124,000 prophets sent by God according to *ḥadīth*, Hindu scriptures as earlier divine revelations. On the one hand, this can all be represented as syncretistic and eclectic. On the other hand, these Sufi writers (whose choice of Bangla as their literary medium did not escape censure) while respecting many aspects of endogenous religion also saw Islam as correcting and perfecting this: *avatars* were prophets not divine incarnations; Muhammad was the culmination of prophetic dispensation; the Qur'ān superseded Hindu scriptures as it did the Bible while also confirming what truths they contain. While the distinction between a Sufi saint and a Hindu guru was blurred in terms of their followers, who might be "Hindu" or "Muslim" or perhaps both, the former were careful to claim intimacy with God, not divinity. However, this approach "connected Islam with Bengal's socio-religious past" rather than repudiating this (Eaton 1993: 269) which meant that those who became disciples of these new teachers remained within existing communities, retaining many practices. In both Bangladesh and Indonesia, some localized expressions of Islam have been labeled "syncretistic." This term has a pejorative connotation. Arguably, provided that beliefs and practices are not explicitly contrary to Islamic norms and values, incorporating customs from Hindu or animism or using the names of spirits derived therefrom (many Muslims believe the spirit world of *djinns* is simply a pragmatic local adaptation. Eaton and others argue that initially people did not so much "convert" from one religion to another but added additional elements to their spiritual worlds. Indeed, they did not rigidly distinguish between religions, a Western concept but drew on whatever they thought would help "them in coping with life's everyday problems" (Eaton 1993: 273) such as a "holy man here, a holy river there –

in order to tap superhuman power" (Eaton 1993: 281). Perhaps the most significant factor in this indigenization process was how Sufi teachers helped extend agricultural space eastward across the delta, clearing forests and settling new territory. Many *pīrs* were later incorporated into the revenue collecting system of the Mughal Administration. This also explains why the larger concentrations of Muslims in Bengal are found in the East not in the West even though the seat of Muslim power was located there. The plough, not the sword, was the instrument that spread Islam across the Ganges delta. On the other hand, there were perhaps fewer women saints involved in this process because of the link with forest clearance and land cultivation.

Banu's research suggests that almost 50% of Bangladeshis express their "primordial loyalty" in terms of the land rather than religion (1992: 98). Loyalty to land here includes "culture" and in Bangladesh Muslims and non-Muslims share love of poetry and song across religious identities. Christians though a small minority also contributed to the Bengali Renaissance. A Hindu, Rabindranath Tagore (1861–1941), a Muslim, Nazrul Islam (1925–75) and a Christian, Michael Madhusudan Datta (1824–73) are almost equally revered as writers; commitment to humanistic, universal values over-and-against religious exclusivism imbues all their work. Nazrul Islam's literary legacy has a great deal of Hindu reference. He regarded Tagore as his mentor. Banu also found that among Muslims almost 50% of urban dwellers report friendships with Hindus while close to 15% of rural and nearly 19% of urban dwellers attend Hindu *pujas* (1992: 97). There are still Muslims who sing Vishnu's praises, and Hindus who sing in honor of Sufi saints. Muslims read the great Hindu epics, while the first Bangla version of the Qur'ān was translated by a Hindu. As a result of reformist activities usually led by Bengalis who spent time in Arabia, Bangladeshi Muslims today are more aware of their Muslim identities than they were in the seventeenth century. However, for many, perhaps the majority, this does not translate into seeing non-Muslims as god-less or as unqualified for full citizenship. Sufism has attracted criticism for alleged heterodoxy (*zandaqa*) and innovation (*Bid'ah*), indeed Bengali-flavored Islam has been dismissed as too Hinduized by various reformers, such as Sharia'tullah (1791–1840) who following time in Arabia called for the purification of Bengali Islam. However, while opposed to saint and shrine veneration and to the teacher-disciple relationship, he did not reject all aspects of Sufi thought or practice, encouraging *dhikr* within his movement. In Arabia, he had been initiated into the *Qādiriyya* order. In recent years, non-Muslims in Bangladesh have been targeted by Islamists who question their loyalty and patriotism, largely because the secular Awami League (AL) attracts their loyalty (Riaz 2004: 57). However, Islamic extremists show no sign of enjoying popular support, failing at the ballot box. Most Muslim Bangladeshis do not favor legal discrimination on the basis of religion; although violent tactics and intimidation could see Islamists achieve their goals. This, though, would be top-down, not bottom-up.

Indonesia

Muslims from India and East Africa trading with the spice-islands, where commercial and cultural contact with India is ancient, preached Islam there from at least the thirteenth century when Islam became well established in Northern Sumatra. However, Islam's origin in Java is traditionally linked with the nine saints (*Wali Sanga*) credited with proselytizing there in the early fifteenth to early sixteenth centuries. Whether historical figures or mythical, each "saint now has a mortuary complex which is often the source of their present-day renown" (Laffan 2011: 9). Some biographers have traced their descent from the Prophet. They are also said to have "created art forms to explain Islam in the local idiom," such as inventing a type of poetical instruction and shadow-puppetry (2011: 8). These have been cited as "examples of Indonesian malleability" that is, an innate tendency to blend and synthesize cultural and religion ideas and practices. Interestingly, as this was taking place in Indonesia, Bengal's cultural mediators were acting similarly. The nine were not, it seems, formally connected with traditional Sufi orders. The "first clear Western reference to tariqa devotees in the archipelago" (Laffan 2011: 21) occurs with the travels of the Aceh born 'Abd al-Ra'uf al-Sinkili (1615–93) who "claimed to have affiliated himself with several tariqas" during the 19 years he spent in Arabia and Egypt "though he is today better known to Arab biographical dictionaries as a Naqshbandi" (Laffan 2011: 18). Subsequently during the seventeenth and eighteenth centuries, orders such as the *Naqshbandi*, *Shadhilya*, *Shattariyya*, *Sanusiyya*, *Qādiriyya* and *Tijananiyya* became established in Indonesia although the majority of Muslim spiritual teachers remained unaffiliated with *ṭarīqahs (tarekats* in Indonesian).

Many of these teachers "had compiled their own eclectic mixture of spiritual techniques and metaphysical speculations from a variety of sources," Islamic and non-Islamic (Laffan 2011: 95). Eclectic orders developed, too, combining pre-Islamic animistic with Islamic concepts, presenting themselves as "alternatives to excessively *shari'a* oriented, exoteric versions of Islam," with some Theosophical influence (Laffan 2011: 97). Since these orders' founders cannot trace their spiritual lineage to Muhammad, they have been called local *ṭarīqahs* (they are also known as *Majlis Dhikr* groups, see Zamhari 2010). As in Bengal, many Sufi teachers became renowned healers, although using the word "sufi" is anachronistic since this does not appear in Indonesia literature until the 1970s (Howell 2000: 707, n. 2). Thus, what became popular in Indonesia was a localized expression of Islam often referred to as *abangan*, rather than a version that closely resembled the type of Islam encountered in the Arab world, although close links were actually maintained with Arabia. *Abangan* holds Islamic and non-Islamic elements in balance; the more Arab-influenced strand of Islam in Indonesia, known as *santri*, gives weight to Islamic elements while *prijaji* favors Indic elements. *Santri* tends to be coastal, *abangan* rural. *Abangan*, often described as syncretistic, includes rituals and beliefs associated with "the agricultural cycle, and local or ancestral spirits" (Van Bruinessen 2007: 93). Use of these three terms was popularized by anthropologist Clifford Geertz (1926–2006) who researched in Java 1952–54 as part of a team from Harvard, later in Bali (57–58) and made many other shorter visits during his career (see Geertz 1960). The more allegedly syncretistic movements are also referred to as *Kebatinan*; (esotericism) (Van Bruinessen 2007: 97). This term is often applied to movements that do not self-define as Muslim. Geertz used the term "scripturalist" for Arab-influenced trends. This carries the assumption that other versions cannot be reconciled with the Qur'ān and should perhaps be avoided.

Sufism in Indonesia, as in Bangladesh, has attracted opposition and criticism from reformists including Geertz's "scripturalists," although traditional orders have tended to identify with a Ghazālīan-type of Sufism and have joined in condemning local *ṭarīqahs* for alleged indifference to exoteric Islam. Zamhari argues that much of this critique is unjustified; these groups offer creative interpretations of Qur'ān and *ḥadīth* within the Indonesian context (2010: 7). Many do observe normative practices, such as daily prayer and the annual fast. Many have strong links with *pesantren* (Islamic schools) which are also strongholds of *santri*. The title *Kiai* (equivalent to *Ālim*), is used for both Sufi teachers and those who run *pesantren* and often overlap. Discussing Salafist criticism of Indonesian Sufis, Van Bruinessen (1999) points out that this was often directed at the perceived chicanery of some Sufi teachers who claimed powers they did not possess, taking advantage of their followers rather than against Sufism *per se*. Howell (2001) says that Sufi devotionalism is flourishing in Indonesia today not only among old men in the villages but also among well-educated urbanites and even "members of the national elite" (2001: 702). This follows a period, especially during the 1980s, when Sufism seemed to be declining and Arab-flavored Islam was resurgent, and *ṭarīqahs* looked like "withering vestiges of the past" (2001: 708). However, her work shows that the traditional orders remain popular, while others are experimenting with "new institutional forms" designed to bridge modernist and traditional styles of Islam (2001: 703). It is, Howell said, the non- *ṭarīqah* forms that are becoming especially attractive to urbanites, "from reading reflective and 'how-to' spiritual books, to attending academically-styled private courses, to joining informal prayer groups or healing workshops using *dzikir* chanting, to accepting the spiritual direction of non-traditional teachers outside the conventional *tarekat*" (2000: 17).

Zamhari describes the continued popularity of local *ṭarīqahs*, which he says are playing important roles in "improving the quality of interfaith dialogue" in Indonesia and attract some who do not find other expressions of Islam very attractive (2010: 3). More members of *Muhammadiyah* (with a membership of roughly 29 million) too, previously critical of Sufism, are now practicing Sufism (Rabasa *et al.* 2004: 372). Kersten (2015) says that "vibrant diversity" is "characteristic of the Indonesian Muslim milieu" (2015: 12). Indonesian Muslims tend to affirm the rights of non-Muslims. How might these localized expressions of Islam, then, have helped shape the political cultures of Bangladesh and of Indonesia, and have Sufis played any identifiable roles in these state's democratic transformations in affirming religious pluralism and political inclusiveness?

HAVE BANGLADESH'S AND INDONESIA'S ISLAMIC TRADITIONS ASSISTED DEMOCRATIZATION?

Bangladesh

East Bengal's Muslims' preference for an independent state based on language, culture and geography as a common home to various religious communities expressed itself in their reluctance to join Pakistan in 1947. Political leaders at the time wanted East and West Bengal to remain unified within an independent state. Even though the British did not allow this option, when the East voted on the issue of partition 107 legislative representatives out of 142 voted against this and in favor of the whole province joining Pakistan. (Chatterji 2007: 21). However, following the rules set by the British, this was overturned by the West's vote in favor of partition and of joining India (2007: 58–21); see the next chapter for further background on this event). Thus, East Bengal (renamed East Pakistan in 1955) became part of Pakistan, separated by 990 miles from West Pakistan, where the government was located. It did not take long for many in East Pakistan to become dissatisfied with what they saw as West Pakistan's hegemony. While most of the GDP was produced in the east, it was mainly spent in the west. Bengalis, too, were underrepresented in the civil and military services (especially in the latter). Efforts to impose Urdu as the national language resulted in pro-Bangla demonstrations during 1952 and by 1966 the Awami League (formed 1949) in the East, led by Sheikh Mujibur Rahman (1920–1975) was campaigning for a federal system that would give the East more autonomy. Resistance to this from the West saw the President, Yahya Khan (1917–1980) override the result of Pakistan's first democratic election in 1970 in which Awami League won 160 out of 300 seats by appointing Zulfikar Ali Bhutto (1928–1979) as Prime Minister (with only 81 seats). Arresting Mujib, Khan launched a military operation in the East to crush what was now regarded as a pro-independence struggle. This provoked the liberation war which began on March 26th 1971 and ended following India's intervention on December 16th 1971 with the creation of Bangladesh. Hindus, Christians and other non-Muslims alongside Muslims supported and fought in the war shouting *Joy Bangla* (Victory to Bengal; the pre-partition slogan had been "Islam in Danger"). Bengali identity, which crosses religions, took priority. They left an Islamic Republic and created a Peoples Republic. This can be seen as culture trumping religion, since although most citizens of Pakistan were Muslims Islam was unable to glue the geographically discontiguous and ethnically diverse state together. However, perhaps what was actually at stake was the East's freedom to practice a type of religiosity that embraced diversity and allowed a certain degree of fluidity between religions, over-and-against an Islam that demanded conformity to a single expression and is viewed as a closed system.

The Awami League won the first election in 1973, gaining all but two seats. Bangladesh's Constitution set out four fundamental principles of state, namely nationalism, socialism, democracy and secularism. There is some similarity between this and Indonesia's Constitution, which established the five principles of *Pancasila* as the state's philosophical foundation. These are belief in the one and only God, just and civilized humanity, Indonesian unity, democracy and social justice. At first sight, Bangladesh's "secularism" seems to be at odds with Indonesia's principle of "belief in One God." However, while Indonesia regards religious belief to be part of national identity, the state does not privilege any single religion. Rather, it officially recognizes six (Catholicism, Confucianism, Buddhism, Hinduism, Islam and Protestantism) despite pressure from some Muslims to replace this with reference to Islam and the role of *shāri'ah* law. "Secularism" (*dharmanirapeksata*) (ধর্ম নিরপেক্ষতা) in the Bangladeshi Constitution means "religious neutrality," that no single religious identity is to be privileged over others (see chapter eight, p. 147). Indeed, under Mujib all the main religions were accommodated in the public square, with readings at the start of Parliamentary sessions from the four main religions' scriptures, and time for each religion on public television. His "secularism" did not totally separate religion from government but rather removed any legislative and judicial function from religion. Article 41 protects freedom of religion. He did, though, take Bangladesh into membership of the OIC in February 1974. Mujib was also influenced by the ideas of Mustafa Kemal Atatürk, whose "guiding principles" were "secularization," "nationalism," "modernization" and Westernization" (Islam 2015: 16). Mujib's governing style, like Atatürk's, was authoritarian. He curtailed freedom of the press. Although democratically elected, he centralized power in his own hands. Ending multi-party politics, he created an executive presidency for himself (4th Constitutional Amnendment, January 25th 1975). His militia arrested dissidents and forcefully implemented his ambitious social program of nationalizing industry and collectivizing farms. Opponents who wanted the state to take a more Islamic direction saw him as pro-Indian, even fearing that he wanted reunification with West Bengal. By emphasizing Bengali culture rather than Islamic identity, they argued, little ground remained for Bangladesh's continued existence as a separate state.

Mujib and almost his entire family were assassinated in a military coup on August 15th 1975. After two short-lived governments and two more coups, Ziaur-Rahman (1936–1981) emerged as military law administrator. He oversaw an Islamization process that some of those behind Mujib's assassination had advocated. Zia prefixed *the Basmala* to the constitution, replaced "secularism" with "absolute trust and faith on Almighty Allah" and "socialism" with "economic and social justice," (Constitution of the People's Republic of Bangladesh 8:1, note similarity with Indonesia's first and fifth principles) changed "Bengali" *citizen* to "Bangladeshi" (Constitution of the People's Republic of Bangladesh 6:2) and ended the reading of non-Muslim scriptures in Parliament (*Jatiya Sangsad*). Lifting the ban on political parties (including sectarian parties) he formed the Bangladesh Nationalist Party (BNP) (1978) to help legitimize his presidency and transformation from a militiary to civilian ruler. The BNP self-defines as center-right, pro-democratic, pro-free-market and aims:

> To preserve the age old human values of the Bangladeshi people through the teaching of Islam-religion of the majority of Bangladeshi people and other religions, expansion of education for the backward people and giving them more facilities and chance to take part in greater national life (BNP Constitution, 2c).

The reference to preserving "old age human values ... through ... Islam" does not necessarily juxtapose Islamic values and those of other faiths; Hindus and Christians can be seen as sharing these. The then president of the largest Protestant denomination served as a cabinet level adviser to Zia. BNP's aim is perhaps similar to that of Turkey's Justice and Development Party, although the BNP has entered alliances with Islamists who call for *shāri'ah* law and the formation of an Islamic state. Following Zia's assassination (May 30th 1981) by army officers who wanted a greater political role for the military, Bangladesh experienced a brief democratic interlude until General Hussain Muhammad Ershad's coup of March 24th 1982. Ershad's rhetoric if not his actual achievements continued Zia's Islamization policy. In 1988, he signed the 8th Amendment that made Islam the state religion (June 7th 1988). Opposition to Ershad's regime drew together Islamists (for example, the *Jamaat-e-Islami* (JI) party, which had sided with West Pakistan during the Liberation War), the BNP under the leadership of Zia's widow, Khaleda Begum and the Awami League, led by Mujib's daughter, Sheikh Hasina. Ershad's resignation (followed by imprisonment for corruption) set the scene for Bangladesh's democratic restoration. In the subsequent 1991 election, BNP won 141 out of 300 seats, JI won 18 and AL 88. Khaleda began her first term as Prime Minister. Although Khaleda preferred to retain an executive presidency she agreed to restoring the Prime Ministerial system (where PM and cabinet in parliament form the executive), with a ceremonial president elected by parliament (12th Amendment, August 6th 1991). Two elections took place in 1996. After the first, in February, boycotted by opposition parties, BNP had 278 seats. Khaleda was forced to resign after a fortnight of days of strikes, demonstrations and violence. The second election, in June saw AL with 146 seats, BNP 116, JI ended up with three seats while the more radical *Islami Oikkya Jote* (IOJ) won one. This election was supervised by a Caretaker Government for which AL and JI had campaigned, established by the 13th Amendment 26 March 1996 (Article 58). Despite her earlier opposition to Ershad, Sheikh Hasina became Bangladesh's second woman PM in an alliance that included his Jatya Party, with 32 seats (Ershad won one seat from his prison cell). Jatya's general secretary received a cabinet post. The 2001 election returned BNP to power with 193 seats. JI gained 14 (and was awarded two cabinet posts), IOJ gained one while AL (at 62) lost 84. The next election was delayed by the intervention of a military-backed caretaker government (October 2006 to December 2008) that attempted to reform the process. A Christian also served at cabinet equivalent rank in that administration. In the 2008, election, AL won a landslide victory with 230 seats, BNP ended up with 30. JI lost 16 seats (retaining two), IOJ lost both seats. Jatya kept 27. During her second term, Sheikh Hasina restored the original four principles to the Constitution, ended the system of Caretaker Governments although she had championed this in 1996 (15th Amendment, June 30th 2011). The Amendment also ordered her father's portrait would replace that of the President and Prime Minister in government buildings and public and private educational institutions (4A) and inserted before "The citizens of Bangladesh shall be known as Bangladeshis," that "The people of Bangladesh shall be known as Bangalees as a nation" (6:2). This followed a Supreme Court on May 15th 2011 decision overturning all amendments passed under military regimes. Islam, however, remains the state religion (2:A). Denouncing the end of the Caretaker Government system and other changes to the Constitution, 18 opposition parties headed by BNP boycotted the 2014 election. The result saw AL with 234 seats, Jatya with 34 (receiving three cabinet seats) and one of the three Sufi-affiliated parties, the BTF with two. The remaining elected seats 32 seats (50 are reserved for women awarded on proportional basis to the parties' nominees) were won by independents and by four other parties. One hundred and fifty-three seats were uncontested. Bangladesh Tarikat Federation (BTF), whose chairman, Syed Najibul Bashar Maizbhandari, attended the launch in London of *Minhaj-al-Quran's* peace and anti-terrorist curriculum June 23rd 2015, describes its mission as "To build an exploitation free, pro-people welfare state maintaining the values of secularism and Sufi way imbued with the spirit of great war of liberation and in the light of Charter of Medina" (Facebook page https://www.facebook.com/pg/Bangladesh-Tariqat-Federation-323370301136129/about/?ref=page_internal). Syed Najibul Bashar, who belongs to the leading family of the Maizbhandari *ṭarīqah*, was initially elected an MP in 1991 for AL. After transferring to BNP before the 2001 election, he became international affairs secretary, resigning in September 2005 over BNP's links with JI which he accused of involvement in attacking Sufi shrines. He also sat on the Hindu-Buddhist Unity Council (Alam 2012: 169).

What has hindered the maturation of democracy in Bangladesh apart from issues about the legitimacy of the 2014 election is absence of the concept of loyal opposition. Opposition members of Parliament rarely attend sessions. The two women party leaders are bitter rivals. Instead of using their seats to critique policy and legislative proposals, they resort to strikes, demonstrations and sometimes incite violent protest. It is difficult to gauge the level of popular support that these express because the same people, for a price, may protest against the government one day and support it the next. This writer's in-laws speak about rent-a-crowd politics. State media broadcasts of parliamentary sessions show empty benches even when there are elected opposition MPs. However, the actual policies of BNP and AL are almost indistinguishable. The main difference lies in how BNP favors a more Muslim Bangladeshi identity, AL an identity that emphasizes a Bengali identity that crosses religious communities and some say the Indian border. BNP's priority may be strengthening relations with Muslim states, AL's with India but how they handle the economy, and the type of legislation they introduce, are similar. The two parties also offer rival narratives about Mujib's secular and Zia's Islamic claims to be the nation's real father and about who declared independence (see Bennett 2010: 148). Yet despite the Islamist rhetoric of some leading politicians, very few laws in Bangladesh are explicitly Islamic, except for Family Law (still essentially the comparatively liberal Family Law Ordinance of 1961, passed during Ayub Khan's presidency in Pakistan, to which Islamists object). A lot of recent legislation draws on various international conventions to which Bangladesh is signatory. Most non-Muslims support AL. A number of non-Muslims have held and hold cabinet posts. Whether the 15th Amendment and secularism's restoration will survive may depend on AL's future political fortunes. A BNP government could reverse this. It is, though, a moderate party and since the 2001 election, the Islamist parties (JI, IOJ) have performed less well at the ballot box while at least one Sufi-affiliated party has had some success. Tariqat "preaches for communal harmony and interfaith dialogue" (Alam 2012: 168). AL also had support from the Sufi-affiliated Zaker Party, whose current leader, the founder's son, "once stated that there is no conflict between secularism and Islam, and that in order to rescue the country from the threats of religious extremists ... secularism should be restored" (Alam 2012: 168). Uddin comments that typically members of the neo-Sufi *Tablighi Jamaat* support AL (Uddin 2006: 162). There are no available statistics on how many people with Sufi-affiliation support AL or indeed BNP but a degree of symmetry does appear to exist between Sufi-inspired traditional Bengali religious inclusivity and the AL's commitment to a political-legal system that does not privilege a single religion, or one interpretation of that religion. Sheikh Hasina's speeches sometimes suggest Sufi sympathies (see Bennett 2010: 161). In 2010, she visited the famous Sufi shrine at Ajmeer in India. She identifies her policy with the Medina Charter that gave non-Muslims co-equal rights with Muslims, also referenced in the High Court decision of August 1st 2013 that revoked JI's registration as a political party. The Court defined the Charter's "philosophical basis as essentially secular and democratic" (Supreme Court of Bangladesh High Court Division, p. 3). In addition to JI's call for a religious state, those petitioning for its de-registration, including BTF, whose General Secretary filed the writ, described it as pursuing "radicalism, extremism and militancy not approved by Islam" (Court of Bangladesh High Court Division, p. 26) that could result in "modern day '*jihad*' and various shades of fanaticism" (Court of Bangladesh High Court Division, p. 4). The three Sufi-related parties all oppose JI, regarding its version of Islam as deviant (the charge that JI makes against Sufism). The Tarikat Council, representing the Sufi orders has "accused JI of endangering Islam" (Al-Alawi 2010). BTF had to amend its own Charter following the verdict. Unfortunately, instability in Bangladesh following the last election has impacted negatively on treatment of minorities, who have experienced an increased number of threats and attacks on property by Islamist-extremists. If they leave the country, their land and businesses can be acquired. The non-Muslim population has declined since this writer first went to Bangladesh, when it was closer to 14%. Attacks were also carried out "on secular writers, foreigners, and Shiites" (Freedom House 2016: 14). In May 2016, al-Qaeda affiliates murdered a Sufi shaykh. Due to these attacks, Freedom House downgraded Bangladesh's freedom score (Freedom House 2016: 18). Bangladesh also dropped from 84 to 86 on the Democracy Index. However, the Economist Intelligence Unit anticipates that AL will complete its present term (which ends in 2019) and reports little public appetite for an earlier election. It seems that many citizens hold the opposition parties responsible for compromising the 2014 result and think that AL should not be blamed (although it had blamed BNP for the dubious February 1996 election) (EIU 2016).

Indonesia

During World War II, Indonesia (a Dutch colony) was occupied by Japan. Sukarno (1901–70) leader of the *Partai Nasional Indonesia* (PNI, Indonesian National Party) and de facto of the independence movement, cooperated with the Japanese when they promised that Indonesia would become a sovereign state. Following Japan's surrender, Sukarno declared Indonesia's independence (August 17th 1945). *Pancasila* was Sukarno's summing up of his own political philosophy, which was adopted as national principles in the 1945 Constitution. Belief in God as a principle gives religion state recognition as part of the identity of Indonesian people but it does not privilege one religion or give religion any official role in the legislative and juridical spheres. Proposed Islamist systems, rather similar to Iran's, tend to vest Muslim jurists or other experts with either sanctioning, revising or vetoing legislation, a term that is also avoided. Legislating is God's prerogative thus the task of an elected or appointed Assembly (*majlis*) is to interpret and apply God's law (by means of ordinances or regulations). Effectively, then, although technically theistic, Indonesia is secular. When the Netherlands attempted to reassert colonial rule, an armed conflict began between Dutch and British troops, there to supervise the Japanese withdrawal, and Indonesian freedom fighters which lasted until the Dutch recognized Indonesia's independence December 27th 1949. Some members of a popular *Kebatinan* movement inspired young fighters during the revolutionary war with a sense of invulnerability and prowess (Van Bruinessen 2007: 98). In the new state's revised 1950 constitution, as the Netherlands insisted, power resided with the Prime Minister and parliament (*Dewan Perwakilan Rakyat* or Peoples Representative Council, DPR) leaving the President with a mainly ceremonial role. Sukarno became President. Until an election took place in 1955, the DPR, which also elected the President, was provisional and unelected. That year, PNI won 57 of the available 257 seats, *Masyumi* (Council of Indonesian Muslim Organizations) also won 57. *Nahdatul Islam* (NU), which functioned at the time as a political party in addition to being a religious organization, won 45 seats. Esposito and Voll describe NU as "a predominantly conservative, rural based, social cultural organization" whose membership represents some "twenty percent of Indonesia's population" (2001: 199). Previously, on the unelected Assembly, it had had only five seats. The Communist Party, which won 39, performed better than predicted. Some members of *Kebatinan* movements actively supported the left, which later resulted in several attracting official suspicion (Van Bruinessen 2007: 98). Christian parties also won seats (one, mainly Protestant, won 8, a Catholic Party won 6) while a number of other parties won a few seats each including the Islamic Union Party and the Islamic Educators Association (known as Perti) with four each. The *Partai Politik Tarekat*

Islam (PPTI), founded by a Sufi shaykh, Haji Jalaluddin only won one seat but polled as high as 10% "in some Sumatran districts" (Van Bruinessen 2007: 99) which boosted Jalaluddin's political standing. Perti also had strong Sufi links; founders included a number of *Naqshbandi* shaykhs. NU, too, counted many Sufis members. Although shaykhs were absent among its founders, they later assumed more active and prominent roles. *Masyumi* traces its beginning to a Japanese initiative to try to "harness Islam to serve their war policy" (Madinier 2015: 51). *Masyumi* set itself the goal of creating a society and state based on Islamic values as "an alternative to the opposition between the imposed collectivism of the Marxist system and the unfettered individualism of capitalism" (Madinier 2015: 400). Though distinctly Islamic, the party envisioned a fairly minimalist role for *shāri'ah* penal laws (Madinier 2015: 307). It drew many members from the *Muhammadiya* (founded 1912), which advocated re-interpreting Islam for the modern world. *Masyumi* avoided using the term "Islamic state" (Madinier 2015: 208) during the 1955 election but, forming an alliance with the other Muslim parties, began to call for this within the DPR, where collectively they held 44.8% of the seats.

The distribution of seats gave no party or alliance enough to form an effective government and a succession of coalitions followed, each in control for brief periods. A *Masyumi* politician led the first, a PNI politician the second, a non-partisan politician the third (formed April 9 1957). Left-right, regional-center, secular versus Islamic and other polarities led to government dysfunction. Violent rebellions in Aceh and elsewhere, led by the Islamist *Darul Islam* (founded 1942) which demanded *shāri'ah* law, hardly helped. Frustrated, Sukarno declared martial law in March 1957, effectively assuming power. He then called for a unity cabinet, which would be guided by a new National Council "chosen from representatives of 'functional groups'… which Indonesian society was composed of" (Madinier 2015: 234) and which represented its diversity. Groups included farmers, the military, academic, religious scholars, women and the regions. This effectively compartmentalized society, isolating those in one group from like-minded people in other groups and women from men (Taylor 2003: 361). Sukarno argued that Western style democracy was failing Indonesia; his new system was supposedly based on a traditional Indonesia leadership style. *Masyumi* was sidelined, receiving no representation on the new body; Sukarno saw *Masyumi* as uncommitted to *Pancasila* and the secular, pluralist society it was designed to support. *Masyumi* saw the Council as undermining democracy, and feared that Sukarno would abrogate even more power to himself. He did. In 1959, Sukarno amended the Constitution to vest power in the presidency, dissolved the DPR and ushered in his "Guided Democracy" experiment. He switched, too, from the federal system enshrined in the 1950 Constitution back to the unitary one of 1945. Pro-Soviet and anti-West,

Sukarno withdrew from the United Nations in 1965. He had ordered *Masyumi's* dissolution in 1960; and later arrested the party's leaders. Reconstituting as an NGO (The Crescent Star Family), members continued to advocate for *sharī'ah*. Suharto's downfall the following year saw Suharto, then army chief of staff, rise to power as a pro-West leader. Suharto's New Order gave the military a prominent role in governance, and reduced popular participation.

While Suharto's pro-West stance attracted US aid, his actual leadership style differed little from Sukarno's. Under Suharto, the recognized functional groups were awarded seats in the DPR or permitted to contest elections but these were carefully controlled to ensure that his chosen political vehicle, *Partai Golangan Kariya* (GOLKAR, comprised of government employees) always won a majority. Only approved political parties could operate, which included NU for the 1971 election in which it was the main opposition to GOLKAR, winning 58 seats to GOLKAR's 236. The Christian parties collectively won seven. Other Muslim parties won an aggregate of 36 seats. PNI won 20. The total number was 360. The Sufi-affiliated PPTI chose to ally itself with GOLKAR becoming "the only Sufi association that enjoyed government recognition" (Van Bruinessen 2007: 99) and the patronage that this brought. Suharto banned the Communist Party. Before the 1974 election, the opposition parties were amalgamated into two, namely the United Development Party (*Partai Persatuan Pebangunan,* PPP) into which the Muslim parties were merged (except for *Partai Politik Tarekat Islam* or Muslim Tarekat Political Party, which had sided with GOLKAR), and the Indonesian Democratic Party-Struggle (*Partai Demokrasi Indonesia Perjuangan*, PDI-P) into which the Christian and nationalist parties were merged. GOLKAR went on to win large rigged majorities in the 1977, 1982, 1987, 1992 and 1997 elections during Suharto's 32 years in power. Suharto tasked the *Majelis Permusyawaratan Rakyat* (MPR or People's Consultative Assembly) in which *Dewan Perwakilan Rakyat* (DPR, Peoples Representative Council, Indonesia) members, members of the Regional Representative Council and 100 members whom he appointed sat with electing the president every five years. Suharto was always elected unopposed. The MPR could also amend the Constitution.

It was during the 1970s that Sufi leaders became more prominent in *Nahdatul Islam* (NU, Awakening of the Scholars). In 1975, Suharto himself opened a congress of NU's affiliated Sufi orders, which had grouped together in 1957 as the *Jam'iyyah Ahlith Thoriqah Mu'tabaroh* to represent a Ghazālīan Sufi orthodoxy over-and-against what they regarded as non-orthodox Sufi orders (the local *ṭarīqahs*). These were declared non-Sufi. The *Jam'iyyah*'s leader at this time, Kiai Musta'in, chose to support Suharto's development philosophy, arguing that material development needed to be accompanied by spiritual growth which the *ṭarīqahs* would lead. Some Sufi shaykhs began to benefit from government patronage; Suharto gained from the religious seal of approval their support represented. Kiai Musta'in campaigned for GOLKAR, although the NU was at this time part of the opposition *Partai Persatuan Pebangunan* (PPP, United Development Party) calling for a greater role for Islam. Some members of *Jam'iyyah* followed Kiai Musta'in's example but others deserted under an alternative leader, forming *Jam'iyyah Ahlith Thoriqah al-Mu`tabaroh al-Nahdliyyah* (JATMN) in 1979, which was more formally allied with NU. Most sheykhs supported PPP, using their influence to attract rural support. Thus, some Sufis reached an accommodation with Suharto's authoritarian regime while others chose to identify with the opposition, demanding more freedoms. Esposito and Voll say Suharto used a "carrot and stick" method to co-opt Muslim support on the one hand and to suppress Muslim opposition on the other. He tried to control and co-opt Islam (Esposito and Voll 2001: 203). Partly, Suharto conscripted backing from Muslim leaders to counter his increasing alienation from the military, which resented how officers had to implement "policies which" they "had no say formulating" despite being ensconced within the political structure (Sukma 2004: 64). Suharto was so confident that he thought he no longer needed a close alliance with the defense forces.

In 1984, the NU withdrew from politics just before a new law was to require all recognized political groups to endorse *Pancasila*. By eschewing politics, NU avoided what may have been a problematic shift from its earlier support for an explicitly Islamic system to one that embraced a *de facto* secular outlook. That year, NU elected Abdurrahman Wahid (also known as *Gus Dur*) as chairman. A former student of Ali Abd al-Raziq at Al-Azhar and a graduate from Baghdad, Wahid had taught at various *pesantren* after returning to Indonesia and was a dean at Hasan al-Ashari University. He had gained national prominence through his writing and efforts to modernize the *pesantren* system. Wahid, affiliated with the *Naqshbandi* of which his grandfather, NU's founder, was a shaykh, would be regarded by millions as a "living saint." From 1979 he had served on NU's Advisory Council where he joined other younger members in attempting to reform the movement. Wahid saw no contradiction between Islam and *Pancasila*, and embraced the national philosophy. However, believing that NU's direct participation in politics compromised its ability to pursue its core educational and social mission, he supported the decision to disengage from politics. He was also wary of how Suharto was attempting to coerce Muslims into backing him. In fact, disengagement made the NU more effective as a pressure group. Seeing his own role primarily as one of a public intellectual, this allowed Wahid to influence thinking on social and religious issues. He may have anticipated that NU could reenter the political arena when circumstances changed, although he was probably a reluctant politician. Nonetheless, when Suharto appointed him an official advocate or indoctrinator for *Pancasila* in 1985, Wahid found himself politically engaged. He was reelected as NU Chair in 1989 and in 1994. His actual relationship with Suharto was complex. His criticism of the Muslim bloc (PPP) during the 1987 election for being too sectarian earned him an MPR seat. Yet he also opposed some of Suharto's projects and turned down joining the Suharto-sponsored Association for Indonesian Muslim Intellectals (ICMA) which was meant to rubber stamp Suharto's initiatives as Islamic. Instead, Wahid set up a Forum for Democracy (1991), which included a number of Christian intellectuals. He saw ICMA's goal of making Indonesia more Islamic as endangering the country's pluralist legacy; ICMA's policy "would mean in-equality and second class citizenship for the minorities and lead to sectarian strife and religious fanaticism" (Esposito and Voll 2001: 214). Suharto saw the Forum as a threat. Wahid argued for what has been called a cosmopolitan Islam that "recognizes the need for a substantial reformulation ... of frameworks of spiritual and human behavior" in response to "universal basic rights" that "recognize and respect other faiths." He regarded the inflexible view of Islam as a legalistic, unchangeable system or Islamic legalism as "a distorted historical reality" that hijacked Islam's original dynamism and reformist outlook, turning it into an institutionalized form of oppression (Esposito and Voll 2001: 206). Cosmopolitan Islam is not a template that must be imposed globally but allows for local adaptations such as Indonesian and Bangladeshi Islam. He championed the Indonesianizing of Islam, rather than the Islamisizing of Indonesia. The latter ran "the risk of degenerating into a religious sectarianism that alienates other national groups and becomes a separatist movement" (Esposito and Voll 2001: 207). He wanted a "more universal, cosmopolitan, pluralistic, Islamically informed worldview" (Esposito and Voll 2001: 206). Islam "should not be the state religion" or "an exclusive state ideology" but "an inclusive, democratic, pluralist force" (Esposito and Voll 2001: 206). However, toward the end of Suharto's rule, Wahid did enter a *quid pro quo* with Suharto by persuading Megawati Sukarnoputri, Sukarno's daughter and PDI-P's leader since 1993, to drop law suits against him in return for Suharto ceasing fomenting discord within the NU.

Although Indonesia's economy grew by an average of 7% annually during Suhato's rule, wealth was unevenly distributed. Suharto, his cronies and the military grew rich and the majority poorer. As inequality increased, so did opposition to the New Order. More people joined in agitating for greater participation in government and protested against Suharto's authoritarian rule. On May 21st 1998, after students had occupied the parliament building, Suharto resigned. Vice-president B. J. Habibie succeeded him. The extent of Suharto's corruption soon became public. Habibie lifted restrictions on parties, released political prisoners and announced new elections. This launched Indonesia's democratic restoration, which so far has seen free and fair elections in 2004, 2009 and 2014. In this new situation, Wahid founded the NU affiliated *Partai Kebangkitan Bangsa* (PKB, National Awakening Party) May 11th, 1998. This affirms *Pancasila* and precludes advocating that Indonesia become an Islamic state, for which NU had earlier campaigned. The NU, though, is not identical with PKB nor is PKB per se a Sufi party, although many Sufis are members. The 1999 election saw PDI-P win the largest number of seats (153) followed by GOLKAR (120). Wahid's PKB won 51 seats (12.61% of the vote), with more seats than any other party with a religious affiliation, which collectively received 33.73% of the vote. The main proponent of a more Islamic polity, the Justice Party (founded 1998) with 1.4% of the vote won seven seats, not enough to participate in the next election. To do this, it reconstituted as the *Partai Keadilan Sejahtera* (PKS, Prosperous Justice Party) in 2002. Still tasked with electing the President, the MPR voted on the parties' nominees. Habibie withdrew as a candidate when the MPR rejected his required accountability speech. The candidates were Megawati, Yusril Mahendra (a former leader of *Muhammadiyah*) nominated by the Crescent Star Party (a revived *Masyumi*) and Wahid, nominated by several Muslim parties. After Muhendra withdrawal, Megawati faced Wahid who won the final vote by 373 to 313. GOLKAR, which did not nominate a candidate, may have supported Wahid to spite Megawati for gaining more seats. Although Wahid's candidacy had strained their earlier good relationship (Megawati had expected Wahid's support) she accepted his nomination for the Vice-Presidency, and was elected by 396 to 284 against Hamzah Haz, who has been described as an Islamic fundamentalist (Suryadinata: 196–97). This saw a Sufi-teacher become Head of State of the world's largest Muslim-majority state with a woman deputy. The gender-card was played against her election but the fact that women had already occupied high office in Pakistan, Turkey and Bangladesh helped to counter this. *Muhammadiyah* and NU both said that gender was not a barrier (Smith 1931: 308).

Wahid did not complete his term. His appointment of a "rainbow cabinet" attempted both to repay those who had supported his candidacy and to unite the nation. However, the many reshuffles that followed were seen as rewarding cronies. Resignations caused instability. His governing style alienated others; he had the presidential residence purified before he moved in and seemed to depend on mystical inspiration rather than expert advice when he made decisions. He saw himself as personally embodying national unity. Indeed, many saw him as their *satria piningit* ("knight and savior") while others thought that he spent more time dreaming than governing. When he fell asleep during his own accountability speech in 2000 (due to his ill health, this was mainly read for him), the hostile reception led him to promise to delegate more responsibility. He appointed Megawati to chair the cabinet. However, corruption scandals involving his administration saw MPR establish a special committee of inquiry. When Wahid tried to dismiss the chief of police, who refused to leave office, he responded by threatening to call a state of emergency. He then dissolved the DPR. Police surrounded the building to protect its members. On July 23th 2001, members unanimously impeached Wahid and elected Megawati as his successor. Haz then defeated two candidates for the vice-presidency. PKB boycotted the session. The world's first female head of a Muslim-majority state in modern time, Megawati continued the "rainbow cabinet" legacy that actually dates from the beginning of the Indonesian state. Her minister for defense and security was a member of PBK (which had held five cabinet posts under Wahid). Assessing her legacy is beyond this chapter's scope (for this, see Bennett 2010: 191–94). However, her government passed the constitutional reform that introduced direct elections for president and vice-president with a two term limit and abolished appointed seats on MPR. She also began to remove the military's political privileges, including its DPR seats. Megawati lost the presidential election in 2004 in the second round. The DPR election saw GOLKAR with the largest number of seats (129), Megawati's PDI-P was second (119) and PBK third (52), again highest of the religious parties.

Megawati stood again but did not win in 2009. She remains Head of PDI-P. Every election since 1999 has seen a peaceful transition of power. Religious parties saw a slight increase in their vote share in 2004 rising to 35.12% although PKB's share fell (to 10. 57%) and the reconstituted Islamist PKS's share rose from 1.36% in 1999 to 7.34%. They performed similarly at local level. This could indicate a decline of support among Muslims for Wahid's Sufi-shaped vision. On the other hand, Sufis might equally choose to vote for GOLKAR or for another party that also affirms *Pancasila* including PDI-P. Thus, his vision continues to dominate the political culture, despite his party's mixed fortunes. The 2009 election saw a sharper overall decline in the Muslim parties' vote share which dropped to 25, 85% although PKS's percentage rose slightly (to 7.8%). Some analysts saw this as indicating the demise of religious parties, including those that advocate a legal role for Islam. However, PKB's loss of vote share may also be explained by how the party's internal problems impact public perception. Founded around Wahid's charismatic personality, it did not develop a strong organizational structure. Dominated by "clientalistic and ascriptive relations" it had no formalized system to renew leadership (Hamayotsu 2011: 153). A split occurred in 2008 between the Wahid-led faction and another headed by his nephew after Wahid had dismissed him as Chair. PKS has developed a more merit-based organizational structure, avoiding the cult of personality. There are regular leadership elections and changes. However, it has also moved closer to the PKB's political philosophy becoming a more moderate, open and centrist party, and has widened its support base from urban areas into some rural areas, PKB's main constituency. In fact, all Muslim parties have moved toward the center. PKB focuses on agrarian reform. Yet predictions of PKB's demise proved premature. In the 2014 election, it again outperformed the other religious parties, receiving 9.4% of the vote to PKS's 6.75%. In the presidential election, PKB supported Megawati's successful nominee, Juoko Widodo, whom most non-Muslims also favored. Widodo has promised new protection for religious minorities. None of the Muslim parties called for *shāri'ah* or for Indonesia to become an Islamic State. Instead, they used "mainstream messaging, focusing on core issues such as education, community and the cost of living" during the 2014 election (Coca 2014). They collectively received 32% of the vote (distributed among BKB, PPS, the Crescent Star Party (*Maysumi's* successor, formed 1998), PPP and the National Mandate Party (f. 1998, linked with *Muhammadiyah*). Four PKB MPs currently serve in the Cabinet, holding the portfolios for Manpower, social affairs, disadvantaged regions and youth and sports. In Indonesia and Bangladesh, the Islamist option is not currently attracting votes, though moderate Islamic parties are. Magnis-Suseno has written about how Christian-Muslim cooperation in NGOs committed to democratic pluralism has contributed to the "almost 100% national consensus that Indonesia has to be a democracy" (Magnis-Suseno 2010: 123).

During 2014 the government of Aceh, a "special territory" since 1959 with more autonomy than provinces, passed a *shāri'ah* law. Some Sufi institutions have been attacked. The Council of Indonesian Islamic Scholars branch in West Sumatra declared *Al-Qiyadah al-Islamiyah*, a *Kebatinan* movement, heretical in 2007. Several leaders were imprisoned for blasphemy. In July 2005, the national *Majelis Ulama Indonesia* (MUI) had issued a *fatwa* (legal opinion) condemning "secularism, liberalism and pluralism as un-Islamic" (known as fatwa 7) (Kersten 2015: 31, 1). In response other scholars cite Q49: 13 to support their conviction that diversity is within God's plan and pluralism "a value system that appreciates religious plurality as a fundamental and inherent part of the human condition" (Kersten 2015: 248). Indonesia's freedom score, too, was lowered from free to party free (by Freedom House) following a 2014 law requiring NGO's to obtain registration with little clarity on either the application or appeal process. All are required to affirm *Pancasiila* and its monotheism principle, to respect and "maintain the value of religion." Espousing atheism, Marxism and communism is prohibited. Critics see this as limiting freedom of conscience, and as contrary to international conventions. The "monotheism" requirement leaves atheists and agnostics vulnerable to the charge that they undermine this national principle. Controversy also swirls around Indonesia's blasphemy law and how this can be used to target specific people or groups.

CONCLUSION: THE IMPORTANCE OF PLURALISM FOR DEMOCRATIC HEALTH

There is probably no objective, scientific measure that could assess the actual contribution that Sufism has made to the formation of Bangladesh's and Indonesia's political cultures today, which affirm pluralism, equal rights and popular participation in politics. However, given the role that Sufis played historically in shaping cultural norms and the generally good relations between Muslims and non-Muslims in the two states, it would be plausible to suggest some link between this legacy and current developments. The decline of Islamists in both contexts, at least at the ballot box and the success of more moderate Muslim parties and of secular parties committed to maintaining existing cultural norms does not challenge but reflects Sufi values. By planting roots in the open, inclusive preexisting cultural milieus of these two South Asian states instead of replacing these, Islam has flourished, and continues to inform national discourse about social and economic justice and the importance of human dignity and freedom. Neither state has sidelined Islam's role as a major, even the major, source of values. Both have removed religion from the legislative process. Both, too, have seen progress in women's political participation, which might owe something to their cultural legacies and to Sufism's relatively good record on gender. In many parts of the Muslim world, what can be understood as the beginning of gender-related reform in the Qur'ān and Muhammad's example, which did not complete the reform but pointed toward the goal, was reversed post-630 when pre-Islamic norms resurfaced. These, in certain places, focused authority in men's hands. Men continued to interpret Islam as a chauvinist system. Islam may have intended power and interpretation to be collective, shared responsibilities, privileging none. Rapid territorial expansion under the early caliphs led to the centralization of authority, so that one man governed and found ways to retain power within his family. Caliphs and other Muslim rulers began to function as autocrats, even though theoretical constraints on their power existed. The survival of authoritarian regimes and of limits on women's rights and liberty in those Arab states where emirs and monarchs wield almost absolute power can be seen as perpetuating this long history of autocratic, dynastic authority. Legalist Islam, framed in certain ways, justifies this. Civil society remains weak, so few mechanisms exist for open and free discussion about rights, problems, solutions and how leaders should be chosen especially where media is restricted. In contrast, Bangladesh and Indonesia appear to have rejected authoritarianism and legalist Islam in favor of Wahid's humanitarian, cosmopolitan Islam, and both affirm pluralism. Some Arab states have such large Muslim majorities that pluralism might seem to be irrelevant but Bangladeshi and Indonesian political cultures importantly accept pluralism within Islam as well as outside. Whether pluralism refers to affirming the equal rights of all regardless of religion, or that differences exist within one religion might well be a pre-condition for building a truly democratic system. Choice is impossible unless more than one option is offered. Thus, one party systems are undemocratic. Pluralism, then, includes the possibility of supporting more than one party.

Pluralism also means that no restrictions exist based on race, religion, sexual orientation or gender. As Mernissi (1992, see Chapter 1) believed, an Islam freed from state control, from the coercive reach of thought police, is likely to result in deeper, more meaningful, personally engaged faith rather than its demise (Mernissi 1992: 65). Where Islam is separate from government there are few signs that religious practice declines among those who voluntarily choose to self-define as Muslim. Iranian thinker Abdolkarim Soroush, a strong advocate of democracy, thinks that the government of any religious society will "have a religious hue" if it is in fact genuinely democratic and should not be "purely secular" (Soroush et al., 2000: 126), which, strictly speaking, neither Bangladesh nor Indonesia are. With Mernissi, he believes that a state with a large religious population will become "more religious as it becomes more free" (Soroush et al., 2000: 145). Muslim-majority states where democracy and acceptance of pluralism are less healthy than in South Asia could learn lessons from that context. Given this chapter's premise, too, that Sufis helped shape these cultures, other spaces might also benefit from Sufi influence in the public square. It seems that Tunisia (see Chapter 1 in this volume) – the Arab Spring's single success story so far – is turning to Sufism to help the healing process following upheaval and hopefully the end of divisive politics. Pointing to the democratic deficit that does exist in Muslim space, some analysts are quick to blame Islam's alleged tendency toward authoritarianism and autocracy. Many point to treatment of non-Muslims in parts of the Muslim world as evidence that Muslims find it difficult to embrace the type of social freedoms that provide the foundations of liberal democracy. By "liberal democracy" we mean separation of powers, free elections open to multiple political parties and the protection of human rights and civil liberties for all citizens regardless of gender, race or religious affiliation. There is room for improvement in Bangladesh and Indonesia. Neither yet qualify as a full "liberal democracy." They do, though, at present represent two Muslim-majority states that challenge the assumptions of those who see "Islam" as ubiquitously problematic, never as part of social or political solutions.

About the Author

Clinton Sarker Bennett holds degrees from Manchester, Birmingham and Oxford Universities. His Birmingham PhD thesis was published as *Victorian Images of Islam* (Grey Seal, 1992; Gorgias, 2009). A Fellow of the

Royal Asiatic Society (FRAS) and of the Royal Anthropological Institute (FRAI), Bennett has combined an academic career with church-related jobs and practical involvement in improving interfaith relations. He is an ordained Baptist minister. In the UK, he helped mosques acquire charitable status and Muslim neighborhood associations funding for community programs. A former missionary in Bangladesh (1979–82), he has served on the staff of the British Council of Churches (1987–92) and took part in several World Council of Churches' interfaith consultations. He currently sits on the Interreligious Convening Table of the National Council of Churches USA. Academic posts include subject leader for Religious Studies at Westminster College, Oxford (1992–98) where he was also an Assistant Chaplain and Associate Professor of Religion at Baylor, TX (1998–2001). Between 1985 and 1992, Bennett was Honorary Associate Minister of a multi-racial, inner-city congregation in Birmingham, UK. He has authored a dozen monographs as well as chapters in edited volumes, book reviews, encyclopedia entries and journal articles. He is Section Editor for North Europe and Team Leader for Western Europe with the Brill series, *Christian-Muslim Relations: a Bibliographical History* (covering 1500 to 1914, directed by David Thomas). His recent work focuses on contemporary Muslim spiritual and political movements, and issues related to citizenship, identity and belonging in multi-cultural contexts. A naturalized US citizen, Bennett teaches Religious Studies at State University of New York at New Paltz. He is also a founder member of the Center for Middle Eastern Dialogue (2008).

7

IN SEARCH OF GOD, IN SEARCH OF HUMANITY: *VILAYAT-E-MUTLAQA* OF HAZRAT DELAOR HUSAYN MAIZBHANDARI[1]

Sarwar Alam

Bangladesh is the third largest Muslim-majority country in the world. It emerged as a nation state in 1971. One of the fundamental principles of the Constitution of this nation state is *dharmanīrapeksatā* or religious neutrality, popularly understood as secularism.[2] Between 1947 and 1971 Bangladesh was a part of Pakistan, a country established in 1947 by parting India on the basis of the religious identity of its population. Upon experiencing the abuse of religion during the Pakistan era and also during the war of liberation, and above all, in order to ensure equality of every individual as a citizen regardless of caste and creed, Bangladesh incorporated *dharmanīrapeksatā* into its constitution as one of the fundamental principles in its fold. However, long before the country's political adoption of this principle, the shaykhs and some adherents of the Maizbhandariyya *Ṭarīqah*, especially Hazrat Sayyid Delaor Husayn, preached an ideal called *jatidharmanirbisese* (regardless of caste and creed), an ideal identical to the political concept of *dharmanīrapeksatā* in upholding the universal value of humanity in lieu of religious identity. Grounded in the Qur'ān and other Sufi genres, Hazrat Delaor Husayn elaborated this concept, among others, in a doctrine called *tawhid-e-adyan* or unity of religions. Husayn analyzed the concept of *jātidharmanirbiśeṣe* as well as the doctrine of *tawhid-e-adyan* in his book *Vilayat-e-Mutlaqa* (VM) published in 1959. In the *Vilayat*, he contends that the doctrine of *tawhid-e-adyan* is capable of eradicating religious conflicts and can unite humanity as it engages every faith and respective laws (*ācārdharmā*) in its fold.

Nevertheless, the ideals of *jātidharmanirbiśeṣe* and *tawhid-e-adyan* were not in conformity with the ideals of the *ulama* and ruling elites of Pakistan. As a new nation, Pakistan experienced the problem of national integration from the very beginning. As a nation it was unable to establish sustainable democratic institutions and overcome the limitations of parochialism. Since an Islamic identity was the driving force in establishing the new country, criticisms of public policy or challenges to political authority were sometimes viewed by the ruling elites, and the *ulama* as threats to the integration of the country as well as Islam. "*Islam khatre mein hai*" (Islam is in danger) was a popular slogan among some ruling elites of Pakistan in containing any political movements. A specific brand of Islam, not humanity or any forms of democratic ideals, eventually emerged as a political tool for national integration. Against this background, Hazrat Delaor Husayn provides a new interpretation of identity that transcends the political slogans of the ruling elites and religious establishments. In this chapter, I argue that Sayyid Delaor Husayn's understanding of Islam and the Qur'ān was counter-hegemonic against the exclusivist perception of Islam that was propagated by both the ruling elites and the *ulama* of the then Pakistan, and that the ideals of *tawhid-e-adyan* and *jātidharmanirbiśeṣe* were more inclusivist, universal and transcendental than the popular understanding of the concepts of communal harmony and ethnic identity promoted by the oppositions and cultural organizations especially of East Pakistan. My argument is mostly based on Hazrat Delaor Husayn's book the *Vilayat-e-Mutlaqa*[3] or the unrestricted sovereignty of sainthood of love. In addition to analyzing the doctrine of *tawhid-e-adyan*, Husayn attempted to establish the authority of the saints[4] as well as the superiority of the founding shaykh of the order Mawlana Sayyid Ahmad Allah. In doing so, I argue that, Husayn also searched for God, one Who not only transcends the conventional understanding as the Supreme Being, but Who also manifests Itself in humanity. At the same time, Husayn projected a commitment of the Maijbhandariyya *ṭarīqah* in humanity, which might be called the Maijbhandariyya humanism.

BIOGRAPHICAL SKETCH

Sayyid Delaor Husayn Maizbhandari was born in 1892 in the district of Chittagong, Bangladesh. He was the grandson of Maulana Sayyid Ahmad Allah Maizbhandari (d. 1906), the founder of the Maizbhandariyya *ṭarīqah*. Husayn lost his father at a very early age and was raised by his grandparents. His grandfather passed away when he was only 13 years-old. Husayn used to sit beside his grandfather at his court (*darbar*) from the age of four or five. He followed his grandfather throughout his life in such a manner that the Maizbhandariyya fellow and scholar Selim Jahangir, in the postscript of the eighth edition of the *Vilayat-e-Mutlaqa*, described Husayn as a mirror of his grandfather Shaykh Ahmad Allah. At the age of 23, Husayn married Sayyida Sajida Khatun, the second daughter of Maulana Sayyid Ghulam ar-Rahman (d. 1937), the second shaykh of the *ṭarīqah*. He fathered five sons and six daughters.

Jahangir informs that Hazrat Delaor Husayn received his first lesson in education at the age of five from his grandfather. In addition to his grandfather, Mawlana *Walī* Allah and later Mawlana Tofajjal Husayn tutored him in mastering the Arabic, Persian, and Urdu languages. During his student life, Husayn excelled in studying the Qur'ān, hadith, Islamic jurisprudence, and philosophy. He wrote at least ten books on the Maizbhandariyya *ṭarīqah*, among which *Ghawthul Azam Maizbhandarir Jibani o Karamat* (Biography and Miracles of Ghawth al-Azam Maizbhandari) and *Vilayat-e-Mutlaqa* are the most prominent. In addition to the Qur'ān and hadith, Husayn consulted 29 books written in Arabic and Persian and three books written in Bengali language while writing the *Vilayat*, in which Husayn described theological, philosophical as well as methodological aspects of the *ṭarīqah*.

Hazrat Delaor Husayn was also a competent organizer and was well known for his social welfare activities. He not only embodied both formal and mystical or inner aspects of the religion of Islam but also a thirst for imparting education. He founded the Ahmadiyya Junior Madrasa in 1914 and established the Maizbhandar Ahmadiyya Primary School in 1943. With the aim of establishing unity among various Sufi paths and advancing the cause of religion of the entire humanity, he founded the Anjuman-e-Mottabein-e-Ghawth-e-Maizbhandari in 1949.

Husayn led a very simple life. He used to describe himself as the servant of those who follow the path of Allah. He died at the age of 89 on January 16th, 1982, with the instruction that there should not be any celebration of his death or birthdays. He also instructed his followers not to erect any mausoleum over his tomb. In honor of his wishes, Husayn's sons and followers refrain from arranging any celebratory programs, but rather organize programs such as tree plantings, mobile eye clinics, and blood donation drives in lieu of traditional birthday or death celebrations (*urs*).

VILAYAT-E-MUTLAQA

The *Vilayat* is comprised of 15 chapters of unequal lengths and an addendum. The first chapter begins with the definition of prophethood and sainthood, while the last chapter ends with the justification of performing dance and music. The chapters in between discuss the various kinds of mystical journeys, the biography of Mawlana Sayyid Ahmad Allah, the Maijbhandariyya path, and the ecstatic statements and miracles of the founding shaykh of the *ṭarīqah*, and other related issues. The addendum summarizes the book. In what follows is a description of the key points of relevant chapters of the *Vilayt*, a section on discussion and analysis, and a conclusion.

In chapter 1, Hazrat Delaor Husayn introduces many forms of *vilayat* or sainthood. He states that God blessed Prophet Muhammad (upon whom be peace) with two great mercies: *nabuwwat* (prophethood) and *vilayat* (sainthood). The term *nabuwwat* means transmitting message. *Nabuwwat* is also a special attribute, one that cannot be acquired. God bestows this attribute to whomever He chooses. *Nabuwwat* is of two kinds: *nabuwwat-e-amma* (usual or general *nabuwwa*) that which is sent down for the entire humanity, while *nabuwwat-e-khassa* (special *nabuwwa*) that which is sent down for a particular nation. The term *vilayat*, on the other hand, derives from the word *wala*,[5] meaning achieving closeness or nearness (for details, see Cornell 1998: xvii-xx). It is a relationship of love. A close relationship with God is called *vilayat*. *Vilayat* is of two types: *vilayat-e-iman* and *vilayat-e-ahsan*. Any faithful person may attain the stage of *vilayat-e-iman*, but *vilayat-e-ahsan* is the closest mysterious relationship with God, and a power. Thus, only prophets and saints (*awliya*) could attain the stage of *vilayat-e-ahsan*. The state of *nabuwwat* ended with the demise of the Prophet Muhammad, but *vilayat-e-ahsan* would continue up until the end of time (VM 12).

Husayn states that there are four ways of attaining *vilayat-e-ahsan*: (a) *bi 'l-isalat* or naturally, which is attained without any effort. It comes naturally from God. This type of *vilayat* is endowed at a certain point of time in accordance with the evolution or changes in nature; (b) *bi 'l-berasat* is a kind of *vilayat* which is earned by a way of spiritual inheritance; in Sufi literature it is known as *bi 'l-walayat*; (c) *bi 'l-darasat* is a kind which is acquired through learning both manifested and secret wisdom; and (d) *bi 'l-malamat* is acquired by restraining the *nafs* or carnal soul (VM 13).

Husayn argues that those who control their carnal self and fight against their ego in order to attain nearness to God can be defined as *malamiyya walī*, or saint. Husayn notes that Abu Saleh Hamd Allah Qassar is the founder of the Malamiyya path (see Toussulis 2010: 75)[6] and Bu Ali Qalander[7] is related to the Qalandariyya path (see Karamustafa 2006: 91).[8] Bu Ali was a follower of a doctrine called *tawhid-e-adyan* (unity of religions) tradition. The doctrine insists that, though there are differences among the various world religions in their outward expression, the core of all religions is the same, as the objective of all religion is God. Other notable scholars and Sufis who are connected to this doctrine are Muhy al-Din ibn al-'Arabi, Amer ibn al-Fares, Jalal al-Din Rumi, Abd al-Karim Jili, and Abu Yazid Bistami (VM 13–14).

Moreover, there are three hierarchical stages of *vilayat*: (a) *vilayat-e-sughra* or those who acquired the status above the ordinary believers, (b) *vilayat-e-wasta* or those who acquired an intermediary status above the angels, and (c) *vilayat-e-'uzma* or the highest level of power, the possessor of which is able to exert power and influence upon the entire creation. The saints belonging to the last stage are known as the great saints or *awliya*. The latter are further divided into two sub-categories: *qutubiyat* (*karmak-attritva* or authority to act) and *ghawthiyat* (*trankatritva* or authority to rescue). The *walī* who possesses *ghawthiyat* or the supreme authority to rescue is known as *ghawth al-azam* or the savior. He is a *bi 'l-isalat* or natural and born *walī*, and by the will of God he emerges as the beneficial savior (*mangalmoy trankarta*) of the creation. The person who becomes a *walī* by virtue of the authority to act is known as *qutb al-aqtab* (the pole of the poles); by the will of God he remains as the supreme authority in maintaining order in the universe (VM 14).

After discussing the categories of saints, Husayn attempts to describe the nature of prophethood. He notes that Prophet Muhammad has two names: Ahmad and Muhammad. In the beginning of the creation, Ahmad was hidden and remained fundamental to the mystery of creation, whereas Muhammad emerged as the beneficial savior of the universe. Because of the influences of the two names, all the prophets and saints are divided into two *mashrab* or categories, i.e. Ahmadi and Muhammadi. The origin of the *ghawthiyat* is Muhammadi and the origin of *qutubiyat* is Ahmadi *mashrab*. The Muhammadi *mashrab* began with Prophet Adam and the Ahmadi *mashrab* began with Prophet Shish (VM 14).[9]

Husayn substantiates his argument by saying that one might understand the above categories by observing the nature of prophethood of Abraham, Jesus and Muhammad. He states that prophet Abraham belongs to Muhammadi category. Prophet Abraham's method of *vilayat* is known as *shahudiyya* or observational method. After observing the sun, moon and other objects, he came to believe in the existence of a supreme permanent power, Allah. His belief belongs to the level of wisdom-philosophy-logic, and closely related to *nabuwwat*. Prominent prophets, such as Adam, Noah and Moses belong to this category; even the faith propagated by Prophet Muhammad is called *Din-i-Ibrahimi* or Abrahamic faith (VM 15).

On the other hand, prophet 'Isa or Jesus belongs to the emaciated realm or Ahmadi category. Angel Jibra'il appeared before Mariam in the form of a human being and transferred to her the spirit of God, leading her to bear Jesus. Prophet Jesus was a mysterious character who preferred a solitary life to sociality and gave preference to love of the heart over formal acts. Prophets, such as Shish, Idris, and Ishaq could be included in the Ahmadi category. In Sufi literature it is described as the *wujudiyya* (self-reflective or self-visioning) method. Thus, the *wujudiyya* path is reflective of the Ahmadi *mashrab* or category (VM 17).

He notes that the Muhammadi prophethood combines the shariat or disciplinary and *tariqat* or mystical paths together, allowing the Muhammadi prophethood to attain *azmiyat* or greatness and completeness. Because of this, Prophet Muhammad is regarded not only as the last prophet but also as *maraj al-bahrain* or the point of confluence for both Ahmadi and Muhammadi streams. However, though *nabuwwat* or the outward (*zahir*) and *vilayat* or the hidden (*batin*) are separate streams, the hidden stream unites in the existence of the Prophet, one that may not apparently follow the command of *shariat* or may transcend the formal aspect of religion. The *vilayati* stream gives preference to God's willpower over the formal decrees and empowered to act in accordance with the benefit and requirement of the religion. The stories of Moses and Khidr as described in the Qur'ān testify God's preference to mysterious willpower over formal decrees (VM 19). Prophet Muhammad embodied both *nabuwwat-i-'uzma* and *vilayat-e-'uzma* in his persona.

Husayn notes that after the demise of the Prophet Muhammad, Hazrat 'Ali inherited all forms of *vilayat*, which continues even today through the perfect *walīs* or *awliya*. The *vilayat-e-'uzma*, which had been inherited by 'Ali, drifted naturally into 'Abd al-Qadir Jilani. Since his time *ghawthiyat* represents both *nabuwwat* and *vilayat* (VM 20). Husayn maintains that historians acknowledge a cycle of the rise and fall of nations in every 500–600 years. Both ibn Khaldun in his *Muqaddima* and Muhy al-Din ibn al-'Arabi in his *Fusus al-Hikm* describe this cycle with examples.[10] History testifies that Prophet Muhammad arrived within 600 years of the demise of Prophet Jesus, while 'Abd al-Qadir arrived within 500 years of the demise of Prophet Muhammad. 'Abd al-Qadir was a reviver (*mujaddid*), a carrier of *vilayat-e-'uzma* state, and the greatest *walī*. Because of his knowledge of the *'alam-e-lahut* (the realm of God) and *'alam-e-nasut* (the realm of humanity) he was recognized as the savior or *ghawth al-azam*. Husayn called the period of 'Abd al-Qadir the era of *vilayat-e-muqayyada* or restricted sainthood. This periodization ended with the beginning of a new era led by the *ghawth al-azam* of the era Mawlana Ahmad Allah Maizbhandari. In contrast to the era of the *vilayat-e-muqayyada*, Husayn called this era *vilayat-e-mutlaqa* or unrestricted sainthood (VM 22).

Husayn continues his effort in establishing the authority of Mawlana Ahmad Allah in chapter 2 of his book. He states that with the strength of spiritual power, humankind's move toward God is called *sayr-e-ruhani* or journey of the soul. There are three types of *sayr-e-ruhani*: *sayr ila Allah*, man's journey to God; *sayr fillah*, journey in God or the state of annihilation in the essence of God; and *sayr ma' Allah*, journey with God or attaining the merit of transfusing God's power into the creation. The greatest *walī* or saint embodies the spiritual strength of all three *sayr*. The spiritual strength may manifest in different ways among the saintly people of *ghawthiyat* and *qutbiyat*, but he who attains both of these qualities is called *ghawth al-azam*. Sayyid 'Abd al-Qadir Jilani and Sayyid Ahmad Allah attained both of these statuses. On top of this, they themselves claimed the status of the *ghawth al-azmiyat* (VM 23).

Husayn states that the word *insan* or human derives from the word *unsun*, which means love, suggesting that God created humankind out of love. God's first creation was the Light of Muhammad or *Nur-e-Muhammad*. The Light of Muhammad reflects the reality of Godly attributes in humanity. Prophet Muhammad, the universal guide, is the mercy of God to humanity. Adam, the primordial man created in the image of Muhammad, was the vicegerent of God and before whom angels prostrated. However, Husayn argues that it is Prophet Muhammad who is the perfect man (*al-insan al-kamil*) and loyalty to him is inevitable (VM 26).

In chapter 3, Husayn argues that Sufism was practiced as the tradition of the Prophet during his lifetime and continued to be practiced by the saints or *awliya* after his demise. However, Sufism in its early days was restricted (*muqayyad*) by the influence of the exoteric *ulama* and governing elites. Therefore this era may be called the sainthood of the restricted Muhammadan era or *muqayyad-e-muhammadi*.

Husayn notes that as time passed, the Islamic system itself became lifeless and weak. About 600 years after the death of the guide 'Abd al-Qadir Jilani, the cracks on the wall of the Islamic world became obvious because of its separation from governance. Humankind fell into confusion once again after the establishment of British rule in Bengal on October 14, 1760. Without the help of a shari'aless state, the Muslim community started experiencing stagnation as well as disaster. In this era of weak and lifeless shari'a, an ethically grounded Ahmadi era of unrestricted sovereignty of sainthood (*Vilayat-e-Mutlaqa-e-Ahmadi*) became a necessity. A person who attains this kind of sainthood embodies sovereignty, gives preference to God's willpower over rituals, ends the era of restricted sainthood and begins the era of unrestricted sainthood; he is a supporter of *tawhid-e-adyan* or unity of religions (VM 27). It is the category of a saint whom ibn al-'Arabi called the seal of sainthood. The Qur'ān says, "And verily the latter portion will be better for thee than the former" (93:4). Many an adherent of Maulana Ahmad Allah believe that the world has not seen such a great saint in last 600 years. The Hindus also believe in the arrival of the *Kalki Avatar* or the savior in a future that resonates the concept of seal of the saints.

In chapter 4 Husayn continues to stress the greatness of Mawlana Ahmad Allah by referring to a prophecy of ibn al-'Arabī (ibn al-'Arabī 1992: 61–62, 70). He argues that ibn al-'Arabi predicts in his book *Fusus al-Hikm* the birth of the *khatam al-walad* or the last saint (VM 31). The signs described in *Fusus al-Hikm* about the arrival of the last saint match the profile of Hazrat Sayyid Ahmad Allah. Ibn al-'Arabī predicted that a sister would be born before the birth of this saint, that he would be born on the edge of China, and that he would speak the language of the local city dwellers. Moreover, ibn al-'Arabī predicted that women would become barren at that time yet the number of marriages would increase. The saint would in vain invite humankind toward God. After his death and the death of other faithfuls of that era, it was predicted that humankind would behave like four-legged animals. People would disregard what is permissible and what is forbidden. They would distance themselves from religion and conscience and engage in fulfilling the desire of their carnal selves.

He emphasizes that the above predictions match with Hazrat Sayyid Ahmad Allah because:

1. According to ibn al-'Arabi, Prophet Shish belongs to Ahmadi *mashrab* as does Sayyid Ahmad Allah
2. A sister was born before his birth
3. He spoke the local dialect
4. Birth control and a sterilization system were introduced during his era
5. Regardless of caste and creed he called humankind toward God
6. Humankind did not understand his message and could not pay heed to his call satisfactorily
7. After his demise, humankind began to lead a life that is far from the ideals of religion
8. Chittagong was the edge of China as it was ruled by the Chinese dynasties during ibn al-'Arabi's time
9. Sayyid Ahmad Allah was adequately aware of the fact that there was no difference in the ethical aspects of various faiths. Regardless of caste and creed, all the contemporary communities were his admirers and were supporters of his greatness.

Husayn goes on to state that God's greatest blessing or *vilayat* was fully developed in the existence of Sayyid Ahmad Allah. Husayn maintains that it is not possible again to develop this in others, because the competency of developing this (*istihaqaq-e-wujudi*) is completed and ended in Ahmad Allah. He is the introducer of the era of unrestricted divine love, and his sevenfold method (*sapta padhati*) is a blueprint for realizing the unity of religions in the world; he is the last savior or *ghawth al-azam* (VM 34).

In chapter 5, Husayn describes the genealogy of Mawlana Ahmad Allah. *Ghawth al-Azam* Shah Sufi Hazrat Maulana Ahmad Allah was born in 1826 in the district of Chittagong of the then Bengal. He was a descendant of Prophet Muhammad. His forefathers arrived in Bengal from Delhi in 1575 CE and settled in the region of Chittagong. Hazrat Ahmad Allah's father Maulana Sayyid Moti Allah moved to Maizbhandar, a village of Fatik-chhari sub-district of Chittagong district. Hazrat Ahmad Allah graduated from the *alia madrasa* in Calcutta, then the capital of British India. He later left the position as *Qadi* of the Jessore district to teach in a madrasa in Mitia Buruz in West Bengal. During that time he met the descendant and Khalifa of the Qadiriyya Order Shaykh Sayyid Abu Shahama Muhammad Saleh Qadiri Lahori, who initiated him into the Qadiriyya Order, subsequently leading him to inherit the spiritual sainthood or *bi 'l-berasat*. Mawlana Ahmad Allah also received the unity of masterhood (*ittehad-e-qutubiyat*) from Shah Sufi Sayyid Delwar Ali Pakbaj Muhajer-e-Madani Lahori, a saint by birth (*bi 'l-isalat*). Because of his companionship with other saints, Mawlana Ahmad Allah was also blessed as a saint of the *bi 'l-berasat* kind. By cultivating both manifested and hidden knowledge, he attained the status of *bi 'l-darasat* sainthood. Moreover, by persevering and fighting against the allurement of the carnal self, he attained the status of *bi 'l-malamat* sainthood. Thus Mawlana Ahmad Allah attained perfectness in all four categories and became the universal saint. He is the reviver (*mujaddid*) of religion and the beginner of *mutlaqa* or the era of unbounded sainthood (VM 39). He died on January 23rd of 1906 at the age of 79.

Husayn goes on to discuss the basic principles of the Maizbhandariyya *tarīqah*, which is popularly known as the Maizbhandariyya philosophy, in chapter 6. He states that God sends down prophets and saints in every era in order to introduce reform, which made the understanding of God easier. After the end of the era of prophethood, when Muslims were going through conflicts, obstacles and confusion, God sends down Sayyid 'Abd al-Qadir Jilani as a religious reformer. He was sent down as the supreme guardian of the era of *vilayat-e-'uzma* and also as the first *ghawth al-azam* and *qutb al-aqtab*. It was the first *dawra* or cycle of the era of religious conflict, which occurred approximately 500 years after the end of the era of prophethood or *nabuwwat*. 'Abd al-Qadir was the introducer of the *bi 'l-isalat* and followed the restricted path or Shari'a. With 'Abd al-Qadir's blessings, Khawaja Muin al-Din Chishti acquired the status of the *qutb al-aqtab* and *bi 'l-berasat ghawthiyat*. There were other *awliya* who also received such blessings and adopted the method of *tariqat* in guiding others that was commensurate to the restricted path of the Shari'a (VM 56).

Following a period of 600 years after the demise of 'Abd al-Qadir, the Islamic governance collapsed due to the emergence of conflicting opinions in the Islamic world. At this point God transformed the *Vilayat-e-Muqayyad-e-Muhammadi* (Sainthood of the Restricted Muhammadi Path) into the *Vilayat-e-Mutalaqa-e-Ahmadi* (Sainthood of the Unrestricted Ahmadi Path) in order to guide and rescue humankind from the world of darkness. This sainthood is all-embracing and is endowed with unrestricted power (VM 56). On principle, it views various religious traditions in the same light; it believes that although there are differences in ideologies and methods among the traditions, they all share the same goal. It could be called the beholder of universal guardianship or world peace, and the eternal Islam. It is able to combine both prophethood and sainthood of Prophet Muhammad and the sainthood of Prophet Jesus together (VM 57).

Husayn contends that the doctrine of the unity of religions (*tawhid-e-adyan*) of the unrestricted sainthood is grounded in the Qur'ān. In support of the doctrine he quoted the following verse of the Qur'ān: "Those who believe (in the Qur'ān), and those who follow the Jewish (scriptures), and the Christians and the Sabians, any who believe in God and the Last Day, and work righteousness, shall have their reward with their Lord: on them shall be no fear, nor shall they grieve" (2:62). Husayn argues that humankind is the trustee of God's knowledge (*marifat*) and unity (*tawhid*);[11] regardless of creed and caste (*dharmajātinirbiśeṣe*), everyone is the bearer of this trusteeship (VM 57). According to the doctrine of the unity of religions, the ethical objective of all religions is the same and no religion is inferior to another. In support of the doctrine, Husayn quoted the following verses of the Qur'ān:[12] "Do ye believe in some books[13] of God and disbelieve in the other books? Who do so amongst you shall be insulted in this life and returned to the grievous punishment on the Day of Judgment. God is surely aware of what ye do" (Qur'ān 2:85); "Those who say none except Christians and Jews shall enter heaven are their futile words. O Muhammad say! Produce proof before you if ye are truthful" (Qur'ān 2:111); "Rather the truth is that, whosoever return to God and do righteousness shall have their rewards from God. No fear shall come upon them, nor shall they grieve" (2:112). Husayn maintains that like those of Jews who think that heaven is assigned only to them also fall under the purview of the same order. In elaborating the message of the above statements of the Qur'ān he summarizes the meaning of *Iman-e-Mujmal*: "I believe in the existence of God; the angels and books of God are true; believe in the prophets and messengers; I do not hold any differences of opinion nor make any differences amongst the prophets and messengers."[14] By quoting Jalal al-Din Rumi, Husayn argues that the differences of laws preached by prophets are due to the differences of time and circumstances therein; nevertheless, there is no difference among them in terms of goal or ethical message (VM 58).

Husayn contends that the doctrine of *tawhid-e-adyan* (unity of religions) is encompassed in the unrestricted sainthood of love or *Vilayat-e-Mutlaqa*. He argues that without preventing adherents of other traditions from following their respective laws, the *Vilayat-e-Mutlaqa* is instead able to unite the people of all faiths on ethical grounds. It does not support any religious conflicts, but rather it judges every religion on the basis of its ultimate objective (VM 60). Though the *Vilayat-e-Mutlaqa* does not always resonate the outward aspect of the Shari'a, it nevertheless maintains a close relationship with the reality or objective; it emphasizes on faith itself. Husayn notes that history has proven that it is absurd to proselytize all of humankind into Islam in order to rescue it from *shirk* and atheism, despite the fact that both atheists and religious conservatives have been trying to take over the entire world in their fold and thus causing conflicts everywhere (VM 60–61). Instead of using force or indulging in conflicts, God emphasizes persuasion, as it is depicted in the following verse: "Call (humankind) to the way of your Lord with good advice or scientific means" (16:125).

The Prophet Muhammad is asked in the Qur'ān to say "I have been commanded to maintain 'adl or justice in dealing with you. Since God is our

Lord as He is your Lord. Our deeds and religious practices are for ours, your deeds and religious practices are for yours. There is no argument or dispute between us and you. God will gather us together in the realm of unicity or non-duality. Because all are subject to return to the Creator" (Qur'ān 42:15). Husayn argues that this ethical message is able to unite humankind and is competent in establishing impartial justice of *'adl-e-mutlaq*. To rescue the world from paganism, atheism, and religious conservatism, it has become necessary for the emergence of an effective great spiritual (*ruhani*) power and a strategy or wisdom under its command. The introduction of that great power is realized through the blessings (*barakat*) of Sayyid Ahmad Allah, and the name of this great strategy or wisdom is *Vilayat-e-Mutlaqa* (VM 62).

In chapter 7 Husayn describes in general terms the categories of *fayd* (divine effulgence), classes of followers or disciples and methods acquiring *fayd*. In chapter 8 Husayn describes in specific terms the sevenfold Maizbhandariyya method. The *sapta paddhati* or the sevenfold method of action is divided into two parts: (i) *Fana-e-tullatha* (The Three Annihilation), and (ii) *Maut-e-arba'* (The Four Deaths). The practice of *Fana-e-tullatha* (The Three Annihilation) is comprised of the following:

1. *Fana an al-khalq* (Annihilation of humanity) means the practice of self-reliance; not to expect any favors from others or not to keep any such desire in mind,
2. *Fana an al-hawa* (Annihilation of desire) means avoidance of unnecessary things, and avoidance of unnecessary activities and utterances in order to make life easy and free of difficulties.
3. *Fana an al-irada* (Annihilation of will) means giving preference to the will of Allah and surrendering personal will or desire in Allah's will.

Maut-e-arba' (The Four Deaths) have four components:

1. *Maut-e-abiyad* (White death). This is achieved through the practice of fasting and abstinence, which enlightens the mind.
2. *Maut-e-aswad* (Black death). This is achieved through opening oneself to the criticism or censures of enemies. This is because criticism and censure help correct a person's faults, which leads the person to repent and beg for the mercy of Allah.
3. *Maut-e-ahmar* (Red death). This is achieved through emancipation from sexual impulses and lust; accomplishing this ensures a person's attainment of the status of a perfect saint.
4. *Maut-e-akhdar* (Green death). This is achieved by leading a simple life. It helps eradicate lust and desire, and generate Divine love in the mind.

Husayn holds that this Qur'ānically grounded method is a faultless easy guidance for human life. Husayn argues that it is easier than the eightfold method of Gautama Buddha. It is not in conflict with the method of other religious traditions; it does not support those who made religion a trade. In this era of diminishing influence of the traders of religion (*pirs*), *Vilayat-e-Mutlaqa* is the lifegiving pole star of the ethical religion (VM 70). Husayn contends that Sayyid Ahmad Allah is the seal of the saints (VM 71). He is the gift of God for the humankind. In this chapter Husayn also argues that he himself is the competent person to disclose the mystery of this sainthood as he is the trustee of Mawlana Sayyid Ahmad Allah who declared Husayn as his spiritual heir before his death (VM 71).

In chapter 9 Husayn describes the superiority of humanity as well as sainthood. He states that God commanded the angels to prostrate themselves before Adam because of the knowledge God provided him. God taught Adam all names and appointed him as His vicegerent. In a similar way, the knowers of the secret knowledge of every era are the deputies of God and representatives of the Prophet Muhammad (VM 72). Husayn notes that Adam fell into misery due to inclinations to his carnal self. Consequently, God assured Adam that He would send down guidance and suggested "whosoever follow the guidance, on them shall be no fear, nor shall they grieve" (Qur'ān 2:38). Moreover Husayn describes various types of prostration in this chapter.

Husayn argues that because of the differences in human wisdom God's guidance is realized by humankind in three different ways. The first way of realization is called '*aql-e-mayash*, which derives from the appetite or desire for food or lust. Eating, drinking or merry-making are a few of its components. '*Aql-e-mayash* is the realm of the revealed world (*nasut*), with God's revealed law or Shari'a as its remedy. The second way is known as '*aql-e-mayad*, which inspires people to become conscious or accountable for their deeds. It helps people to become self-conscious and seek God's mercy. This state of human consciousness is known as *lawwama* or reproachful state, and it is called *malkut* or angelic state. The third way is called '*aql-e-kulli* or universal intellect. People of this state are the knowers of all things. No other existence but God is the characteristic of this state. People of this state may transcend the Shari'a (VM 76–79).

These three categories of people deserve differential leadership. A competent leader is in fact the representative of God. He is the greatest person who acquires such competency, and that person is known as the *khilafat-e-uluhiyat* or the Vicegerent of the Divine (VM 80). He is free of tension and devoted to establishing religious unity. He is the guide for the God-seeking people. Opposing such a person or leader is synonymous to opposing the eternal Islam. In order to reach the summit of humanity, it is imperative that everyone recognizes and follows the lead of the prophet, saint or the reviver of the era (VM 80). Husayn notes that there is no difference between the principles of the unrestricted or universal sainthood (*Vilayat-e-Mutlaqa*) and the principles of God because the universal sainthood derives from God's will. *Ghawth al-Azam* Shah Sufi Mawlana Sayyid Ahmad Allah Maizbhandari Malamiyya Qaderi is the reformer of the era (*mujaddid-e-zaman*), bearer of the universal intellect of the ethical religion, and a saint with the supreme personality. Regardless of their caste and creed, Mawlana Sayyid Ahmad Allah drew everyone's attention to the doctrine of the *tawhid-e-adyan* or unity of religions and undivided love for God. He preferred ethics to religious law and rituals (*ācārdharmā*) and supported the state's tolerance or neutrality towards the practices of various traditions. Among his concerns were the remembrance of God, cultivation of the self, and freedom of religion in the world civilization; he viewed individualism as the key to the development of humanity (VM 81). He noted again that Sayyid Ahmad Allah was the seal of the era of restricted sainthood (*Vilayat-e-Muqayyada*) and the beginner of the era of unrestricted sainthood (*Vilayat-e-Mutlaqa*) and *ghawth al-azam*. The strength and principles of this *vilayat* is called all-embracing guardianship (*Vilayat-e-Muhith*). It is the easiest and most approachable path to realize the religious goal of every nation and every religion (VM 87).

In chapter 10 Husayn describes the importance of the *Vilayat-e-Mutlaqa* in eradicating religious conflicts. Despite the fact that Islam is the latest reform of divine religions and the Qur'ān is a pure, faultless, and unchanged divine revelation, the *Vilayat-e-Mutlaqa* insists that regardless of creed, its adherents should remain committed to their respective faith (VM 89). The Qur'ān offers a progressive and universal religious system, with Prophet Muhammad as the symbol of the best character and universal humanity. That is why Islam is the acceptable religion to all. Yet anyone can choose a religion according to his conscience and taste. Those Shari'a-minded Muslims that are unable to maintain a balance between themselves and others have become habituated to forgetting the loving aspect of God even in their prayer. God warns them in the Qur'ān (107:5). The literal meaning of *salat* or prayer is igniting the fire, which means igniting the concealed love of God. A prayer that does not ignite the love of God cannot be termed as a prayer. A love for God is the key of any prayer regardless of the differences amongst religions; as such, religious conflicts would be purged if one understands this. Thus, Husayn argues that the *Vilayat-e-Mutlaqa-e-Ahmadi* is the best path for abolishing religious conflicts and integrating every religion of the world (VM 90). The influence of this *vilayat* may remove religious conflicts and eradicate degeneration of human character. People of different nations have dissimilar ways of worship, yet the common goal of every religion is to create a human race with ideal character traits by stopping the degeneration of the human character (VM 91). This is just a fundamental and common goal. That is why Prophet Muhammad said that he arrived on earth to help humankind reach the highest standard of character.

Husayn notes that the *awliya* or saints have been propagating Islam in this world without inflicting any conflicts. Islam was not spread with the rulers' sword, but rather with the exemplary speech, behavior, manner and etiquette of the holy men, which are in conformity with the eternal Islam. Bengal and other peripheral and remote islands where the existence of any political authority was barely felt would testify to this historical fact. Nevertheless, some *nasuti* or worldly-minded people criticize the Sufis without having any historical grounding or understanding of them (VM 91).

In chapter 11, Husayn states that the *vilayat* is a close, intimate and eternal state of one's relationship with God. Therefore the flag of friendship or the *Liwa-e-Ahmadi* will be the last sign or flag on the Day of Judgement (VM 93). In chapter 12, Husayn narrates how Sayyid Ahmad Allah used to give advice to his disciples by using similes or allegories. He advised people to lead an honest, simple and pure God-loving life, to lead a life of an angel, to say supererogatory prayers, to refrain from sinful acts, and to avoid activities that have little or no worth. Husayn informs that Mawlana Sayyid Ahmad Allah did not like ornaments and fashions, so much so that he ordered people to remove ornaments from their hands, noses or ears.

The *Vilayat-e-Mutlaqa* is the God-approved flow of peace for humanity. It is a guide against rivalries and competition in earning wealth. It is a method of contentment and free of excitement. It is a guide for the welfare of humanity. It removes the roots of both capitalism and atheism.[15] It is a symbol of equality and peace. God suggests not to circuit wealth between the wealthy alone (Qur'ān 59:7). Husayn contends that there is no room for discrimination on the basis of race, ethnicity or region in the reign of the unrestricted sainthood (*Vilayat-e-Mutlaqa*); rather, it is a universal system and a message of justice for the have-nots (VM 99). Therefore, the *Vilayat-e-Mutlaqa* is the symbol of a welfare-laden society and the redeemer of a universal humanity. It is intended to establish the supreme Godly justice (*'adl-e-mutlaq*), love, unity and brotherhood by upholding the sevenfold method.

In chapter 13, Husayn describes the Vision of the Self. He also describes the kinds of *fayd* or divine effulgence in this chapter. He states that people used to receive three kinds of *foyd* from the company of the Prophet: (1) *Ṭarīqah-e-abrar-e-mujahidin*, (2) *Ṭarīqah-e-abrar-e-salehin*, and (3) *Ṭarīqah-e-shohada-e-asheqin*, meaning those who helped the Prophet by fighting and spending their wealth for him, those who became followers by honest deeds, and those who sacrificed their lives because of their love for him (VM 104). Hazrat Ali inherited the Prophet's esoteric wisdom (*Ilm al-batin*). He gave the leadership of *bi 'l-berasat Ṭarīqah-e-abrar-e-mujahidin* to his own son Imam Hasan, *Ṭarīqah-e-abrar-e-salehin* to Hasan Basri, and the trusteeship of the *Ṭarīqah-e-shohada-e-asheqin* to Hazrat Uways

Qarani. These three *vilayati* traditions gave birth to several branches and sub-branches. They developed in diverse ways, but their goal was the same – the love for the creator.

During the period of *nabuwwat* or prophethood, the way in which the threefold branch of the *Nabuwwat-e-Muhammadi* was manifested in the last prophet, the same way it was manifested in the *Ghawth al-Azam* Mawlana Shah Sufi Sayyid Ahmad Allah Malamiyya Qaderi during this period of the *Vilayat-e-Mutlaqa-e-Ahmadi*. Because of this, Mawlana Ahmad Allah is known as integrator of the preceding *adiyan-e-sabiqa* or preceding past religions and different scattered paths. By following his own method he was able to accord *fayd* among the adherents of the paths of all religions without asking them to change their faith or religion (VM 104).

Husayn argues that one should not quarrel over religion, as the Qur'ān says, "If God had so willed, He would have made you a single People, but (His plan is) to test you in what He hath given you: so strive as in a race in all virtues. The goal of you all is to God; it is He that will show you the truth of the matters in which ye dispute" (Qur'ān 5:48). God also says, "Did not God check one set of people by means of another, there would surely have been pulled down monasteries, churches, synagogues, and mosques, in which the name of God is commemorated in abundant measure" (Qur'ān 22:40). By ignoring these stipulations in the Qur'ān, some people engage themselves in squabbles over religion; they are moving toward destruction without being conscious of it (VM 107). Similar to the light of the prophethood of the Perfect Prophet, the light of the *vilayat* inspired by the light of God's love had been removing the darkness of humankind (VM 107).

In chapter 14 Husayn describes the right methods of performing prayers as well as the importance of fasting. In this chapter he reiterates human agency and freedom of religion in choosing a faith in accordance with his or her own taste (VM 129). In chapter 15 Husayn describes the importance of music and ecstatic dance. He argues that music is able to help a wayfarer refrain from engaging in dirty activities and find guidance to the right path. It helps to concentrate the mind or *hujur-e-qalb*, without which a prayer does not get accepted by God (VM 131). The Qur'ān mentions those people who remember God in any postures, whether it be standing, sitting, or laying. There is a Prophetic narrative that says that a state of intoxication in God is greater than the prayer of two worlds (VM 132). Thus it is understood that the tactic of dhikr-in-dance is a classical Islamic wisdom; it is not a new discovery or an un-Islamic method (VM 132).

DISCUSSION AND ANALYSIS

The *Vilayat-e-Mutlaqa* is a pedagogy of sainthood, more precisely the sainthood of Sayyid Ahmad Allah. The book portrays a continuation of the medieval paradigm of sainthood, which was embodied in his grandfather, to whom he claims himself as a legitimate trustee. Yet, it appears that Husayn did not claim the status of the supreme sainthood for himself. In establishing the sainthood of Sayyid Ahmad Allah, the Maijbhandariyya *ṭarīqah*, and the doctrine of *tawhid-e-adyan*, Husayn addresses several issues in his book that may be summarized in the following categories with some overlappings: (a) theological, (b) historical, and (c) social.

Theological

Since there is no specific reference to Sufism in the Qur'ān or Prophetic traditions, it remains a center of controversy throughout centuries among both Muslim *ulama* and non-Muslim scholars (Karamustafa 2004: xi). Husayn discusses in detail the roots of Sufism in Islam. He discusses the types and differences of prophethood (*nabuwwa*) and the types and differences of sainthood and their relationships with one another. In addition, he discusses the categories of faith (*iman*) and knowledge. He notes that the very objective of the creation of humanity is love. In this regard, he refers to a *hadith qudsi*[16] or a sacred hadith in which God says, "I was a hidden treasure, and I wanted to be known, so I created the world."[17] Husayn argues that God first created the Light of Muhammad (*Nur-e-Muhammad*) out of love. The reality of humanity (*haqiqa al-insani*) embodies God's light. Muhammad is the savior of the worldly realm as well as the mercy of God to humanity (VM 26).[18] Adam, as the first human and God's vicegerent before whom angels prostrated, beholds the Muhammadi image. In another sacred hadith God says, "I have created Adam in My image" (VM 75). The greatness of humanity lies between the love of God and love of creation (VM 76). In this regard, he quoted Jalal ad-Din Rumi who says that fools honor the mosque – a creation made by man – and give hardships to the possessor of a heart – a creation made by God (VM 92), and that the human body is the real book, so one should discover the signs in it by oneself (VM 123). Husayn states in another booklet (Husayn 2012: 11) that the clay-made human being is the mirror of God's essence. It is mentioned in a sacred hadith in which God says: "My servant ceases not to draw nigh unto Me by works of devotion until I love him, and when I love him I am the eye by which he sees, the ear by which he hears, the tongue by which he talks, the hands by which he grasps, the foot by which he walks, and by Me he attains and imparts knowledge. It means the servant annihilates its self in God, only God's existence remains" (Husayn 2012: 19; see also Nasr 2007: 115). There are differences in the methods among the lovers of God but every religion shares the essence of this message. All agree that, when a human being makes itself free of weakness and temptation, it moves nearer to God; no one could separate God from it or separate it from God (Husayn 2012: 19). God says that it is indeed humanity that undertook the trust of God (Qur'ān 33:72). The Qur'ān depicts that God has put signs into nature and into the human soul (Qur'ān 51:20–21). Grounded in the Qur'ān, prophetic traditions and other Sufi literature, Husayn describes the importance of knowing both God and humanity in order to know the world. God loves humanity and humanity's goal is to attain the love of God. It is not the wrathful God who only rewards or punishes, but a loving God Who emanates His light of love in humankind and in return humankind loves Him. There is another sacred hadith in which God says that he who knows his self knows his Lord.[19] Nevertheless, knowing one's own self is not enough, as God enlightens humanity with His own light, one should love others too. Husayn admits the superiority of the Qur'ān as it is the latest revelation from God for humanity and Islam supersedes previously revealed religions; yet, he did not deny the validity of other faiths. Thus, it appears that Husayn went beyond the traditional Islamic views on other faiths as projected in the phrase *ahl al-kitab* (People of the Book, which generally includes Jews and Christians). For him humanity is not confined to the Muslim community alone; it includes Hindus, Buddhists, and even idol worshippers.

Historical

In establishing the authority of Mawlana Sayyid Ahmad Allah, Husayn introduced a historical narrative beginning with Prophet Muhammad. He divided the Islamic historical periods into three eras: the era of the Prophet, the era of the restricted sainthood (*Vilayat-e-Muqayyada*), and the era of the unrestricted sainthood (*Vilayat-e-Mutlaqa*). He argues that when the Islamic society became degenerated and corrupted, God appointed Abd al-Qadir Jilani (d. 1166) as the reviver of the faith. Abd al-Qadir Jilani was blessed with the authority of *ghawth al-azam* or as the savior. The era of restricted sainthood began with him, continuing up until the birth of Mawlana Ahmad Allah, who began the era of unrestricted sainthood. Like Abd al-Qadir, Mawlana Ahmad Allah also carried the authority of *ghawth al-azam*. The basic difference between the restricted and unrestricted sainthood is that the former worked for the Muslim community within the framework of the Shari'a and the latter worked for the entire humanity and transcends the Shari'a. Husayn notes that the unrestricted sainthood integrates both the prophethood and sainthood of Prophet Muhammad and also the saintly aspect of Prophet Jesus (VM 57). His narratives reflect the sufferings and persecution the Sufis experienced over centuries. Husayn also acknowledged the roles Sufis played in proselytization, especially in South Asia. It may be mentioned here that Husayn includes both written and oral narratives in his discourse; by following other Sufi discourses of South Asia, he also took oral narratives as a source of history.

Social

The book describes the social activism of the *ṭarīqah* as a whole and provides a subtle description of the author's engagement in this regard. The author used to call himself *"khadem al-fokra"* or the servant of the poor. The book highlights one of the important aspects of the tradition: establishing absolute justice (*'adl-e-mutlaq*) or a just society in terms of equality by erasing social barriers and discrimination. It argues that all human beings are equal regardless of differences in faith. It attempts to uphold not only a peaceful coexistence of people of differing faiths but also of cohabitation (for details, see Butler 2011b: 84). The book cites several instances in which the adherents of other faiths wanted to convert to Islam; they were given acceptance to the *ṭarīqah* but advised to remain in their own faith (VM 81). Husayn lists Gurudas Fakir (Hindu), Manmohan Dutta (Hindu), and Dhananjoy Barua (Buddhist) as khalifa or deputy of the *ṭarīqah* in another book (see Jahangir 2012: 350–51). Other non-Muslim prominent figures include Kavial Ramesh Chandra Shil, Kalachand Sadhu, and Michael Penaru (Jahangir 2012: 335).

The Maizbhandariyya *ṭarīqah* propagates an open spirituality that transcends religious boundaries and attempts to establish a human community based on morality rather than on religious practices (VM 60, 70). This open spirituality has created confusion and controversy about the *ṭarīqah* among some circles of the Islamic religious establishment; nevertheless, it continues to attract not only Muslims but also people of other faiths in its fold.

The audience of the book comprises four categories of people: followers of the order, those who are suspicious of Sufi practices, learned readers, and the general public. For the followers of the *ṭarīqah*, there are devotional writings, for those who are suspicious of Sufi practices there are polemical counter-arguments in favor of Sufism, for the learned readers there are historical narratives of Sufism grounded in Islamic historicity as well as its appeal to non-Muslim people and its potential for establishing a harmonious society, and for the general public there are didactic stories and narratives. However, one of the fundamental objectives of the Maizbhandariyya or the Ahmadi order, as described in the book, is to eradicate religious conflict, as the Qur'ān says that "conflict is worse than killing" (Qur'ān 2:191). God warns those who are inclined to conflict and are forgetful of the loving aspect of God (Qur'ān 107:5). According to the book, the method of erasing conflict is the faith in *tawhid-e-adiyan* or unicity of religions. It stipulates that one ought not to consider his own understanding as the final truth and engage himself in conflict with another's practiced truth (VM 80). In this regard Husayn quotes the Qur'ānic verse that states, "To each among you have We prescribed a Law and an Open Way. If God had so willed He would have made you a single people" (Qur'ān 5:48). Following this message,

Husayn argues, the *ṭarīqah* upholds the doctrine of the unity of religions that acknowledges pluralism and cohabitation over conflict. The doctrine insists that without interfering in another's practice (*acardharma*) humankind can be united on the basis of ethics (Also see Ernst 1999: 5, 118). Instead of emphasizing only the Islamic faith, it promotes faith in general terms.[20] Husayn even appreciates idol worshippers as well as those who create partnerships with God (*shirk*), because they uphold those with faiths over the faithless, or atheists (VM 61). Respect for other faiths is reflected in Delaor Husayn's praise of Gautam Buddha (VM 17). During the Arab-Israeli war of 1967, when one of his devotees called for the destruction of Israel, Husayn asked him, "Are [Israelis] not creatures of Allah too?" He concluded by saying that the solution to the Palestinian crisis would come through coexistence with and recognition of Israel, not through war (Sikder 2005: 76).

However, in establishing the authority of sainthood, the author engaged in polemics with other authoritative narratives of the Islamic traditions. As discussed earlier, following the traditional Sufi genre, Husayn argues that Prophet Muhammad was endowed with two blessings: *nabuwwat* or prophethood and *vilayat* or sainthood. The prophethood ended with the demise of Prophet Muhammad whereas the *vilayat*, which is a state of mysterious relation between God and certain people as well as a state of power, would continue up until the end of time. In order to rescue Islam from degeneration, corruption and conflict,[21] God endowed Abd al-Qadir Jilani with supreme *vilayat* or *ghawthiyat* with the responsibility of reviving Islam within the framework of Shari'a. The era of the Shari'a-bounded *vilayat* concluded with the birth of Mawlana Ahmad Allah, who was endowed with another kind of *vilayat* in order to rescue all of humanity, which was experiencing a different kind of degeneration and conflict. This time the conflict was mostly caused by European colonialism. God blessed Saint Ahmad Allah with the highest authority or *ghawthiyat* and made him responsible of uniting all of humanity on the basis of morality rather than on reviving a specific faith. After the demise of Shaykh Ahmad Allah, this *Vilayat-e-Muhith* or all-embracing *vilayat* passed to Sayyid Ghulam ar-Rahman. After Ghulam ar-Rahman it passed to the author himself as he was declared the trustee by his grandfather Sayyid Ahmad Allah (VM 71).

One may notice a crisis of legitimacy in Husayn's narratives. A twofold crisis of authoritativeness (see El Fadl 2003: 92–94) is reflected in his arguments, a crisis of legitimacy and authoritativeness of saint Ahmad Allah, and a crisis of establishing his own authority as a legitimate heir to his grandfather Ahmad Allah. Husayn attempts to overcome the first crisis by grounding Mawlana Ahmad Allah in a historical setting, and compiles the sayings, practices, teachings, oral narratives on miracles as well as statements and quotes of others, especially those of ibn al-'Arabi, in justifying the claim of *ghawthiyat* of Sayyid Ahmad Allah in the book.[22] It may be mentioned here that saint Ahmad Allah did not leave any writings of his own behind. However, the sole source of Husayn's own legitimacy was that he was the grandson of Sayyid Ahmad Allah, and that before his death Sayyid Ahmad Allah declared Husayn as his trustee. In establishing legitimacy of this twofold authoritativeness, Husayn also encountered other fronts. He engaged himself with polemical arguments against the *ulama* who traditionally possess a negative view of Sufism. Different groups of authorities of exoteric traditions question the authority of the Sufi shaykhs as well as the legitimacy of some practices such as saint veneration, prostration, audition and dance. Thus, in establishing the authority of sainthood Husayn encountered four groups of people: the *ulama*, political elites, fundamentalists such as the Wahhabis, reformists such as the Deobandis and the Tablighis. In addition, he was critical of some so-called Sufi shaykhs who practiced Sufism as a trade or a means of making a living. In doing so, Husayn came up with a genre which is now known to most adherents of the *ṭarīqah* as the *Maizbhandari darsan* or the Maizbhandari philosophy.

One of the characteristics of the Maizbhandari philosophy as outlined in the book is that it is didactic in nature. It compiles the important comments, practices and instructions of saint Ahmad Allah along with the views of scholarly followers and admirers of the saint. The book also describes the goals, justification and practices to be followed by the adherents of the *ṭarīqah*. It describes in detail the nature and categories of self (*nafs*) and the methods of controlling and purifying the human self. Husayn provides a biographical sketch of Mawlana Ahmad Allah, portrays him as a historical figure, and highlights the ethical aspects of his life and teachings. He also incorporates miracles performed by the Shaykh in order to edify both the religious and ethical messages of the saint (see Delehaye 1961: 2; Hefferman 1988; Olsen 1981: 7; Rozehnal 2007: 41–42). Based on the teachings of saint Ahmad Allah, his personal experience of piety as well as the collective memory of the community, Husayn constructed the sainthood of saint Ahmad Allah a living memory and a collective representation (see Delooz 1983: 195; Cornell 1998: 63).

The humanity persuaded by the Maizbhandariyya *ṭarīqah* resonates, to a great degree, the doctrine of the unity of being (*wahdat al-wujud*).[23] Grounded mostly in ibn al-'Arabi and Rumi, Husayn made several statements indicating that the human heart is the dwelling place of God; He resides everywhere but the most sacred place is the human heart, as one of the sacred hadith's narrates: "My earth and My heaven contain Me not, but the heart of My faithful servant containeth Me" (Quoted in Nicholson 1963: 68). It transcends differences in terms of discrimination and at the same time it accepts differences in terms of diversity. Sayyid Ahmad Allah embodied this spirit, which is reflected in his response to a request of Dhananjoy

Barua, a Buddhist who wanted to convert to Islam. Sayyid Ahmad Allah said to him, "I made you Muslim, but you stay in your religion" (VM 81). What Husayn meant by this anecdote was that the Maizbhandariyya *ṭarīqah* honors diversity and pluralism, and at the same time that Mawlana Ahmad Allah and the *ṭarīqah* he founded were able to transcend outward rituals.

The *ṭarīqah* introduced a new phrase "*jātidharmanirbiśeṣe*" (regardless of caste and creed) while preaching *tawhid-e-adyan*. It is difficult to track the beginning of the usage of the phrase *jātidharmanirbiśeṣe*, though it seems that the phrase is the end product of colonialism and its discursive offshoot orientalism. Colonial administrative policies sometimes benefited a specific community at the cost of the benefits of others and thus created, sometimes deliberately, conflicts and distrust among the communities. Moreover, intellectual discourses of orientalists on the Hindu golden past or the communalist interpretation of the Indian history, which in some cases demonizes the pre-colonial Muslim period, agitated Muslims. Added to these were the internal political dynamics, such as the reactions of the Indian National Congress and the All India Muslim League to the Communal Award, Khilaphate Movement and its aftermath, Roundtable Conferences, election results and power sharing in 1937 among others, that ultimately gave birth to religious nationalism or communalism (Hasan 1993; Jalal 1994; Pandey 1990; Veer 1994: 18–24, 133). The end result was the partition of India. The justification of the partition of India and the establishment of the state of Pakistan in 1947 as the homeland for an imagined nation (see Anderson 2006, and Veer 1994: 19–23) was that Hindus and Muslims were two different nations due to the differences in their faiths and in every sphere of their personal and social life. Among the Muslim thinkers, the poet-philosopher Muhammad Iqbal, similar to some of his Hindu and Muslim predecessors and contemporaries (see Sarkar 1996) was one of the pioneering figures who believed that Muslims are different from Hindus and proposed a separate homeland for Muslims within India.[24] Convinced by this idea, Muhammad Ali Jinnah, the founding father of Pakistan (see among others, Jalal 1994; Hasan 1993) and other leading figures of the Muslim League[25] organized a movement for a separate homeland for Muslims at the northwestern part of the colonial India.[26] Proposed by A.K. Fazlul Haq of Bengal at the Muslim League's convention held in Lahore in 1940, a resolution was passed to divide India on the basis of communal identity and to establish two separate independent Muslim states: one on the northwestern part of India and the other on the eastern part of India. However, the language of the resolution was changed in 1946 and demand for a single country was placed instead (see Bennett, chapter 6 in this volume on this event). The British would not permit a vote on East Bengal's independence because they feared that other provinces would also opt to join neither India nor Pakistan, creating chaos. India was partitioned on August 14, 1947. The Muslim-majority East Bengal joined the dominion of Pakistan. Conflict soon followed between the two wings of Pakistan on a secular issue: language. During the early days of Pakistan the ruling political elites attempted to make Urdu the official language of Pakistan despite Bengali being the vernacular of the majority of people. Most political figures as well as the Islamic religious establishment viewed Bengali as a non-Islamic language and too closely related to Hindu culture, which agitated Bengalis. Added to the growing tension were the steadily lowering prices of the cash crop jute in East Bengal as well as the increasing frustration among the middle class due to unemployment and discrimination (for detail, see, among others, Umar 2000).

Consequently, a language movement was organized in East Pakistan. On February 21st and 22nd of 1952, police opened fire on protesting rallies, leaving several people dead. Later Bengali was granted status as the second official language of Pakistan. Precisely this was the political environment that stipulated the popularity of the twin concepts of *jātidharmanirbiśeṣe* and *dharmanirapekhsata* (religious neutrality, popularly understood as secularism), though it was not until the late 1960s that *dharmanīrapeksatā* became widely used as a political slogan. It was included in the constitution of Bangladesh in 1972 as one of its basic principles. Bangladesh's secession from Pakistan can be seen, as Bennett says, as culture trumping Islam. He argues, though, that it also has roots in a religious current that has long flowed in East Bengal that affirms the value of diversity over one dominant in West Pakistan that demanded conformity.

As mentioned earlier, Husayn published the *Vilayat-e-Mutlaqa* (Harder 2011: 69) in 1959, in which he argues that the state should observe tolerance toward diversity and maintain neutrality toward various traditions and practices or *ācārdharmā* (VM 81). The concept of "regardless of caste and creed" or *jātidharmanirbiśeṣe* appears a number of times in the book in order to emphasize the openness of the *ṭarīqah* as well as to set Mawlana Ahmad Allah apart from other saints. It should be mentioned here that the period between the 1940s and 1960s was full of communal tensions and riots throughout the Indian sub-continent (see among others, Pandey 1990, and Hasan 1993). Grounded in the Qur'ānic stipulations[27] on diversity and best conduct, *jātidharmanirbiśeṣe* upholds the values of pluralism and adds the notions of unity of religions (*tawhid-e-adyan*) and fair justice ('*adl-e-mutlaq*). The concept also advocates one should not impose one's belief upon others, as ibn al-'Arabī maintains "for God is too vast and too immense to be enclosed in one credo that excludes all the others" (see Geoffroy 2010: 185, and Chapter 10 below). Considering the ethnic and communal tensions and political environment during the publication of the book, it appears that Husayn put forward a parallel discourse and attempted to contextualize Islam (see Ayoub 2008: 2) against the authoritative Islamic discourses advanced by the Sunni *ulama*, fundamentalists, and political elites of postcolonial Pakistan. Some of the ideas and concepts in his discourse took shape in the works of earlier authors, though other ideas such as religious pluralism, diversity and humanism might be seen not only as an attempt at producing an alternative discourse, but as a counter-hegemonic discourse as well (see Harder 2011: 170). Against the rhetoric of Islamization advanced by the ruling elites, Husayn propagated for *dharmasamya* or equality of religions and unity of religions. The literary productions as well as the practices the *ṭarīqah* established, as reflected in the book, attempted to encounter and compete with both state and Western ideologies.[28] His use of the Bengali language in writing religious discourses may be viewed as a sign of resistance, as the use of Urdu, Persian or Arabic was considered the norm.

The phrase *jātidharmanirbiśeṣe*, which is closely related to the doctrine of *tawhid-e-adyan*, is also important from a different perspective. The declaration of Pakistan as an Islamic republic in its 1956 constitution[29] created a two-prone crisis of citizenship. Only Muslims were eligible to hold the highest offices of the republic, which meant that non-Muslim citizens as well as women became marginalized. Secondly, the framers of the constitution attempted to originate a general definition of a Muslim, thereby designating some Muslims as better than others, or some Muslims as "true" Muslims, and the rest as heretics.[30] The state thus damaged its arbitrational role as a neutral institution and skewed to a specific version of Islam, and thus tended to take control of the public space and became coercive to dissenters. As such, the state transformed into a superimposed institution and further became an instrument in promoting and shaping ideology. It has been argued that "when a pluralist state can no longer project its transcendent, arbitrational image, conflicts can only be solved through violence" (see Veer 1994: 23).

The failure of both the pre- and post-colonial state to be a neutral arbiter made the doctrine of *tawhid-e-adyan* and its discursive offshoot *jātidharmanirbiśeṣe* popular to a certain segment of the populous. This counter-hegemonic discourse is advantageous on two accounts: first, it could be easily tailored to rather traditional, pre-reformist forms of religion as practiced in Maizbhandar; secondly, its dictum of general acceptability could easily be harmonized with democratic principles, and thus conveys to Maizbhandar a novel type of political correctness especially in the context of the liberated and democratic Bangladesh (see Harder 2011: 170–71).

CONCLUSION

Sayyid Delaor Husayn published ten books among which *Vilayat-e-Mutlaqa* is the most prominent. The primary objective of writing *Vilayat-e-Mutlaqa* is to inform its readers about the *Vilayat-e-Mutlaqa-e-Ahmadi*, popularly known as the Maizbhandariyya *ṭarīqah*, and its founder Maulana Sayyid Ahmad Allah. Husayn includes Sufi historiography, a biographical sketch of Sayyid Ahmad Allah and the *ṭarīqah* itself, and a description of the methods of following the *ṭarīqah* in the book. In addition to depending on the Qur'ān and hadith and written sources, Husayn also depended on collective memories and oral narratives in making his arguments. The book not only describes the emergence of Sufism as the Prophetic tradition but also describes how the Sufi tradition differs from the so-called traditions of the *ulama*. In this polemics, the book also justifies the practices of audition and prostration, the two most controversial issues of the *ṭarīqah* that often upset the followers of exoteric traditions of Islam. In its attempt to establish Maulana Ahmad Allah as the savior (*ghawth al-azam*) and Husayn as the legitimate trustee of the founder of the *ṭarīqah*, the book also highlights that the ultimate objective of the *ṭarīqah* is to eradicate religious conflicts, a feat that could only be achieved by believing and practicing *tawhid-e-adyan* or unity of religions. It emphasizes the ethics of religion, respect for other faiths, cohabitation, and humanity. Men, among others, should search God in humanity, as it embodies the light of God. The book is didactic and protean in character.

The book describes how the *ṭarīqah* accommodates people of other faiths in its fold without insisting on conversion; anybody can choose a religion according to her or his conscience and taste, as the Qur'ān says that there is no compulsion in religion and that God could have created only one community of faith if He willed. The Maizbhandariyya *ṭarīqah* believes in the unity in diversity and it is a tradition of love. It emphasizes the compassion and mercy (*rahman* and *rahim*) of God for humanity instead of His wrath. In doing so, it criticizes the Wahhabis, Tablighis, Deobandis, religious extremists and those so-called Sufis who practiced Sufism as a trade, and those who are forgetful of the merciful aspect of God. It thus explicitly encounters the internal challenges that question the validity of Sufism and at the same time implicitly encounters challenges such as the orientalists' arguments that emphasize the exteriority of Sufi tradition. In this sense, the *ṭarīqah* is the defender of the spiritual humanism and universalism of Islam. It is at the same time also a fundamentalist tradition, as it remains faithful to the scriptures but defends Islam from both parochial interpretations of the *ulama* and the materialism of the West (see Geoffroy 2010: 22).

Unlike the preceding writers about the *ṭarīqah* who preferred Arabic, Persian or Urdu in writing their treatise, Sayyid Delaor Husayn preferred Bengali. He insisted on celebrating anniversaries based on the Bengali calendar. He supported the War of Liberation; in fact, one of his sons participated in the war against the forces of Pakistan in 1971 (see Jahangir 2005: 103–105). Instead of only supporting the Islamic creed, Husayn used the phrase *jātidharmanirbiśeṣe* (regardless of caste and creed) and the doctrine of *tawhid-e-adyan* in propagating the message of the *ṭarīqah*. Husayn was not a political figure, yet, it appears that he was a politically conscious person that attempted to resist the hegemony of the exoteric *ulama* and the ruling elites. He contextualized his narratives both in history as well as his contemporary socio-political grounds and described the emergence of the great savior Sayyid Ahmad Allah, the legitimacy of his own authority, and the relations between God and humanity. In addition, his preference for ethics, to ritual practice of religions (*ācārdharmā*), attitude towards other faiths, projection of the loving and merciful aspect of God, and social activism as portrayed in the book reflect, among others, the commitment and confidence of the Maijbhandariyya *ṭarīqah* in humanity, which might be called the Maijbhandariyya humanism. The preference for religious pluralism and accommodation over conflict as projected in the book might be a model for national integration, which in turn may resolve the tension between the secular and the religious in modern Bangladesh. As Bennett describes in chapter 6 of this volume, the pluralist-inclusive, secular current in Bangladesh was vulnerable following the 2014 election. This, it seems, is not true at the ballot box given the poor performance of Islamists. Rather, it is from attempts to foment suspicion of non-Muslims and of some Muslims too, including Sufis, and to replace the type of religion that Sayyid Delaor Husayn represented with a single, exclusive, and intolerant of diversity version of Islam.

About the Author

Sarwar Alam teaches at the King Fahd Center for Middle East Studies at the University of Arkansas in the USA. He received his doctorate from the same university in 2006. Alam also holds Masters degrees from Chittagong and Pittsburg State Universities. He was a member of Bangladesh Civil Service and worked as an assistant secretary, and also as a magistrate before moving to the USA. He was a postdoctoral fellow in the department of Middle Eastern and South Asian Studies at Emory University, Atlanta, Georgia between 2007 and 2010. He submitted a manuscript for publication titled *Jewels of Honor: the Perception of the Self, Power, and Gender Among Muslim Women of a Rural Community in Bangladesh*. He contributed two chapters on Sufi historiography and political activism in Bangladesh in *South Asian Sufis: Devotion, Deviation and Destiny*, eds., Clinton Bennett and Charles Ramsey (Continuum, 2012). His other publications include "Sufism Without Boundaries: Pluralism, Coexistence, and Interfaith Dialogue in Bangladesh" *Comparative Islamic Studies*, 9, no. 1 (2013), "Sufi Pluralism in Bangladesh: The Case of Maizbhandariyya Tariqa," *Journal of South Asian and Middle Eastern Studies*, xxxiv, no. 1 (Fall 2010), "Contesting the Shari'a: The Prospect of CEDAW in Eliminating Gender Discrimination in Bangladesh," *Law Vision* 10 (2008), and "Islam, Culture, and the Power of Women in a Bangladesh Village," *Voices of Islam*, 5 vols., ed., Vincent J. Cornell (Praeger, 2007). He has regularly presented papers at American Academy of Religion's annual meetings.

Notes

1. A synopsis of the chapter was first presented at the South-East Regional Middle East and Islamic Studies Seminar (SERMEISS), Valle Crucis, North Carolina, on October 8, 2014. A revised version of the same chapter was presented at the XXI Quinquennial World Congress of the International Association for the History of Religions (IAHR) at Erfurt University, Germany on August 24th 2015. I thank Dr Hüseyin Altındiş *(Selçuk Üniversitesi, Turkey)* and Annika Tabassum (a medical student of the University of Arkansas Medical Sciences) for reading the drafts and making comments. However, any errors in the final draft are mine.
2. The Bengali word *dharmanirapeksata* is translated as secularism in the Constitution of the country (*dharmanīrapeksatā* 12). For a discussion on secularism in South Asian context, see Riaz (2004: 21–22).
3. I have used the eighth edition of the book.
4. I have used saint, sainthood, *walī*, *wilāyat*, waliyat interchangeably. For details, see Cornell (1998: xvii-xxi).
5. Waw-lam-ya.
6. For contrasting views of two prominent medieval Sufi authors on the Malamatis, see al-Hujwiri (1999: 62–69, especially 67), 183–84 and al-Qushayri 2007: 42–43. Also see the comments of Arberry on al-Hujwiri and al-Qushayri in Arberry (1950: 70–71, 74) and Schimmel (1975: 86–87). An analysis of the medieval treatises on the Malamatis can be found in Sviri (1999). For a synthesis of all the contrary views, see Seale (1968).
7. Sharaf al-Din Bu 'Ali Qalander Panipati (d. 1324?).
8. See, Karamustafa (2006: 91). It was probably Abu Sa'id Abi'l-Khayr (d. 1049) who blended the Malamati and the Qalandari modes of mysticism together. For details, see Toussulis (2010: 82–89).
9. For a discussion on the categories as well as hierarchy of sainthood among the prominent Sufi masters, see Renard (2008: 260–75).
10. Husayn did not provide any citations.
11. Qur'ān 33:72.
12. I have translated the Bengali translation of the Qur'ān provided by Husayn. I am taking the responsibility for any mistakes in translating the Bengali.
13. It appears that Husayn translated the word al-Kitab as the books instead of the book. The generally agreed upon translations indicate the book as the Torah and parts of it.
14. Translated from Bengali provided by Husayn.
15. The Bengali word for atheism is *nastikatabad*, which also means communism.
16. Hadith Qudsi or Divine saying means a body of utterances of the Prophet which are of direct Divine inspiration and in which God speaks in the first person through the mouth of the Prophet. Divine sayings are God's words but not a part of the Qur'ān. See, Nasr (2007: 166 n. 67).
17. *kuntu kanzan makhfian.* See Schimmel (1975: 189).
18. Muhammad was sent as "mercy for the worlds" or rahmatanlil'alamin (Qur'ān 21:107). See Schimmel (1975: 217).
19. *man 'arafa nafsahu faqad 'arafa rabbahu.* Husayn (2012: 11). Also Schimmel (1975: 189).
20. The most frequently used term in the Qur'ān is *mu'minun* or believers which occurs almost 1,000 times, whereas the term *muslimun* appears fewer than 75 times. For details, see Donner (2010: 57); Watt (1968: 59–60).

21. Although he did not describe the conflicts in detail, from his passing comments on the role of the *ulama*, Hallaj, Dhun-nun al-Misri and Junaid we may assume that he indicates the conflicts among the *ulama* and the Sufis, Sunnis and Shi'is, Mutajilites and Asharites, *kalām* and *falasafa*, and the political instability of Baghdad.
22. The details are compiled in Husayn's 2004 book, *Hazrat Ghawthul Azam Shah Sufi Mawlana Sayyid Ahmad Allah (K) Maizbhandari: Jiboni o Karamat* (Biography and Miracles).
23. For details, see, among others, Chittick (1998, especially chapter I); Cornell (2007: 34); Morewedge (2003: 225–27); Nasr (2007: 104–108); Nicholson (1921: 77–142).
24. Before him, Sir Sayyid Ahmad Khan (d. 1898) also viewed Muslims as a separate community. See Khan (2012: 58); Sevea (2012: 152); Sirriyeh (2003: 136).
25. The party that led the Pakistan movement.
26. Iqbal did not include the eastern region, more precisely, the province of Bengal in his dreamland, although Bengal was a Muslim majority territory. See Jalal (1994: 12); Noorani (2010: 165); and Sirriyeh (2003: 136).
27. Qur'ān 5:48, 30:22, 49:13.
28. It encountered the so called "Islamic" of the state ideology (Pakistan was renamed as the Islamic Republic of Pakistan in 1956) and at the same time Western capitalism and communism as well (VM 99).
29. The Objective Resolution moved toward the direction of establishing an Islamic state. See Khan (2012: 94–99).
30. See An-Na'im (2008: 30–34, 84–88, 125–39); Khan (2012: 99–104); Justice Munir Commission Report on the Anti-Ahmadi Riots of Punjab in 1953 (Munir Commission 1954: 211–20).

SECTION V

Literary & Theoretical Underpinnings

8

TWO BELOVED SUFI POETS OF THE PUNJAB: A CASE OF "HEARING WITHOUT LISTENING"[1]

Nikky-Guninder Kaur Singh

> Whereas all the other senses have no immediate share in the universality of the verbal experience of the world, but only offer the key to their own specific fields, hearing is an avenue to the whole because it is able to listen to the logos.
>
> Gadamer, *Truth and Method*

> Everybody hears and plays the notes of your flute,
>   But rarely does anybody understand them.
> Whoever hears its unstruck sound,
>   Your flute mesmerizes them.
> *Krishna plays the magic flute*
>
> Bullhe Shah

The Sufi poets Bullhe Shah (1680–1758) and Waris Shah (1722–1798) are loved by people from both sides of the Indo-Pakistan border. There is not much historical documentation on either of them, but popular stories about their lives are still a living force in all segments of society. For generations, Muslims, Sikhs, and Hindus of the Punjab have been enchanted by their lyrics, and interestingly, each community has appropriated them as their own. Their mausoleums have become important sites of pilgrimage for people of all faiths, and their poetry is an essential part of the folk culture of both sides of the Punjab. Contemporary Indian and Pakistani singers are synthesizing their lyrics with reggae and hip-hop. Their powerful themes expressed in accessible vernacular Punjabi are played not only in *qawalli* sessions but also in rock bands, Bollywood films, weddings, and social events. From amateur singers at dinner parties to renowned masters like Nusrat Fateh Ali Khan sing their songs and mesmerize their audiences. The ecumenical pulsations of the Sufi poets have acquired a new poignancy of cultural unity lost to the Punjabis on both sides of the Border.

And yet audiences have not absorbed their lyrics, for we do not hear them resonate in the personal, social, or political life of the Punjabis. Evidently, they have not been put into use! The Punjab at the time of Bullhe Shah and Waris Shah was fraught with internal battles and external invasions by the Persian Nadir Shah and the Afghani Ahmad Shah Durrani. The religious extremism of Emperor Aurangzeb (1618–1707) had demoralized the people. The Mughal Empire founded by Babur in 1526 was shrinking, Akbar's pluralism (1542–1605) was slipping away from people's consciousness, and the commercial East India Company was expanding its military dominance. Eighteenth-century Punjab became a battleground for the Persians, Afghanis, the British, and Sikhs – each group fighting to establish its own empire. Responding to this violent background, our Sufi poets tried to spread the message of peace and harmony. They were deeply drawn to the contemporary currents of love expressed in Sufism, Islam, Sikhism, Hinduism, and Bhakti. Even though Arabic was the language of the holy Qur'ān and of theology, and Persian was the language of administration and that of "elite" Sufism, Bullhe Shah and Waris Shah produced poetry in the local Punjabi. While their lyrics in simple everyday language immediately imprinted on the lips and hearts of the people, their meaning has not been understood to date. In the tragically divided Punjab of 1947, the postcolonial identity of politics, and the global situation, an understanding of their poetry is all the more necessary today.

"Understanding" is a complex phenomenon, involving both the cognitive and practical dimensions. "*Understanding proves to be an event*," says literary critic Gadamer, for "understanding always involves something like applying the text to be understood to the interpreter's present situation" (Gadamer 1982: 309–10). As he explains in his influential *Truth and Method*, understanding, interpretation, and application together constitute the hermeneutic process. Furthermore, Gadamer underscores the importance of "hearing": "Whereas all the other senses have no immediate share in the universality of the verbal experience of the world, but only offer the key to their own specific fields, hearing is an avenue to the whole because it is able to listen to the logos" (cited as prelude to this chapter). Hearing opens us to the profound dimension of language and puts us in touch with our past. It is through hearing that we absorb our tradition and belong to history. So forceful is this sensibility that we have no control over it: we turn away from seeing something by looking in another direction, but we cannot "hear away" (Gadamer 1982: 462).

Unfortunately something has gone awry in this important aural process. As listeners we have not been able to interpret Sufi verse from our own particular situation; we have not been able to receive its empowering message. Like parrots it seems we have been singing and reciting the exquisite lyrics. This is a case of "hearing without listening." The audiences have been hearing the sound waves as they strike the ear, and their brains process them into a sequence such that brings them either intense joy or sadness. In joy of the rustic humor and elemental beauty of the landscapes portrayed by our poets, Punjabis dance until they drop; in sympathy with the protagonist Heer, Punjabis drown themselves in tears. But there has been a lack of existential seriousness. The hermeneutic circuit has a blockage. There is a severe hearing impediment.

According to Gadamer's diagnosis, hidden prejudices are the cause of this malady. "It is the tyranny of hidden prejudices that makes us deaf to what speaks to us in tradition" (Gadamer 1982: 270). Each of us hears from our own horizon; we have our assumptions, our knowledge, our prejudices, our fore-meanings. Inevitably we are "prejudiced." For Gadamer, however, "prejudice" does not have a negative connotation. He regards it simply as prejudgment, which is the reality of our historical inheritance; "prejudice against prejudice" only "denies tradition its power," he says (Gadamer 1982). Since each us of belongs to a tradition, our understanding is shaped by our personal proclivities, by the immediate families we grow up in, by the long and complex past of our society, and by our political state. Indeed, the intellectual habits of Punjabi audiences have been constructed by their muscular patriarchal tradition, so naturally they have been hearing and reading the Sufi songs with meanings and expectations that go way back in their past. The otherness and newness of Waris Shah and Bullhe Shah's message is lost.

Gadamer also helps us resolve our problem: we need to hermeneutically train our consciousness. This involves being sensitive to the text's "alterity," a sensitivity that is neither neutrality for the literary content, nor the extinction of the listener's self" (Gadamer 1982: 269). The cure Gadamer prescribes for our deafness is a double dose of "tension" – tension between listener and text, tension between the past and the present. As listeners then we must self-examine our biases and recognize the *otherness* of the Sufi poetry. We must also acknowledge the norms we inherited from our families, society, politics, so that we can hear the lyrics from our present situation. This double tension would break the spell of our "fore-meanings" and clear out our auditory canals. And thus we would retrieve the meaning of the precious Sufi lyrics in all their difference and newness.

In this chapter I really want us to "listen" to the visionary poets so we can respond to them responsibly. From the vast repertoire of Bullhe Shah and Waris Shah, I am particularly drawn to their message of human wholeness, religious unity, and gender justice. These three themes are extremely relevant to us in our present twenty-first century reality, and I will choose verses to highlight them. As far as their oeuvre is concerned, we know very little for certain about what actually belongs to them. My selections from Bullhe Shah come from his famous *Kafian* (short lyric stanzas interspersed by a refrain), which continue to be sung in formal sessions of Sufi singing (*qawalli*).[2] Numerous collections of verses attributed to Bullhe Shah in Indo-Persian and Gurmukhi scripts first appear in the late nineteenth century. As Robin Rinehart alerts us, these collections were transcribed from poems of his that were sung at qawalli sessions, and so they include alterations and interpolations by the singers. There is no reliable text of his poetry; instead, there is "only a Bullhe Shah tradition, a body of poetry attributed to Bullhe Shah" (Rinehart 1999: 48). There is a similar problem with Waris Shah, since there is a gap of several decades between the time his text was composed (1766) and the earliest manuscript to date (1821). According to Jeevan Deol, a specialist in Punjabi manuscripts, the other extant manuscripts are longer, and the numerous printed editions use these long manuscripts, which also interpolate verses from famous poets Deol (2002:150). Though their verses have come down to us in a "notoriously corrupt"[3] manuscript tradition, they still play powerfully, and can serve as an important moral guide.

HUMAN WHOLENESS

Waris Shah and Bullhe Shah shatter the Descartian split between mind and body/the sacred and the secular, which only devalues the body and shifts the attention from life on earth to an afterlife and heaven beyond. As feminist philosophers and postcolonial scholars have informed us from numerous different angles, this dualism has been harmful to human subjectivity. Our Sufi poets desire the Divine most romantically, most tenderly, opening new possibilities for living spiritually in this very world of ours. Erotic and sublime elements fuse brilliantly as they exalt *ishq* or *muhabbat* (love) their supreme religious principle (Shackle 2006). These Muslim poets seem to profess their faith as *la ilaha illa'l-'ishq* ("There is no God but Love"), and thus they poetically identify Allah with Love in their new version of the first pillar of Islam.[4] Belonging to its open and mystical dimension, Bullhe Shah and Waris Shah approach Islam in a personal and experiential way. Their verse is sustained by their powerful human love for Allah, the Prophet Muhammad, and Sufi Masters (for further details, see Singh 2012: 79–80).

For the poets, passionate love is the highest form of religious experience, and so they simultaneously spin the erotic and divine fibers into their literary texture. Physical love (*ishq-e majazi*) is essential for metaphysical love (*ishq-e haqiqi*), a material thread that binds us with the Divine: "can a needle sew without thread?" questions Bullhe Shah,

> How can we love without physical love?
> How can a needle sew without thread?
> Physical love is a blessing –
> Spinning everything into ecstasy.
>
> As love seeps into the marrow,
> We die living our very best.
> Love is our father and mother,
> Love spins everything into ecstasy.

> A lover's body may age, yet here
> I stand in the shadow
>   Of my moon-like beloved
> Watching lovers laugh with gusto.
>   Love teaches us to cross all rules, so
> Those who are suffused with its flow
>   They are utterly helpless
> Their every cell melts with rapture.
>
> There is no secret whatsoever:
> The Divine is seen everywhere
> O Bullah, lovers thus swim across.
> Those who recall their lover's abode,
> The Divine sees and speaks to them
> Even peeks into their inner self
> And spins everything into ecstasy.
>
> How can we love without physical love?
> How can a needle sew without thread?
>
> *A Needle without a Thread*

The chemical ingredient of love seeps into the marrow, it runs through the various organs of our body, colors our emotional responses, impassions the imagination, and consequently, sews us snugly with the Divine.

In their deceptively simple idioms and metaphors, we discover highly sophisticated Sufi ideals of *wahdat al-wujud* (oneness of being), *fana* (annihilation of the individual ego), and *baqa* (subsistence in the Divine); complex human emotions of love, hate, jealousy; and experiences religious and sexual. Of course, being rapt in love is not a fool's paradise; paradoxically, the oblivion to traditional rites and rituals, produces for the Sufi poets an excruciating experience – analogous to being "fried," "grinded," "burnt," "pierced." As Bullhe Shah admits,

> O friend, I am struck by eternal love
> That love from the beginning of time
> It is frying me in a pan
> The fried is being fried over again
> O friend, I am struck by primal love
> That love from the beginning of time.
>
> It kills the dead over and over
> It crushes the crushed over and over
> O I am struck by eternal love
> That love from the beginning of time.
>
> My skin is burning like straw on fire
> My inside is stinging with thorns
> O I am struck by eternal love
> That love from the beginning of time.

> The arrow of love has struck my heart
> But it won't move despite all motion
> O I am struck by eternal love
> That love from the beginning of time.
>
> Bullhe Shah's love is unique
> It does not dissolve
>   No matter how much you crush it
> O I am struck by eternal love
> That love from the beginning of time.

Frying in the Pan

Rather than doubt or denounce or transcend the body, a norm amongst most intellectuals and the religious, Bullhe Shah celebrates it. His body is on fire with the timeless love – his skin burns like straw, his inside stings with thorns. The functioning body experiences the Divine. He knows his body as himself.

Likewise, multi-dimensional love is the nub of Waris Shah's reproduction of the legendary romance between Heer and Ranjha – the Juliet and Romeo of the Punjab. Emperor Akbar's courtier, Damodar, had popularized the story of Heer and Ranjha at the beginning of the seventeenth century. Numerous other versions of the story, including those of Hafiz Shah Mukbal, Piloo, and Hafiz Barkhurdar, were also in circulation. Waris Shah retells this classic tale of the star-crossed lovers that had been a part of the Punjab's written and oral tradition, and with his unique aesthetic sensibility, makes their archetypal romance into a masterpiece of Punjabi literature. His *qissah* (lyric narrative) of *Heer* begins with a paean on love. The *qissah* is a narrative lyric, which combines Perso-Islamic and regional literary forms, and typically begins with an invocation (*hamad*). Flowing out from Allah, Waris Shah glorifies love as the ontological "root of the universe" – "*jagu da mool.*" The birth of the cosmos, its reality, its space and time, and its entire functioning are therefore contingent on its force. Waris Shah invokes his divine subject while repeatedly drawing in his audience (four times he uses the term *mian*, a title of respect that connotes intimacy; translated below as "O friend"). His story is prefaced with the reminder that the archetypal lover is Allah and the primordial beloved is the Prophet Muhammad:

> *Aval hamad khuda da virad kije*
> *Ishq kita su jag da mool mian*
> *Pahilan aap Allah ne ishq kita*
> *Te mashuk hai nabi rasul mian*
> *Ishq pir faqir da martaba hai,*
> *Marad ishq da bhala ranjool mian*
> *Khule tinhan de bab kaloob andar*
> *Jinhan kita hai ishq kabool mian*

> First recite the praise for Khuda,
> For love is the root of the universe, O friend
> At the beginning Allah was the lover, and
> Prophet-messenger, the beloved, O friend
> Love marks the saint and the ascetic,
> Love is the honor of humans, O friend
> Those who welcome love within,
> Their hearts open to infinite realms, O friend

Their primal divine relationship opens up the horizon for human protagonists. In love the heart unlocks and takes lovers to those depths of richness and fullness where there is freedom from all sorts of limitations and barriers.

Love for the poets works out as that potent hormone which dissolves the individual ego and opens up the pores so wide that we savor the Other – divine and human – with utmost bliss. They overcome the Descartian split between body and mind: spiritual love carries many physiological associations. They give us confidence in our own bodies and incite us to forge connections with fellow humans across centuries and continents and genders. After reading their works we feel a closeness with the Chisti poet Amir Khusrau (d 1325 CE) who said, "love came and spread like blood in my veins." Similarly, we relate with Walt Whitman's "Body Electric" in which the American transcendentalist poet affirms the erotic and spiritual connection of his physical body, and celebrates male and female bodies for their "sacred" status. The holy Qur'ān and the experience of the Prophet remain the constant inspiration for our Sufi poets. In a popularly quoted verse, Allah expresses love for humanity through the analogy of the jugular vein: "We are closer to him than his jugular vein" (Qur'ān 50:16). With Bullhe Shah and Waris Shah, we learn and we remember to appreciate our body and experience the Divine in it, with it, – most palpably. They give us ammunition to reconstruct our broken selves.

RELIGIOUS PLURALISM

Bullhe Shah and Waris Shah lived in the Punjab, where the West Asian tradition of Islam encountered South Asian civilization. Since Punjab was the gateway to the Indian Subcontinent, people from various regions, religions, and ethnicities settled on its soil. Raised in this culturally diverse environment, our Sufi poets invite audiences from different backgrounds to be themselves, and engage with one another. They provide us with important insights into creating a common society with all the plurality of our global world.

First of all they help us to see beyond our fractured selves. Bullhe Shah and Waris Shah witnessed the conflict between Hindus and Muslims, they witnessed the conflict between Sunni and Shia Muslims. Sadly, these "inter" and "intra" religious conflicts continue to flare in our dangerously divided and polarized world. But the poets categorically say that there is nothing essential that divides Hindu from Muslim, or Sunni from Shia. To cite Bullhe Shah,

> We are not Hindu, we are not Muslim,
> So let us give up our pride, and do our spinning;
> We are neither Sunni nor Shia;
> We are a family, so let us live in harmony.
>
> We are not hungry,
>   we are not full;
> We are not naked,
>   we have no clothes;
> We are not crying,
>   we are not happy;
> We are not deserted;
>   we have no home.
>
> We are not sinners, we are not saints,
> I do not know of sin, I do not know of sainthood;
> Says Bullhe: when we are in tune with the Divine,
> Hindu and Muslim lose their difference.
>
> Neither Sinners nor Saints

According to our Sufi poets, the root of religious conflicts around the world is inflated egotism. Artificial pride gets densely congealed, and obstructs people from recognizing their unity. Narcissistic obsessions and power games shut out genuine love for the Divine, the absolute singular One – common to each and all. Of course we have different features, complexions, and personalities, but we belong to the same human family. We must therefore have mutual respect, trust, and love.

"Such is my enlightenment: Hindu or Muslim is irrelevant," declares Bullhe Shah loud and clear. As he goes on to say in his poem entitled "There is a Thief in my Shawl," Hindus cremate their dead and Muslims bury their dead, but they needlessly scorn the *other*'s way:

> *There is a thief in my shawl*
> *Who should I call to alert O saints*
>   *There is a thief in my shawl*
>
> Here Ram Das, there Fateh Muhammad –
>   So goes the ancient brawl;
> Muslims scorn the crematory fire,
>   Hindus scorn the grave;
> Fights and arguments go on
>   While somebody else escapes.
> *Who should I call to alert O saints*
> *There is a thief in my shawl*

> The One I searched for
>   I did not find;
> But a person sought by
>   The Divine is strong.
> The writ on our forehead
>   Who can break or tear it?
> *Who should I call to alert O saints*
> *There is a thief in my shawl*
>
> Our ancestral master is in Baghdad,
>   My master's seat is in Lahore
> But we are all the same:
>   The kite and the string are the same.
> Keep this in mind, I tell you,
>   Bullhe Shah spreads this news.
> *Who should I call to alert O saints*
> *There is a thief in my shawl*
>
> *There is a Thief in my Shawl*

Due to external factors like geography and climate, communities may develop different patterns and customs, but they are all alike at the essential human self. Our different names – Ram Das (Hindu) or Fateh Muhammad (Muslim) – identify us at the individual level, but they cannot conceal our common human identity. Sufi poetry evokes a pluralistic society where we do not hide our differences but acknowledge them, and even celebrate them together.

In a cotton-growing region, the ubiquitous household chore of spinning, naturally becomes significant for the Punjabi poets; its syncopated rhythm symbolizes divine contemplation. The movement of the stars and planets, the whirl of electrons and protons, the ebb and tide of life, the flow of the infinite into the finite – are choreographed in spinning cotton into thread at the spinning wheel. The mesmerizing circularity dissolves the selfish ego, opening conduits of freedom, gratitude, and love. The poet's call to sit and spin together (that we hear in *"Neither Sinners nor Saints"*) is extremely relevant in the mechanically operated and fundamentally disjointed world we inhabit.

Second, their courage is most admirable. They were devout Muslims and yet they boldly reject institutional rituals and doctrines that repress the human spirit. They denounce religious orthodoxy; they reject formalism and ceremonies, and even substitute the essential pillars of Islam with the rapture of love. "Why must I turn towards the Ka'ba, when my lover lives in Takht Hazara?" asks Bullhe Shah. His lover's village stands in for the Ka'ba, the prototypical Islamic shrine, and a visit there possesses the religious efficacy of pilgrimage to Mecca:

> Why must I turn towards the Ka'ba,
> When my heart longs for Takht Hazara?
>
> People say their prayers facing Ka'ba,
> I say my prayers facing my lover;
> My heart longs for Takht Hazara
>
> If you find any flaws in me, dear Ranjha,
> Don't forget my deeds flow from my desire –
> My heart longs for Takht Hazara
>
> Untrained, I don't know how to swim –
> My savior, shame would be yours if I drown
> My heart longs for Takht Hazara
>
> I have not found anybody your equal,
> Though I have searched the world over;
> My heart longs for Takht Hazara
>
> Bullhe Shah says: love is exceptional;
> It redeems the worthless.
> Why must I turn towards the Ka'ba
>
> *Why Turn to the Ka'ba?*

These Punjabi Sufi poets reject the cultural ethos cultivated by many Mecca-oriented Muslim theologians, scholars, and saints living on the Subcontinent, as their "extra-territorial cultural ethos" is shifted to the local Punjabi territory" (Asani 1988: 82). Paradise is not a promise after death either; paradise is right here, in the lover Ranjha's natal village.

Institutional religion with all its formalities, doctrines, and modes of worship is made redundant. "Those who drink from the cup of love, why should they care about fasts or prayers?"

> I am smitten by true love, O
> Show me the way to my Beloved
> I was a naïve little girl in my parents' home,
> When he stole my heart away, O
> Show me the way to my Beloved
> I studied logic, grammar, laws, and texts
>   But I am bereft of love, O
> Show me the way to my Beloved
> Those who drink from the cup of love
>   What do they care about fasts or prayers? O
> Show me the way to my Beloved
> Says Bullhe: when I sat with the Divine,
>   All rituals and discipline left me. O
> Show me the way to my Beloved
>
> *Show Me the Way*

In another poem, addressing his psyche as a maternal subject, Bullhe Shah says,

> Fasts, pilgrimage, prayers, O mother,
>   My beloved came and made me forget
>
> When I heard the news of my lover
> I forgot all about logic and syntax
> As he struck the soundless chord
> Fasting, pilgrimage, prayers, O mother
> My beloved made me forget them all
>
> When my lover entered my home
> I forgot the *sharia* and its laws
> I see my lover in each and every thing
>   That radiance sparkling inside and out
> How can people not see
>
> Fasting, pilgrimage, prayers O mother
> My beloved has made me forget them all
>
> *All Forgotten*

The poets endorse the pure emotion of love, for all other means pose restrictions. With a flash of the lover, the individual is freed from societal and religious obligations and experiences true religion. Pluralism is grounded in that shared human emotion.

And those who impose restrictions on the flow of love are vehemently criticized. These include religious officials, community members, and the immediate family. For instance, Waris Shah's protagonist Ranjha cheekily confronts the Mullah and chastises him for his self-righteousness and hypocrisy:

> With the beard of a Sheikh,
> The deeds of Satan,
> You ensnare passers by;
> With the Qur'ān in hand,
> Perched on the *minbar*,
> You cast the nets of deceit...
>
> (Heer Waris Shah cited in Sekhon 2002: 40)

Not only the Mullahs – caretakers of mosques and leaders in prayers, but also the Qazis – public officials who propagate the legalities of Islam, emerge as reprehensible figures in Waris Shah's text. After all, only a lover can know the *sharia*, the divine law! The clergy with their dogmatic insistence miss out on the inner vibrations of the heart and merely stress the exoteric codes of behavior. In many parts of the world today clergy are promoting exclusivist practices and ideologies and fanning divisive emotions in youngsters. The solidarity of love is threatening for them.[5]

Third, the poets offer us a pluralistic kaleidoscope that widens our aesthetic sensibility. We see images from West Asia and South Asia magically spliced in their verse. For instance we find Ranjha, the Punjabi Romeo, in a pastoral setting playing the flute – a primordial Krishna figure from the Hindu tradition. But when driven away from his beloved, the imagery comes from the Islamic tradition: he is compared with Adam expelled from the Garden of Eden, his bewilderment rendered analogous to Noah caught in the Flood.

> Hurled away from his beloved Heer,
>   Ranjha was in utter shock.
> He felt pushed away
>   From his paradise –
> Like Adam expelled
>   From the Garden of Eden,
> Like Satan
>   Pushed away by God.
> Was he Shaddad
>   Banned from heaven?
> Or king Nimrud
>   Destroyed by a mosquito?
> Says Waris Shah,
>   This lover was utterly bewildered
> Like Noah caught in the Flood.
>
> *Punjabi Noah*

Rather than irreconcilable differences, we recover equality and convergence between the Islamic and Hindu religions.

In the context of our own insular twenty-first century their pluralistic imagination is a remarkable gift. Their tender strokes sweep away all jagged conflicts between aniconic Islam and representational Hinduism. Both Bullhe Shah and Waris Shah firmly belong to the aniconic tradition of Islam, yet they sumptuously utilize Hindu imagery. However, instead of appreciating the novel multivalency of their poetics, scholars frequently try to find chain-link patterns of historical influence and dependency. Regarding Bullhe Shah, Rinehart discusses the claims made by respective scholars that he is either a "Vedantic Sufi," "Vaisnava Vedantic Sufi," or a "strictly orthodox Muslim," and concludes that the authors appropriate him for their own agendas, give little attention to the actual content of his compositions, even misinterpret him, and end up providing "more about their own religious preferences than those of Bullhe Shah's" (Rinehart 1999: 46, 57). The application of the genetic thrust to label the poets in *either/or* categories blocks the dazzling diversity of the human spirit. Bennett and Alam's chapters in this book describe Muslim-majority contexts where Sufis have opened up to truth "outside" as well as "Inside" Islam because as did these poets they do not see "religion" as closed off and insular. There is no doubt that Bulhe Shah and Waris Shah participated in an intellectually vibrant milieu; in fact their vocabulary and imagery attests to their exposure to an environment charged with a spiritual dynamic and diversity. Without being chauvinistic or afraid of the "other," they enjoy the pluralistic patterns of us humans. For instance, in "Krishna Plays the Magic Flute," Bullhe Shah concretely visualizes the handsome cowherd and acutely hears his mesmerizing melodies.

Krishna plays the magic flute
O Ranjha with the flute –
  O cowherd Ranjha
You are in tune
  With all of us
You make your delights
  Chime with our consciousness
Krishna plays the magic flute

O flute player,
  You are called Krishna
You are our virtue
  You are our inner self
Yet our eyes cannot quite see you
  How complex your sport.
Krishna plays the magic flute

Everybody hears and plays the notes of your flute,
  But rarely does anybody grasp their meaning;
Whoever hears its unstruck sound,
  Your flute mesmerizes that person.
Krishna plays the magic flute

Hearing your melodious flute,
  Mind and body cry out like peacocks;
Your rhythmic twists and turns reveal
  That solo note sustaining your great art.
Krishna plays the magic flute

This flute has a long writ
  If we search we can find it
Simple is its style for it has gathered
  Its attributes from its essential Being.
Krishna plays the magic flute

This flute has some five or seven stars
  Each plays its own part
The one note that vibrates in all
  It has blown away our senses.
Krishna plays the magic flute

> Says Bullhe: end all this conflict
>   Welcome friends to the door
> Do keep your deal with the Kalma,
>   So the Master will stand as your witness.
> *Krishna plays the magic flute*
>
> *Krishna Plays the Magic Flute*

As the poem progresses, the popular Hindu figure is spliced with his Muslim Prophet (Hazrat), just as the sound of Krishna's flute is fused in with the language of Islamic prayer (Kalma). In fact, the attributes (*sifat*) of the magical flute flow from Being Itself (*wujud*); its singular note (*ikk sur*) breathes life (*dam mare*) into each and all (*sabh de vic*). Such magical confluences of the West Asian and Indian worlds filter throughout Punjabi Sufi poetry and give an exciting new impetus to conventional tropes and future relationships.

Professor Denis Matringe, an eminent scholar of Punjabi literature, explores many interesting Hindu elements in Bullhe Shah's mystical message, (see Matringe 1992) but again, if we look closely, each instance embraces multiple cultural allusions that defy any one religious label. For instance who is the thief hiding in Bullhe's shawl in the following poem?

> *Bullah wonders who he is*
> I am not seated with the pious in the mosque
>   I am not sinking in acts of vice;
> I am not with the pure
>   I am not with the polluted;
> I am not Moses
>   I am not Pharaoh
> *Bullah wonders who he is*
>
> I do not follow Indian scriptures
>   I do not follow Western scriptures;
> I do not take drugs
>   I do not take alcohol;
> I am not decadent
>   Nor licentious;
> I am neither asleep
>   Nor awake
> *Bullah wonders who he is*
>
> I am neither happy
>   Nor am I sad
> I am not clean
>   I am not dirty
> I am neither on land
>   Nor in the sea
> I am not made of fire
>   I am not made of air
> *Bullah wonders who he is*

> I do not belong to Arabia
> > I do not belong to Lahore
> I am not from the city
> > Nor from the district of Nagaur
> I am not Hindu
> > I am not Muslim
> I am not from Peshawar
> I do not live in Nadaun
> > *Bullah wonders who he is*
>
> I do not know the mystery of faith
> > I am not the child of Adam and Eve
> I have no name for myself
> > I am not among the settled or the migrants
> *Bullah wonders who he is*
>
> From A to Z –
> > All of that I am;
> Anybody else,
> > I do not perceive;
> More intelligent than me
> > There is no one.
> Asks Bullah: Who is the Sovereign?
> > Who stands there?
> *Bullah wonders who he is*
>
> *But Bullah: who stands there?*
> > *Is that the Sovereign?*
>
> > > > *Bullah wonders who he is*

The thief here could be the naughty Krishna playing hide and seek with his beautiful maidens, just as it could be the majestic Hidden Treasure from the author's West Asian Sufi inheritance. As we know from a popular Islamic tradition, God speaks in the first person through the voice of the Prophet to explain the purpose of creation: "I was a Hidden Treasure. I loved to be known. Therefore I created the creation" (Nasr 2004: 10–11).

Likewise, in Bullhe Shah's references to dance, readers can discover their own and different meaning:

> Those touched by perfect love,
> They dance out of tune
> > They dance out of step.
>
> Do not disturb the distressed,
> Let them suffer their anguish;
> They escape birth and death,
> They know themselves.
> Those touched by perfect love,
> They dance out of tune
> > They dance out of step.

> Those who wear the robe of love,
> They receive the *fatwa*
>   From the divine court;
> As they sip the cup of revelation,
> Their questions and doubts die out.
> Those touched by perfect love,
> They dance out of tune
>   They dance out of step.
>
> In whom dwells the divine,
> They jump up calling,
>   "Beloved! O' Beloved!"
> They do not care for rules
>   They do not care for tunes,
> They play their own sports.
> Those touched by perfect love,
> They dance out of tune
>   They dance out of step.
>
> O Bullah, I have found
>   My lover's true town,
> Din and falsity have fizzled out;
> For truthful people I tell the truth:
> I see immaculate light.
> Those touched by perfect love,
> They dance out of tune,
> They dance out of step.
>
> *Out of Tune, Out of Step*

For those tuned into the popular Vaishnava devotional dances of *raslila* on the north Indian stage, Lord Krishna may quickly flash; for Shaivites, the image of Shiva Nataraja all whirl and twirl dancing in the circle of flames, may appear. But the movement of freedom and rapture could as easily belong to the Sufi *dhikr* practiced by the Whirling Dervishes or the "unveiled dancer" in Guru Nanak's poetry.[6] Christians could even read in it the primal paradox expressed by T.S. Eliot, "at the still point that is where the dance is" (*Four Quartets*). With Bullhe Shah, the primordial form of religiosity acquires a strong nonconformist message: the choreography of dance lies not in following external rules and patterns that confine movement, but in the "physical touch" (*tan lagia*) of "perfect love" (*ishq kamal*) which tears apart all fetters. While pointing out the absolute unicity of the Divine, the multiple cultural references fusing organically in Punjabi Sufi lyrics usher us into a fantastic pluralistic horizon. We break out of our shell, inspired to relate with one another in mutuality and trust.

GENDER JUSTICE

Living in a patriarchal society, the poets disclose great awareness of the role and status of women. Several feminist issues that are critical even in the twenty-first century, are brought to the surface by these pre-modern poets. In fact their depiction of protagonist Heer is quite admirable. Though contemporary feminists would find a great deal lacking in Heer, for her time and place she is quite radical. A literary critic from Pakistan observes that Heer is probably the only heroine in romantic literature who had to face the Shariat Court and hear the threat of flogging from a stern Qazi. Yet "she refused to surrender her fundamental right – freedom to marry a man of her own choice, the right recognized by Islam unambiguously" (Mirza 1992: 9; see also Matringe 2003).

For Shafqat Tanveer Mirza, Heer based her argument on the Qur'ānic principles. Clearly the heroine is an intelligent woman who knows her rights, who claims them for herself, and discerns the abuse of religion for the upkeep of social and economic values.

Waris Shah named the work *Heer*, after her alone. She drives the plot and owns the epic. The plot centers on the illicit love affair between the children of two village chiefs: Dhido, the youngest and favorite son of Mauju Ranjha, and Heer, the daughter of Chuchak Syal. Because his jealous brothers allot him barren land upon the death of their father, Ranjha is forced to leave his village of Takht Hazara. As he sleeps in a boat after departing, Heer happens to come across him and instantly falls madly in love. With her recommendation, Ranjha gets a job as a herdsman for her snobbish family. Tending buffaloes in pastoral landscapes, the mischievous and seductive Ranjha has ample opportunity to meet with his beloved and her bevy of friends – much like Krishna dallying with Radha and the Gopis in Brindaban. But Heer's nasty uncle Kaido spies on them, and warns the parents of Heer's ignoble behavior. Chuchak and his wife Maliki are deeply ashamed of their daughter staining the family name, and marry her off against all her pleading to another fellow in another village. Ranjha then disguises as an austere yogi: with his ears pierced and body smeared in ashes, he arrives in Heer's marital village. Here Heer's sister-in-law Sahiti, herself in love with a Baloch merchant, is instrumental in their secret rendezvous. With her masterminding, both couples manage to elope; however, Heer and Ranjha are caught. Through his yogic powers, Ranjha is able to win Heer back, and her parents consent to their marriage. Sadly, just as she is waiting for her groom's party, the beautiful Heer is treacherously poisoned by her natal family. Ranjha hears the news of his beloved's death and dies from the shock.

Within the framework of a patriarchal society, Waris Shah releases Heer from the stereotypical male-female roles, and endows her with a powerful personality. Heer's beauty far surpasses the dainty rhetoric of romantic damsels: "Her eyebrows are arched like the bows of Lahore... the kolh in her eyes digs in fiercely like the armies of the Punjab... her gait is like that of an intoxicated elephant... her features are honed like the calligraphy of book... beholding her face is like making a pilgrimage during Laylat al-qadr..." (See Sekhon 2002: 47–88). The poet's similes betray not only a Sufi's reverence for the art of calligraphy and the Laylat al-qadr ("Night of Might" when the holy Qur'ān was first revealed in the final days of Ramadan), but also his pride in the Punjab with its famed city of Lahore and its fierce armies.

Heer's physical strength is important for Waris Shah. In a rather amusing scene she takes on the lame Kaido (her uncle), who she deems as the source of conflict and heartbreaks:

> Heer hurried to meet him on the way
> Pretending to address him amiably at first
> But coming closer she roared like a lion
> With drops of anger flooding her cheeks
> She pulled his cap from his head
> She wrenched his locket
> From round his neck
> Grabbing him by the waist
> She threw Kaido
> On the ground in rage
> Like a washerman whacks *khes* against a board
>   Says Waris Shah, an angel from the heavens
>   Pitched Satan down on the floor
>
> *Heer Whacks Kaido*

She approaches him deceptively, and then roaring at him like a lion, thrashes him on the ground. The simile of the washerman whacking a cotton-blanket (*khes*) against a board graphically describes the ease with which Heer accomplishes her feat. Later, her friends join in, and they beat him up again. The poet seems to really enjoy the satanic Kaido being thrashed by Heer and her friends.

Heer is mentally and emotionally sturdy. She seethes with passion and sexuality. Leprosy was common in that age, so in her courageous pledge for Ranjha she vows,

> I swear upon my father, O Ranjha,
> Upon my mother too,
>   I will never leave you
> Without you, life is sin for me,
> My eyes will meet no man's body.
> I swear by saint Khwaja Khizr,
> I am a pig if I break my pledge of love;
> If ever I take another lover,
> Let my eyes and life, like a leper's, wither.
>
> *Heer's Pledge of Love*

8 Two Beloved Sufi Poets of the Punjab

She boldly stands up to her family, society, and religious leaders. To her father she asserts that Ranjha is Khuda's own gift to her and she is addicted to him: "This love-sickness is such that my life may go, but my love will not":

> Says Heer, dear father, addicts
> Cannot live without their drug;
> I cannot live without Ranjha, sir,
> Incorrigible habits do not change.
> Lions and leopards can't live without meat
> With a single pounce they earn their meal.
> I made my wish for Ranjha at the *dargah*
> – The herdsman is Khuda's own blessing
> A gift written in my destiny
> How can anybody erase it?
> Such is my love-sickness that
> Life may go, but love will not.
>
> *Heer's Addiction*

She recommends Ranjha to her father, which gets him his job with her family: "*vasai nur allah da mukhre te, muhon rabb hi rabb citarda hai* – On his face dwells Allah's light; his lips recite *rabb*, and *rabb* alone" (Heer Waris Shah in Sekhon 2002: 56). Qur'ānic epithets for the Divine – Khuda, Allah, Rabb emerge in Heer's introduction of her lover, whose inner devotion radiates externally, and spiritual exercises (*dhikr*) slip out incessantly. A determined Heer reiterates her resolve to her mother: "*na murangi ranjare ton bhaven bap de bap da bap ave* – I will not turn away from Ranjha even if father's father's father were to come in my way" ("Enough Mother"). In a dynamic repetition, Heer audaciously rejects the rules coming down from the fathers.

> Mother, it's enough! Curse no more!
>   Cursing incurs grave demerits.
> To dishonor what is Divine is horrible,
>   We sin when we kill our daughters.
> May some fever or plague take me
>   Away from this wretched place
> But I will not turn away from Ranjah
> Even if father's father's father
> Were to come in my way.
>
> *"Enough Mother"*

The daughter conveys a moral sense to her mother who blindly follows androcenric codes. By warning her against the murder of daughters, Heer tries to awaken Maliki from the stupor of false consciousness: "*jinhan betian marian roz kiamat/sir tinhan de vadda gunah mae/milan khanian tinhan nun phar kar ke/jivain marian je tivain khah mae* – Those who kill their daughters/Are heavily fined on the Judgment Day;/They are served the flesh torn from their victims/Just what they destroyed that is what they must eat, O mother" (Heer Waris Shah in Sekhon 2002: 73). She undergirds it with a profound social awareness of injustice against women. In her dialogues she denounces conventional beliefs and practices centered on external authorities and outward response. Tracing her intoxication to the Divine source, Heer uses Qur'ānic expressions and concepts to affirm passionate love as the sole religious practice. With her Sufi infused vocabulary she too espouses fundamental human principles. Of course Heer's family did not hear her arguments then, and neither has Heer's patriarchal Indo-Pak society to date.

Heer's daring speeches and deeds are depicted throughout the narrative text. With her sister-in-law Sahiti's support, Heer clandestinely meets with her lover, and even feigns a snake-bite so the yogi with occult powers (Ranjha in disguise) would be brought over. Heer demonstrates superb dramatic skills: she clenches her teeth, twists her body into a knot, she goes into concussions, and turns her eyes "blue and yellow." The family is convinced that Heer has been bitten by the most venomous of snakes, and bring in all sorts of physicians and snake charmers to cure her. They try countless antidotes, but all in vain. Heer and Sahiti's strategy succeeds: their family calls upon the "yogi" (disguised Ranjha), and together the lovers manage to run away. All along Heer thinks, speaks, walks, and does everything in accordance with her desire. Heer's authentic subjectivity is quite an anomaly in her sexist Punjabi society that has idealized docile and submissive women who live entirely for their husbands and their families, without any desire of their own. In breathtaking imagery, Waris Shah depicts his fiery heroine:

> Heer bathes herself, she dresses up in silks,
> She massages her hair with scented oils;
> She twists up her seductive braids,
> Coaxing a few wisps around her fair face.
> Eyes with liner, laden with lust,
> She gets ready with her weapons of beauty.
> She cleanses her face with a mask,
>   On her lips she puts crimson red –
> Coating them anew over and over.
> She covers her head with a diaphanous scarf,
> She decks her ears with big dangling hoops,
> Her brocade bodice fits her snug and tight,
> Her bangles chime, her jewels sparkle.
> With anklets haughtily jingling,
> Her forehead glowing with gold and red,
> Heer from the Syal family saunters over.
> A peacock, she dances seductively,
> An elephant in heat, she plunges ahead,
> Killing every naïve fellow on the way.

> Eyes intoxicating, lips lethal with red bark,
> A fairy arrives jingle jangling.
> At times she veils her face
> At times she shows her face –
>   Striking her beholders dead.
> Lifting off her veil, a sensual Heer,
> Tries to win her lover again;
> To the master who owns her pleasure,
> She shows off her treasures one by one.
>
> *Preparations*

The more we read Waris Shah, the more we realize that Heer's confidence and empowerment are a direct result of her being in touch with her erotic self.

But as we have been observing all along, Waris Shah is equally good at exposing the rampant subjugation and victimization of women. In the Punjabi patriarchal social structure, family honor (*izzat*) is centered on the bodies and sexuality of women. Control over the daughter's reproductive rights leads to the reproduction of her family's identity and prestige. Religious and social rules conflate as the Qazi and her mother-brother-father exhort Heer to marry the suitor of their choice. Heer's escapades with Ranjha bring much disgrace to the upper-class Syals. The poet quotes the parents asking: Why did we not strangle her at birth? Give her poison? Drown her in a well? Float her away?

> Kuchak asks his wife Maliki,
> Why did we not strangle her at birth?
> Why did we not give her a drop of poison,
> Which today would have been our savior?
> Why did we not drown her in some deep well?
> Why did we not float her away in the river?
> Says Waris, with the fear of Khuda,
> Why did we not lay her to rest
>   In the bed of the river Karun?
>
> *Why Did We Not?*

The father's regret for losing out on the manifold opportunities to kill his fearless daughter brings a chuckle to the eavesdropping reader. But it also makes the stomach churn. How easy it is to kill a baby daughter! How men and women internalize and perpetuate horrific sexist values! How the mother in her false consciousness is an equal partner in the brutal practices of honor killing and infanticide.

> Pull out her braids, cut off her hair
> Wring her neck and bury her far below
> Crack her head with the churn

> Break her back with the club
> Take a sickle – tear open her stomach
> And gouge her eyes with those needles.
>
> No way will she turn away from him
> Says Waris, try as much as we may

Says the Father

Such a conversation in Heer's family brings home the stark reality of women who are being killed by their families right at this moment in the name of "honor" – only because they have fallen in love with somebody of their own choice. They explain the dwindling population of baby girls due to sex-specific abortions eliminating female fetuses. The conversation also serves as a tragic foreshadowing of her family's ultimate victory – their poisoning of Heer just when she is happily awaiting Ranjha's wedding party. A radical heroine has no place in society.

As in the case of Bullhe Shah, many of Waris Shah's passages could very well have been composed today. We hear him incisively criticize the suffocating and oppressive custom of veiling. Instead of *burqa* he uses the north Indian word *ghundh* for veil, which is found in Punjabi, Hindi, and Urdu. Waris Shah does not merely see it as a piece of material with which women cover their hair, their faces and their bodies, but as a bundle of complex norms involving patriarchal control of female sexuality. He compares this abusive female practice to putting birds in a cage:

> This veil is full of woes,
> So burn it away
> It hides the glory of beauty,
> It shows the abuse of woman.
> The veil sinks the ship of lovers,
> It suffocates lovers like birds in a cage.
> The world opens up
> When the veil slips down.
> A veil blinds even those with eyes,
> So take it off your face, young one
> Says Waris Shah, do not bury pearls,
>   Nor set the flower on fire.

Burn the Veil

The poet poignantly declares, "The world opens up when the veil slips down." Waris Shah's imperative "*agg laike ghundh nun sarieh ni* – let us burn the veil in the fire" bears a striking resonance with that of the contemporary radically feminist Muslim, Taslima Nasrin, who is famous for her slogan, "Let's Burn the Burqa."

CONCLUSION

To conclude we must be aware of our own biases – be they Descartian, religious, or androcentric. Only then will we be able to understand the "alterity" of our beloved Sufi poetics and utilize their ideas to fight against the horribly contagious diseases of sexism, sectarianism, and snobbery around us. Religious conflicts abound across the globe. Sexism festers. Honor killings are so frequently reported in the media. Infanticide (in the form of gender-selective abortions) is widespread. In India's population of 1.027 billion, a recent Census showed only 927 girls for every 1,000 boys. Many women continue to wear the veil, and those who do not still live as though they were encaged – being excluded from the public sphere, and from all kinds of political and economic processes and interactions. We don't want other Heers to be murdered; we want them to live and fulfill their hopes and dreams. Therefore we must recognize our personal fore-meanings and cultural norms, which have made us deaf to the true vitality of our poets. Gadamer's discourse made us realize that listening involves a good deal more than hearing. It entails an understanding of the *otherness* the poets speak of, and practically responding to what they say. In fact Bullhe Shah himself was well aware of people hearing without listening. Centuries ago he poetically alerted us, *"bansi sabh koi sune sunavai, arth is da koi virala pave* – everybody hears and plays the notes of your flute, but rarely does anybody understand them." It's time we listened to our beloved Punjabi Sufi poets.

About the Author

Nikky-Guninder Kaur Singh is the Crawford Family Professor of Religious Studies at Colby College in Maine, USA. Her interests focus on poetics and feminist issues. Dr. Kaur Singh has published extensively in the field of Sikhism. Her books include *Of Sacred and Secular Desire: An Anthology of Lyrical Writings from the Punjab* (IB Tauris, 2012*)*, *Sikhism: An Introduction* (I.B. Tauris, 2011), *Cosmic Symphony* (Sahitya Akademy, 2008), *The Birth of the Khalsa* (SUNY, 2005), *Feminine Principle in the Sikh Vision of the Transcendent* (Cambridge University Press, 1993), *Metaphysics and Physics of the Guru Granth Sahib* (Sterling, 1981). Her translation of Sikh scriptural hymns entitled *The Name of My Beloved: Verses of the Sikh Gurus* was first published by HarperCollins in 1995, and by Penguin in 2001. She has lectured internationally, and appeared on television and radio in America, Canada, Ireland, Bangladesh, and India. She serves as a delegate for the American Institute for Indian Studies, and is on the editorial board of several journals including the *History of Religions*, the *Journal of the American Academy of Religion*, and *Sikh Formations*. She was born in the Punjab, and received her BA in Philosophy and Religion from Wellesley

College, her MA from the University of Pennsylvania, and her PhD from Temple University.

Notes

1. This chapter draws upon my translations of the original Punjabi verses and their introduction from my book *Of Sacred and Secular Desire: An Anthology of Punjabi Lyrical Writings from the Punjab* (New York and London: I.B. Tauris, 2012), pp. 70–118.
2. The edition I used is *Bullhe Shah dian Kafian* (published by Mehtab Singh; Jullundur: New Book Company, n.d.). For Waris Shah's narrative, I used Sant Singh Sekhon's edition *Heer Waris Shah* (New Delhi: Sahitya Akademi, 2002).
3. Used by Shackle for Waris Shah's text. See Shackle 1992: 262.
4. The change was first made by the Persian mystic Fakhuruddin Iraqi. See Schimmel (1975: 137).
5. An insightful example is Hanif Kureshi's short story "My Son the fanatic" which first appeared in the *New Yorker* in 1994, and was later made into a film by Udayan Prasad in 1997.
6. Guru Nanak's verse from Sikh scripture:

    jab nachi tab ghughat kaisa
    matuki phor nirari

    (GG: 1112)

9

LOOKING INSIDE THE HEART: THE UNIVERSAL APPEAL OF GOD AND HUMANITY AS REFLECTED IN IBN AL-'ARABĪ'S *FUSUS AL-HIKAM* AND MAULANA RŪMĪ'S *MATHNAWI MANAWI*

Sayed Hassan Akhlaq Hussaini

Sufism, as one school of Islamic intellectualism that tried to answer new questions and encourage people to have richer experiences of Islam, has made a long journey from its beginnings to the height of its accomplishment. Apparently, this journey was inspired by Qur'ānic verses and Islamic preaching on asceticism, piety, complete devotion and submission to God, and emphasis on the transitory nature of this world versus the eternal nature of the world hereafter. However, Sufism, similar to other Islamic principles including theology (Kalām) or philosophy was affected by non-Islamic schools of thought as well as the mentalities and backgrounds of those who traveled its path. It was a natural outcome of evolving during different times and locations. But what encourages us to concentrate on this traditional school is the fact that it serves as an inspiration for a better life in our time. For example, in regard to the topic of religious pluralism, Sufism decrees that an individual can not view every path toward God as equally correct for him, but insists that there is one correct path for each person, though it is no better than the path that is correct for another person. In this perspective, these paths to truth are not far from us or without relation to our souls, but they are within each of us, inviting us to a rich and meaningful life.

Muhiyddin Ibn 'al-Arabī (known as Ibn 'al-Arabī) (1165–1240) and Jalal ad-Din Muhammad Balkhi Rūmī (1207–1273) are two masters of Islamic Mysticism, which is known as Sufism, who brought Sufism,[1] to the peak of its perfection, and their works, *Fusus al-Hikam* and *Mathnawi*, are the best examples of the Sufi system and ideas. Both figures experienced deep love for a person and reflected it in their mystical poems. Ibn 'al-Arabī fell in love with an Isfahani lady and created *Tarjoman al-Ashwaq*; Rūmī fell in love with Shams and created *Divan-e Kabir* (though Rūmī's *Mathnawi* is more influenced by his love than Ibn 'Arabī's *Fusus*.) They are also different in their methods, orders and particular points. One well-known story exemplifies the difference in their styles. One day, Rūmī and

Sadr al-Din al-Qunawi (1207–74), the well-known disciple and first interpreter of Ibn 'al-Arabī, discussed the relationship between God and being. Qunawi explained the subject using scholarly and complex terms, but Rūmī explained it simply and clearly. Qunawi wondered at Rūmī's explanation, asking: How do you explain this hard topic in that simple way that everyone can understand? Rūmī answered: I'm wondering how you explain that simple point in a way that no one can understand it! Ibn 'al-Arabī explains Sufi ideas in an academic, systematic and professional method for a specific sphere, while Rūmī explains them in a plain speech using many metaphors and stories for the public sphere. The first is more speculative and theoretic, while the second is more illuminative and emotionally compelling.

In addition, Rūmī is a representative of the eastern Islamic world's non-Arab form of Sufism who tries to expand his mystical ideas independently from religion. For example, he started his book without using "in the name of God, the merciful, the compassionate,"[2] which is the standard and expected opening to any work or text in the Islamic world. He does not mention the names and stories of prophets including Muhammad, and prominent caliphs as often as he mentions the names of Shams and Muslim Sufis. Ibn 'al-Arabī is a representative of the western Islamic world and of the Arab form who claimed that his most significant book, *Fusus al-Hikam*, was inspired by the Prophet Muhammad and who used the names of Islamic prophets to title his book's chapters! However, it is important to note that they both belong to same school of thought, namely Sufism, with the same principles, such as the unity of being, the descent and ascent of being, spiritual journey, intuition and revelation, rebirth, love, and the mysterious path. The similarity of their ideas led some scholars to consider Mathnawi Manawi as the best interpretation of Ibn 'al-Arabī's ideas. This chapter seeks to illuminate the approach to, belief in, reasoning for, and explanation of religious pluralism found in both Ibn 'al-Arabī's and Rūmī's most significant works.

In other words, the chapter intends to discuss how their understanding of God, the world, and humanity creates a platform for moving toward religious pluralism based not only on a pragmatic approach leading to practical tolerance, but also on an existential approach. What does religious pluralism mean here? What is the origin of visible diversity among people, their emotions, their intellects, their rationalities, their capacities and finally their faiths? What points of their Islamic doctrines allow them to interpret this diversity and lead them to religious pluralism?

The chapter goes on to examine the following points in order in both Ibn 'al-Arabī and Rūmī:

1. The concept of God and its manifestations
2. The relationship between humans and God
3. The relationship between God and different faiths
4. The existential approach towards Jesus

Finally, it concentrates on *Fusus al-Hikam*, which literally means "the seals of wisdoms,"[3] and *Mathanawi Manawi*, which literally means "the spiritual couplet." They are considered significant because each contains the complete ideas of its respective author and discusses them in a almost didactic fashion. Tabatabaii, a great modern-day Muslim philosopher and an interpreter of the holy Qur'ān once said that no one in the Islamic world has ever been able to write even one line similar to Ibn 'al-Arabī's writing. Ayatollah Khomeini, the supreme leader of the Iranian revolution and an eminent religious authority, suggested in a letter to Soviet President Mikhail Gorbachev that he should study Ibn 'al-Arabī's ideas in order to understand the Muslim world because these teachings represented the pinnacle of Islamic philosophy and wisdom. The sheer number of interpretations that have been written on *Fusus* – more than 110 in the history of Islamic mysticism – shows the special status of this book. Rūmī has the same position in the non-Arab Islamic world among speakers of Farsi, Turkish and Indian languages and Sufi orders. Great Sunni and Shia scholars such as Nur ad-Din Abd ar-Rahman Jami (1414–1492) and Shaykh Bahaii (1547–1621) described *Mathnawi* as the Persian Qur'ān.

In this chapter, I will analyze the above mentioned points directly from the original texts, without constantly referring to their different interpretations. Further, I aim to present these mystical points in a clear way for Western readers and new minds that are more concerned with concrete notions.

1. THE CONCEPT OF GOD AND HIS MANIFESTATIONS

In the Sufi doctrine, the main concept of Abrahamic religions clearly changes from creator and creature to manifestor and manifestations, such as the sun and its rays (Rūmī 1381/2002: 3.3715–18; 3.3578). Sufi doctrine tries to solve the problem of obvious plurality by reducing all entities to the One and its different manifestations. In doing so, it answers the questions of when creation occurred, what its purpose, and what the relationship between God and creatures is. Based on the Sufi viewpoint, there is only one being who is absolute beauty and perfection. His beauty causes Him to appear. As Jami said:

> The beautiful one can't remain concealed. If you try to close the door against her, she will show off from inside the window.

Therefore, the world is the mirror of God (Ibn 'al-Arabī 1946: 48–49). I will later explain that "world" here is a "macro-human" and "human" is a "microcosm." This is another form of "God created man in his image, in the divine image he created him; male and female he created them" (The New American Bible, Genesis 1.27). Rūmī says:

> God created us in His image: our qualities are instructed by (and modeled upon) His qualities (Rūmī 1381/2002: 4.1194).[4]
>
> Those progenies are not (produced) by means of these four (elements); consequently they are not seen by these eyes.
>
> Those progenies are born of (Divine) illumination; consequently they are covered (from sight) by a pure veil.
>
> We said 'born,' but in reality they are not born, and this expression is only (used) in order to guide (understanding) (Rūmī 1381/2002: 6.1812–14).

God constantly wants to manifest, because of this desire, He then appears. The world is in a state of permanent production, ceaselessly alternating between annihilation and creation (Ibn 'al-Arabī 1946: 49). Here, "creation" and "annihilation" merely refer to manifestation in different levels regarding the descent and ascent of being. In this perspective, the world does not exist independently from God; moreover, existence is merely a reflection of divine. The world is only humans' "imagination" originating from our insufficient knowledge of truth. All entities and their implications belong to God, and all aspects of their beings are imaginary. Ibn 'al-Arabī writes that there is nothing except the imagination. Everything that can be conceived or named, save for God, all is imagination (Ibn 'al-Arabī 1946: 104, 159). The absolute being is like light that itself is clear and makes all other things clear. This one being transforms into the plurality that we can see. The point is that the plurality of the world is but the different modes, states, names, attributes, and phases of the unity of the divine, similar to waves and the sea. God exists, and others are only manifestations. Though we think we exist, only God exists, and we can only find ourselves in Him as His appearance. The absolute being enacts its desires to show off and love by descending in different forms through three phases and five worlds,[5] from absolute to concrete and from general to particular, to reach the level of "human." From this position, He begins His ascent back to point of origin:

> Know that the wheeling heavens are turned by waves of Love: were it not for Love, the world would be frozen (inanimate) (Rūmī 1381/2002: 5.3854 also see 1.1–18; Ibn 'al-Arabī 1946: 48–58).

The ascending stage is begun and advanced by love as well. That which makes the absolute being expand and manifest in the obvious plurality that ends in the human stage, causes it to collect all worlds and phases and realize them in real unity through the human journey from physic to metaphysic, soil to soul, and ray to sun (Ibn 'al-Arabī 1946, Fass-e Musa). Therefore, the human's essence is not a body as a materialist thinks, nor a mind as the idealist thinks, but a divine entity, as a Sufi thinks; human body and mind are merely different manifestations of that divine entity. Something that merits discussion is that this divine entity – the human – has a paradoxical identity; all entities and identities are simultaneously mirrors for him as well as veils over him – mirrors, because they show a bit of his capacity and perfection, and veils, because they distract him from his true journey unity in God by encouraging him to lose himself in the plurality of worldly affairs. The Persian poet, Hafiz (1325–1390) relates this paradoxical status most beautifully:

> In this path, every drop of night dew is a hundred fiery waves
> Alas! Explanation, or interpretation, this 'puzzle' hath not.

However, in contrast to descending, the ascent is the journey of abandoning limitations and determinations; here, the lowest level of existence – the pure potential phase – starts moving toward the highest level of existence – the infinite actuality. The human becomes more human by freeing himself from different implications and limitations. Sufis call this passing phase death and annihilation. Rūmī explains how it differs from common viewpoints:

> Hence all the world have taken the wrong way, for they are afraid of non-existence, though it is (really) the refuge (in which they find salvation).
> Whence shall we seek (true) knowledge? From renouncing (our false) knowledge. Whence shall we seek (true) peace? From renouncing peace (with our carnal selves).
> Whence shall we seek (real) existence? From renouncing (illusory) existence. Whence shall we seek the apple (of Truth)? From renouncing the hand (of self-assertion and self-interest) (Rūmī 1381/2002: 6.822–24).

Annihilation and death is a positive point: the other side of rebirth! Because the spiritual traveler breaks the tight boundary and receives a vast one in each step. This journey happens within human existence, since the human has all horizons and spheres within. He is the true bridge among all worlds and hierarchies of being. Here, Rūmī explains the variety of spheres through which the human passes:

> I died to the inorganic state and became endowed with growth, and (then) I died to (vegetable) growth and attained to the animal.
> I died from animality and became Adam (man): why, then, should I fear? When have I become less by dying?
> At the next remove I shall die to man, that I may soar and lift up my head amongst the angels;
> And I must escape even from (the state of) the angel: *everything is perishing except His Face.*
> Once more I shall be sacrificed and die to the angel: I shall become that which enters not into the imagination.
> Then I shall become non-existence: non-existence saith to me, (in tones loud) as an organ, Verily, unto Him shall we return (Rūmī 1381/2002: 3.3901–906).

The last point is that in Sufi cosmology, everything, even the smallest thing that can be overlooked, is a representative of God's name and being. Therefore, everything is valued by God's attributes of knowledge, power, mercy, and will. Doubtless, all things deserve respect! We can understand this point by a spiritual journey, not a conceptual contact. This is not formal knowledge available in books, but an existential understanding that is reachable after inwardly traveling through different worlds and experiencing various levels of existence. In regards to Sufi doctrine, we cannot understand anything without approaching these levels of existence in their world and within the bounds of their identity:

> Do thou, then, become the (spiritual) resurrection and (thereby) see (experience) the resurrection: this (becoming) is the necessary condition for seeing (knowing and experiencing the real nature of) anything.
> Until thou become it, thou wilt not know it completely, whether it be light or darkness (Rūmī 1381/2002: 6.756–57).

2. THE RELATIONSHIP BETWEEN HUMANS AND GOD

The true knowledge, accompanied with existential struggling originates from within person. He passes a journey of love that is looking for God's presence, mercy, manifestations, and ideas everywhere. A Sufi's journey moves between the human's actual position and his ideal position. The main concern of Sufism deals with our passion for life, which occurs between freedom and limitation. On one side, we were not born in a vacuum; we were born in and are influenced by a particular nature, community, culture, history, and location. Our natural life, social coexistence, and communications require keeping our identity recognized separately from others, caring for ourselves, and looking after our desires. All these issues imprison us in a particular classification. On the other hand, we wish to fly in the heavens, break the chains, and realize a limitless sphere of love, beauty, virtue, and knowledge.

Ibn 'al-Arabī began his book, *Fusus Al-Hikam*, with the following:

> Once God – glory be to Him! – willed that regarding to His most Beautiful Names – which are beyond enumeration – be seen (or you can equally say that He willed His nature to be seen), He willed that they be seen in a comprehensive being which contained the entire matter, endowed with existence, and through which His secret was manifested to Him (Ibn 'al-Arabī 1946: 48).

The chapter, "Fas Adamiyah," is the most significant part of the book; what it contains is detailed in later chapters (Mosleh 1384: 56). It describes the human, in his ideal position, as the "comprehensive being" – meaning that human essence includes (1) all levels of the existence, (2) a mirror for God, (3) the spirit of the world, (4) the medium through which God deals with the world, (5) the king of the angels, (6) the vice president of God, and (7) the sum of God. The surprising thing, though, is that the human, in his actual position, is not at all far from his ideal position. The above-mentioned characteristics are manifested in different phases, though in different levels. The human is vice president of God in any level. He acts as his position requires in that level and within the scope of his existential horizon. For example, he enacts his status of "vice president" in his community, or family, or body; s/he cares for the environment, plants in the field, governs a nation, builds or destroys, writes and sings, etc. This position helps him to make the leap from earth to heaven, from physical to metaphysical, from particular to general, from reason to love, and from diversity to identity. However, the origin, path, and end all are within the human. His ascent is but an expansion of his existence and exploration of his hidden capacities. In spite of the significant diversity and plurality in regard to people's existential status, they are nonetheless all the same. Although the ideal human – which, according to Sufi tradition, has been actualized in the mind of God – comprises vast and rich infinite dimensions, when he is made manifest in the tight and narrow format of nature, these constraints lead to a reality where his particular manifestations become the plurality in unity or differences in indifferences (Mosleh 1384: 134).

"The plurality of things" refers to differences that lead to inconsistent elements. When these inconsistent elements are gathering in a special place such as an individual, the challenge of reconciling between limitation and limitlessness will appear. The paradoxes within the human demonstrate the collection of opposite capacities and powers (Rūmī 4.1008–11). The awareness of his deficiencies motivates the human to substitute his perspective with God's perspective (Rūmī 1381/2002: 2.3714–51) As much as other things are determined and identified, the human by contrast, is undetermined and unidentified. This is a sign of opportunity, rather than a problem; opportunity to self-realization as we want, not as is wanted by a separated creator. Here the sphere of the human exists from zero to infinity. We are but continuously changing entities. Everyone has a direct intuition of growth, characteristic change, and different moods within.

One might attribute these changes to society, education and circumstances. This is absolutely true, but merely as a part of reality. If there is not a capacity for change within the human, he does not face them at all. There are as many individuals calling themselves "I" as there are human beings. The child who wants his or her toy uses "I," as does the saint who explains his divine findings. Both perceive "I" as their identity, though there are different implications and manifestations for each "I" because of their existence in different levels. This situation is applicable in the sphere of cultures and religions. Religions and culture are related to the human; there is no culture or religion without human beings.

Sufi books must be read as the itinerary of a spiritual journey among different worlds where the Sufi faces a variety of moods and minds. *Fusus Al-Hikam* consists of 27 chapters, each of which is called "Fas." The Arabic word "Fas" means seal. It is applied to cover two points: (1) the ringstone that is the center of a ring, referring to the central position of the human in the world, and (2) the seal that completes a verdict, referring to the ability of the human to act as a medium linking the kingdom of God to the realm of the worlds. Consequently, Ibn 'al-Arabī follows the names of the prophets with "the word," meaning that each prophet is a unique appearance of God, because the word signifies the intention and meaning. As we can understand words in their context, we also understand the prophets in their contextures only. All things are the words of God that reveal themselves to us. The world is the macro-human. It talks to us, asking us to listen to it. However, the main speech of the world belongs to the human, because he is the semi-God. The prophets are at the top and reveal the profound names of God. Therefore, the prophets' story is the story of revealing human capacities at the highest level. Sufis recite the holy Qur'ān from this viewpoint to discover the manifestations of truths through the prophets:

> When you have fled (for refuge) to the Qur'án of God, you have mingled with the spirit of the prophets.
> The Qur'án is (a description of) the states of the prophets, (who are) the fishes of the holy sea of (Divine) Majesty.
> And if you read and do not accept (take to heart) the Qur'án, suppose you have seen the prophets and saints (what will that avail you?);
> But if you are accepting (the Qur'án), when you read the stories (of the prophets), the bird, your soul, will be distressed in its cage (Rūmī 1381/2002: 1.1537–40).

Why then, are there different prophets with different paths, known in Islamic terms as al-Sharia? Ibn 'al-Arabī answers explicitly: "The differences among nations and religions have originated from the differences among people" (Ibn 'al-Arabī 1946: 47). The different prophets' paths are different lines connecting the circle to the core. This quotation makes clear the interconnection between the prophets and their followers.

The *Mathnawi* of Rūmī is summarized in the first 18 verses of the book, *Nay Naamah*. They are reflections of the human situation that places man far from his origin as well as his end. All of Rūmī's other poems and stories remind us of this issue and tell us how to solve the problem. Rūmī's concept of religion, prophets, and saints must be observed in this context. His discussion of the prophets and saints motivates us to discover our inner prophets and saints:

> The mention of Moses serves for a mask, but the Light of Moses is thy actual concern, O good man.

Moses and Pharaoh are in thy being: thou must seek these two adversaries in thyself (Rūmī 1381/2002: 3.1252–54).

The prophets' and saints' paths or Sharia are the methods for self-realization. This self-realization begins with characteristic changes, which Rūmī depicts as follows:

> Since colorlessness (pure Unity) became the captive of color (manifestation in the phenomenal world), a Moses came into conflict with a Moses. When you attain unto the colorlessness which you (originally) possessed, Moses and Pharaoh are at peace (with each other) (Rūmī 1381/2002: 1.2467–68).

This self-realization reaches different realms of existence that are beyond the common division of popular dualistic doctrines such as believers and non-believers, good and bad, paradise and hell, and obedience and disobedience. These two opposite sides refer only to a portion of the human capacity:

> Do not judge from the (normal) state of man, do not abide in wrong-doing and in well-doing.
> Wrong-doing and well-doing, grief and joy, are things that come into existence; those who come into existence die; God is their heir (Rūmī 1381/2002: 1.1805–806 also see 2.3322; 3.4724 also see Mosleh 1384: 117; Akhlaq 1386: 63–89).

As a result, the relationship between God and humans is an existential relationship that links the human to his vast inner worlds as well as his path towards God by looking to the prophets and their path with an existential approach. The prophets will appear for the spiritual traveler, or *Saalek*, in relation to his capacity, struggles, and goal. He sees them as aspects of his soul meant to enlighten him.[6]

3. THE RELATIONSHIP BETWEEN GOD AND DIFFERENT FAITHS

Sufism has a firm faith in "unity of being" when they analyze humans and the prophets in this context. "Unity of being" means that only one being exists; He is God. Other things we imagine to exist are merely different manifestations of God. Ibn 'al-Arabī clearly mentions unity of being in "The Seal of the Wisdom of Sanctification (*Quddûs*) in the Word of Idris." He discussed God's elevation referring to a quotation of al-Kharraz,[7] who said, "I only knew Allah by joining the opposites. He is the First and the Last, the Outwardly Manifest and the Inwardly Hidden." Ibn 'al-Arabī adds,

> He is the source of what appears and the source of what is hidden in the state of its manifestation. There is none who sees Him other than

> Him and there is none who is hidden from Him. So He is manifest to Himself and hidden from Himself. He is called Abu Sa'id, al-Kharraz and other than that from the names of things in-time (Ibn 'al-Arabī 1946: 77).

This poem from *Mathnawi* also declares the unity of being:

> We and our existences are (really) non-existences: thou art the absolute Being which manifests the perishable (causes phenomena to appear).
>
> We all are lions, but lions on a banner: because of the wind they are rushing onward from moment to moment (Rūmī 1381/2002: 1.602–603 also see 2.54–55).

Rūmī also explains the unity of seemingly diverse entities by encouraging us to understand this matter with the clearness of vision that only comes from seeing with one's heart from of path of love (Rūmī 1381/2002: 1.682–84). He believes that if a person is sufficiently introspective, he can compare his unity and variety of attributes to the unity of God and the world (Rūmī 1381/2002: 1.1290; also see: 2.54–59).

Therefore, if there is only one true being who constantly is demonstrating Himself, all religions who call on Him are the same, despite their different faces and varied rituals. There is no one to call on except Him. There is only one object of worship whose presence is boundless. Many of Ibn 'al-Arabī's and Rūmī's writings encompass this notion. Here I mention just one example from each:

> So, Allah makes it clear to you that He is in the 'where-ness' of every direction. There are only creeds, so all directions are correct. Every correct thing has a reward. Every rewarded thing is happy. Every happy one is approved. (Ibn 'al-Arabī 1946: 114) (Rūmī: 1.493, 2545 and 2547)
>
> Whether love be from this (earthly) side or from that (heavenly) side, in the end it leads us yonder (Rūmī 1381/2002: 1.111).
> Inasmuch as God comes not into sight, these prophets are the vicars of God (Rūmī 1381/2002: 1.673).

In reality, we face different religions with muliple rites that simultaneously claim themselves to be the only truth, devaluing others. What is the origin of this diversity? And how can each one undrestand the others? Ibn 'al-'Arabī's speculative Sufism contains enough substance to answer the first question, and Rūmī's more pragmatic Sufism helps us with the second question. The differences and even inconsistencies between all things – including human desires and inner powers, and culture, civilization, and non-human beings – have originated from God's plurality of names and their essential desires to manifist themselves.[8] An example of this is the positive conflict between the names of God such as *Mumit*, which means "the giver of death," *Muhii*, "the giver of life," *Hadi*, "the guider," and *Muzil*, "the misleader." This conflict leads to the best order of the world and has been judged by the "Perfect Man," who is a manifistation of God, the "Comprehensive name." The "General Names" of God are limited, while the "Particular Names" are unlimited (Ibn 'al-Arabī 1946: 65) as the prophets and the main religions are limited and we, the people are unlimited. Here, the actual plurality of God's names leads to the variety of the prophets and their paths, or *Sharia*. *Fusus al-Hikam* is the story of the prophets as God has manifested within them in accordance with their share of God's names.

Ibn 'al-Arabī expands his idea with a focus on a "believed God." As there is diversity between essence and attribute, there is also a diversity between God and belief in God, and faith and the object of faith. God is an absolute that manifests in each form within the limits of its boundaries. Each faithful person – even perfect Sufi – is satisfied with his own form of God, not absolute God: "He sees Him in the form of his belief in God. God, who is in the belief, is He whose form the heart contains. He is the One who gives it a *Tajalli* (Manifestation), and so it knows Him. The eye only sees by belief" (Ibn 'al-Arabī 1946: 121).

People cannot go further than themselves when they are talking of or believing in God,

> On the whole, each person must have some idea of his Lord by which he refers to Him and in which he seeks Him. So, when God manifests Himself to him in it, he knows Him and goes near Him. If He manifests Himself to him in other than it, he denies Him and takes refuge from Him and has bad attitude in that matter while claiming he shows attitude with Him. He only believes in a divinity according to the form he built that in himself. The belief in divinity is based on subjective positing. People only see themselves and what they formulate in themselves (Ibn 'al-Arabī 1946: 113). They venerate themselves when they venerate God (Ibn 'al-Arabī 1946: 226).

Ibn 'al-Arabī also demonstrates that all beliefs in God are matters of strong conjecture, not certainty, because knowledge of the absolute is impossible,

> He has opinion but does not know Him. For that reason, God says, 'I am in My slave's opinion of Me', that is, I only appear to him in the form of his belief […] and He is the God which the heart of His slave encompasses. The Absolute Divinity is not encompassed by anything because He is the identity of things and the nature of Himself (Ibn 'al-Arabī 1946: 226).

Then, he explicitly encourages people to be open to different ideas and faiths with the following:

> In this view, each faithful person is awarded with God's grace, is said to be in the right way, *Sirat al-Mustaqim*, He is with us by open declaration. God said, He is with you wherever you are (Qur'ān, 57.4) and we are with Him as He takes us by our forelocks (Qur'ān, 11.56). Then He – may He be exalted – is with Himself wherever He goes with us on His path. So everyone in the world is on a straight path, and it is the path of the exalted Lord (Ibn 'al-Arabī 1946: 158).

Furthermore, Ibn 'al-Arabī declares that worshipping any God is acceptable (Ibn 'al-Arabī 1946: 72); each worshipped one is one mirror of God, "The complete gnostic is the one who sees that every idol is a locus of God's Manifestation in which He is worshipped" (Ibn 'al-Arabī 1946: 195) that is not avoidable, "The manifestation occurs in forms. They must be manifestation and form, and the one who sees Him by his passion must worship Him" (Ibn 'al-Arabī 1946: 196).

Lastly, he looks deeply in worshipping the idols, as in the story of Noah, "The Seal of the Wisdom of the Breath of Divine Inspiration In the Word of Nuh (Noah)" (Ibn 'al-Arabī 1946: 68–74 also see Afifi 1946: 31–43) and admires in an extremely pluralistic way the non-divine religions as much as they have wisdom and use (Ibn 'al-Arabī 1946: 95). Thus, Ibn 'Arabī's poem in *Shawareq al-Elahm* enthusiastically presents his personal feeling toward this pluralistic approach:

> My heart has become capable of every form: it is a pasture for gazelles and a convent for Christian monks,
> And a temple for idols and the pilgrim's *Ka'ba* and the tables of the *Torah* and the book of the Qur'ān.
> I follow the religion of Love: whatever way Love's camels take, that is my religion and my faith" (Ibn 'al-Arabī 1911: 67).

Otherwise, Rūmī emphasizes the unity among multicolored manifestations of God in a variety religions, encouraging a move beyond this situation as follows:

> There is a way from many-coloredness to colorlessness: color is like the clouds, and colorlessness is a moon (Rūmī 1381/2002: 1.3476).
> Thou art (still) of the same complexion with which thou wast born: thou hast not taken one step forward (Rūmī 1381/2002: 6.1784).

> People are advised to transcend their subjective boundaries and become involved in pure truth (Rūmī 1381/2002: 3.1225–28). Rūmī analogies religions as ships, truth as water, the faithful people as passengers, and the conflict among religions as a battle among ships. People are bystanders distarcted by watching the battle and pitting those on the ships against one another, instead of exploring the water of the truth (Rūmī 1381/2002: 3.1273–77). They are looking for and talking about the same human transcendence without strong decisions or a correct approach (Rūmī 1381/2002: 3.1259–56).

The benefit of religiosity is the ability to find new vision that expands the human horizon and existence (Rūmī 1381/2002: 6.812). This is a criterion that Rūmī uses in evaluating any religion and venerating any prophet or saint, including gathering in the martyrdom of the Prophet Muhammad's grandson by saying:

> Mourn for thy corrupt heart and religion, for it (thy heart) sees naught but this old earth.
> Or if it is seeing (the spiritual world), why is it not brave and supporting (others) and self-sacrificing and fully contented?
> In thy countenance where is the happiness (which is the effect) of the wine of (true) religion? If thou hast beheld the Ocean (of Bounty), where is the bounteous hand?
> He that has beheld the River does not grudge water (to the thirsty), especially he that has beheld that Sea and (those) Clouds (Rūmī 1381/2002: 6.802–805).

Changing a person through religion, which leads to new perspectives, will offer the same ideas about other faiths, as mentioned below:

> The mention of Moses serves for a mask, but the Light of Moses is thy actual concern, O good man.
> Moses and Pharaoh are in thy being: thou must seek these two adversaries in thyself.
> The (process of) generation from Moses is (continuing) till the Resurrection: the Light is not different, (though) the lamp has become different (Rūmī 1381/2002: 3.1250–52 also see: 1.2480).

In other words, by leaving the varied colors of our limited circumstances and moving toward absolute and true being, we will obtain an alternative view and "non-colored" position that shows different religious paths as varied radii directed to the core of the same circle. Rūmī says that we have to leave the colors that make us vibrant without our choice – as we have no choice in our racial identity – in favor of the permanent color of the truth. Obviously, it is not a simple step toward humanity, but it is possible. He explains the accidental state of these local colors by picturing death (Rūmī 1381/2002: 6.4709–15). Death makes one more appearance in *Mathnawi* when it is depicted as "a removal (during life) from one place to another." With this in mind, Rūmī concludes the following points: (1) saints and prophets are people who have passed the ordinary levels of life in favor of the life hereafter, which is not far from daily affairs; (2) following a religion or spiritual order means accomplishing self-realization to the level of saints or prophets; and (3) evaluating or judging extraordinary individuals and states using ordinary criteria, such as calculative reasoning is not permissible (Rūmī 1381/2002: 6.723–61). This existential transcendence transfers believers from the realm of inconstancy and disloyalty to the realm of friendship and reliability:

> The son of the world (the worldling) is faithless like the world: though he turn the face towards thee, that face is (really) the nape (back).
> The people of that (other) world, like that world, on account of (their) probity continue forever in (observance of their) covenant and promise.
> When, in sooth, did two prophets oppose each other? When did they wrest (their) evidential miracles (spiritual powers and privileges) from one another? (Rūmī 1381/2002: 4.1650–52).

Thus, the belief in inconsistency among prophets is the result of formalism (Rūmī 1381/2002: 5.2884, also see 1.674–89, and for conflict between religious formalism and religious true experience, see "How Moses, on whom be peace, took offence at the prayer of the shepherd" (Rūmī 1381/2002: 2.1710–1805). This poem clearly talks about unity among the founders of all religions:

> In the salutations and benedictions addressed to the righteous (saints) praise of all the prophets is blended.
> The praises are all commingled (and united): the jugs are poured into one basin.
> Inasmuch as the object of praise Himself is not more than One, from this point of view (all) religions are but one religion.
> Know that every praise goes (belongs) to the Light of God and is (only) lent to (created) forms and persons (Rūmī 1381/2002: 3.2122–25).

In further detail, Rūmī extends the unity among prophets over unity among their true believers so that disrespecting any believer leads to disrespecting all, and destroying another believer's house equals destroying all our faiths' houses (4.407–18). When people unite their spirits with their saints' spirits, there will not be any conflict and inconsistency, because "on that account these companions of ours are all at war, (but) no one (ever) heard of war amongst the prophets" (Rūmī 1381/2002: 4.447–66).

Rūmī uses a story about three individuals who want grapes, but because they are talking in different languages, they do not understand, and subsequently they fight one another (Rūmī 1381/2002: 2.3668–3673, also see Rūmī 1381/2002: 2.3689). Also, the story of "The disagreement as to the description and shape of the elephant" in *Mathnawi* presents knowledge's limitations as one extra source of fighting and conflict (Rūmī 1381/2002: 3.1257–67). Language, location, historical period, personal interests, cultural implications, intellectual viewpoints, and business positions are all colors that make our perspectives bright in sighting both our religion and other religions. In fact, we are enchanted by these boundaries, which is why we turn to religion (Rūmī 1381/2002: 6.4504 and 4541). Also, there is an opportunity to evaluate anyone's weight in accordance with the question, "Do I determine myself, or do others determine who I am?" (Rūmī 1381/2002: 2.283–87; 4.2303–304).

One point worth pondering is that Rūmī motivates us to view from a higher level what is behind the fight among faiths; there is a huge incentive treasure for spiritual travelers, far from ordinary people who are satisfied with watching the battle. Of course, treasure is always behind the battlefield, but the battle is sited to evaluate each person looking for truth or involved in the fight:

> Sing, like nightingales, in the presence of the Rose, in order that you may divert them from the scent of the Rose (Rūmī 1381/2002: 6.700).

All religions make creeds and doctrines, while truth lies in colorless love (Rūmī 1381/2002: 1.2472–248; 5.3214–3250). Truth merely arises from within, the real location of the living Moses and Pharaoh:

> Moses and Pharaoh are in thy being: thou must seek these two adversaries in thyself (3.1251).

Rūmī emphasizes that we have to reach our living Moses instead of limiting our minds and arguing about the prophets and saints or criticizing other faiths that are another ray of truth; this misconception requires exchanging the lantern and the light (Rūmī 1381/2002: 3.1249–57). *Mathnawi* spreads the ideas of unity of religions, although it accepts that the actual differences among religious founders lead us to one truth in regard to this poem:

> We are dashing against each other, like boats: our eyes are darkened, though we are in the clear water.
> O thou that hast gone to sleep in the body's boat, thou hast seen the water, (but) look on the Water of the water.
> The water hath a Water that is driving it; the spirit hath a Spirit that is calling it.
> Where were Moses and Jesus when the (Divine) Sun was giving water to the sown field of existent things?
> Where were Adam and Eve at the time when God fitted this string to the bow? (Rūmī 1381/2002: 3.1273–76).

The author justifies the different religious paths, or *Sharia*, corresponding to a variety of situations (Rūmī 1381/2002: 4.494–96). Finally, Rūmī describes his faith as the faith of a lover separated from ordinary religious beliefs:

> The religion of Love is apart from all religions: for lovers, the (only) religion and creed is – God (2.1760).

In summary, Ibn 'al-Arabī believes that God's names are manifested in different faces among diverse religions, which Rūmī considers to be different expressions of the Truth. The former tries to theorize his thoughts, while the later seeks to motivate us more. Both Ibn 'al-Arabī and Rūmī look at different religions as a variety of paths toward God that call upon our existential movement, more so than analytical attempts. God, through diverse religions, invites people to recreate as they want, instead of standing at their given position. Contemplation on the plurality of religions helps us to see the richness of truth in thought and become inspired to move beyond the everyday by different faith-builders. Now, let us look to how Ibn 'al-Arabī and Rūmī examine the case of Jesus in this aim.

4. THE EXISTENTIAL APPROACH TOWARDS JESUS

As the above-mentioned points demonstrate Sufism tries to transcend from peoples in the world to the characteristics within them. The existential approach here merely examines Jesus in terms of those people's existential levels, their share of gradual being. Saints and prophets as well as infidels and pagans are but different aspects of our existence. Referring to the verse 64.2 of the Qur'ān, Rūmī substitutes the outward category of people with the inward category of aspects:

> Whoever sees the former half spurns (him); whoever sees the latter half seeks (after him).
> Joseph was like a beast of burden in the eyes of his brethren; at the same time in the eyes of a Jacob he was like a houri.
> Through evil fancy the (bodily) derivative eye and the original unseen eye (of the mind) regarded him (Joseph) as ugly (Rūmī 1381/2002: 2.608–610 also see 1.1598–99).

He believes in the prophets and saints who live in our lives, present in daily experiences of up and down, and sadness and happiness, directly talking with and hearing from God – and not only in our imagination or dreams. Therefore, Rūmī's approach to Jesus is a mystical and esoteric approach that discovers and explains Jesus by describing our inner side. Jesus is the symbol of eternity who leads us to permanent life and raises us from our temporary at-present existence (Rūmī 1381/2002: 1.4258). Evoking a popular Islamic narration, Rūmī portrays Jesus as our true self, the purpose that we are leaving in favor of tools and devices. Unfortunately, we are listening to machines' voices and demonstrating our eagerness to serve techniques and desires rather than hearing from our soul – Jesus – and accompanying him in the higher levels of being, happiness, and knowledge (Rūmī 2.1850–53).

With Rūmī, we approach Jesus as the perfect man[9] who (1) does not take a side in facing a variety of colors and characteristics, and (2) teaches us a unity that digests all pluralities that separate us from each other. Therefore, his religion points to the unity of faiths (1.500–503; 6.1855). Jesus' inspiration is still applicable; this is our mission, Muslims and Christians, to receive benefits from his altar:

> How excellent is the Messiah's table of food without stint! How excellent is Mary's fruit (that was produced) without an orchard! (Rūmī 1381/2002:, 6.1307).

Finally, Rūmī expresses his sorrow at the lack of awareness among humankind about their inner angels and the Messiac aspect of their beings. This deficiency failed them, leading to two huge sicknesses: a formalism that caused them to limit God's house to one religious place, and an inversion that made them become servants of their servants, exchanging the place of tool and goal (Rūmī 1381/2002: 6.4584).

However, both Ibn 'al-Arabī and Rūmī look at Jesus as one level of Muhammad's existence, meaning that (1) followers of Christ follow Muhammad as much as their levels allow; and (2) if we cannot apply the comprehensive being of Muhammad to our lives, why do we choose not to apply that of Jesus instead? "If you cannot go by the Mohammedan way, at least go by the way of Jesus, so you will not remain completely outside the spiritual path" (Mawlawi 1386: 104; see also Rūmī 1381/2002: 6.494).

In opposition to the practical approach of Rūmī, Ibn 'Arabī, as his theorizing method depicts, deals with Jesus and the Trinity in a more detailed manner. Ibn 'al-Arabī approaches Jesus and Christianity by discussing three issues: the Trinity, a redefinition of *Kufr*, and the concept of *Khaatam-e Awliya*. Through this discussion he hopes to sympathize more with Christian people and open a path toward religious pluralism which I will elaborate in order. Since Sufis consider One to be the origin of numbers, rather than a number itself, Ibn 'al-Arabī states, "The first singular is three, and what is more than this firstness of individuals comes from three." He extends this triple structure of being across ontology – meaning God's substance, attributes, and names; cosmology – meaning love, beloved and lover, or knowledge, knower, and knowable; the creation process – meaning God's essence, will, and commend; epistemology – meaning the minor premise, major premise, and the conclusion; human family – meaning male, female, and child; and his knowledge of Muhammad's spiritual position in the origin, middle, and end of the manifestation, as well as his depiction of the Trinity in Muhammad's love for woman, perfume, and praying so that we can say that the chapter of Muhammad in the *Fusus al-Hikam* is an interpretation of the Trinity (Ibn 'al-Arabī 1946: 214–26).[10] Explicitly, this system of thought struggles with the concept of trinity to understand the manifestation of truth in Christianity.

Moreover, Ibn 'al-Arabī narrates his personal meeting with Jesus in several spiritual positions in his magnum opus and great Sufi encyclopedia, *al-Futuhat al-Makkiyyah*, "The Meccan Openings."[11] *Fusus* also includes a chapter entitled "The Seal of the Wisdom of Prophethood in the Word of Isa (Jesus)." In addition to a discussion of the Trinity, this chapter covers two important points: (1) the innovative interpretation of the

Qur'ānic description of Christians as *Kafir*; and (2) the unique position of Jesus among prophets and saints.

In regard to the first point, there is a Qur'ānic verse which says, "Certainly they disbelieve, *Kafara*, who say: 'Surely God, he is the Messiah, son of Mary'; and the messiah said: 'O children of Israel! serve God, my lord and your lord. Surely whoever associates (others) with God, then God has forbidden to him the garden, and his abode is the fire; and there shall be no helpers for the unjust'" (5.72). The Qur'ān used the word *Kafara*, which means "does not believe" in Islamic law. But Ibn 'al-Arabī returns to the literal meaning of *Kafara*, – meaning *Satara*, or cover. Then, he expresses that what is wrong with Christianity based on the Qur'ānic verse is not Christians' belief in the divinity of Jesus but their belief in the non-divinity of others. Since Christians limit God's manifestation to Jesus' being, they fail to recognize manifestations of God in the wide world. In fact, they are "covered" from other manifestations of God – a situation that is not acceptable by Ibn 'al-'Arabī, who wrote:[12]

> The complete mystic is the one who sees that every idol is a locus of the truth and God's place of manifestation in which He is worshipped. For that reason, they are all called 'god' in spite of having a particular name such as 'stone', 'tree', 'animal', 'human', 'star', or 'angel' (Ibn 'al-Arabī 1946: 195).

In regard to the second point, we have to more closely examine Ibn 'al-Arabī as well as Islamic terminology. *Fas* in *Fusus al-Hikam* applies the wisdom attributed to only one prophet in regard to his unique position and potential. The wisdom of prophethood, reserved for Jesus, explores Jesus' special position. The inner side of prophet is *Wilaya*, the annihilation in God. Jesus is the end, or Seal of *Awliya* – they who reach the *Wilaya*. Ibn 'al-Arabī rationalizes his belief in both Jesus' position and Muhammad's position as follows:

> The Message and Prophethood – by which I mean the Prophethood of bringing the Sharia and its message – ceases, but *Wilaya* never ceases. Thus the Messengers, in much as they are *Awliya*, see what we mentioned only from the niche of the ender/seal of the *Awliya*. How could it be different for other *Awliya*? Although the ender of the *Awliya* is subject to the judgment which the ender of the Messengers (namely Muhammad) brought through the Sharia, that does not diminish his station nor does it detract from what we have said, for something which is lower from one point of view can be higher from another (Ibn 'al-Arabī 1946: 62).[13]

Thus Ibn 'al-'Arabī, by referring to verses 5.44 and 34.28 of the Qur'ān, deduces that all followers of all prophets are Muhammad's followers – namely non-titled Muslims, upholding Muhammad's Sharia. Because their

Sharia paths originated from Muhammad's Sharia path, and Muslims are ordered to judge among them according to their path. Therefore the finality of Muhammad in the chain of messengers gives them credit and validation, as opposed to merely signifying that he came after them (Ibn 'al-Arabī 1985: 13.237–239, also, see 2.293). In other words, the idea of "the truth of Muhammad," causes Ibn 'al-Arabī to consider each prophet, including Jesus, as the one level and aspect of Muhammad's truth. Therefore, Ibn 'al-Arabī obviously counts all people as Muslims that are forgiven by God, as narrated in the Qur'ānic enunciation 48.1–2. Therefore, here is a vast salvation for all ('al-Arabī 1985:13.266–267).

As a result, Rūmī's practical approach and Ibn 'Arabī's speculative approach toward Jesus represent clear Sufism voices that raise significant points: (1) religious people have to discover the inner side of their beliefs in order to move forward – meaning that the heart of their founders gather them, while clinging to the outer ritual affairs separate them; (2) there is a unity among diverse spiritual paths, Sharia, that is available only to the true seeker of transcendence, rather than dogmatic believers of stable notions; and (3) there are two ways of looking to other faiths: empathically and strangely; both ways go from our hearts and decisions and lead to a sweeter or bitterer world and life. Ibn 'al-Arabī and Rūmī examine other religions to gain a richer and more comprehensive understanding of their own faith. For them, other faiths, including Christianity, are mirrors that make visible futures of Islamic potentiality that would otherwise be mostly ignored.

CONCLUSION

After the above analytical account, I can conclude that Ibn 'al-Arabī and Rūmī explain religious pluralism by discussing the unique relationship of God and His manifestations, including their worlds, human beings, religions and founders, such as Jesus or Muhammad. *Fusus al-Hikam* and *Mathnawi Manawi* formulate the relationship between God and His worlds, including subjective or objective ones, like sun and its rays. All prophets and saints are God's strong expressions inviting people to become involved in discovering themselves through the path of love. Both Ibn 'al-Arabī and Rūmī believe in hierarchy among prophets and saints, although the aim and origin are the same. Therefore, their approaches to religious pluralism are not mere points or sermons that are beneficial for society. They are based on their existential experiences and systems of thought that firstly are mixed with their level of being and secondly develop new ideas on religion, God, people and relationships. Thus the notion of tolerance is substantial, rather than accidental. This is the positive pluralism that encourages people to observe more faces of God's manifestations through religions, be more inspired, and realize themselves more comprehensively, in opposition to the negative pluralism that expands a kind of relativism, skepticism, and lack of discretion leading to everydayness, or life's meaninglessness. Sufi pluralism is the realm of activity and evangelism that originated from our relationship with God and our own special share of God.

The visible diversity among people, their emotions, their intellects, their rationalities, their capacities and finally their faiths expresses how God's manifestations can attract people in favor of beauty, goodness, friendliness, peace, and wisdom. Ibn 'al-Arabī and Rūmī promote a pluralistic viewpoint on salvation, the paths toward God, and His manifestations. Furthermore, since everyone is unique and has to follow his own special path, and since every spiritual master has his own status with regard to his path and education, this religious pluralism covers the diversity of rites and rituals as well. Ibn 'al-'Arabī's and Rūmī's perspectives approach other religions empathically, not critically, to discover their share of the truth, as we saw in the discussion of Jesus. Instead, they criticize the dominant reading of Islam and the Qur'ān, limiting it to formalism. Always the last point in regard to Sufism is its invitation to introspection, realizing our share of being that is involved in love, enjoying the unity of plurality, and helping others to do the same. Without diversity, we lack God's manifestation! Drawing on the philosophical but existentially derived teaching of these two Sufi masters, where Sufis today embrace and even champion pluralism, often in the context of democratic movements, they can claim to stand on an historical foundation that these masters laid down.

About the Author

Sayed Hassan "Akhlaq" Hussaini earned his PhD in Philosophy in 2009 from Allameh Tabatabaii University in Tehran, Iran. He acted as an academic advisor to the Afghanistan Academy of Sciences in 2010. He taught at Al-Mustafa International University and Payam-e Noor University in Iran during 2007–2010 and worked as the Chancellor of Gharjistan University in Afghanistan in 2011. Hussaini is the Religious Advisor of American Councils for International Education in Washington D.C. He conducted many pieces of reseach as a Visiting Scholar at George Washington University from 2013–2016. Since 2012 he has been a Visiting Research Fellow at the Catholic University of America. His paper entitled "The Theoretical Foundation of Tolerance in Rumi's Viewpoint" was published in *Philosophy, Culture, and Traditions*, Vol. 12 (2012): 165–88. He has published some scholarly papers on Islamic Sufism and Philosophy in Iran and Afghanistan's national Encyclopedia and professional journals. Akhlaq, moreover, co-edited "the Secular and the Sacred: Complementary and/or Conflictual?" (Washington DC: CRVP, 2017). His most recent book *The Intellectual Foundations of Islamic Culture: An Introduction* is forthcoming.

Notes

1. A small but important point to note regarding the term "Sufism" was best articulated by Ibn Sarraj Tusi. He pointed out that we do not call Sufis philosophers, theologians, historians of the Prophet's speeches (Hadith), or even ascetics, because they are not limited to a profession, position or status. They have in-depth knowledge of philosophy, theology and history and they enact the virtues that each of these disciplines teach. Sufis transcend the fixed limitations of these fields and are constantly progressing in their spiritual attainment. Therefore, we call them Sufi because of their physical appearance (al-Sarraj al-Tusi 1960: 41–42). "Sufi" is an Arabic term that comes from the word *Sawf*, meaning wool, so "sufi" means "one who wears wool." Present-day Sufis do not wear this type of cloth for the most part, so we can only identify them by their wisdom.
2. *Bismillah al-Rahman al-Rahim.*
3. Other scholars translate *fusus* as "ringstones" or "bezels" instead of "seals," and use "wisdom" in its singular form to follow English convention, although the original Arabic is intentionally plural.
4. All Rūmī's poems from *Mathnawi* are cited from the translation by Reynold Alleyne Nicholson, the great translator of Mathnawi in English.
5. Three phases of God's descending are: *Huwiyyat* (unsaying phase), *Ahadiyyat* (manifestation for self), and *Wahediyyat* (manifestation of names and attributes). The five worlds (*Hazarat Khams*) include *Ayane-Thabitah* (the absolute unseen world), *Jabarut* (supernatural world), *Malakut* (Ideal world), *Mulk* (material world), and the perfect human.
6. For a detailed discussion on Rumi's concepts of differences, tolerance and their relationship with mystical approach see my article titled, "The Theoretical Foundations of Tolerance in Rumi," in *Philosophy, Culture, and Traditions: A Journal of the World Union of Catholic Philosophical Societies* 8 (2012): 165–88.
7. Abu Sa'id Ahmad ibn 'Isa al-Kharraz (died in 899) is a Sufi of Baghdad.
8. This poem of the great Sufi, Sa'd ud-Din Mahmud Shabistari (1288–1340) expresses the subject directly, "Each creature has its being from the One Name, From which it comes forth, and to which it return, with praises unending" (Cranmer-Byng and Kapadia 1920: 72). Also, for an in-depth discussion of this subject in Sufism see, Mosleh 1384: 137–50.
9. Rūmī repeatedly describes his beloved spiritual leader, Shams of Tabriz, as a then-modern day Jesus in *Divan-e Kabir*.
10. Ibn 'al-Arabī's poem in the *Tarjuman al-Ashwaq* portrays his beloved as a trinity who was originally one: *My Beloved is three although He is One, even as the (three) Persons (of the Trinity) are made one Person in essence.*
    Ibn 'al-Arabī offers a brief comment on his poem with the following: "Number does not beget multiplicity in the Divine substance, as the Christians declare that the Three Persons of the Trinity are One God, and as the Qur'ān declares (17.110): '*Call on God or call on the Merciful; however ye invoke Him, it is well, for to Him belong the most excellent Names.*' The cardinal Names in the Qur'ān are three, viz. *Allah* and *ar-Rahman* and *ar-Rabb*, by which One God is signified, and the rest of the Names serve as epithets of those three." Therefore, there is a unity among the Trinity and plurality of God's names (Ibn 'al-Arabī 1911: 70–71).
11. Ibn 'al-Arabī reports plenty of his meetings with Jesus, his returning to God because of his presence, and obtaining his advice (Ibn 'al-Arabi 1985: 12.123).

Then, he adds that he passed from this level of existence to that of Moses, Hud and other prophets to reach the level of Muhammad, the final level (Ibn 'al-Arabi 1985: 3.362).

12. Ibn 'al-Arabī presented a mystical interpretation about the Qur'ānic verses 5.116–18.

13. See, also, Ibn 'al-Arabī 1985: 13.136–37. Ibn 'al-Arabī describing Jesus' spiritual position in relation to Muhammad's one, writes: "After I told you Jesus' position when he will return back, you can say what you want. You can say Muhammad and Jesus' paths are paths toward same source; and you can say they are same path, *Sharia*" (Ibn 'al-Arabī 1985: 3.177).

CONCLUSION

"CORPORATE ISLAM" VERSUS SUFI ISLAM AND THE ARTICULATION OF THE PRESENT

Sarwar Alam

How should we approach Islam: follow the juridico-legal tradition or the mystical tradition? We chose the latter in this book. This book is an attempt to reopen a dialogue with the often-sidelined Islamic tradition, Sufism (*taṣawwuf*) or the mystical dimension of Islam. It is an attempt to engage Sufi practices and treatises in defining the "present" and "time." While mainstream Islamic scholarship tends to view various Islamic traditions as "an" Islamic one that resists changes, Sufi traditions of different eras and countries, it appears, remained open in addressing issues related to time and context. There are opposite views between two streams of Islam, especially the so-called monolithic mainstream Sunni Islam, which Vincent J. Cornell (2014) convincingly has labeled as "corporate Islam," and the Sufi Islam, in their articulation of the present. Our view is that while the former tends to view Islam as something pristine and immune to changes, Sufis tend to face the challenge of the present mostly in creative fashions, even though they are no less orthodox than those of normative Muslims.[1] Because of their creativity and dynamism, the adherents of mainstream (normative tradition) Islam often blame Sufis for the decline of Islam, Sufi doctrines as *bid'a* (innovation), and label Sufism sometimes as a disease.[2]

Frozen in the past, the present mainstream Islamic followers, it has been argued, often reduce the personal belief to a creed, synonymous to the millet of the Ottoman period, "a hermetic, self-contained religious community that exists concurrently with but in nearly total separation from the millets of other religions" (Cornell 2014: 129). Practice and perception of this type underscore the original meaning of Islam, individual submission to the will of God. With few exceptions (such as legal theories), the corporate Islam has failed or has had little to do with theology, philosophy, Sufism, or other Islamic disciplines of the past. This failure seals Islam off from the rest of the world. The failure of engaging the past scholarship in fashioning the present fuels the emergence of the Islamic version of fundamentalism, "on the one hand it has lost sight of the Qur'ānic concept of the universality of revelation and on the other hand its perspective of the world is badly skewed," as it views Islam as the "only" tradition that contains normative truth. It is an epistemological crisis (Cornell 2014) that Muslims of the contemporary world should encounter, but not by discarding the legacies of the past scholarship; rather, by reengaging them to face the present moment.

We believe that the prime character of the present is modernity along with its characteristic signature of pluralism and democracy. It is said that a Sufi is the "son of the moment or time" (*Ibn al-Waqt*) (Schuon 2006: 13), which means that "he situated in God's Present without concern for yesterday or tomorrow, and this Present is none other than a reflection of Unity; the One projected into time becomes the "Now" of God, which coincides with Eternity" (Schuon 2006). It also means that "he keeps himself all times in the divine Will, that is to say, he realizes that the present moment is what God wants of him" (Schuon 1998: 187). Keeping this want in mind, some Sufi masters have been engaging themselves in promoting pluralism, encouraging interfaith dialogue, participating in the democratic process by organizing political parties, and in some cases, preaching that there is no inherent conflict between secularism and Islam (see Alam 2012). It is a new form of *ijtihad*, it appears, through which they are perceiving the present, contextualizing Islam, and encountering the Islamists not only theologically, but also socially and politically. This challenges Islamist ideas of Islam as monolithic, immutable and the top-down, authoritarian type political systems they wish to establish.

Sufis insist on remembering God not only in a contemplative way, but also by witnessing (*mushahada*) the "signs" (*ayat*) around them. Because, as some Sufis believe, God discloses Himself in every existing thing (see Murata 1992: 192). One of the signs of such disclosure (*tajalli*) is the time itself; signs are also revealed in the Book and in the nature (See Schuon 1998 [1961]: 161, 165). Witnessing as well as embodying the signs, which is a cultivated virtue, is called *ihsan* or "doing the beautiful," to quote William C. Chittick (2000: 4–6), is also a method of becoming a Muslim (see Schimmel in Schuon 1998 [1961]: vi–vii). It emphasizes on knowing, knowing one's own self. This *ihsan* or "doing the beautiful" along with sincerity or *ikhlas* constitutes *taṣawwuf*.

One of the early Egyptian Sufi, mufti, and *faqīh*, ibn 'Ata Allah (d. 1309) (see Mohamed 2013) suggested his fellow co-religionists to go along with the present time in which they live and accept the consequences of the present time as a manifestation of the divine will. According to him, a true believer should have absolute trust (*tawakkul*) in God and adapt himself to present circumstances, "go with the flow," and trust that God will see him through the changing times. As one of the Prophetic tradition states that God is time (see Cornell 2014: 146). Ibn 'Ata Allah expressed this view in a quatrain:

> When I saw destiny flowing
> There was no doubt or hesitation about it.
> So I entrusted all of my rights to my Creator
> And threw myself into the current (cited in Cornell 2014: 146).

We choose Sufi tradition instead of the mainstream exoteric or normative tradition with a view that the former is more dynamic and challenging, as from the very beginning, it was creative and innovative in its endeavors in challenging the hegemony of the latter by contextualizing Islam with its present. Compared to the normative tradition, the Sufi tradition, we believe, is more prone to interreligious openness, as some Sufi masters (such as Delaor Husayn Maizbhandari) argue that Islam is not the only chosen path for humanity to reach God. This is how, in our view, Sufism "contributes to opening up Muslims' field of vision through its encouragement of interreligious exchanges and the intermingling of cultures" (Geoffroy 2010: 198).

We wanted to emphasize that Islam as a whole, and Sufism in particular, considers diversity of peoples and religions as an expression of the divine plan. In fact, "there exists a theology of religious pluralism in Islam," (Geoffroy 2010: 183) as the Qur'ān depicts "And unto thee have We revealed the Scripture with the truth, confirming whatever Scripture was before it, and a watcher over it... For each We have appointed a divine law and a traced-out way. Had Allah willed He could have made you one community... So vie one with another in good works" (5:48), "For every community there is a Messenger" (10:47), and "Surely the believers and the Jews, and Christians, and Sabaeans, whoever believes in God and the Last Day, and whosoever does right, shall have his reward with his Lord and will neither have fear nor regret" (2:62). Diversity thus reflects divine wisdom, and the Qur'ān insists believers on accepting the differences in humanity in terms of language, color, nations and tribes as signs of God. Based on the Qur'ānic spirit of diversity and pluralism, some Muslim scholars recognize Buddha, Zoroaster or even Akhenaton as prophets; some South Asian scholars regard the Vedas, the sacred texts of Hinduism, as inspired by God and consider Hindus as among the "People of the Book" (*ahl al-bayt*) (Geoffroy 2010: 182). One of the mystics of Islam, ibn al-'Arabī (d. 1240), moved further and furnished a doctrinal framework for the concept of the "transcendent unity of religions" (*wahdat al-adyan*). To him, all beliefs, and therefore all religions, are true because each is a response to the manifestation of a divine Name (Geoffroy 2010: 184). Engaging ibn al-'Arabi, another contemporary Sufi master formulated doctrines of *tawhid-e-adyan* or unicity of religions and *'adl-e-mutlaq* or the supreme justice that view every religion with the same light, and argue that no religion is superior to another.[3] Although there are variations and differences among the Sufi doctrines and traditions, it appears that Sufism as a whole embodies some of the Qur'ānic principles of diversity, pluralism, and coexistence of other faiths more than the exoteric Islamic tradition.

Asked once whether Rabi'a al-'Adawiya (d. 801) loved God and hated the Devil, she replied: "My love of God has prevented me from the hatred of Satan" (quoted in Fakhry 1997: 92). Sufism is a tradition of extinction in the love of God. There is a hadith *qudsi* (holy utterances) that refers to God who says, "I was a hidden treasure, and I wanted to be known; hence I created the world." Sufis endeavor to discover the hidden treasure by deciphering the signs of God. Did not God say He is nearer to man than human's jugular vein (Qur'ān 50:16)? The Qur'ān also states reciprocal love between God and humanity. However, the notion of reciprocal love between God and humans is sharply objected to by the scholars of normative tradition. According to this view, love means loving God's commands, that is, strict obedience. Yet, it remained the central issue with the Sufi-minded people, whose love was not only directed to God but also to God's beloved, the Prophet, "love for whom became a highly important ingredient in Muslim life" (Schimmel 1994: 251). "As the first sura of the Koran begins with words *al-hamdu lillah*, 'Praise be to God', thus praise of God fills the created world, audible to those who understand the signs. Is not Muhammad's very name derived from the root h-m-d, 'to praise'?" (Schimmel 1994: 252). The mutuality of love expressed in the Qur'ān (5:54) (see Ernst 1999a: 435–47) oftentimes is sidelined in the exoteric tradition. On the contrary, Sufis long for God's love but also long for the love of humanity and vice versa. To them, love is transcendent.

Sufism resembles not only outward practices, but also inward beliefs and ideals with other religious traditions. It views Jesus ('*Īsā* in Arabic) as the role model of love, sacrifice, and asceticism. Some early mystics of Islam quoted so much of Christ (Geoffroy 2010: 184) and other Christian monks and saints that some scholars believe that not only Sufism but Islam as a whole is an offshoot of Christianity.[4] Sufi asceticism, humility, and also humiliation sometimes viewed as an imitation of Christianity.[5] Some of Sufism's ideals and doctrines also resemble Neoplatonic rationalistic theology. The Sufi doctrine of *fanā'* (annihilation) so much resembles the Buddhist doctrine of *nibbana* (passing away) that an absence of comparison of these two phenomena seems to make any discussion or analysis of Sufism incomplete. Some of the prominent Sufi figures' ideals, practices, and utterances resemble Vedantic philosophy in such a way that some scholars believe that Sufism, especially Persianate Sufism, is the product of the Vedentic philosophy.[6] In some cases, scholars draw their conclusions by comparing Sufism with their own traditions while others compare Sufi ideals with the Qur'ān. In defense, some scholars also argue that "Far from being dependent on or derivative of Neoplatonism, Christianity, Buddhism, or Hindu yoga, Sufism is an original, comprehensive, and hence authentic form of knowledge" (Ernst and Lawrence 2002: 8). There are traceable resemblances, even influences, of other traditions in Sufism but with these resemblances Sufism has inadvertently created the rooms to accommodate the ideals of other traditions in its fold. Because of the similarities and resemblances it is more approachable and understandable by others compared to the exoteric Islamic tradition. It creates common grounds and opens up opportunities for dialogue.

There is a stark difference of perception between the two streams of Islam in another area, and it is the view of the standing of women. The standing of men and women before God is expressed in the following verse (Qur'ān 33:35):

> For Muslim men and women, for believing men and women, for devout men and women, for true men and women, for men and women who are patient and constant, for men and women who humble themselves, for men and women who give in charity, for men and women who fast (and deny themselves), for men and women who guard their chastity, and for men and women who engage much in God's praise, for them has God prepared forgiveness and great reward (Yusuf Ali's translation).

Not very long after the Prophet Muhammad's death, this Qur'ānic depiction of gender balance was replaced by the old Arab misogyny, examples of which are abundant. The veil was rediscovered and reinforced upon and thus a gender imparity was enforced in the society contrary to the Qur'ān's repeated assertion of maintaining balance in everything and following a middle path (see El Fadl 2003 [2001], among others). It was challenged theologically, among others, by ibn al-'Arabī, who argues that the Arabic name of God is masculine, but His essence is feminine, which includes His creative power. In this sense one may witness God in women (see Shaikh 2012: 173–79). Similarly Rūmī wrote, "She is the radiance of God, she is not your beloved. She is the creator – you could say that she is not created" (quoted in Murata 1992: 185). Sufi poetries, sacred biographies, and Qur'ān commentaries of the Sufis unveiled women's standing time and again in Islam.[7] Because of this, it has been argued that "Sufism was more favorable to the development of feminine activities than were other branches of Islam" (Schimmel 1975: 426).

In mystical traditions of Islam, the greatest form of jihad (striving) or *jihad al-akbar* is to purify the soul and refine its disposition. This is regarded as the utmost and momentous struggle. The Prophetic tradition in this regard, as described in the treatise of mystic al-Hujwiri (d. 1073), is that the *mujahid* (who engages in a jihad) is he who struggles with all his might against himself (*jahada nafsahu*) for God's sake. The Prophet adjudged the mortification of the lower soul to be superior to the holy war, because the fomer is more painful (Al-Hijwiri [trans. Nicholson] 1999: 200–201). It is the greatest struggle to purify the carnal self (*nafs*) so that humans may know themselves and know God. One of the hadith qudsi narrates, he who knows his self knows his Lord (*man 'arafa nafsahu faqad 'arafa rabbahu*). God resides in the heart of the believers. The following is a famous quote from Mawlana Jalal al-Din Rūmī (d. 1273): "I looked for God. I went to a temple, and I didn't find him there. Then I went to a church, and I didn't find him there. And then I went to a mosque, and I didn't find him there. And then finally I looked in my heart, and there he was." This loving aspect God as well as the striving (jihad) for purifying one's soul is mostly absent in exoteric tradition.

Some juridical concepts relevant to pluralism and democracy, such as *khilaf* (divergence) and *ijm'a* (consensus), have not yet been fully elaborated as an Islamic theoretical framework in facing modernity. Sufism's openness to diversity and difference might provide a foundation for democratizing Muslim-majority spaces. A parliament or consultative assembly could be an institutional setup for upholding divergence and consensus. The corporate Islam tends to deny any Islamic legitimacy to such institutions and does its best to stifle divergence. Believing in "an" or "the" Islam, as a pristine and idealized tradition without taking the present into account is a backward looking perception. As ibn al-'Arabī perceives, to God today's present is no less important than the present of the yesterday (see Cornell 2014: 135). Following the Islamic mystics' construction of time (*waqt*), one could say that modernity is another name of the present, in which God discloses Himself. It could be interpreted as a sign (*aya*) of God. Apart from the exoteric Islamic tradition, this book is an attempt at a conversation between the past and the present using both modern and pre-modern Sufi discourses that appreciate pluralism, tolerance, and diversity as parts of the belief system to see how they could be used in interpreting our own time.

About the Author

Sarwar Alam teaches at the King Fahd Center for Middle East Studies at the University of Arkansas in the USA. He received his doctorate from the same university in 2006. Alam also holds Masters degrees from Chittagong and Pittsburg State Universities. He was a member of Bangladesh Civil Service and worked as an assistant secretary, and also as a magistrate before moving to the USA. He was a postdoctoral fellow in the department of Middle Eastern and South Asian Studies at Emory University, Atlanta, Georgia between 2007 and 2010. He submitted a manuscript for publication titled *Jewels of Honor: the Perception of the Self, Power, and Gender Among Muslim Women of a Rural Community in Bangladesh*. Alam contributed two chapters on Sufi historiography and political activism in Bangladesh in *South Asian Sufis: Devotion, Deviation and Destiny*, eds., Clinton Bennett and Charles Ramsey (Continuum, 2012). His other publications include "Sufism Without Boundaries: Pluralism, Coexistence, and Interfaith

Dialogue in Bangladesh" *Comparative Islamic Studies*, 9. 1 (2013), "Sufi Pluralism in Bangladesh: The Case of Maizbhandariyya Tariqa," *Journal of South Asian and Middle Eastern Studies*, xxxiv, no. 1 (2010), "Contesting the Shari'a: The Prospect of CEDAW in Eliminating Gender Discrimination in Bangladesh," *Law Vision* 10 (2008), and "Islam, Culture, and the Power of Women in a Bangladesh Village," *Voices of Islam*, 5 vols., ed., Vincent J. Cornell (Praeger, 2007). He has regularly presented papers at the American Academy of Religion's annual meetings.

Notes

1. See Schuon 1998 [1961]: 167; Stoddart 1985 [1976]: 42–43.
2. Ernst and Lawrence 2002: 12; also see Chittick 2000: 3. Muslim modernist Muhammad Iqbal's view in Sirriyeh 2003: 132. Ernst (2003: 115, 108–18) shows how colonialism, European orientalist writings as well as Muslim fundamentalists contributed in negative projections of Sufism.
3. See Alam's chapter in this collection.
4. See Baldick 1989, Smith 1931. For Islamic origins, see among others, Hodgson 1974, 1: 393.
5. For a comparison between Christian and Islamic mysticism, see Stoddart 1985 [1976]: 44–48.
6. See Zaehner 1960. For a comparison, see Schuon 1998 [1961]: 172–73, 182–83.
7. See also As-Sulami (trans. Cornell 1999), Helminski 2003, among others.

BIBLIOGRAPHY

Abdelaziz, Mohamed Mosad. 2013. "Ibn ʿAṭāʾ Allāh al-Sakandarī: A Sufi, ʿĀlim and Faqīh." *Comparative Islamic Studies* 9:1: 41–66.
Afifi, Abu al-Ala. 1946. Taliqat ala Fusus al-Hikam. Beirut: Dar al-Kitab al-Arabi.
Ahram Online. 2015. "Sufi Party Demands Probe into Egypt's Salafist Nour Party." Ahram, 18 January. Available at: https://tinyurl.com/proble-salafist
Akhlaq, Sayed Hassan. 1386. Az Mawlana ta Nietzsche (From Rumi to Nietzsche). Qum: Soluk-e Jawan.
Al-Alawi, Irfan. 2010. "Bangladesh Ban's Arch-Jihadist's Writings." New York: Gatestone Institute. Available at: http://www.gatestoneinstitute.org/1430/bangladesh-bans-jihadist-writings
Al-Qushayri, Abu 'l-Qasim. 2007. *Al-Qushayri's Epistle on Sufism: Al-Risala al-qushayriyya fi ʿilm al-tasawwuf*, trans. Alexander D. Knysh. Reading: Garnet.
Al-Turabi, Hassan. 1983. "The Islamic State." In: *Voices of Resurgent Islam*, ed. John L. Esposito, 21–51. New York: Oxford University Press.
Alam, Arshad. 2006. 'Understanding Deoband Locally: Interrogating Madrasat diya' al- 'Ulum.' In: Jan-Peter Hartung and Helmut Reifeld, eds. *Islamic Education, Diversity, and National Identity: Dini Madaris in India Post 9/11*. New Delhi: Sage Publications.
Alam, Sarwar. 2012. "Encountering the Unholy: The Establishment of Political Parties by Sufi Masters in Modern Bangladesh." In: *South Asian Sufis: Devotion, Deviation, and Destiny*, eds Clinton Bennett and Charles M. Ramsey, 163–80. London: Continuum.
Anderson, Benedict. 2006. *Imagined Communities: Reflections on the Origin and Spread of Nationalism*, Revised Edition. London and New York: Verso.
An-Naʿim, Abdullahi A. 2008. *Islam and the Secular State: Negotiating the Future of Shariʿa*. Cambridge, MA: Harvard University Press.
Ansari, Sarah F. 1992. *Sufi Saints and State Power: the Pirs of Sind, 1843–1947*. Cambridge: Cambridge University Press.
Arberry, Arthur J. 1950. *Sufism: An Account of the Mystics of Islam*. New York: The Macmillan Company.
As-Sulami, Abu ʿAbd ar-Rahman. 1999. *Early Sufi Women: Dhikr an-Niswa al-mutaʿabbidat as as-sufiyyat* (Memorial of Female Sufi Devotees), trans. Rkia E. Cornell. Louisville, KY: Fons Vitae.
Asani, Ali Asani. 1988. "Sufi Poetry in the Folk Tradition of Indo-Pakistan." *Religion and Literature* 20(1): 81–94.
Axiarlis, Evangelia. 2014. *Political Islam and the Secular State in Turkey: Democracy, Reform and the Justice and Development Party*. London: I.B. Tauris.
Ayoub, Mohammed. 2008. *The Many Faces of Political Islam: Religion and Politics in the Beyond*. New York: Palgrave Macmillan.
Balci, Tamer. 2012. "Islam and Democracy in the Thought of Nursi and *Gülen*." In: *The Gülen Hizmet Movement: Circumspect Activism in Faith-Based Reform*, eds Tamer Balci and Christopher L. Miller. Cambridge: Cambridge Scholars Publishing.

Baldick, Julian. 1989. *Mystical Islam: An Introduction to Sufism*. New York: New York University Press.
Banu, Razia Akter U.A.B. 1992. *Islam in Bangladesh*. Leiden: Brill.
Baskan, Filiz. 2004. "The Political Economy of Islamic Finance in Turkey: The Role of Fethullah Gülen and Asya Finans." In: *The Politics of Islamic Finance*, eds Clement M. Henry and Rodney Wilson. Edinburgh: Edinburgh University Press.
Bashir, Shahzad. 2011. *Sufi Bodies: Religion and Society in Medieval Islam*. New York: Columbia University Press.
Beqiri, Baba Rexheb. 1970. *Mistiçizma Islame dhe Bektashizma* [Alternative title: *Misticizmi Islam dhe Bektashizmi*]. New York: Waldon Press [Urtësia, Tirana, 2006]. The sole reliable English translation of this work is Baba Rexheb, *The Mysticism of Islam and Bektashism*. Dragotti, Naples, 1984.
Bennett, Clinton. 2015. *Muslims and Modernity: An Introduction to the Issues and Debates*. London: Continuum.
—2010. *Muslim Women of Power: Gender, Politics and Culture in Islam*. London: Continuum.
—2014. *In Search of Solutions: The Problem of Religion and Conflict*. Abingdon: Routledge.
Bennett, Clinton and Charles M. Ramsey, eds. 2012. *South Asian Sufis: Devotion, Deviation, and Destiny*. London: Continuum.
Birge, John Kingsley. 1937. *The Bektashi Order of Dervishes*. London: Luzac.
Black, Antony. 2011. *The History of Islamic Political Thought from the Prophet to the Present*. Edinburgh: Edinburgh University Press.
Blackburn, Susan. 2004. *Women and The State in Modern Indonesia*. Cambridge: Cambridge Universirty Press.
Borsatti, Luciana. 2010. "Sufi Leader, Our Influence is Crucial against Jihadism." *ANSA*, July 5. Available at: http://www.ansamed.info/ansamed/en/news/sections/politics/2014/07/05/sufi-leader-our-influence-is-crucial-against-jihadism_6a2b83e2-a807-4312-b694-476f9f965419.html
Bourdieu, Pierre. 1984. *Distinction: A Social Critique of the Judgement of Taste*. London: Routledge.
Brinton, Jacquelene Gottlieb. 2016. *Preaching Islamic Renewal: Religious Authority and Media in Contemporary Egypt*. Oakland, CA: University of California Press.
Buehler, Arthur F. 1997. *Sufi Heirs of the Prophet: the Indian Naqshbandiyya and the Rise of the Mediating Sufi Shaykh*. Columbia, SC: University of South Carolina Press.
Butler, Judith. 2011a. "Is Judaism Zionism?" In: *The Power of Religion in the Public Sphere*. Cambridge, MA: Harvard University Press.
—2011b. "Is Judaism Zionism?" In: *The Power of Religion in the Public Sphere*, eds Eduardo Mendieta and Jonathan Vanantwerpen, 70–91. New York: Columbia University Press.
Can, Eyup. 1997. *Fethullah Gülen Hocaefendi ile Ufuk Turu*. Istanbul: AD Publishing.
Carroll, B. Jill. 2007. *A Dialogue of Civilizations: Gülen's Islamic Ideals and Humanistic Discourse*. Somerset, NJ: The Light.
Çelebi, Evliya, Robert Dankoff and Robert Elsie. 2000. *Evliya Çelebi in Albania and Adjacent Regions Kossovo, Montenegro, Ohrid: the Relevant Sections of the Seyahatname*. Leiden: Brill.
Cemal, Mehment. 1974. "Yuzaltmisuc." *The Milli Gazette*. April 10–30.

Cesari, Jocelyne. 2014. *The Awakening of Muslim Democracy: Religion, Modernity, and the State*. New York: Cambridge University Press.

Chatterji, Joya. 2007. *The Spoils of Partition: Bengal and India, 1947–1967*. Cambridge: Cambridge University Press.

Chittick, William C. 1998. *The Self-Disclosure of God: Principles of Ibn al-'Arabi's Cosmology*. Albany, NY: State University of New York Press.

—2000. *Sufism*. Oxford: Oneworld.

Choufi, Firas. 2013. "Lebanon: Al-Ahbash Retreat from Politics." *Al-Akhbar*, 29 January. Available at: http://english.al-akhbar.com/node/14719

Coca, Nina. 2014. *Al-Jazeerra*. 12 May. Available at: http://www.aljazeera.com/indepth/features/2014/04/political-islam-rising-indonesia-201442913253417235.html

Corbett, Rosemary R. 2017. *Making Moderate Islam: Sufism, Service, and the "Ground Zero Mosque" Controversy*. Stanford, CA: Stanford University Press.

Cornell, Svente E., and M.K. Kaya. 2015. "The Naqshbandi-Khalidi Order and Political Islam in Turkey." The Hudson Institute. Available at: http://hudson.org/research/11601-the-naqshbandi-khalidi-order-and-political-islam-in-turkey

Cornell, Vincent J. 1998. *Realm of the Saint: Power and Authority in Moroccan Sufism*. Austin, TX: University of Texas Press.

—2007. "The All-Comprehensive Circle (al-Ihata): Soul, Intellect, and the Oneness of Existence in the Doctrine of Ibn Saba'in." In: *Sufism and Theology*, ed. Ayman Shihadeh, 31–48. Edinburgh: Edinburgh University Press.

—2014. "Islam." In: *The Crisis of the Holy: Challenges and Transformations in World Religions*, ed. Alon Goshen-Gottstein, 125–49. Lanham, MD: Lexington Books.

Cranmer-Byng, L., and S.A. Kapadia, eds. 1920. *The Secret Rose Garden of Sa'd ud Din Mahmud Shabistari. Rendered from the Persian with an Introduction by Florence Lederer*. London: John Murray.

Delehaye, Hippolyte. 1961. *The Legends of the Saints: An Introduction to Hagiography*, trans. V.M. Crawford. London: University of Notre Dame Press.

Delooz, Pierre. 1983. "Towards a Sociological Study of Canonized Sainthood in the Catholic Church." In: *Saints and Their Cults: Studies in Religious Sociology, Folklore and History*, ed. Stephan Wilson, 189–215. Cambridge: Cambridge University Press.

Deol, Jeevan. 2002. "Sex, Social Critique and the Female Figure in Premodern Punjabi Poetry: Varis Sahh's Hir." *Modern Asian Studies* 36(1): 141–71.

Diouf, Mamadou. 2013. "Introduction. The Public Role of 'Good Islam': Sufi Islam and the Administration of Pluralism." In: *Tolerance, Democracy, and Sufis in Senegal*, ed. M. Diouf, 1–35. New York: Columbia University Press.

Donner, Fred M. 2010. *Muhammad and the Believers: At the Origins of Islam*. Cambridge, MA: Harvard University Press.

Economist Intelligence Unit. 2016. *Democracy Index 2015: Democracy in An Age of Anxiety*. London, New York, Hong Kong, Geneva and Dubai: The Economist Intelligence Unit.

—2016. *Country Report: Bangladesh*. London: Economist Intelligence Unit. Available at: http://country.eiu.com/bangladesh

—2017. *Democracy Index 2016: Revenge of the Deplorables*. London, New York, Hong Kong, Geneva and Dubai: The Economist Intelligence Unit.

Eaton, Richard Maxwell. 1993. *The Rise of Islam and the Bengal Frontier, 1204–1760*. Berkeley, CA: University of California Press.

—2003. *India's Islamic Traditions 711–1750*. New Delhi: Oxford University Press.

El Fadl, Khalid A. 2003 [2001]. *Speaking in God's Name: Islamic Law, Authority and Women*, reprinted. Oxford: Oneworld.
Elmasry, Mohamed. 2015. "Ali Gumah: El Sisi's Most Loyal Islamic Scholar." *Middle East Eye*, 27 June. Available at: http://www.middleeasteye.net/columns/ali-gumah-sisi-s-most-loyal-islamic-scholar-1205811558
Elsie, Robert. 2005. *Albanian Literature: A Short History*. London: I.B. Tauris and Centre for Albanian Studies, London.
—2000. *A Dictionary of Albanian Religion, Mythology, and Folk Culture*. New York: New York University Press.
Erdoğan, Latif. 1995. *Fethullah Gülen Hocaefendi: Küçük Dünyam*. Istanbul: AD Yayıncılık.
Ernst, Carl, and Bruce B. Lawrence. 2002. *Sufi Martyrs of Love: Chishti Sufism in South Asia and Beyond*. New York: Palgrave Macmillan.
—1992. *Eternal Garden: Mysticism, History, and Politics at a South Asian Sufi Center*. Albany, NY: State University of New York Press.
—1993. Preface in Michael A. Sells, *Early Islamic Mysticism: Sufi, Qur'an, Miraj, Poetic and Theological Writings*. Mahwah, NJ: Paulist Press, 3.
—1999a. "The Stages of Love in Early Persian Sufism, from Rabi'a to Ruzbihan." In: *The Heritage of Sufism*, Vol. 1, ed. Leonard Lewisohn, 435–47. Oxford: Oneworld.
—1999b. *Teachings of Sufism*. Boston, MA: Shambhala.
—2003. "Between Orientalism and Fundamentalism: Problematizing the Teaching of Sufism." In: *Mysticism and Language*, ed. Brannon Wheeler, 108–23. New York: Oxford University Press.
Esposito, John L., and John O. Voll. 2001. *Makers of Contemporary Islam*. Oxford: Oxford University Press.
Fakhry, Majid. 1997. *Islamic Philosophy*. Oxford: Oneworld.
Findley, Carter V. 2015. "Hizmet Among the Most Influential Religious Renewals of Late Ottoman and Modern Turkish History." In: *Hizmet Means Service*: *Perspectives on an Alternative Path within Islam*, ed. Martin E. Marty, 14. Berkeley, CA: University of California Press.
Forum. (2007). [online]. Available at: https://groups.google.com/forum/#!msg/alt.sufi/LduKU6y_DWY/LZ-jY34974wJ
Freedom House. *Freedom in the World.* 2016. Freedom House, Washington, DC. https://freedomhouse.org/report/freedom-world/freedom-world-2016
Gadamer, Hans-Georg. 1982 [1975]. *Truth and Method*, trans. Joel Weinsheimer. New York: Crossroads.
Gauvain, Richard. 2013. *Salafi Ritual Purity: In the Presence of God*. London: Routledge.
Gawrych, George W. 2006. *The Crescent and the Eagle: Ottoman Rule, Islam, and the Albanians, 1874–1913*. London: I.B. Tauris. [The author depends exclusively on non-Albanian sources.]
Geertz, Clifford. 1968. *Islam Observed: Religious Developments in Morocco and Indonesia*. Chicago, IL: University of Chicago Press.
—1960. *The Religion of Java*. Glencoe, IL: Free Press.
Geertz, Clifford, and Walter W. Ross. 1992. "CA Interview." *Contemporary Authors*, New Revision Series, 36, 150–54. Farmington Hills, MI: Gale Research.
Geoffroy, Eric. 2010. *Introduction to Sufism: The Inner Path of Islam*, trans. Roger Gaetami. Bloomington, IN, World Wisdom.
Ghanmi, Lamine. 2016. "In Tunisia, Sufism is here to stay." *The Arab Weekly*, 12 February. Available at: http://www.thearabweekly.com/?id=3790

Gilmartin, D. 1984. "Shrines, Succession, and Sources of Moral Authority". In: Barbara Daly Metcalf ed., *Moral Conduct and Authority: The Place of Adab in South Asian Islam.* Berkeley, CA: University of California Press.

Al-Ghazālī, and W.H.T. Gairdner. 2010. *The Miskhat al-anwar, the Niche for Lights.* Cosimo, NY facsimile of 1923 edition.

Graham, Terry. 1999. "Shah Nimatullah Wali: The Founder of the Nimatullah Sufi Order," in Leonard Lewisohn, ed, The Heritrage of Sufism, 2, Oxford: Oneworld.

Gülen, Fethullah. M. 1997a. *Prizma 2*, Izmir: Nil.

—1997b. "Altın Neslin Vasıfları." *Sızıntı* 19 (March).

—1998a. 2004a. 2006a. *The Emerald Hills of the Heart: Key Concepts in the Practice of Sufism 1*, trans. Ali Ünal. Somerset, NJ: The Light.

—1998b. "Claims and Answers." *Aksiyon*, June 6.

—2004b. *Toward a Global Civilization of Love and Tolerance.* Clifton, NJ: Light.

—2004c. *Emerald Hills of the Heart: Key Concepts in the Practice of Sufism 2.* Clifton, NJ: Light.

—2006b. "Respect for Humankind." *The Fountain*, Issue 53. Available at: http://www.fountainmagazine.com/Issue/detail/Respect-For-Humankind

—2007. *Pearls of Wisdom.* Clifton, NJ: Light.

Guy, Nicola. 2012. *The Birth of Albania.* London: I.B. Tauris.

Hamayotsu, Kikue. 2011. "The End of Political Islam? A Comparative Analysis of the Religious Parties in the Muslim Democracy of Indonesia." *Journal of Current South East Asian Studies* 30:3: 133–59.

Hameed, Syeda Saiyidain. 1993. *Contemporary Relevance of Sufism.* New Delhi: Indian Council for Cultural Relations.

Hamid, Sadek. 2016. *Sufis, Salafis and Islamists: the Contested Ground of British Islamic Activism.* London: I.B. Tauris.

Hamka. 2015. *Tasawuf Modern.* Jakarta: Republika Penerbit (originally published 1939).

Hamzeh, A. Nizar, and R. Hrair Dekmejian. 1996. "A Sufi Response to Political Islamism: Al-Ahbash of Lebanon." *International Journal of Middle East Studies*, 28: 2, 217–229.

Harder, Hans. 2011. *Sufism and Saint Veneration in Contemporary Bangladesh: The Maijbhandaris of Chittagong.* London and New York: Routledge.

Haroon, Sana. 2007. *Frontier of Faith: Islam in the Indo-Afghan Borderland.* New York: Columbia University Press.

Harvard Divinity School Religious Literacy Project. "Sufism in Egypt." Available at: http://rlp.hds.harvard.edu/faq/sufism-egypt

Hasluck, F.W. 1929. *Christianity and Islam Under the Sultans.* Oxford: Clarendon Press.

Hasan, Mushirul, ed. 1993. *India's Partition: Process, Strategy and Mobilization.* Delhi: Oxford University Press.

Hassan, Ammar Ali. 2011. *Political Role of Sufi Orders in Egypt after the January 25 Revolution.* Doha: Al Jazeera.

Hayat, Khizar, 2012. *Akabir ka baghi kon?* Attock: Maktab Hussainiyya, 18–19.

Helminski, Camille A. 2003. *Women of Sufism: A Hidden Treasure.* Boston and London: Shambhala.

Hefferman, Thomas J. 1988. *Sacred Biography: Saints and Their Biographers in the Middle Ages.* Oxford: Oxford University Press.

Hermansen, Marcia. 2012. "South Asian Sufism in America." In: *South Asian Sufis: Devotion, Deviation, and Destiny*, eds Clinton Bennett and Charles M. Ramsey, 247–68. London: Continuum.

—2015. "Who is Fethullah Gülen? An Overview of His Life." In: *Hizmet Means Service: Perspectives on An Alternative Path within Islam*, ed. Martin E. Marty. Berkeley, CA: University of California Press.
Hodgson, Marshall G.S. 1974. *The Venture of Islam: Conscience and History in a World Civilization*, 3 vols. Vol. 1. Chicago, IL: The University of Chicago Press.
Hoffman, Valerie. 1995. *Sufism, Mystics, and Saints in Modern Egypt*. Columbia, NC: University of South Carolina Press.
Howell, Julia Day. 2000. "Indonesia's Urban Sufis: Challenging Stereotypes of Islamic Revival," *ISIM* [International Institute for the Study of Islam in the Modern World] *Newsletter*, 6, 17.
—2001. "Sufism and the Indonesian Islamic Revival." *The Journal of Asian Studies* 6(3): 701–29.
Hujwírí, Alí ibu Usmán and Reynold Alleyne Nicholson. 1976. *The Kashf al-Mahjúb: the Oldest Persian Treatise on Sufiism by Alí B. Uthmán al-Jullábi al-Hujwírí*. London: Luzac.
—1999. *Revelation of the Mystery (Kasf al-Mahjub)*, trans. Reynold A. Nicholson. New York: Pir Press.
Huntington, Samuel P. 1993. "The Clash of Civilizations?" *Foreign Affairs* 72/3 (Summer): 22–49.
Hussain, Mahmud. 1957. "Sayyid Ahman Khan." In: *A History of the Freedom Movement*, ed. Mahmud Hussain. Karachi: Pakistan Historical Society.
Hussaini, Sayed Hassan Akhlaq. 2013. "The Theoretical Foundations of Tolerance in Rumi." *Philosophy, Culture, and Traditions*: A Journal of the World Union of Catholic Philosophical Societies 9: 165–87.
Husayn, Sayyid Delaor. 2001. *Velayat-e-Mutlaqa*, 8th edition. Chittagong, Bangladesh: Anjuman-e- Mottabe'in-e-Ghawth-e-Maizbhandari.
—2004. *Hazrat Ghawthul Azam Shah Sufi Mawlana Sayyid Ahmad Ullah (K) Maizbhandari: Jiboni o Karamat* [Biography and Miracles of Hazrat GhawthulAzam Shah Sufi Mawlana Sayyid Ahmad Ullah (K) Maijbhandari], 15th reprint]. Chittagong, Bangladesh: Maizbhandar Darbar Sharif.
—2012. *Multattva* [Basic Theory], part one, 9th edition. Chittagong, Bangladesh: Anjuman-e-Muttaba'in-e-Ghawth-e-Maizbhandari.
Ibn 'al-Arabī Muhii al-Din. 1911. The Tarjuman al-Ashwaq: A Collection of Mystical Odes, ed. and trans. Reynold A. Nicholson. London: Royal Asiatic Society.
—1946. Fusus al-Hikam, ed. abu al-Ala Afifi. Beirut: Dar al-Kitab al-Arabi.
—1985. al-Futuhat al-Makkiyyah, ed. and reviewed by Uthman Yahya and Ibrahim Madkur. Cairo: al-Maktabat al-Arabia.
—1992. *The Bezels of Wisdom*, trans. R.W.J. Austin (The Classics of Western Spirituality Series). New York: Paulist Press.
Ingram, Brannon. 2009. "Sufis, Scholars and Scapegoats: Rashid Ahmad Gangohi and the Deobandi Critique of Sufism," *The Muslim World* 99: 3, 478–501.
Institute of Statistics. 2011. *Njoftim (n.d.) per Media: Fjala e Drejtorit të Përgjithshëm të INSTAT, Ines Nurja gjatë prezantimit të rezultateve kryesore të Censusit të Popullsisë dhe Banesave 2011 (Press Release: Remarks By the Director General of* INSTAT [Institute of Statistics], Ines Nurja On Presentation of Main Results of the 2011 Census of People and Housing), Tirana, INSTAT, http://www.instat.gov.al/media/177358/njoftim_per_media_-_fjala_e_drejtorit_te_instat_ines_nurja_per_rezultatet_finale_te_census_2011.pdf

Islam, Maidul. 2015. *The Limits of Islamism: Jamaat-e-Islami in Contemporary India and Bangladesh.* Delhi: Cambridge University Press.

Ismaʿil, Muhammad. 1824. *Taqwiyyat al-Iman.* Multan: Kutub Khana-i Majidiyya.

Iqbal, Muhammad and M. Saeed Sheikh. 2012. *The Reconstruction of Religious Thought in Islam.* Stanford, CA: Stanford University Press.

Jaffer, Maulana Muhammad. 1981. *Kala Pani.* Lahore: Sang-e-Meel

Jaffrelot, Christopje. 2015. *The Pakistan Paradox: Instability and Resilience.* New Delhi: Random House, 544–46.

Jahan, Rounaq. 1972. *Pakistan: Failure in National Integration.* New York: Columbia University Press.

Jahangir, Selim. 2005. *Maizbhandari Tariqar Tatvik Bislesion* [Theoretical Analysis of the Maijbhandari Path], reprint. Chittagong, Bangladesh: Anzuman-e-Mottabeyeen-e-Ghawth-e-Maizbhandari.

—2012. *Ghawthul Azam Maizbhandari: Satobarser Aloke* [Ghawthul Azam Maizbhandari: On Flaming Centenary], reprint. Chittagong, Bangladesh: Anzuman-e-Mottabeyeen-e-Ghawth-e-Maizbhandari.

Jalal, Ayesha. 1994 [1985]. *The Sole Spokesman: Jinnah, the Muslim League and the Demand for Pakistan.* Cambridge: Cambridge University Press.

Jones, Sophia, "Egypt's Sufi Muslims, Facing Increased Persecution, Put Faith in Former Military Chief." *The World Post*, May 23 2014. Available at: http://www.huffingtonpost.com/2014/05/23/egypt-sufi-muslims_n_5372577.html

Justice Munir Commission Report on the Anti-Ahmadi Riots of Punjab in 1953. Available at: hhttps://tinyurl.com/k6ndldf

Kahn, Joel S. 2014. "Modern Gnostics: The Pursuit of the Sacred in Indonesian Islam." *Heritage of NUSANTARA. International Journal of Religious Literature and Heritage* 3(2): 171–94.

Karamustafa, Ahmet T. 2004. "Preface." In: *Knowledge of God in Classical Sufism: Foundations of Islamic Mystical Theology*, ed. and trans. John Renard. New York: Paulist Press.

—2006. *God's Unruly Friends: Dervish Groups in the Islamic Middle Period 1200–1550.* Oxford: Oneworld.

Keles, Ozgan, and Ismail Mesut Sejkic. 2015. *A Hizmet Approach to Rooting Out Terrorism.* London: Centre for Hizmet Studies.

Kersten, C. 2015. *Islam in Indonesia: The Contest for Society, Ideas and Values.* London: C. Hurst & Co.

Khan, M.A. Muqtedar. 2009. "Islamic Governance and Democracy." In: *Islam and Democratization in Asia*, ed. Shiping Hua, 13–27. Amherst, NY: Cambria.

Khan, Muhammad Sarfraz, 2017. *Taskin as-sadur fi tahqiq hawal al-mutafil barzikh wal qabur*, 12th edition. Maktaba Safdariyya; Gujranwala.

Khan, Naveeda. 2012. *Muslim Becoming: Aspiration and Skepticism in Pakistan.* Durham, NC and London: Duke University Press.

Kim, Heon Choul. 2008. *The Nature and Role of Sufism in Contemporary Islam: A Case Study of the Life, Thought and Teachings of Fehtullah Güllen.* Ann Arbor, MI: University of Michigan.

Koç, Doğan. 2012. *Strategic Defamation of Fethullah Gülen: English vs. Turkish.* Lanham, MD: University Press of America.

Kosova, Parim. 2006. *The Complex of Monuments of the Albanian League of Prizren – Its Challenges.* [Albanian]. Prizren: n.p.

Ladjal, Tarek, and Benaouda Bensaid. 2011. "Sufism and Politics in Contemporary

Egypt: A Study of Sufi Political Engagement in the Pre and Post-Revolutionary Reality of January 2011." *Journal of Asian and African Studies*: 1–19.
Laffan, Michael Francis. 2011. *The Makings of Indonesian Islam: Orientalism and the Narration of a Sufi Past*. Princeton, NJ: Princeton University Press.
Lapidus, Ira M. 2014. *A History of Islamic Societies*. Cambridge: Cambridge University Press.
Lewis, Bernard. 1937. "The Islamic Guilds." *The Economic History Review* 8(1): 20–37.
—1968. *The Emergence of Modern Turkey*. New York: Oxford University Press.
Lewisohn, Leonard. 2006. "Persian Sufism in the Contemporary West." In: *Sufism in the West*, ed. Jamal Malik and John Hinnells. London: Routledge.
Liebeskind, Claudia. 1998. *Piety on Its Knees: Three Sufi Traditions in South Asia*. Delhi: Oxford University Press.
Lieven, Anatol. 1998. *Chechnya: Tombstone of Russian Power*. New Haven, CT: Yale University Press.
Lindholm, Charles. Revised ed. 2002. *The Islamic Middle East: Tradition and Change*. Oxford: Blackwell.
Lombardi, Marco, Eman Ragab, Vivienne Chin, Yvon Dandurand, Valerio de Divitiis and Alessandro Burato (2012) *Countering Radicalisation and Violent Extremism among Youth to Prevent Terrorism*. Amsterdam: IOS Press.
Madinier, Rémy, and Jeremy Desmond. 2015. *Islam and Politics in Indonesia: the Masyumi Party between Democracy and Integralism*. Singapore: NUSD Press.
Magnis-Suseno, Franz. 2010. "Pancacila and Inter-religious Dialogue: How Christians and Muslims in Indonesia Learned to Accept Each Other." In: *Austrian-Indonesian Dialogue Symposium*, ed. R. Potz, S. Kroissenbrunner and A. Hafner. *State, Law and Religion in Pluralistic Societies Austrian and Indonesian Perspectives: Austrian-Indonesian Dialogue Symposium, 27–29 May, 2009, Vienna*, 113–28. Göttingen: V & R Unipress.
Malcolm, Noel. 1998. *Kosovo: A Short History*. London: Macmillan.
Marty, Martin. E., ed. 2015. *Hizmet Means Service*: *Perspectives on an Alternative Path within Islam*. Berkeley, CA: University of California Press.
Massignon, Louis, and Louis Gardet. 1986. "Al-Halladj," *Encyclopedia of Islam*, 2nd edn, Vol. 3, 99–104. Leiden: Brill.
Matton, Karl. 2008. "Habitus." In: *Pierre Bourdieu Key Concepts*, ed. Michael Grenfell, 49–65. Durham: Acumen Publishing.
Matringe, Denis. 1992. "Krsnaite and Nath Elements in the Poetry of the Eighteenth-Century Punjabi Sufi Bullhe Sah." In: *Devotional Literature in South Asia*: *Current Research 1985–1988*, ed. R.S. McGregor, 190–206. Cambridge: Cambridge University Press.
—2003. "*Hir* Waris Shah." In: *On Becoming an Indian Muslim: French Essays on Aspects of Syncretism*, ed. M. Waseem, 208–37. New Delhi: Oxford University Press.
Mawlawi, Jalal ad-Din Muhammad. 1386. *Fihi Ma Fihi*, ed. Baii al-Zaman Furozanfar. Tehran: Nigah.
—1384. *Divan-e Shams-e Tabrizi*. Tehran: Talayeh.
Mernissi, Fatima. 1992. *Islam and Democracy: Fear of the Modern World*, trans. Mary Jo Lakeland. Cambridge, MA: Perseus.
—1993. *The Forgotten Queens of Islam*, trans. Mary Jo Lakeland. Minneapolis, MN: University of Minnesota Press.

Metcalf, Barbara Daly. 1994. *Islamic Revival in British India: Deoband, 1860–1900*: Princeton; Princeton University Press.

Milani, Milad, and Adam Possamai. 2016 "Sufism, Spirituality and Consumerism: the Case Study of the Nimatullahiya and Naqshbandiya Sufi Orders in Australia," *Contemporary Islam: Dynamics of Muslim Life* 10: 67. Doi:10.1007/s11562-015-0335-1

Mirza, Shafqat T. 1992. *Resistance Themes in Punjabi Literature*. Lahore: Sane-meel Publications.

Mohamed, Mohamed Mosaad Abdelaziz. 2013. "Ibn 'Ata Allah al-Sakandari: A Sufi, 'Alim and Faqih." *Comparative Islamic Studies* 9(1): 41–65.

Moosa, Matti. 1988. *Extremist Shiites: the Ghulat Sects*. Syracuse, NY: Syracuse University Press, 1988.

Morewedge, Parviz. 2003. *Essays in Islamic Philosophy, Theology, and Mysticism*. New York: Global Scholarly Publications.

Mosleh, Ali Asghar. 1384. *Porsesh Az Haqiqat-e Insan* (The Question Concerning The Truth of Man: A Comparative Study in Ibn al-Arabi's and Heidegger's Thought). Qum: Kitab-e Taha.

Muedini, Fait. 2015. *Sponsoring Sufism: How Governments Promote "Mystical Islam" in Their Domestic and Foreign Policies.* New York: Palgrave.

Murata, Sachiko. 1992. *The Tao of Islam: A Sourcebook on Gender Relationships in Islamic Thought*. New York: State University of New York Press.

Myzyri, Hysni. 2007. *National Education During the Albanian Renaissance*. Tirana: Milenium i Ri.

Nanautivi, Qasim. 1992. *Ab-i hayat, dar asbat hayat-i babarkat sarvar-i qainat ahla salat wa hayat.* Multan: Idara talifat-i Ashrafiyya,

Nasr, Seyyed Hossain. 2004. *The Heart of Islam: Enduring Values for Humanity*. New York: HarperCollins.

Nasr, Seyyed H. 2007. *Three Muslim Sages*. Reprint. Ann Arbor, MI: Caravan.

Neelvi, Muhammad Hussain, nd. *Nida-i haqq*. New Delhi: Maktaba ishaat-i islam, 18–19.

Nicholson, Reynold A. 1921. *Studies in Islamic Mysticism*. Cambridge: Cambridge University Press.

—1963. *The Mystics of Islam*. London: Routledge and Kegan Paul.

Nimtz, August H. 1980. *Islam and Politics in East Africa the Sufi Order in Tanzania*. Minneapolis, MN: University of Minnesota Press.

Noorani, Abdul Majeed. 2010. *Jinnah and Tilak: Comrades in the Freedom Struggle*. Karachi, Pakistan: Oxford University Press.

Nurbakhsh, Javed. 1993. *The Psychology of Sufism*. London: Khaniqahi-Nimatullahi Publications.

—1996. *Discourses on the Sufi Path*. London: Khaniqahi Nimatullahi Publications.

Olsen, Alexandra H. 1981. *Guthlac of Croyland: A Study of Heroic Hagiography*. Washington, DC: University Press of America.

Ozkok, Ertugrul. 1995. "Fethullahçılık ve Tarikat." *Hurriyet* (January): 23–30.

Özdalga, Elisabeth. 2000. "Worldly Asceticism in Islamic Casting: Fethullah Gülen's Inspired Piety and Activism." *Critique: Critical Middle Eastern Studies* 17.

Pandey, Gyanendra. 1990. *The Construction of Communalism in Colonial North India*. Delhi: Oxford University Press.

Pemberton, Kelly. 2012. "Sufis and Social Activism: A Chīshtī Response to Communal

Strife in India Today." In: *South Asian Sufis*, ed. Clinton Bennett and Charles M. Ramsey. London: Continuum.
Pew Research Centre. 2010. Muslim Networks and Movements in Central Europe. Available at: http://www.pewforum.org/2010/09/15/muslim-networks-and-movements-in-western-europe/
—2012a. The World's Muslims: Unity and Diversity, 9 August 2012 Available at: http://www.pewforum.org/2012/08/09/the-worlds-muslims-unity-and-diversity-1-religious-affiliation/
—2012b. *The Global Religious Landscape: A Report on the Size and Distribution of the World's Major Religious Groups as of 2010*. Available at: http://www.pewforum.org/2012/12/18/global-religious-landscape-exec/
Pope, Nicole. 1998. "Interview with Gülen." *Fransız Le Monde Gazetesi*, 28 April.
Pourjavady, Nashrollah. 1978. *The Kings of Love*. Tehran: Imperial Iranian Academy of Philosophy.
Qutb, Sayyid. 2006. *Milestones*. Birmingham: Maktabah. Available at: http://www.kalamullah.com/Books/Milestones%20Special%20Edition.pdf
Quinn, George. 2016. "Islam: Saints and Sacred Geographies: Indonesia." In: *Encyclopedia of Women & Islamic Cultures Online Edition*, ed. Suad Joseph. Available at: https://tinyurl.com/lx5s43z
Quinn, Sholeh, A. 1999. "Rewriting Nimatullahi History in Safavid Chronicles." In: *The Heritage of Sufism (Volume 3)*, ed. Leonard Lewisohn. Oxford: Oneworld.
Quraeshi, Samina. 2010. "Storytelling as Imaginative History." In: Samina Quraeshi, S. Asani, Carl W. Ernst and Kamil Khan Mumtaz, *Sacred Spaces: a Journey with the Sufis of the Indus*, 69–264. Cambridge, MA: Peabody Museum Press.
Rabasa, Angel, Cheryl Benard, Lowell H. Schwartz, and Peter Sickle. 2007. *Building Moderate Muslim Networks*. Santa Monica, CA: RAND Corp.
Renard, John. 2008. *Friends of God: Islamic Images of Piety, Commitment, and Servanthood*. Berkeley, CA: University of California Press.
Riaz, Ali. 2004. *God Willing: The Politics of Islamism in Bangladesh*. Lanham, MD: Rowman & Littlefield.
Ramsey, Charles M. 2015. "Elucidating the Word: Sayyid Ahmad Khan (1817–1898), Revelation, and Coherence." Unpublished PhD thesis, University of Birmingham [forthcoming as *God's Word, Spoken and Otherwise: Sayyid Ahmad Khan (1817–1898), Revelation, and Coherence*. Leiden: Brill].
Rinehart, Robin. 1999. "Interpretations of the Poetry of Bullhe Shah." *International Journal of Punjab Studies* 3(1): 45–63.
Ridgeon, Lloyd, V.J. 2006. *Sufi Castigator: Ahmad Kasravi and the Iranian Mystical Tradition*. London: Routledge.
—2015a. "Mysticism in Medieval Sufism." In: *Cambridge Companion to Sufism*, ed. Lloyd Ridgeon, 125–40. New York: Cambridge University Press.
—ed. 2015b. *Sufis and Salafis in the Contemporary Age*. New York: Bloomsbury.
Roy, Asim. 1983. *The Islamic Syncretistic Tradition in Bengal*. Princeton, NJ: Princeton University Press.
Royal Al-Bayt Institute for Islamic Thought. 2012. *A Common Word: Between Us and You. 5th Anniversary Edition.* English Monograph Series No. 20. Amman, Jordan: The Royal Aal Al-Bayt Institute for Islamic Thought. Available at: http://rissc.jo/docs/20-acw/20-ACW-5.pdf
Rozehnal, Robert Thomas. 2007. *Islamic Sufism Unbound: Politics and Piety in Twenty-first Century Pakistan*. New York: Palgrave Macmillan.

Rumi, Jalal ud-din. 1381/2002. *The Mathnawi of Jalal ud-din Rumi*, ed. and trans. Reynold Alleyne Nicholson. Tehran: Research Center of Booteh Publication Co.

Saharanpuri, Maluana Khalil Ahmad. 1907. *Al-muhannad ala al-mufannad.* Deoband: Dar ul-Uloom.

Sanyal, Usha. 1996. "Are Wahhabis Kafirs? Ahmad Riza Khan Barelvi and His Sword of the Haramayn." In: *Islamic Legal Interpretation: Muftis and Their Fatwas*, ed. Brinkley Messick Muhammad Khalid Masud, and David S. Powers. Karachi: Oxford University Press, 204–14.

Sarkar, Tanika. 1996. "Imagining Hindurashtra: The Hindu and the Muslim in Bankim Chandra's Writings." In: *Contesting the Nation: Religion, Community, and the Politics of Democracy in India*, ed. David Ludden, 162–84. Philadelphia, PA: University of Pennsylvania Press.

Sarıtoprak, Zeki. 2003. "Fethullah Gülen: A Sufi in His Own Way." In: *Turkish Islam and the Secular State: The Gülen Movement*, ed. Yavuz, M. Hakan and John L. Esposito. New York: Syracuse University Press.

Saritoprak, Zeki, and Ali Ünal. 2005. "An interview with Gülen." *The Muslim World* (Special Issue) 95(3): 452–53.

al-Sarraj al-Tusi, Abi Nasr. 1960. Kitab *al-luma* ed. abd al-Hakim Mahmud and al-Baqi Sorur. Cairo: Dar al-Kutub al-Hadithah.

Sayyid Ahmad Khan. 2002. "Lecture on Islam." In: *Liberal Islam, 1840–1940: A Sourcebook*, ed. Charles Kurzman, 291–313. New York: Oxford University Press.

Sekhon, Sant Singh. 2002. *Heer Warris Shah*. New Delhi, India: Sahitya Akademy.

Shackle, Christopher S. 1992. "Transition and Transformation in Varis Shah's Hir." In: *The Indian Narrative: Perspectives and Patterns*, eds. Christopher Shackle and Rupert Snell, 241–64. Wiesbaden: Otto Harrosowitz.

—2006. "The Shifting Sands of Love." In: *Love in South Asia: A Cultural History*, ed. Francesca Orsini, 87–108. Cambridge: Cambridge University Press.

Schimmel, Annemarie. 1975. *Mystical Dimensions of Islam*. Chapel Hill, NC: University of North Carolina Press.

—1994. *Deciphering the Signs of God: A Phenomenological Approach to Islam*. New York: State University of New York Press.

Schuon, Frithjof. 1998. *Understanding Islam*. Bloomington, IN: World Wisdom.

—2006. *Sufism: Veil and Quintessence: A New Translation with Selected Letters*, ed. James S. Cutsinger. Bloomington, IN: World Wisdom.

Schwartz, Stephen. 2008. *The Other Islam*. New York: Doubleday.

—2009. "Bektashi Sufis in the Albanian National Renaissance: The Universal Significance of the League of Prizren." *Illyria* (New York), 28 November. Available at: http://www.islamicpluralism.org/1425/bektashi-sufis-in-the-albanian-national.

—2010. "On the 800th Birthday of Haxhi Bektash Veli: The Challenges of Bektashism In the New Millennium." *Illyria* [New York], March 2 – Presented to International Symposium on Bektashism, Tirana, Albania, 29 January 2010. Available at: http://www.islamicpluralism.org/1491/on-the-800th-birthday-of-haxhi-bektash-veli

—2012. "*Rahmetli* Baba Rexheb Beqiri, 1901–1995: A Balkan and American Sufi Saint." *The Huffington Post*, 23 August. Available at: http://www.islamicpluralism.org/2088/rahmetli-baba-rexheb-beqiri-1901-1995

—2015. "The Bektashi Sufis Should Join the Kosova Sufi Union [BTK]." *Illyria* [New York], 22 June. Available at: http://www.islamicpluralism.org/2499/the-bektashi-sufis-should-join-the-kosova-sufi

Schwartz, Stephen, with Shpëtim Mahmudi. 2008. "We Must Recognize in Baba Rexheb the Founder of Authentic Sufism in the U.S." *Urtësia* [Tirana], December (periodical of the Court of the World Supreme Grandfather [*Kryegjyshata*] of the Bektashi Community in Tirana, Albania), *Illyria* [New York], 27 March 2009. Available at: http://www.islamicpluralism.org/788/we-must-recognize-in-baba-rexheb-the-founder

Seale, Morris S. 1968. "The Ethics of Malamatiya Sufism and the Sermon on the Mount." *The Muslim World* 58(1): 12–23.

Sedgwick, Mark. 2015. "The Support of Sufism as a Counterweight to Radicalization." In: Marco Lombardi, Eman Ragab, Vivienne Chin, Yvon Dandurand, Valerio de Divitiis and Alessandro Burato. *Countering Radicalisation and Violent Extremism among Youth to Prevent Terrorism*, 113–19. Amsterdam: IOS Press.

Sevea, Iqbal Singh. 2012. *The Political Philosophy of Muhammad Iqbal: Islam and Nationalism in Late Colonial India*. Cambridge: Cambridge University Press.

Shaikh, Sa'diyya. 2012. *Sufi Narratives of Intimacy: Ibn 'Arabi, Gender, and Sexuality*. Chapel Hill, NC: The University of North Carolina Press.

Shoebat, Walid. 2015. "Shocking: Muslims are Now Declaring Erdogan as God." Shoebat Foundation, 30 March. Available at: http://shoebat.com/2015/03/30/shocking-muslims-are-now-declaring-erdogan-as-god/

Shukriu, Shukriu. 2001. *Prizreni i Lashtë*. [Albanian]. Prizren: n.p.

Sial, Safdar. 2012. ed. *Critical Ideologies: A Debate on Takfeer and Khurooj/* Islamabad: Narratives.

Sikand, Yoginder. 2002. *The Origins and Development of the Tablighi Jama'at, 1920–2000: A Cross-Country Comparative Survey*. Hyderabad: Orient Longman, 2002.

Sikder, Jamal A. 2005. *Shahan Shah Ziaul Haqq Maizbhandari (K)* [King of Kings Ziaul Haqq Maizbhandari (K)], 6th edition. Chittagong: Ghawthia Haqq Manzil.

Singh, Nikky-Guninder K. 2012. *Of Sacred and Secular Desire: An Anthology of Punjabi Lyrical Writings from the Punjab*. New York and London: I.B. Tauris.

Sirriyeh, Elizabeth. 2003 [1999]. *Sufis and Ant-Sufis: The Defence, Rethinking and Rejection of Sufism in the Modern World*, reprinted. London: RoutledgeCurzon.

Smith, Llew. (2008a). *Interview with Dr Javad Nurbakhsh 1*. [Online] Available at: http://www.nimatullahi.org/media-library/video/interview-with-dr-javad-nurbakhsh-part-1.php

Smith, Llew. (2008b). *Interview with Dr Javad Nurbakhsh 2*. [Online] Available at: http://www.nimatullahi.org/media-library/video/interview-with-dr-javad-nurbakhsh-part-2.php

Smith, Margaret. 1931. *Studies in Early Mysticism in the Near and Middle East*. London: The Sheldon Press.

Soroush, Abdolkarim, Mahmoud Sadri and Ahmad Sadri. 2000. *Reason, Freedom, & Democracy in Islam: Essential Writings of 'Abdolkarim Soroush*. New York: Oxford University Press.

Spellman, Kathryn. 2004. *Religion and Nation: Iranian Local and Transnational Networks in Britain*. New York and Oxford: Berghahn.

Stoddart, William. 1985. *Sufism: Mystical Doctrines and Methods of Islam*. New York: Paragon House.

Sukma, Rizal. 2004. *Islam in Indonesian Foreign Policy: Domestic Weakness and the Dilemma of Dual Identity*. London: Routledge.

Supreme Court of Bangladesh High Court Division High Court. 2013. "Chadpuri and Others v *Jamaat-e-Islami* (verdict)." Available at: http://www.supremecourt.gov.bd/resources/documents/179191_WP630of2009final.pdf

Suvorova, Anna. 1999. *Muslim Saints of South Asia: The Eleventh to Fifteenth Centuries*. London: Routledge.

Sviri, Sara. 1999. "Hakim Tirmidhi and the Malamati Movement in Early Sufism." In: *The Heritage of Sufism, Volume 1: Classical Persian Sufism from its Origins to Rumi (700–1300)*, ed. Leonard Lewisohn, 583–613. Oxford: Oneworld.

Tahir ul-Qadri, Muhammad. 2010. *Fatwa on Terrorism and Suicide Bombings*. London: Minhaj-ul-Quran Publications.

Tanchi, Tahir Hameed. 2013. "A Forgotten Debate on *Wahdat ul-Wajud* in Contemporary Perspective." In: *Mysticism in East and West: The Concept of the Unity of Being*. Loyola Hall, Lahore, 202–204.

Taylor, Jean Gelman. 2003. *Indonesia: Peoples and Histories*. New Haven, CT: Yale University Press.

The Amman Message. 2004. Available at: http://ammanmessage.com/the-amman-message-full/

The Amman Interfaith Message. 2005. Amman: The Royal Hashemite Court. Available at: http://ammanmessage.com/the-amman-interfaith-message/

The New American Bible. 1991. Saint Joseph Edition. New York: Catholic Book Publishing Co.

The World FactBook. 2016. Washington, DC, VA: Central Intelligence Agency. Available at: https://www.cia.gov/library/publications/resources/the-world-factbook/index.html. Last accessed 13 June 2016.

Toprak, Binnaz. 2005. "A Secular Democracy in the Muslim World: The Turkish Model." In: *Modernization, Democracy, and Islam*, ed. Shireen Hunter and Huma Malik. New York: Praeger.

Toussulis, Yannis. 2010. *Sufism and the Way of Blame: Hidden Sources of a Sacred Psychology*. Wheaton, IL: Quest.

Trimingham, J. Spencer, and John Obert Voll. 1998. *The Sufi Orders in Islam*. New York: Oxford University Press.

Trix, Frances. 1994. "The Resurfacing of Islam in Albania." *East European Quarterly* (Winter).

—2009. *The Sufi Journey of Baba Rexheb*. Philadelphia, PA: University of Pennsylvania Press.

Trompf, Garry, W. 1994. *Payback*. Cambridge: Cambridge University Press; Wheaton, IL: Quest Books.

Uddin, Sufia M. 2006. *Constructing Bangladesh Religion, Ethnicity, and Language in an Islamic Nation*. Chapel Hill, NC: University of North Carolina Press.

Umar, Badruddin. 2000. *Language Movement in East Bengal*. Dhaka: Jatiya Grontho Prakashan.

Ünal, Ali, and Alphonse Williams. 2000. *Advocate of Dialogue*. Fairfax, VA: The Fountain.

Van Bruinessen, Martin. 1999. "Controversies and Polemics Involving the Sufi Orders in Twentieth Century Indonesia." In: *Islamic Mysticism Contested: Thirteen Centuries of Controversies and Polemics*, eds. Frederick de Jong and Bernd Radtke, 705–28. Leiden: Brill.

—2007. "Saints, Politicians and Sufi Bureaucrats: Mysticism and Politics in Indonesia's New Order." In: *Sufism and 'The Modern' in Islam*, eds. Martin van Bruinessen and Julia Day Howell, 92–112. London: I.B. Tauris.

Van Bruinessen, Martin, and Julia Day Howell, eds. 2007. *Sufism and the Modern in Islam*. London: I.B. Tauris.

Veer, Peter van der. 1994. *Religious Nationalism: Hindus and Muslims in India*. Berkeley, CA: University of California Press.
Watt, W. Montgomery. 1968. *Islamic Political Thought*. Edinburgh: Edinburgh University Press.
Weismann, Itzchak. 2007. "Sufi Fundamentalism in India and the Middle East." In: *Sufism and the Modern in Islam*, ed. M. van Bruinessen and J. Howell. London: I.B. Tauris.
—2015. "Modernity from Within: Islamic Fundamentalism and Sufism." In: *Sufis and Salafis in the Contemporary Age*, ed. Lloyd V.J. Ridgeon, 9–32. New York: Bloomsbury.
Werbner, Pnina. 2003. *Pilgrims of Love: the Anthropology of a Global Ṣūfī Cult*. Bloomington, IN: Indiana University Press.
—2012. "Du'a: Popular Culture and Powerful Blessing at the 'URS'." In: *South Asian Sufis: Devotion, Deviation, and Destiny*, eds. Clinton Bennett and Charles M. Ramsey, 83–94. London: Continuum.
Werenfels, Isabelle. 2014. "Beyond Authoritarian Upgrading: the Re-emergence of Sufi Orders in Maghrebi Politics." *The Journal of North African Studies* 19(3): 275–95.
Wiegand, Krista E. 2016. *Bombs and Ballots: Governance by Islamist Terrorist and Guerilla Groups*. Abingdon: Routledge.
Yasrebi, Sayed Yahya. 1384. *Erfan-e Nazari (Theoretical Gnosis: a Research on Sufism's Development Principles and Matters)*. Qum: Daftar-e Tabliqat-e Islami Huze Elmiye Qum.
Yavuz, Hakan. 2003. *Islamic Political Identity in Turkey*. New York: Oxford University Press.
Zaehner, Robert C. 1960. *Hindu and Muslim Mysticism*. London: University of London.
Zaman, Muhammad Qasim. 2004. *The Ulama in Contemporary Islam: Custodians of Change*. Karachi: Oxford University Press.
–2007. *Ashraf 'Ali Thanwi: Islam in Modern South Asia*. Oxford: Oneworld.
Zamhari, Arif. 2010. *Rituals of Islamic Spirituality: A Study of Majlis Dhikr Groups in East Java*. Canberra: Australian National University Press.

INDEX

Abdelaziz, Mohamed Mosaad 27
Abduh, Muhammad 54
Abdyl Frashëri 77–79, 84–86
Abraham 151
Adam 151–52
al-Afghānī, Sayyid Jamāl al-Dīn 54
Afghanistan 2, 45. 116. 122, 220
Ahbash 5, 31
Ajmeer 135
Akbar, Mughal emperor 178, 182
AKP 7, 11, 31–33, 35, 37
Arshad Alam 103
Alam, Sarwar 7, 8, 17–18, 19, 134–35, 188
Albania 12, 14, 44, 46, 71–87
Algeria 13, 34–35, 45
'Ali ibn Abi Talib, Imam 72–73, 85, 152, 160
Asir, Emirate of 26
Atatürk, Kemal Mustafa 131
Awami League 30–34, 127, 130–35
Axiarli, Evangelia 14, 32
Ayyubids 27
Al-Azhar 28, 69, 139

Bangladesh 4, 8. 10, 11, 17–18, 30, 33–35, 42–44, 46, 48, 71, 121–28, 130–35, 140–45, 148–71
   Sufi-related political parties in Banngladesh 11, 33, 35, 134–35
baqā' (union) 2, 92, 181
Banu, Razia Akter U.A.B. 123, 127
Barelvis 71, 105–107, 110, 114–15, 117–18
Bennett, Clinton 7, 14, 17, 34, 55, 134, 135, 142, 167–68, 171, 188
Bektashi 14–16, 54–90
Bhutto, Zulfikar Ali 130
Bid'ah (innovation) 54, 111, 124, 127, 161, 224
BNP 11, 17, 132, 135
Bosnia-Hercegovina 76, 77, 81, 86
Bourdieu, Pierre 15, 92–93
Buddhism 4, 80, 131, 226
Bullhe Shah 18, 177–200

Chechnya 13, 27
Chistiyya 2, 105, 110, 183
Corbett, Rosemary R. 29
Cornell, Vincent J. 166, 171–73, 223–25, 228–29
Crescent Star Party 138, 141, 143

Demirel, Suleyman 32, 57
Deoband 16–17, 36, 54, 103–120
Dharmanirapeksata 1 (religious neutrality) 131, 47, 168, 172
Diouf 13, 28

Eaton, Richard R. 39, 106, 125–27
Economic Intelligence Unit (EIU) 5, 17, 21, 28, 30, 43, 45–48, 135
Egypt 5, 8, 10, 11, 12, 13, 27, 31
   Sufi-related political parties in Egyot 8, 32–33, 35
   Supreme Council of Sufi Orders, Egypt 28–29
Eliot, T. S. 192
Elsie, Robert 73, 77
El-Sis, Abdel Fattahi 33
Erbakan, Necmettin 31–32, 37, 57, 64
Erdoğan, Recep Tayyip 31–32
Ernst, Carl W. 27, 27–38, 164–65, 226–27, 229
Ershad, Hussain Muhamamdd 30, 33, 132–33
Esposito, John L. 136, 139–40

fanā' (passing away) 2, 92, 157, 181, 226
Farīd al-*Dīn 'Aṭṭār* 42
France 9, 19, 64, 93
Futuwwa 27, 40

Gadamer, Hans-Georg 18, 177–79, 199
Geertz, Clifford 13, 17, 35, 39, 129
Geoffrey, Eric 4, 36, 43, 168, 170, 225, 226
al-Ghazālī, Abū Ḥāmid Muḥammad ibn Muḥammad 2, 82, 129, 138

Gucia, Ali Pash 77–80
Gülen, Fethullah 14, 26, 41, 53–70
Gumah, Ali 28
Guru Nanak 192, 200

Habibie, B. J. 140–41
al-Hallaj, Mansur 2, 5, 37. 62. 173
HAMAS 10–11, 137, 139–41
Hamid, Sadek 13
Hamka (Abdul Malik Karim Amrullah) 36
Hamzeh, A. Nizar 31
Hasan of Basra 3
Hasina, Sheikh 132–33
Hawwā, Saāīd 4
Hermansen, Marcia 43, 58, 63–64
Hezbollah 5, 10–11, 35, 46
Hindu/Hinduism 16, 18, 42–43, 111, 123, 125, 126–27, 131–32, 134, 153, 163–64, 167–68, 177–78, 183–85, 188, 190–91, 225–26
Hizmet 4, 14, 53–70
Howell, Julia Day 37, 54–55, 128–29
Human rights 26, 30, 34, 41, 108, 145
Al-Ḥusayn ibn ʿAlī ibn Abī Ṭālib, Imam 72–73, 83, 85
Hussaini, Sayed Hassan Akhlaq 2, 4, 5, 18
al-Hujwiri (Abul Hassan Ali Ibn Usman al-Jullabi al-Hajveri al-Ghaznawi) 39, 172, 227

ibn ʿAta Allah 224–25
Ibn al-ʿArabi, Muhy al-Din 5, 18, 42–43, 73, 150, 152–54, 165–66, 168, 225, 227–78
Ibn al-Hassan ʿAbbasi 111
ibn Khaldun (Abū Zayd ʿAbd ar-Raḥmān ibn Muḥammad ibn Khaldūn al-Ḥaḍramī) 152
ICMA 140
Ijtihad (mental effort) 54, 224
India 2, 6, 28, 42, 43, 55, 55, 71, 80, 103, 105, 128, 178, 183, 193, 198–99
  Partition of India (1947) 130, 167–68, 178
Indonesia 4, 3, 5, 9, 12, 13, 15, 16, 18. 30, 31, 35, 121–25, 128–30, 135–45
Iqbal, Alim Muhammad 5–6, 167, 173, 229
Iran 8, 12, 15, 25, 45–46, 72, 91–105
Iraq 6, 12, 38, 44, 47, 71
Iskander, Muhammad 31

Islamic State (IS) 6, 38, 101
Islamist/Islamism 6, 8, 10, 11, 13, 19, 25, 30, 33–35, 40, 54, 61, 93–94, 97, 116, 121, 127–28, 132–37, 142–44, 171, 224
Israel 35, 46, 86, 165, 218
Jahangir, Selim 148, 164, 170
Jam'iyyah Ahlith Thoriqah al-Muʿtabaroh al-Nahdliyyah 3, 138–39
Jamaat-e-Islami (JI) 10, 11, 33, 34, 132–35
Jami, Nur ad-Din Abd ar-Rahman 203
Jesus 5, 151–52, 155, 163, 202, 215–29, 220–22, 226
Jibra'il (Gabriel) 151
Jihad/jihadis 6–7, 9, 16, 71–72, 135, 227–28
Jilani, ʿAbd al-Qadir Jilani 152–55, 163, 165
Jinnah, Muhammad Ali 167
Jordan 12–13, 45
  A Common Word initiative from Jordan 13

Kalām 173, 201
Khan, Ayub 28, 134
Khan, Hazrat Inayat 34, 92
Khan, M. A. Muqtedar 8, 9
Khan, Sir Sayyid 16–17, 40, 106, 173
Khan, Yahya 130
Lodges/Khanaqahs/*tekke* 1, 3, 27, 32, 56, 73–74
Khomeini, Ruhollah 71, 95, 203
Kiai Musta'in 138–39
Kim, Heon C. 14, 41
Kosovo 14–16, 71–90
Kosovo Sufi Union 15, 79, 80, 82, 89
Krishna 177, 188–93

Ladjal, Tarek 11, 29, 22
Lawrence, Bruce 227, 229
League of Prizren 75–79
Lebanon 5, 8, 12, 31, 35, 44, 46, 47
Lewis, Bernard 40, 55
Libya 26, 27, 45, 47, 48
Lindholm, Charles 25, 27, 38–40

Macedonia 72, 73, 76, 77, 80, 82, 86
Mahdi 60, 71
Maizbhandari, Hazrat Sayyid Delaor Husayn 17–18, 42, 147–76
Maizbhandariyya 17–18, 33, 134, 147–76, 230
Malaysia 12, 44, 121

Mathnawi 138, 201–222
Matringe, Denis 190, 193
Maysumi 136–38, 143
Medina Charter 134–35
MENA 12–13, 44–45
Mernissi, Fatema 26, 41–42, 123, 145
Metcalf, Barbara D. 106–107
Mevlevi 2, 72, 82
Milani, Milad 4, 6, 15, 17, 20, 26, 41, 95, 100
Minhaj-al-Quran 34, 133–34
Montenegro 75, 76, 78
Morocco 8, 12, 13. 39, 41, 44, 47, 48
Moses 151–52, 190, 208–209, 213–15, 222
Mubarak, Hosno 28, 29, 22, 53
Muedini, Fait 7, 13, 26, 28, 29, 43
Mughal Empire 93, 38, 127, 178
Muhammad ibn Abdullah 1, 3, 11, 20, 39–40, 43, 108, 114–15, 126, 128, 144, 149–56, 158–59, 162–63, 165, 172, 180, 182, 202, 213, 217–19, 222
    Light of Muhammad 114, 152, 152
Muhammadiyah 5, 36, 125, 130, 141, 143
Mujibir Rahman, Sheikh 130–32, 134
Muslim Brotherhood 5, 10, 28, 36–37

Nafs (ego) 1, 2, 150, 166, 227
Nahlatul Ulama 3, 15–16, 30, 35, 71, 125, 136–41
Naqhsbandiyya 2, 8, 30, 31, 32, 35, 37, 55, 59, 71, 72, 74, 82, 100, 105, 110, 119, 128, 137, 139
Al-Nasir, Caliph 27
Nazrul Islam 127
Neo-sufis 3–4, 6–7, 34–35, 41, 96, 135
Noah 151, 181, 212
Nurbakhsh, Javad 25, 92–100
Nursi, Bediuzzaman Said 56
Nyi Roro Kidul 124–25

Organization of Islamic Cooperation 10, 44, 47, 131
Ottoman empire/Ottomans 2, 15, 44, 55, 72–80, 105, 223
Özal, Turgut 31–32, 58

Pakistan 3, 12, 13, 16, 17, 28, 34–35, 38, 40, 42–44, 46, 71, 105–119, 123, 130–34, 141, 147–48, 167–70, 173, 177
Palestine 12, 44, 46–47
Pancasila 11, 131, 137, 139–41

Pew Research 4, 29, 30, 31, 33, 47
PKB 11, 30, 31, 35, 141–43
PKS 141–42

Muhammad Tahir-ul-Qadri 33–34
    Awami Tehreek 34, 35
    Minhaj-al-Quran 34, 133–34
Qadiriyya 35, 37, 71, 127–28
Al-Qaeda 10, 38, 135
Al-Qassabi 29, 33
Qassar, Abu Saleh Hamd Allah 150
Quinn, George 124
Qur'ān 9, 11, 19, 20, 36, 41, 43, 51, 62, 69, 91, 94, 108, 110, 114, 116, 126–27, 129, 144, 147–49, 152–64, 168, 170, 172–73, 178, 218–222, 238, 225–26
Qutb, Sayyid 36
Qutb, the 39, 99, 151–52, 155

Rabi'a al-'Adawiyya al-Qaysiyya 3, 226
Rahman, Tariq 107
Ramsey, Charles 3, 7, 16–17, 36
Al-Raziq, Abd 40, 59
Ridgeon, Lloyd 3, 7, 13, 36–37, 98
Rifa'iyyah 32, 36–37, 79
Royal Hashemite Court 13
Rozehnal, Robert Thomas 13, 166
Rūmī, Jalāl ad-Dīn Muhammad 2, 4, 5, 18, 65, 67. 72–73, 92, 150, 156, 162, 166, 201–217, 219–20

Salafists/Salafism 5, 6, 7, 10, 13, 19, 25, 29, 30, 31, 33, 36–37, 39–40
Salman the Farsi 3
San Stefano Treaty 76–77
Saudi Arabia 45, 47
Sayyid Ahmad Barelvi 105–106
Schwatrz, Stephen S. 7, 14–15, 38, 81, 87
Senegal 4, 28, 44, 46, 121
Sepoy rebellion, 1857 16, 103, 106, 119
Shah Isma'il 105, 111
Shah Jalal 126
Shāh Walī Allāh 105, 107, 114, 119
shāri'ah, sharia 15, 62, 74, 78, 84, 85, 98, 104, 111, 116, 128, 131, 132, 137, 138, 143, 163, 187
Schuon, Fritjof 224, 229
Secularism 9, 14, 131–32, 134–35, 143, 147, 168, 172, 224
Shūrā 40

Silsilah 1, 37, 107, 116
Singh, Nikky 18, 42, 180, 200
Sirhindī, Shaykh Ahmad 56, 106
Soroush, Abdolkarim 145
Sufi, origin of term 3, 221
Suharto 130–40
Suhrawardiyya 2, 27, 105, 106, 110
Sukarno 136–38
Sukarnoputri, Magawati 140–43
Suvorova, Anna 105
Syncretism, Sufism accused of 3, 4, 15, 118, 126, 129
Syria 6, 10, 12, 27, 43, 45–47, 55

Tablighi Jamaat 34, 27, 41, 113, 135, 166, 170
Tagore, Rabindranath 123, 127
Taliban 17, 112, 116–17
Tanzania 13
Tawhid (unity) 60, 62, 114, 136
Tawhid-e-adyan (unity of religions) 147–48, 150, 153, 155–70, 225
Tijaniyyah 2
Al-Turabi, Hasan 10
Trabulsi, Adnan 31
Trimngham, J. Spencer 27, 37, 41, 54–55
Trompf, Garry 91, 93–94, 99
Tunisia 6, 12, 36, 44, 46, 121, 145
Turkey 11, 12, 14, 17, 32–33, 35, 41, 44, 46, 54–58, 63–65, 69–70, 72, 76, 80, 84, 121
Uddin, Sofia 33, 135

United Kingdom (UK) 9, 29, 71, 95, 98
United Nations (UN) 138
United States of America (USA) 7, 19, 29, 46, 72, 83, 98, 138
Uzbekistan 13, 45

Van Bruinessen, Martin 129, 136–38
Vilayat 18, 147–76
Voll, John O. 27, 37, 41, 136, 139–40

Wahdat-al-wujud 2, 114, 119, 166, 181
Wahhab, Ibn 5
Wahhabi/Wahhhabism 5, 71, 80, 84, 114, 115, 166, 170
Wahid 30, 31, 40, 139–42, 144
Wali, awila, wilayat 39, 150–52, 172
Wali Sanga, the 128
Waris Shah 18, 171, 200
Weismann, Itzchak 36, 55
Werbner, Pnina 38, 40
Werenfel 38, 40
World Federation of Sufi Orders 32–33

Yasir, Muhammad 108, 119
Yemen 6, 12, 45, 47, 126
Yoginder Sikand 103–104

Zaman, Muhammad Qasim 103, 104
Zia, Khaleda 132–33
Zia al-Haq 40
Zia-ur-Rahman 132, 134

www.ingramcontent.com/pod-product-compliance
Lightning Source LLC
Chambersburg PA
CBHW032021230426
43671CB00005B/162